Interrogating Xenophobia and Nativism in Twenty-First-Century Africa

Interrogating Xenophobia and Nativism in Twenty-First-Century Africa

Edited by
Emmanuel Matambo

LEXINGTON BOOKS
Lanham • Boulder • New York • London

Published by Lexington Books
An imprint of The Rowman & Littlefield Publishing Group, Inc.
4501 Forbes Boulevard, Suite 200, Lanham, Maryland 20706
www.rowman.com

86-90 Paul Street, London EC2A 4NE

British Library Cataloguing in Publication Information Available

Library of Congress Cataloging-in-Publication Data

Names: Matambo, Emmanuel, 1987- editor.
Title: Interrogating xenophobia and nativism in twenty-first-century Africa / edited by Emmanuel Matambo.
Description: Lanham : Lexington Books, [2022] | Includes bibliographical references and index.
Identifiers: LCCN 2022001756 (print) | LCCN 2022001757 (ebook) | ISBN 9781793645319 (cloth) | ISBN 9781793645333 (paperback) | ISBN 9781793645326 (epub)
Subjects: LCSH: Xenophobia—Political aspects—Africa. | Nativistic movements—Africa. | Pan-Africanism. | Africa—Ethnic relations. | Africa—Emigration and immigration—Government policy. | Africa—Politics and government—1960-
Classification: LCC DT15 .I588 2022 (print) | LCC DT15 (ebook) | DDC 305.80096—dc23/eng/20220311
LC record available at https://lccn.loc.gov/2022001756
LC ebook record available at https://lccn.loc.gov/2022001757

As this book project was nearing completion, Kenneth Kaunda, the founding president of the Republic of Zambia, passed away at the age of 97. Notwithstanding his blemishes as a leader, Kaunda's commitment to Pan-Africanism cannot be besmirched, even by his most ardent critics. It is to his memory that this book is dedicated.

Contents

Acknowledgments

As I type these sentences, the world is still reeling from the devastation of a pandemic such as the world has never seen, certainly not since the turn of the millennium. The emergence and spread of the coronavirus pandemic has substantially changed the world, collapsing the barriers that previously separated compartments of human activity such as work, social life, religious fellowship, and other dimensions that comprise daily living. These unprecedented and unforeseen circumstances have summoned all the powers of adjustment that are humanly possible. I am thus heartily grateful to the 16 authors who weathered an uncertain world to find time to commit themselves to a cause that is much more than an academic undertaking. The pages you are about to read bear a frank assessment of the problems facing Africa, some of which at first glance take on the nature of insuperable hurdles to the realization of Pan-Africanism. However, the authors who brought those pages to life do not have a despondent fiber in them. Indeed, while they are candid about the continent's culpability in failing to prevent and then contain xenophobia and nativism, they all converge on the conviction that Africa is capable of beating back these vices in pursuit of a united and prosperous continent. I commend this group of talented writers; their diligence and commitment made this book a joy and a manageable project for a first ever single-edited book by this editor.

At Rowman, my publisher, I render my wholehearted appreciation to Shelby Russell, Sydney Wedbush and the production team. Shelby guided this project from the time it was an idea to its current form. It is much her project as it is mine and of the authors who contributed to it. In the same vein, I direct my acclaim at the anonymous peer-reviewers, whose insights enhanced the quality of this project. I am also thankful to Nivethitha Tamilselvan, Project Manager at Deanta Publishing Services for overseeing the production of the book.

I am also indebted to my employer, the University of Johannesburg (UJ), for introducing me to a competitive and exacting but rewarding academic and work environment. Dr. Bhaso Ndzendze, my head of department at UJ and my predecessor in my current position, has offered me advice and support to be bold enough in my academic pursuits. I hope this project will be a befitting response to his expectations of me.

To the Centre for Africa-China (CACS), which I serve as director of research, words are a feeble attempt to capture the profundity of my gratitude. Alas, they are the only facility at my disposal, so Thank You! CACS has given me the plenitude of its generosity. My colleagues not only helped to shape my ideas about this project but provided a convivial work environment through which I was not afraid or shy to risk raising these ideas. Dr. David Monyae, the CACS director, has been a constant and encouraging voice during the compilation of this book and, under his aegis, I was never short of needed resources to produce a quality work. For this, my gratitude to him is total. The same goes to my colleagues, Professor Peng Yi, Lebogang Mosebua, Zizipho Masiza, and Goitseone Maswabi, who have supported this book in different respects.

At the time when I was frightened of the arduous task of editing a book, and the attendant management of contributors that devolves upon this responsibility, Professor Sabella O. Abidde, was the first to "decide," not encourage, that I could do it. His confidence in me is a reality that I cherish, and it has been the bedrock of his presence in my life as editor, mentor, brother, and colleague. I thank him dearly.

Finally, I would like to thank my mother, siblings, and extended family who, though at times not fully understanding why I chose "a life of always staring at the computer and reading books," have supported me, convinced that my pursuits have well-meaning intent.

The ensuing book does not pretend to provide all solutions to the issues raised. It would have succeeded in its mission if it will ignite a new way of looking at the origins, nature, and sustenance of xenophobia and nativism and how they occlude the noble pursuit of a stable and self-loving African continent. For this reason, the authors answered the call not to make their contributions arcane and hence only comprehensible by a select few. Therefore, this book is meant for people of all socioeconomic stations and, judging by how insular politics are infecting the global international system, it will hopefully benefit readers even beyond the confines of the African continent. Enjoy!

Emmanuel Matambo
Johannesburg, July 23, 2021

Introduction

Vying for Prominence: Xenophobia, Nativism, and the Prospects of Pan-Africanism in Twenty-First-Century Africa

Emmanuel Kasonde Matambo

XENOPHOBIA AND NATIVISM AS GLOBAL OCCURRENCES

The intent of this book is to interrogate xenophobia and nativism in twenty-first-century Africa. Naturally, those engaging with the book will ponder the prospects of fulfilling Africa's Pan-African quest amid persisting levels of xenophobic violence and nativism on the African continent. Xenophobia and nativism, if left unchecked, could also occlude a successful implementation of the African Continental Free Trade Agreement (AfCFTA), on of the biggest of its kind in the world and a possible thoroughgoing solution to anemic intra-African trade. The AfCFTA is more than a trade pact; it has the potential of going beyond trade and entrenching the tenets of Pan-Africanism. For this to happen, however, Africa needs to foreswear actions and policies that restrict and discourage free movement of persons, goods, and ideas. To be fair, while Africa's ethnic realities compound the continent's difficulties with curbing identity strife, they form a part of the post–Cold War struggles with cultural clashes.

In 1993, a few years after the collapse of the Berlin Wall and the dissolution of the Union of Soviet Socialist Republics (USSR/Soviet Union), Samuel Huntington, a prominent American political scientist, wrote an article in *Foreign Affairs* titled "The Clash of Civilizations?" In the article, Huntington added his voice to speculation on what would be the patterns of conflict in a world that had apparently left behind ideology as a basis for discord, as it was between the capitalist and socialist blocs during the Cold War. Huntington's piece came at the back of Francis Fukuyama's *The End of History and the*

Last Man which argued that with the seeming triumph of Western liberal democracy, humankind has reached its ideological evolution.

Huntington argued that economic ambition and ideological discord would not be the main casus belli in the post–Cold War international system. Instead, he argued that cultural differences would form the basis for disharmony in the ensuing international system. He used the word "civilizational" as an adjective of the clashes in post–Cold War international affairs. It was easy to surmise that Huntington was a doomsayer, accusing humanity of being prone to atavistic identity clashes. His brief, however, as Richard K. Betts argues, was "to prevent the growing clash of civilizations from becoming a war of civilizations."[1] The rise of Islamic extremism and terror, especially after the September 11, 2001 attacks on America has fueled the prominence of cultural and civilizational impulses for war and xenophobia.

This background underlines the fact that xenophobia, nativism, and extreme nationalism are not exclusively African. Socioeconomic and sociocultural factors form a formidable basis on which nativism and xenophobia thrive. Nativism comes in the form of nationalism and xenophobia, and usually emanates from a feeling of disenchantment, alienation from political and economic establishments, or widespread inequality. Nativists abhor signs that show state institutions' willingness to accept the inflow of non-native persons and ideas. Income inequality and unstinting levels of poverty are usually blamed on foreign nationals and governments that seem not to be assertive to keep them out. Thus, nativists argue that only those who are indigenous should inhabit states. Their sentiment plays successfully in the hands of populists, claiming to be opposed to state establishments that are allegedly willing to cede national sovereignty and thereby allow transnational institutions that call for the free passage of persons to hold sway. In other words, nativists, or the populists and opportunists that claim to be their champions and spokespersons, loath globalization. Nat O'Connor asserts that their "rhetoric typically involves anti-globalisation and 'welfare chauvinist' messages that blame minorities, migrants and foreigners for the decline of economic circumstances experienced by 'natives.'"[2]

The election of Donald Trump as American president in 2016 and the withdrawal of Britain from the European Union (EU) demonstrate the presence of populism in the West in concert with anti-immigrant and anti-foreign sentiment. Donald Trump successfully demonized immigrants for his political ends, presenting them as threats to America's economy, security, and the country's way of life. His tirades against China as a mortal threat to America's economic preeminence mask a more troubling inkling or stereotype against non-Americans. Trump even used the coronavirus pandemic as another avenue for mobilizing his nationalist adherents. He called the virus the China flu. Such characterizations provoked attacks on people of Asian descent because of the Asian provenance of the virus. In 2016, Trump won converts among the many Americans who felt estranged from Washington and those who believed that America's troubles were partly a result of foreign nationals. Indeed, there are Americans who want to create an America that is Caucasian, protestant, and prosperous. The rising number of non-white immigrants, many of them non-protestant and from poor countries, sent shivers to those attuned to the Trump mold. In addition, the rise of terrorism, especially that of an extreme Islamic brand, has opened up antipathy toward people of Arab stock, and this is seen more in EU debates about immigrants fleeing from Arab countries, most of which are Islam-dominated.

While countries such as Germany have been amenable to the acceptance of desperate migrants fleeing their troubled countries, others, like Poland, have been unequivocal in their hostility to the immigrants that are both non-white and non-Christian. In Italy, the 2020 Human Rights Watch Report noted "an increase in intolerance, racial and religious hatred and xenophobia, and the role of political leaders and members of government in allowing or encouraging these phenomena."[3] This elicited condemnation from the United Nations High Commission for Refugees. The growing profile and success of those espousing xenophobic views accord with the assertion that xenophobia and nativism are seeping into Western politics, with measurable levels of success. Arguably, Britain's withdrawal from the EU could also shield the UK from accepting the free passage of immigrants from the developing world who, once admitted in the EU countries, could easily gain access to the UK and hence bring with them new ideas and cultures. From this viewpoint, Brexit (as Britain's exit from the EU is also called) was not born only out of economic impulses and Britain's quest to recapture state sovereignty rather than deferring to the EU. These realities bear out Huntington's observation, made almost three decades ago, that "rising immigration from non-Western sources is provoking rising concern in both Europe and America."[4]

From the foregoing, any society that has rising levels of economic inequality and a fear of cultural dilution, if not annihilation, brought by immigrants is likely to lend itself to deep-seated nativist and xenophobic elements. These conditions have been perennial in Africa. They explain not only the presence of xenophobia but ethnic strife as well. While postcolonial African leaders are culpable in failing to stem inequalities between the native elite and the rest of the citizens, Africa's woes are partly because immediate postcolonial or postapartheid governments inherited proverbial poisoned chalices that were not designed to favor the masses.

THE POSTCOLONIAL SOCIOECONOMIC AND
POLITICAL FABRIC: A POISONED CHALICE

A combination of factors conspires to hobble Africa's effort to develop as a unified continent. History no doubt plays a part in besetting the continent because postcolonial leaders inherited the proverbial poisoned chalice. Postcolonial Africa remained stubbornly structured along colonial-era lines. The change from colonial to indigenous leadership was cosmetic in its depth and Frantz Fanon's prescient predictions about what facile changes could breed in Africa give an impression that myopia on the part of postcolonial leaders would doom Africa for years to come. A system that is based on identity be it racial, ethnic, religious, or national is bound to be fractured. In *The Wretched of the Earth*, Fanon urged Africans not to create "states, institutions, and societies that draw their inspiration from [Europe]."[5] To Fanon's misfortune, anti-colonial activists, including himself, were educated in Western (i.e., European) institutions and hence were to a great extent bound to Western systems. The same discriminatory manner of distributing public goods during colonialism continued to feature in independent Africa, only that this time around ethnicity and nationality, rather than colonial-cum-racial bias, became more salient. It is noteworthy that colonialism demarcated Africa using borders, and within borders certain ethnic groups were preferred over others. For example, in countries such as Nigeria and Ghana, ethnic groups that had converted to Christianity (the dominant religion of colonizers) received favorable treatment from the colonial edifice. This favoritism has had an enduring impact on postcolonial Africa.

The Rwandan genocide of 1994 is one of the most ghastly expressions of the salience of ethnicity in fractured postcolonial polities. As Rwanda was awash with blood in May 1994, 3,000 kilometers to the south, Nelson Mandela was being installed as the first democratically elected president of South Africa. This was one of the defining moments of the past decade of the twentieth century. Despite being a pariah from the rest of Southern Africa for almost half a century, South Africa was the undisputed giant of the region in economic size, military might, and some measure of moral leadership. For more than a century, South Africa attracted human labor from as far as Malawi. The discovery of diamonds and a cartload of other minerals triggered a massive demand for labor. The long history of migration to South Africa received a fillip with Mandela's inauguration, but this further compounded the task that the incoming government had of addressing age-old economic, political, and social injustices. Thus far, this has proved to be a Sisyphean task despite the adoption of policies such as affirmative action. The long-suffering black South Africans whose hopes have been dashed by government corruption, myopia, and lethargy are understandably hostile to sharing their meager resources with the growing numbers of desperate and ambitious foreign nationals. The violence that occasionally ensues from this complex has tarnished South Africa's standing and all but eliminated the euphoria that characterized Mandela's accession to power.

XENOPHOBIA IN SOUTH AFRICA: AN UNCOMFORTABLE REALITY

Xenophobia abounds across Africa. In April 2020, Zambian musicians called by pseudonyms 705 Empire and General Kanene sang a song in which they warned foreigners not to be commandeering Zambian women, failing which they would be forced to flee back to their countries.[6] This has resonance with one of the oft-repeated justifications for attacking foreign nationals in South Africa on grounds that they commandeer and sometimes traffic South African girls and women. Growing economic inequality (South Africa is the most unequal society in the world) and the stubbornly high numbers of unemployment add to South Africa's difficulties with fighting anti-foreign sentiment. According to Statistics South Africa, the country's general unemployment rate in the first quarter of 2021 was 32.6%, while among the youth (aged between 15 and 34) it was 46.3% "implying that almost one in every two young people in the labour force did not have a job in the first quarter of 2021."[7] One of the rallying cries of those who take umbrage at the presence of foreign nationals in South Africa is that their prospects of employment, already diminished, are almost totally eliminated by foreign nationals,[8] eager to work for very competitive (read low) wages. This has provoked the rise of groups such as the All Truck Drivers Foundation that call for the total expulsion of foreign truck drivers in South Africa. Between 2018 and 2019, 200 truck drivers, mostly foreign nationals, were killed during attacks on South African roads.

It is thus not by happenstance that 7 of the 13 chapters in this book focus on South Africa. South Africa's xenophobia commands attention due to the scope, frequency, and ferocity with which it occurs. In addition, South Africa, as a prominent African country with a relatively free media, is easily recognizable. Furthermore, attacks on foreign nationals (mainly of black African extraction) usually evoke the solidarity that oppressed (mainly black) South Africans under apartheid enjoyed from the rest of the continent. As the last victims of a minority regime in Africa, black South Africans depended largely on the political support of independent Africa.

Exiled and proscribed South African liberation movements, including the now ruling African National Congress (ANC), were ensconced in some African countries, where they established their military bases and political headquarters. The death of Kenneth Kaunda, Zambia's founding president and a seminal figure in offering succor to South Africa's liberation movements, saw a rejuvenation in South Africa's Pan-African rhetoric, with South Africa's former president, Thabo Mbeki, referring to Kaunda as one of the architects of South Africa's democracy.[9] Unsurprisingly, postapartheid South Africa vowed to uphold the importance of Pan-Africanism and Africa in South Africa's domestic and foreign policy and affairs. Alas, the reality of both the South African government and ordinary citizens honors this vow occasionally in the breach.

Adekeye Adebajo points to the paradox of South Africa as Africa's most Pan-Africanist but also most xenophobic nation. He states that South Africa's

> national anthem starts with the words 'God bless Africa'; its ruling party is the African National Congress (ANC); its other main black liberation movement is called the Pan Africanist Congress (PAC); and many of the leaders of its liberation movement grew up in exile elsewhere on the continent.[10]

In addition, postapartheid and democratic South Africa sought to build a rainbow nation in which people of different hues would live in harmony. Despite this history and perspective, from 1994 to June 2021, there were 818 incidents against foreign nationals, 121,945 displacements of immigrants, 4,770 of their shops looted, and at least 605 deaths, according to Xenowatch.[11] It is noteworthy that the seven-year period from 2008 to 2015 was particularly violent toward foreign nationals, claiming an estimate of 350 lives, which is almost 58% of the total number of foreign nationals killed in 27 years. According to Human Rights Watch, during 2008 spate of xenophobic violence alone "40,000 foreign nationals left the country and a further 50,000" were internally displaced.[12]

By far one of the most notable and influential proponents of Pan-Africanism in twenty-first-century Africa has been Thabo Mbeki, South Africa's president from 1999 to 2008. However, not even he is immune to criticism of just how deep his stated commitment to Pan-Africanism runs. His customary denialism to the presence of xenophobia in South Africa deprives the country of an opportunity to embark on a candid search for solutions to xenophobia and nativism. As far back as 2007, before the 2008 widespread attacks on foreign nationals, African Peer Review Mechanism (APRM) issued a cautionary report on the disturbing xenophobic sentiment in South Africa and how it could lead to violence. The South African government traduced the report as "simply not true." The events of May 2008 demonstrated that South Africa's denial was a costly mistake both in human life and the country's international standing and Pan-African credentials.

In March 2017, Mbeki delivered the keynote address on the occasion of the 13th year anniversary of the APRM at which he was asked whether he was remorseful about the 2007 denial. He maintained his 2007 response, which is contrary to reality and to views such as those of the Human Rights Watch that the 2008 attacks were "indicative of growing xenophobia in South Africa" and that "the government's commitment to address them is inadequate."[13] Mbeki's manner of (mis)characterizing attacks on foreign nationals has become the orthodox stance of the ruling ANC. The Mbeki-ANC line has been to interpret attacks on foreign nationals simply as "criminal" rather than "xenophobic." Adekeye Adebajo has described this as a "false distinction that [Mbeki] and many South African leaders continue to insist on."[14] Indeed, xenophobic violence is innately criminal in that it happens outside the ambit of the law. To deny the presence of xenophobia only defers if not aggravates one of the biggest impediments to creating a Pan-African climate. In addition, the use of pejorative terms such as *amakwerekwere* to describe mainly African foreign nationals betrays deep-seated resentment for foreign nationals and draws an unfortunate comparison to apartheid-era epithets such as *kaffir* that Afrikaner racists used to describe black South Africans. While xenophobia as an attitude is rife and knows no social boundaries, xenophobic violence is usually visited on migrants (chiefly black Africans) at the socioeconomic stations of poor South Africans, in townships and places of small-scale entrepreneurship.

According the Human Rights Watch, xenophobia has continued unabated in South Africa. In March 2019, xenophobic attacks in South Africa's port city of Durban forced hundreds of immigrants to flee their homes and places of business. This came a year after South Africa's Department of Justice crafted the Anti Xenophobia Pledge, which implores South Africans to "reject all violence and discrimination against people from other countries."[15] Despite usual denials by the then minister of International Relations, Lindiwe Sisulu, another minister, Nkosazana Dlamini-Zuma, condemned what she called "all kinds of Xenophobia [*sic*]".[16] A further positive development was when the South African government adopted The National Action Plan to Combat Racism, Racial Discrimination, Xenophobia and Related Intolerance on March 25, 2019. Awkwardly, this happened on the very day that attacks on foreign nationals erupted in Durban. However, the success of such well-meaning measures will rest largely on attitudinal change, aided by victory over South Africa's trinity of systemic problems: poverty, inequality, and unemployment. The coronavirus pandemic, which has sucked even more South Africans in the unemployment pit, will test social cohesion among South Africans and foreign nationals. The slow pace of economic recovery and reclamation of employment will continuously put foreign nationals in peril. Indubitably, studies are in the offing to address how this could come about.

STRUCTURE AND CONTENT

In chapter 1, Adeniyi S. Basiru cites citizenship crisis, pervasive nativity, and rising Afrophobia as a trilemma that has assailed the African states in the past two decades and exposed their failings in dealing with rights-oriented conflicts. In a rapidly globalizing world, it is imperative to critically engage these challenges and their corollaries. The chapter is a frank analysis of how postcolonial African states treat their citizens and African foreign nationals within their borders. The fact that attacks on foreign nationals are usually visited on African foreign nationals justifies the increasing use of the word "Afrophobia" rather than the more general term "xenophobia."

In the second chapter, Kizito N. C. Okeke examines the psychological impacts of the activities of xenophobes and nativists on the African people and in the development of African nations. The author suggests a way forward for a stronger African identity and solidarity in the African continent, a much brighter future for the African people through a renewed African conscious-ness, and the reconstruction of the African nations for more meaningful and purposeful participation in the politics and the economy of nations.

The third chapter looks at how colonial legacies still shape African poli-tics, with a focus on how apartheid still haunts democratic South Africa. The author, Robert Maseko, asks some searching questions: How did South Africa end up in such a situation, where black-on-black violence has become the order of the day? Why are black African nationals targeted in xenophobic violence, while other racial groups of lighter skin are not victims of native rage? The answers, Maseko argues, are found in the continued legacies of coloniality and apartheid divisions which promote the insider-outsider mentality on citizens, the creation of superior and inferior people, and the influences of national policy. The coverage of white-controlled media, an influential white population, and the surfeit of blacks educated in Western institutions has aided the regrettable legacies of apartheid in South Africa. In apportioning blame for postapartheid South Africa's xenophobia, Maseko fingers what he describes as the failed nationalist project of the ANC govern-ment after the end of apartheid.

Seun Bamidele in chapter 4 looks at xenophobia and Afrophobia from a policy perspective. The chapter uses empirical data collected in the South African cities of Durban, Johannesburg, and Pretoria. Research participants comprised African migrants and black South Africans, the two groups that are typically at the center of spates of xenophobic violence. The paper is an interrogation of how and why attacks on foreign nationals continue unabated despite numerous initiatives to stem them. The unstintingly high levels of unemployment in postapartheid South Africa account for much of the disillusionment among unemployed and historically disadvantaged

South Africans. Naturally, the presence of foreign nationals, seemingly competing with South Africa's economically marginalized for employment and entrepreneurial opportunities, inflames the sensibilities of locals and occasionally drives them toward attacking foreign nationals in an attempt to monopolize South Africa's limited opportunities.

South Africa has a sizable Nigerian population that has been very visible and vocal. Allegations of drug and human trafficking by foreign nationals are usually made against Nigerians residing in South Africa. In 2020, aggrieved South Africans took to social media network Twitter to support a #NigeriansMustFall trend against Nigerian nationals in South Africa. This is what Janet Abosede Ogundairo, Victor Onyilor Achem, and Feyisitan Ijimakinwa address in chapter 5. The chapter is a reminder of how powerful communication in general and social media in particular, is in influencing people's perceptions. The chapter adopts the Group Conflict theory to cogently explain the dynamics of new media and how it served as a vehicle that drove the xenophobic attacks against Nigerians in South Africa, as well the secessionist agitations of the Igbo ethnic nationality in Nigeria. The Group Conflict theory is also used to deconstruct perceptions attached to xenophobia and secession-inciting tweets using the trend #NigeriaMustFall.

As mentioned earlier, focus on South Africa has dominated this book because of the scale, depth, and frequency of attacks on foreign nationals in South Africa, which are unmatched anywhere in Africa. However, because of the many raging debates regarding the characterization of such attacks in South Africa, with some claiming they are criminal rather than xenophobic, Happy Mathew Tirivangasi and Samukezi Mrubula-Ngwenya in the sixth chapter seek to probe whether South Africans are really anti-heterogeneity. They arrive at the crux of this question in historical and cascading fashion, by placing xenophobia in the global context (e.g., anti-Semitism in Germany), Africa, and then South Africa. The chapter is a discourse analysis of the extent of xenophobia in South Africa. The authors arrive at the fact that xenophobic sentiment has been consistent in postapartheid South Africa and that widely reported spates such as the 2008 and 2015 ones claim more attention because of their magnitude. Many more xenophobic incidents happen, but at a small scale that they go unreported. The authors enjoin the South African government to tackle the issue of xenophobia with more consistency and vigor; short of doing this, attacks on foreign nationals will damage relations between South Africa and affected African countries, as it was the case with Nigeria in 2019.

In chapter 7, Sunday Paul Onwuegbuchulam proposes the Siswati adage *Live Liyengcayelwa* as an African philosophico-ethical resource and basis on which mutual respect among citizens and immigrants in South Africa could be built toward eschewing all xenophobic tendencies. *Live liyengcayelwa* could be literally translated as "land is respectable." Thus, people are urged to respect places that offer hearth and home or refuge. The chapter offers what qualifies to be an Afrocentric approach to curbing animosity among Africans of different national extractions. It draws some of its inspiration from the African ethic of Ubuntu (humanness), which emphasizes the relational nature of human interaction and that one's sense of humanness coexists and to some extent depends on the existence of the other. While some chapters offer a more pragmatic way of solving xenophobic sentiment (such as improving the quality of governance by ruling parties), Onwuegbuchulam looks at other underlying causes of xenophobia (such as the departure from African ethics and their emphasis on hospitality and care for nature in general). The strength of that chapter resides in the fact that it does not only condemn violence on the part of native-born nationals; the logic of *live liyengcayelwa* also puts some responsibility on foreign nationals—who are expected to respect host countries that offer them succor. This means pursuing peaceful coexistence with their hosts and adhering to local laws.

Chapter 8 is another chapter that focuses on the scourge of xenophobia in South Africa, but it trains its focus on how the governing party, the ANC, responds to allegations that attacks on foreign nationals in South Africa are xenophobic. The ANC often denies the existence of xenophobia and characterizes attacks on foreign nationals as criminal rather than xenophobic. Judging from the intensity of violence and crime in South Africa, this stance, however erroneous and misleading it is, is understandable. Nevertheless, in chapter 8, Emmanuel Matambo characterizes the ANC's stance as a dangerous denial that inadvertently excuses and eschews the presence of anti-foreign sentiment among South Africans. The chapter concedes that socioeconomic factors, such as historical exclusion of previously disadvantaged groups and alarming levels of unemployment and inequality, are contributing factors to anti-foreign antipathy. However, these social economic factors, which occasionally breed crime toward foreign nationals, are not mutually exclusive to covert feelings of xenophobia among South Africans.

In chapter 9, Steve Siziba debates the relevance of Pan-Africanism in twenty-first-century Africa. As a concept, Pan-Africanism preceded Africa's decolonization, and was present beyond the continent's physical confines. As a continent that is the least integrated in terms of trade, it is explicable that some Africans have doubts about the reality and possibility of instituting Pan-Africanism. To some, Pan-African ideals are an unrealistic and wistful attempt to recapture a pristine African past, untainted by foreign and colonial domination and mores. To these skeptics, Pan-Africanism is neither possible nor realistic. Siziba challenges such skeptics and detractors of Pan-Africanism and argues that, in twenty-first-century Africa, Pan-Africanism is more relevant than ever. Achievements such as the AfCFTA testify to the presence of Pan-African quests in Africa. In sum, chapter 9 espouses the aspirations of Pan-Africanists in the mold of Kwame Nkrumah and Nelson Mandela who envisioned an Africa that seeks to surmount its challenges using a continental rather than a national approach.

Following Siziba's call for rejuvenating Pan-Africanism in twenty-first-century Africa, Lehasa Moloi in chapter 10 follows it up by arguing that Africa's road to development should follow an Afrocentric approach. Moloi uses the critical social theory of Afrocentricity to negotiate Africa's space at the center of the discourse of development, taking it back from the West, which has long arrogated that space. The basic assumption of the chapter is that the dominance of colonial and Eurocentric models in Africa has con-tributed to dismembering the continent, and this in turn has led to deepening xenophobia and Afrophobia. Therefore, an Afrocentric approach that builds on Pan-Africanist zeal could forge an Africa that is united and largely free of the specters of intra-African animosity across the continent's nations.

In chapter 11 Sky Mkuti continues to reflect on the fate of Pan-Africanism in Africa, against the backdrop of xenophobia in South Africa, especially after the highly publicized 2008 attacks. More pointedly, the author asks whether Pan-Africanism is alive or dead. Attacks on African foreign nation-als residing in South Africa could seem to seal the fate of Pan-Africanism, but Mkuti argues that, notwithstanding Afrophobic attacks, Africa's attempts to fortify Regional Economic Communities and the African Union (AU) demonstrate that Africa still hankers for Pan-Africanism.

The quest for Pan-Africanism encounters difficulties that are both of foreign and African making. In chapter 12 Akinkunmi Afeez Akinlabi argues that foreign-imposed difficulties to achieving Pan-Africanism stem from the identities that colonial structures imposed on their subjects. Before the onset of colonial control, identity in Africa mainly followed ethnic kinship. However, the onset of colonial rule divided the continent into artificial territories which were maintained even after the continent gained independence. National identities have ultimately calcified into seemingly inflexible compartments that breed a "we versus them" mentality, with nationality often the determinant. Akinlabi advocates a common African citizenship that could only be attained if prevailing divisive identities are transformed into more pliable characteristics.

The final chapter, chapter 13, continues a continental focus on Pan-Africanism and xenophobia. The author, Festus Chibuike Onuegbu, discusses the role of the AU in addressing the problem of xenophobia in South Africa. Onuegbu argues that the AU has the moral and political obligation to resolve sporadic xenophobic attacks. However, there is a paucity of academic literature on the role of the AU in stemming xenophobia in South Africa, and chapter 13 is an attempt to reduce that lacuna. The author argues that while the AU has made some commendable efforts to deal with xenophobia, its approach still needs more decisiveness.

Finally, the book has been written by scholars and academics spanning a host of expertise. Thus there is a variety of angles and perspectives on the subject at hand, but the converging attempt of all the 13 chapters was to make the book accessible and comprehensible to scholars, policymakers, workers in government institutions, and general readers. The topics addressed in this book are so important as to require the attention and efforts of all Africans and the world at large.

NOTES

1. Richard K. Betts, "Conflict or Cooperation? Three Visions Revisited," *African Affairs* 89, no. 6 (2010): 186–194, 189.

2. Nat O'Connor, "Three Connections between Rising Economic Inequality and the Rise of Populism," *Irish Studies in International Affairs* 28 (2017): 29–43.

3. Human Rights Watch. *World Report*. 2020, 223.

4. Huntington, Samuel P, "If Not Civilizations, What? Paradigms of the Post-Cold War World," *Foreign Affairs* 72, no. 5 (1993): 186–194.

5. Frantz Fanon, *The Wretched of the Earth* (New York: Grove Press, 1968), 315.

6. 705 Empire and General Kanene. *Banyamulenge*. 2020. https://www.youtube .com/watch?v=-W0vxY4yuFM.

7. Statistics South Africa. Quarterly Labour Force Survey, Quarter1: 2021. http:// www.statssa.gov.za/?p=14415.

8. Adeleke Olumide Ogunnoiki and Ademola Adefisayo Adeyemi, "The Impact of Xenophobic Attacks on Nigeria-South Africa Relations," *African Journal of Social Sciences and Humanities Research* 2, no. 2 (2019): 1–18.

9. SABC News. *RIP Kenneth Kaunda: Reflecting on the Life and Times of "KK" with Thabo Mbeki*. 2021. https://www.youtube.com/watch?v=hKjmTTfnLW0.

10. Adekeye Adebajo, "Vanquishing the Ghost of Cecil Rhodes: Historical Struggles to Transform South Africa's Humanities Curriculum." In *From Ivory Towers to Ebony Towers: Transforming Humanities Curricula in South Africa, Africa and African-American Studies*, ed. Oluwaseun Tella amd Shireen Motala (Sunnyside: Fanele, 2020), 13–29.

11. Xenowatch. 2021. *Incidents of Xenophobic Violence in South Africa: 1994-June 2021*. http://www.xenowatch.ac.za/statistics-dashboard/.

12. Human Rights Watch. *World Report*. (2009), 115. https://www.hrw.org/sites/ default/files/reports/wr2009_web_1.pdf.

13. Human Rights Watch. World, 2009 115.

14. Adekeye Adebajo, "Thabo Mbeki: The Pan-African Philosopher King." In *The Pan-African Pantheon: Prophets, Poets, and Philosophers*, ed. Adebajo, Adekeye (Auckland Park: Jacana Media, 2020): 167–181.

15. Department of Justice. *Anti-Xenophobia Pledge.* 2018. https://www.justice
.gov.za/nap/docs/Poster-AntiXenophobiaPledge-Feb2018.pdf.
16. Nkosazana Dlamini-Zuma. 2019. https://bit.ly/2TY5lh1.

REFERENCES

705 Empire and General Kanene. *Banyamulenge.* 2020. https://www.youtube.com/watch?v=-W0vxY4yuFM

Adebajo, Adekeye. "Thabo Mbeki: The Pan-African Philosopher King." In *The Pan-African Pantheon: Prophets, Poets, and Philosophers*, edited by Adekeye Adebajo, 167–181. Auckland Park: Jacana Media, 2020.

Adebajo, Adekeye. "Vanquishing the ghost of Cecil Rhodes: Historical struggles to transform South Africa's humanities curriculum." In *From Ivory Towers to Ebony Towers: Transforming Humanities Curricula in South Africa, Africa and African-American Studies*, edited by Oluwaseun Tella amd Shireen Motala, 13–29. Sunnyside: Fanele, 2020.

Betts, Richard K. 2010. "Conflict or Cooperation? Three Visions Revisited." *Foreign Affairs* 89 no. 6 (2010): 186–194.

Department of Justice. *Anti-Xenophobia Pledge.* 2018. https://www.justice.gov.za/nap/docs/Poster-AntiXenophobiaPledge-Feb2018.pdf

Fanon, Frantz. *The Wretched of the Earth.* New York: Grove Press, 1968.

Human Rights Watch. *World Report.* 2009. https://www.hrw.org/sites/default/files/reports/wr2009_web_1.pdf

Human Rights Watch. *World Report.* 2020, 223.

Huntington, Samuel P. "If Not Civilizations, What? Paradigms of the Post-Cold War World." Foreign Affairs 72, no. 5 (1993): 186–194. doi: 10.2307/20045880.

Nkosazana Dlamini-Zuma. 2019. https://bit.ly/2TY5lh1

O'Connor, Nat. "Three Connections between Rising Economic Inequality and the Rise of Populism." *Irish Studies in International Affairs* 28 (2017): 29–43.

Ogunnoiki, Adeleke Olumide and Ademola Adefisayo Adeyemi. "The Impact of Xenophobic attacks on Nigeria-South Africa Relations." *African Journal of Social Sciences and Humanities Research* 2, no. 2 (2019): 1–18.

SABC News. *RIP Kenneth Kaunda: Reflecting on the Life and Times of "KK" with Thabo Mbeki.* 2021. https://www.youtube.com/watch?v=hKjmTTfnLW0

Statistics South Africa. *Quarterly Labour Force Survey, Quarter1: 2021.* http://www.statssa.gov.za/?p=14415

Xenowatch. 2021. *Incidents of Xenophobic Violence in South Africa: 1994 - June 2021.* http://www.xenowatch.ac.za/statistics-dashboard/

Part I

NATIVISM AND XENOPHOBIA IN AFRICA

HISTORICAL CONTEXTS

Chapter 1

Citizenship Crisis, Pervasive Nativism, and Rising Afrophobia

Engaging Africa's "Trilemma" and Their Drivers in the Age of Globalization

Adeniyi S. Basiru

Following the Cold War, the system of states witnessed a monumental upsurge in a new genre of conflicts whose nature was markedly different from the Cold War epoch.[1] Driven by identities and rights concerns, mostly intrastate and low-intensity in nature, this mode of conflicts, or "new wars" to borrow Mary Kaldor's[2] elegant phrase, has become the dominant feature of the post–Cold War international security landscape. Interestingly, while few states appear to have performed exceptionally well in dealing with these conflicts, a vast majority would seem to have performed abysmally low and thus attracted epithets like "fragilestates" and "weakstates" among others.[3]

No area within the world's geopolitical space symbolizes this reality more fittingly than Africa. According to the Fund for Peace's Fragile State Index for 2020, except Botswana, Mauritius, and Seychelles, all African countries are on the watch list of weak, failing, or failed states.[4] Observably, among the "monsters" that have assailed the African states, in the past two decades, and exposed their failings in dealing with rights-oriented conflicts are the trilemma of citizenship crisis, pervasive nativity, and rising Afrophobia. To be sure, the common tragedy of all of these is the cyclical insecurity that they have visited on the African state system.

In the context of the foregoing, it is imperative to critically engage these challenges and their corollaries. This is more compelling in a rapidly globalizing world in which many nations are striving to meet up with the Sustainable Development Goals. How have postcolonial African states historically and generally related to the citizens within the territories? How do the citizens of African states view their fellow citizens and foreigners?

Deploying documentary data sourced through library search, this chapter examines these triple manifestations of state failure in Africa within the context of rising incidences of xenophobia on the continent. Specifically, the chapter attempts to unearth the drivers of citizenship crisis, pervasive nativity, and rising Afrophobia in Africa in a globalizing world.

The chapter proceeds in six sections. Following this introductory preamble is the second section which clarifies the concepts that are germane to this discourse with the intent to situating their operational meanings. This is followed by the theoretical framework whereby the "globalization" thesis is appropriated as an analytical anchor for the study. The section following that explores the nature of the post-African states and how the societies and the political economies that they have engendered have interacted with the contours of citizenship, promote nativism, and reinforce xenophobia (Afrophobia). The aim here is to show how the character of the state-citizens relations has been constructed over the years. The section following that engages and discusses the contextual issues and drivers of citizenship crisis, xenophobism, and other rights-oriented struggles in Africa. The sixth section concludes the chapter with a number of submissions.

CONCEPTUAL AND DEFINITIONAL ISSUES

Before delving into the intricacies of the subject of concern in this chapter, it is apposite to conceptualize the terms "citizenship crisis," "pervasive nativism," and "xenophobia/Afrophobia." This is crucial to gain a better understanding of their meanings in the context of the issues being discussed in this chapter. However, suffice to stress that these concepts, like most of their counterparts in social analysis, are essentially contested.[5] Given this reality and based on the fact that they are compound concepts, the methodology adopted for the purpose of clearing the undergrowths beneath these concepts is to aggregate and then disaggregate them to have a better understanding.

The concept of citizenship conveys different interpretations.[6] This, as Adepoju and Basiru note, may be unconnected to the fact that it has an organic connection to the concept of the state whose definition is also nebulous.[7] Notwithstanding, citizenship has generally been viewed as the domain of rights in which a segment of the population of a state, the citizens, connect with the state and its agents. By citizens here, it means a substratum of the population of the state that enjoys certain rights and privileges that are not enjoyed by the other substratum of the population (the aliens). Perhaps it is in this context that Charles Tilly[8] views citizenship as entailing a continuing series of transactions between persons and agents of a given state in which each has enforceable rights and obligations. More cogently, Adejumobi[9] avers that it is a form of social pact constituted by the dual elements of reciprocity and exchange between the individual and the state.

The point being made here is that citizenship has two sides: those of rights and obligations. To be sure, as citizens enjoy certain rights[10] by virtue of the constitution of the state, they must also render obligations[11] to the state and its agents. In the words of Dragger, "citizenship may be a matter of legal status that confers various privileges and immunities on the citizens. . . . 'Real' or 'true' citizenship requires commitment to the common goods and active participation in public affairs. It requires a civic virtue."[12] Viewed this way, therefore, it may be plausible to decipher a situation of stable citizenship in which both the state and the citizens dispense their historic mandates. According to Adepoju and Basiru,[13] drawing from the works of Heater[14] and Ifidon,[15] it is citizens reciprocating in terms of loyalty to the state and its officials for safeguarding and guaranteeing their rights. Adepoju and Basiru add further that should both sides in the citizenship equation renege in fulfilling their historic mandates, harmony would appear to break down, manifesting in all genres of contradictions and crises.[16] In the light of the foregoing, citizenship crisis suggests an immanent disconnect between the state and the citizens which often manifests in state failure and other state exiting strategies.[17] As it will soon be demonstrated, its ubiquity, in recent times, has contributed to increasing transnational migrations, xenophobia (Afrophobia), and different genres of violent ethno-nationalism across Africa.

From the foregoing, the state is central to the construction of citizenship. It is also pivotal to its deconstruction through its action and those of its agents. Put differently, state policies and programs instead of promoting social inclusivity among the citizenry could rather promote exclusivity and ethnic injustice and contribute to further deepening the citizenship crisis.[18] Conceptually, these tendencies in literature constitute "nativism." Generally, it depicts policy or regulation put in place by the state and its custodians to protect the rights and interests of native-born citizens or a privileged ethnic group within a country. Either way, it is discriminatory and exclusionary in nature as it seeks to marginalize a segment of the population from participating in certain aspects of the societal life. As regards the latter, it is often targeted, via immigration laws and regulations, against immigrants to prevent them from enjoying some rights that the custodians of the state think should be reserved for citizens. In the latter sense, immigrants are not the focus but rather the ruling elites, via nationalist policy, target fellow citizens for electoral exclusion, land deprivation, and so on.[19] In the context of foregoing and for the purpose of this discourse, pervasive nativism would then suggest a condition in which the afore-explained practices have become so widespread to the extent that they have been institutionalized as part of the political game.[20]

The concept of Afrophobia cannot be unearthed without grasping the concept of xenophobia. Indeed, it has been contended that the term "Afrophobia" is an Africanization of the concept of xenophobia. Xenophobia, a linguistic contraction of two Latin words "xeno" and "phobia," has been assailed with several interpretations in literature. According to one source, it is fear or hatred of strangers or foreigners or of anything foreign or strange.[21] At another level, it is defined as an irrational fear of foreigners or of anything foreign.[22] For Miller, "it is the attitudes, prejudices and behavior that reject, exclude often vilify persons, based on the perception that they are outsiders or foreigners to the community, society or national identity."[23] What could be deduced from the foregoing is that xenophobia is an attitudinal system that is hinged on disdain and hatred for others that are not from one's in-group. While it has generally and historically been conceived as a vile disposition toward foreigners (migrants, refugees, etc.), its meaning now includes ethnocentrist dispositions. Put differently, it is now linked with a disposition that sees one's group or culture as superior to others. Viewed in the foregoing context, therefore, Afrophobia would suggest fears and hatred of Africans toward other Africans.

THEORETICAL FRAMEWORK

The trilemma of citizenship crisis, pervasive nativism, and rising Afrophobia that has assailed the postcolonial African national states could be analyzed from a variety of theoretical standpoints. To be sure, this could be attributed to seemingly multitudes of agential and structural challenges. This writer is not oblivious of this reality. However, in this study, globalization theoretical perspective is adopted. This is informed by the fact that, since the end of the Cold War, no exogenous force would seem to have shaped the behavior of the state, on the one hand, and its relations with the society, subnationally and transnationally, on the other hand, as globalization.[24] Although like most time-tested theoretical paradigms in the social sciences, globalization, here defined as the growing interconnectedness and interrelatedness of all aspects of society,[25] has different theoretical sects.[26]

Notwithstanding, there seems to be a consensus that the Westphalia state has been a major victim of the force of globalization.[27] This thesis, as promoted by Rosenau,[28] Strange,[29] Held and McGrew,[30] Cox,[31] and Kofman and Youngs[32], contends that while globalization has no doubt aided global transformation and integration of societies, it has also fundamentally undermined the territorial state. Putting this more succinctly, Castells[33] remarks,

The nation-state is increasingly submitted to a more subtle, and more troubling competition from sources of power that are undefined, and sometimes, undefinable. These are networks of capital, production, communication, crime, international institutions, supranational military apparatuses, non-governmental organizations, transnational religious and public opinion movements. And below the state, there are communities, tribes, localities, cults, and gangs. So, while nation-states continue to exist, and they will continue to do so in the foreseeable future, there are, and there will increasingly be, *nodes of a broader networks of power*. They will often be confronted by other flows of power in the network, which directly contradict the exercise of their authority. (Castells's emphasis)

Reechoing this, Adejumobi[34] posits that "the content and character of globalization promote social fragmentation, disintegration and disaggregation; split groups and identities into warring factions; undermine the state by emptying it of its social content and relevance." What could be deduced from the foregoing is that this thesis posits that nation-state is not a dinosaur waiting to die as Kenichi Ohmae[35] once noted but rather does not exercise sovereignty as it used to.[36] As Jones[37] contends, globalization has removed the ability of the central states to effect changes in their nominally sovereign territories. In a similar vein, Held et al.[38] are of the view that the flow of illegal and undocumented migrants, economic and noneconomic, further attests to the reality of the limited capacity of many nation-states to secure independently their own borders.

More fundamentally, it is further posited that, courtesy of the triumph of neoliberalism, the ideological underpinning of globalization, the state has succumbed to the fundamentalism of the market.[39] Thus, it is contended, the state has abandoned its historic role of social provisioning, and this has led to inequality within and between countries.[40] To be sure, as the central state downsizes its social provisioning role in deference to the dictate of market, a new model of state-society relations has developed in many societies of the world.[41] From the foregoing, it is apt to infer that the globalization thesis would appear to offer a plausible explanatory framework for understanding the state-society relations in Africa in a neoliberal world order.

By keying into the globalization-oriented framework of development in the past three decades, as part of aid conditionality, postcolonial African states would appear not only to have lost the sovereignties to manage their national economies to the custodians of global capitalism but to have also abandoned their social provisioning roles.[42] As it would soon be demonstrated, as the state winds down the social aspect of citizenship, citizens are pushed to withdraw their support for the state and invest same in subnational and transnational entities; whereupon citizenship crisis and nativism increase in salience.

STATES-CITIZENS RELATIONS IN AFRICA: A HISTORIOGRAPHY AND POLITICAL ECONOMY

To start with, the states that today superintend the populations in various territories in Africa were creations of an imperialist force.[43] Indeed, as Opello and
Rosow[44] remark, "it is impossible to understand the development of modern
states without taking into account the way European States constructed an
interconnected global order by means of conquest, trade, religious conversion
and diplomacy." Prior to this era, various communities had evolved various
forms of political organizations. To be sure, while some had evolved into
mega centralized states, others were many mini states in terms of governing
structures and administrative sizes.[45] Irrespective of the forms, by the first
decades of the twentieth century, they were all territorialized into extroverted
state systems superintended by the metropolitan states. In the words of
Adepoju and Basiru,

> By 1900, Africans, courtesy of the firepower of the Europeans lost their
> territories and independence to the invaders.
>   The consequence of the losses of Africans to the invaders was the imposition
> of superstructure states, which were totally alien to the people.[46]

Interestingly, given the way they were floated and coupled with their raison
d'être, which was to exploit the natives for the benefit of the metropoles,[47]
the colonial states had to depend majorly but not exclusively on raw force.
In French Africa, for instance, it was operationalized massively through the
indigenenant policy. To be sure, as long as the indigenenant policy lasted, it
was justified on the rationale of "mission civilisatrice."[48] Beyond a system of
coercive rule, a system of rule that bifurcated the society was institutionalized
by the colonial states in Africa.[49] Such a system, as Ekeh[50] and Mamdani[51]
have extensively dealt with in their seminal works, created a disjointed
model of citizenship which later became the albatross of many countries after
independence.[52]

Colonial rule, however, with the passage of time, generated its own
internal contradictions that heralded its winding down starting with the
independence of Ghana in 1957. Indeed, by 1960s, most colonies had attained
their independence as liberal democratic states.[53] By these transitions, the
burden of developing Africa and its people now fell on the shoulders of the
nascent ruling elites who were the torchbearers of the nationalist struggles.
These leaders individually and collectively, through the auspices of the
Organization of African Unity (OAU), made efforts to develop their countries
to the extent that modest economic growths were recorded in the 1960s and
1970s.[54] However, by the 1980s and 1990s, the continent had been gripped

by excruciating debts and developmental crisis with serious implications for governance and state-society relations.[55] This raises the question "How did this arise?" This calls for the historicization of the continent's political economy.

At independence, African countries were ushered into Weberian state systems under multiparty models.[56] Soonest, however, under the guise of promoting national integration and curtailing ethnicity, the inherited multiparty systems were jettisoned for one-party systems.[57] Justifying this, leaders like Julius Nyerere and Léopold Senghor of Tanzania and Senegal, respectively, contended that adversarial politics, synonymous with multiparty democracies, was alien to Africa's sociocultural milieu.[58] By institutionalizing one-party systems, politics became more contentious and warlike as the oppositions and the ruling parties battled one another to control the souls of the states. To be sure, this development paved the way for the "specialist" in violence, the military, to abandon their constitutional role to intervene in African politics. As Claude Ake has rightly argued, it was the warlike character of politics that predisposes the African military to intervene in African politics.[59] More tragically, by the latter part of the 1960s and early 1970s, a system of neo-patrimonial rule, in which the leaders deploy patronage as the basis of legitimacy, has become the norm in Africa.[60]

The point being made here is that many countries by this period descended into neo-patrimonial rule under one-party regimes or military juntas. Under this model of rule, as explained by Thomson,[61] except the few (clients) that have access to state resources and thus benefit from the state, the majority of the citizens were left to wait for their time when their kinsmen may take charge of power. Ivory Coast under Houphouët Boigny offers an illustration here. In the heyday of Boigny's one-party rule in Côte d'Ivoire, not only did he centralize power in the presidency, organically linked to his clique of clients, but he also deployed the machinery of his party, Democratic Party of Ivory Coast, to coordinate the distribution of patronage to supporters across the country.[62] To be sure, the chief beneficiaries in all of these are his kinsmen who were rewarded with the location of the country's capital and the largest Basilica in the world, both sited in Yamoussoukro—Boigny's hometown.

Interestingly, this model of rule aside disconnecting the state from the society also had implications for the economies. This is explained as follows: since patronage and its corollary, clientelism, is the vertebra for sustaining this form of rule,[63] the personal rulers often move to control the national economies by centralizing the development processes. Indeed, until the early 1990s, parastatals and state-owned enterprises came to dominate all large-scale economic activities across many countries in Africa.[64] Unfortunately, given the motives behind their formation and proliferations, these entities became conduit pipes for siphoning state resources for patronage. Putting this in perspective, Thomson writes,

> With political considerations overriding administrative or economic needs in these neo-patriomonial institutions, efficiency inevitably suffered. Public servants were often employed because of their loyalty or faction or ethnic links, not for their skills, experience or ability to do the job. Indeed, the need to provide patronage often left these institutions considerably overstaffed.[65]

However, by the 1990s, as a result of dwindling revenues and the loss of Cold War patronage, there were not enough resources to sustain this practice. Consequently, as the resources of the state dwindled and the state also keyed into neoliberal globalization and its ideology which enjoins the state to divest from public provisioning, the distribution capacity of the state was further weakened.[66] Observably, this resulted in the states inverting their social responsibilities to the citizens. As the crisis of governance and the economy further deepened, African states would appear to have lost the sovereignties to control their citizens and territories.[67] The outcome of this state of affairs is that citizens recalibrated their relations with the states via engagements and disengagements.

Suffice to stress that while some engage the state by obeying it when it was in their interests to do so and avoid it when it was not,[68] others disengage (exit) the state by migrating to other jurisdictions.[69] In most extreme cases, the citizens resorted to armed insurgencies directed against the state.[70] A clear case is the Tuaregs, an itinerant group in the Sahel region that had engaged the central states in Bamako and Niamey for almost three decades for inclusion in the states.[71] Irrespective of the strategies, citizens' alienation has been manifesting in citizenship crisis in postcolonial Africa.[72] Interestingly, beyond vertical engagements with the state, citizens observably often do respond horizontally to loss of opportunities, arising from state incapacity, by "scapegoating" noncitizens and immigrants.[73] Added to this is the fact state elites themselves often hide their failures by adopting a policy of nativism in order to whip nationalistic sentiments and been seen as protecting the interests of citizens against foreigners.[74]

CITIZENSHIP CRISIS, PERVASIVE NATIVISM, RISING AFRO-PHOBIA: DRIVERS AND CONTEXTS

It should be clear from the discussions in the last section that the state-citizens schism and its throwbacks have been features of Africa's development trajectory. It is thus germane to decipher and engage some of the contextual issues that are probably the drivers of citizenship crisis, pervasive nativism, and rising Afro-phobia. The first is the force of globalization which has impacted on the way the postcolonial African states and their functionaries have conducted their affairs internally and externally.[75] Politically, the postcolonial African states and their superintendents, in the past three decades, had embraced the political framework of globalization (democratization) as part of the "political conditionalities" of the Bretton Woods Institutions.[76] Although the postcolonial African states have not been democratized, the political elites, would seem to have, accepted liberal democracy as a fait accompli.[77] Indeed, not only that elections have become regular features of the continent's political landscape, in the past three decades, liberal democratic norms have also been codified in the extant Charter of the OAU/AU.[78]

The implication of the institutionalization of democracy is that people now have wider latitude in the enjoyment of their democratic rights as citizens than ever before. It would be recalled that before the democratic third wave, the authoritarian regimes of all shapes that pervaded Africa's polities gave little room for people to ventilate their rights.[79] With democracy, however, this changed as individuals and groups that have been guillotined during the praetorian era now had the greater temerity to voice out their demands against the state. Aside improved "hygiene environment" for ventilating individual and groups' political rights, the demands for economic rights (rights to job, decent living, housing, etc.) in many countries also heightened.

Unfortunately, this era coincided with the era of structural adjustment programs (economic globalization). As briefly teased out earlier, by keying into neoliberal globalization, the ideological anchorage of Stuctural Adjustment Programs (SAP), African states introduced the logic of the market into the public and social services sector. Mustapha,[80] following Mkandawire,[81] has argued that globalization, encapsulated as neoliberal reforms, introduced by African leaders have resulted in eroding the developmental capacities of African states. Joining issue with Mustapha, Amuwo[82] remarks, "The neoliberal onslaught against African political economies in the past three decades has almost everywhere incapacitated the neo-colonial state, jeopardized its performance legitimacy and emptied it of its content."

To be sure, the failures of the African states to effectively meet the socioeconomic demands of the people, as a result of their weakened developmental capacities, may have contributed to citizenship crisis, xenophobia, hatred, and instabilities in Africa. In South Africa, for instance, the failure of the authorities to meet up with the citizens' demands for certain economic benefits would have created wedge between the citizens and migrants leading to xenophobia.[83] Put differently, most citizens would have perceived that their brethren from other African countries have been taken over their jobs.

Related to the force of globalization and the attendant weakened capacities of the African states is the contextual issue of the proliferation of ungoverned spaces across the continent.[84] As the African states abandon their historic roles in social provisioning, many swaths of the African territories have, in the three decades, remained ungoverned. For instance, some exciting studies have demonstrated how some citizens in the North-East region of Nigeria have transferred their loyalties to groups other than the Nigerian state.[85] Perhaps, this is unconnected to the failure of the Nigerian state, over the years, to meet the needs of this category of citizen and as such any entity that fills this gap is regarded as the "the state" by them.[86]

The state-society schism in postcolonial Africa is another lens through which the problem can be x-rayed. This, however, has to be situated in a proper historical context. It would be recalled that colonial rule in Africa left an inheritance in which the state sees the society as entity that needs to caged. That is why the postcolonial African states and their custodians would seem not to have really considered the society as a partner in nation-building. Indeed, in Africa, to paraphrase to Rothchild and Chazan,[87] the state and society are in a precarious balance. Again, as Mafeje[88] notes, a state in order to have a firm root must develop organically out of society and must construct hegemony and legitimacy for itself in society. Unfortunately, the postcolonial state in Africa would appear not to have been able to do this. Resultantly, the citizens that should be the beneficiaries of the functional synergy between the state and the society have been at the receiving end.

CONCLUDING REMARKS

This chapter set out to examine the triple manifestations of state failure in Africa within the context of mounting citizenship crisis and rising xenophobia (Afro-phobia). It also sought to unravel the contextual drivers of these challenges. In furtherance of these objectives, it undertook a conceptual analysis, teased out a theoretical framework, and historicized the trajectories of state-citizens relations in Africa. Really, the state should connect with the society and the citizens under its watch. However, as this chapter has demonstrated, this is not the case in postcolonial Africa. In Africa, the state does not connect with the society and the citizens. This is unconnected with the prevalence of states whose capacities to deliver social provisions to the citizens have been weakened by the force of neoliberal globalization. Yet, peace, security, and stability are sine qua non for sustainable development. More importantly, these challenges are antithetical to the continent's quest for Pan-African integration as envisaged in Agenda 2063. In the context of the foregoing, putting things back together will require the re-legitimization and re-democratization of the postcolonial African states so that they can be partners with the societies and the citizens.

NOTES

1. Tamuno Tekena, *Peace and Violence in Nigeria* (Ibadan: History Project, 1991), 10.

2. See Mary Kaldor, *New and Old Wars: Organized Violence in a Global Era* (London: Polity Press, 1998).

3. Eghosa Osaghae, "Revisiting the Concepts of State fragility and State building in Africa." In *Fifty years of Nationhood? State, Society and Politics in Nigeria (1960-2010).* eds. S. O. Akinboye and M. M. Fadakinte (Lagos: Concept Publications Limited, 2010), 75–131.

4. Fund for Peace, *Fragile State Index* (Washington, DC: Fund for Peace (FFP) Publishers, 2020).

5. Williams B. Gallie, "Essentially Contested Concepts," in *The Importance of Language*, ed. M. Black (New Jersey: Prentice Hall, 1962), 170.

6. Said Adejumobi, "Identity, Citizenship and Conflict: The African Experience," in *The Crisis of the State and Regionalism in West Africa*, ed. Alade Fawole and Charles Ukeje (Dakar: CODESRIA, 2005), 21.

7. Adewale Adepoju and Adeniyi Basiru, "The State and Crisis of Citizenship in Contemporary Africa: Revisiting the Globalization Thesis," *African Journal of Democracy & Governance*, 6, no. 2 & 3 (2019), 205.

8. Charles Tilly "Citizen, Identity and Social History," *International Review of Social History*, 3 (1996), 8.

9. Adejumobi, "Identity, Citizenship and Conflict: The African Experience," 206.

10. These rights are usually enshrined in national constitutions. They include rights to freedom of movement, residence, association, due process, and equality before the law, franchise, and social welfare.

11. Some of the obligations expected from citizens include payment of taxes; military conscriptions; if need arises, loyalty to the state; and so on.

12. R. Dragger, "Republican Citizenship," in *Handbook of Citizenship Studies*, ed. E. Isin and B. Turner (London: Sage, 2002), 149.

13. Adepoju and Basiru, "The State and Crisis of Citizenship in Contemporary Africa: Revisiting the Globalization Thesis," 207.

14. D. Heater, *What is Citizenship?* (Cambridge: Polity Press, 1999).

15. E. Ifidon, "Citizenship, Statehood and the Problem of Democratization," *Africa Development*, XXI, no. 1 & 2 (1996).

16. Adepoju and Basiru, "The State and Crisis of Citizenship in Contemporary Africa: Revisiting the Globalization Thesis", 207.

17. See Jeffrey Herbst and Richard Joseph, "Correspondence: Responding to State Failure in Africa," *International Security*, 22, no. 2 (1997).

18. See M. Mamdani, *Citizen and Subject: Contemporary Africa and the Legacy of Late Colonialism* (Princeton: Princeton University Press, 1996); T. Kuran, "Ethnic

Norms and their Transformation through reputational Cascade," *Journal of Legal Studies*, 27 (1998).

19. See C. Boone and N. Kriger, "Land Patronage and Elections: Winners and Losers in Zimbabwe and Côte d'Ivoire," in *Voting in Fear: Electoral Violence in Sub-Saharan Africa*. ed. D. A. Bekoe (Washington, DC: United States Institute for Peace Press, 2012); R. Banegas and R. Marshall-Fratani, "Cote d'Ivoire: Negotiating Identity and Citizenship," in *African Guerrillas: Raging against the Machine*. ed. M. Boas and K. C. Dunn (Boulder, CO: Lynne Rienner, 2007); I. Cote and M. I. Mitchell "Elections and 'Sons of the Soil': Conflict Dynamics in Africa and Asia," *Democratization* 23, no. 4 (2016): 657–677.

20. Mahmood Mamdani, *When Victims Become Killers: Colonialism, Nativism and the Genocide in Rwanda* (Kampala: Fountain Publishers/Oxford: James Currey, 2001).

21. www.yourdictionary.com/ xenophobia (accessed November10, 2020).

22. www.macmillandictionary.com/ xenophobia (accessed November 8, 2020).

23. Sarah D. Miller, *Xenophobia Toward Refugees and Other Forced Migrants* (Ontario: Centre for International Governance Innovation, 2018), 2.

24. See Ali Mazrui, "Identity Politics and the Nation-State under Siege: Towards a Theory of Reverse Evolution," *Social Dynamics*, 35, no. 2 (1999).

25. Andrew Jones, *Dictionary of Globalization* (Cambridge: Polity Press, 2006), 12–13.

26. A. Tidwell and C. Lerche, "Globalization and Conflict Resolution," *International Journal of Peace Studies*, 9, no. 1 (2004): 48.

27. Jones, "Dictionary of Globalization," 12–13.

28. James Rosenau, *The Study of World Politics, Volume 2: Globalization and Governance* (London/New York: Routledge, 2006).

29. S. Strange, "The Declining Authority of States," in *The Globalization Reader*, ed. J. Lechner and F. Boli (Oxford: Blackwell, 2004).

30. D. Held and A. McGrew, *The Global Transformations Readers* (Cambridge: Polity, 2003).

31. R. Cox, "A Perspective on Globalization," in *Globalization: Critical Reflections*, ed. J. Mittelman (New York: Lynne Reinner, 1997).

32. E. Kofman and C. Youngs, *Globalization: Theory and Practice* (London: Pinter, 2001).

33. Quoted in James Rosenau, "The Study of World Politics, Volume 2: Globalization and Governance," 24.

34. Adejumobi, "Identity, Citizenship and Conflict: The African Experience," 19.

35. See Kenichi Ohmae, "The End of the Nation State," in *The Globalization Reader*, ed. J. Lechner and F. Boli (Oxford: Blackwell, 2004).

36. See S. Krasner, "Compromising Westphalia," in *The Global Transformations Readers*, ed. D. Held and A. McGrew (Cambridge: Polity, 2003).

37. Jones, "Dictionary of Globalization," 45.

38. D. Held et al., "People on the Move," in *Global Transformations*, ed. D. Held et al. (Cambridge: Polity, 1999).

39. See S. E. Khan, "Bringing the State Back In: Critique of Neo-liberal Globalization," *African Journal of International Affairs and Development*, 3, no. 1 (1995).

40. See M. Khor, *Rethinking Globalization: Critical Issues and Policy Choices* (London: Zed Books, 2001).

41. See R. Robertson, *Globalization: Social Theory and Global Culture* (London: Sage Publication, 1993).

42. See Dani Nabudere, "Globalization, the African Post-Colonial State, Post Traditionalism and the New World Order," in *Globalization and the African Post-Colonial State*, ed. Dani Nabudere (Harare: AAPS Books, 2001); K. Ninsin, *Globalization and the Future of the Africa* (Harare: AAPS Occasional Paper Series, 4, 1, 2000).

43. Adepoju and Basiru, "The State and Crisis of Citizenship in Contemporary Africa: Revisiting the Globalization Thesis," 211.

44. W. Opello and S. Rosow, *The Nation-State and Global Order: A Historical Introduction to Contemporary Politics* (London: Lynne Reiner, 2000), 121.

45. A. Thomson, *An Introduction to African Politics* (London/New York: Routledge, 2000), 8.

46. Adepoju and Basiru, "The State and Crisis of Citizenship in Contemporary Africa: Revisiting the Globalization Thesis," 212.

47. See W. Rodney, *How Europe Underdeveloped Africa* (Dar-es-Salam: Tanzania Publishing House, 1972).

48. A. Basiru, "Extra-African Powers and the Crisis of Regionalism in Africa: Background to and Reflections on France's Engagement with Africa," *Africa Review*, 8, no. 2 (2016): 101.

49. Adepoju and Basiru, "The State and Crisis of Citizenship in Contemporary Africa: Revisiting the Globalization Thesis," 213.

50. See P. Ekeh, "Colonialism and the Two Publics in Africa: A Theoretical Statement," *Comparative Studies in Society and History*, 17, no. 1 (1975).

51. See M. Mamdani, *Citizen and Subject: Contemporary Africa and the Legacy of Late Colonialism*.

52. Adepoju and Basiru, "The State and Crisis of Citizenship in Contemporary Africa: Revisiting the Globalization Thesis."

53. A. Thomson, *An Introduction to African Politics* (London/New York: Routledge, 2000), 17.

54. Blessing Chinsinga, "Resurrecting the Developmental State in Malawi," in *Reforming the Malawian Public Sector*. ed. R. Tambulasi (Dakar: CODESRIA, 2010), 92.

55. Bayo Adekanye, *Linking Conflict Diagnosis, Conflict Prevention, Conflict Management in Contemporary Africa* (Lagos: Ababa Press Ltd, 2007), 16–36.

56. A. Thomson, *An Introduction to African Politics*, 110.

57. Adeniyi Basiru and Olusesan Osunkoya, "Between the Rock and a Hard Place: The Africa Union and Democracy Promotion in Africa," *Journal of Governance and Development*, 16, no. 1, (June 2020): 50.

Claude Ake, *Democracy and Development in Africa* (Washington, DC: The Brookings Institution, 1996), 6.

58. See Julius Nyerere, "Spearhead," in *The Ideologies of Developing Nations*, ed. Paul Sigmund (New York: Praeger, 1963), 188.

59. Claude Ake, *Democracy and Development in Africa* (Washington, DC: The Brookings Institution, 1996), 6.

60. Jean Medard, "The Underdeveloped State in Tropical Africa: Political Clientelism or Neo-Patrimonialism," in *Private Patronage and Public Power*, ed. C. Clapham (London: Pinter, 1982).

61. A. Thomson, *An Introduction To African Politics*, 119–120.

62. Ibid.

63. Ibid.

64. See G. Harrison, *The World Bank and Africa: The Construction of Governance States* (London: Routledge, 2004).

65. A. Thomson, *An Introduction to African Politics*, 204.

66. See T. Lumumba-Kasongo, "Reconceptualizing the State as the Leading Agent of Development in the Context of Globalization in Africa," *African Journal of Political Science*, 7, no. 1 (2002).

67. Adeniyi Basiru et al., "Nigeria's Quadrilemma: Globalization, State Delegitimization, Religious Fundamentalism and Insecurity," *Journal of International Studies*, 12 (2016).

68. A. Thomson, *An Introduction to African Politics*, 207.

69. See Eghosa Osaghae, "Exiting from the State in Nigeria," *Journal of African Political Science*, 4, no. 1 (1999).

70. Herbert Wulf, *Challenging the Weberian Concept of the State: The Future of the Monopoly of Violence*. The Australian Centre for Peace and Conflict Studies Occasional Papers Series. Number 9, December 2007. Available from: http://www.wulf-herbert.de/ACPACS-occpaper9. pdf (Accessed October 21, 2018).

71. Charles Thomas and Toyin Falola, *Secession and Separatist Conflicts in Postcolonial Africa* (Calgary: University of Calgary Press , 2020), 231.

72. See Adeniyi Basiru, "Globalization and the State: Implications for the State of Human Rights in Africa," *Inkanyiso: Humanities and Social Sciences Journal*, 7, no. 1 (2015): 53–59.

73. See Loren Landau, "Loving the Alien? Citizenship, Law, and the Future in South Africa's Demonic Society," *African Affairs* 109, no. 435 (2010), 213–230; Jean Pierre Misago, "Politics by Other Means? The Political Economy of Xenophobic in Post-apartheid South Africa," *The Black Scholar*, 47, no. 2 (2017), 40–53.

74. See Loren Landau, *Exorcising the Demons Within: Xenophobia, Violence and Statecraft in Contemporary South Africa* (Johannesburg: Wits University Press, 2011).

75. See K. Mengisteab, "Globalization and State-Society Relations in Africa," *African Development*, 33, no. 2 (2008).

76. Adekanye, *Linking Conflict Diagnosis, Conflict Prevention, Conflict Management in Contemporary Africa*.

77. See N. J. Udombana, "Articulating the Right to Democratic Governance in Africa," *Michigan Journal of International Law*, 24, no. 4 (2003): 1209–1287.

78. See P. J. Glen, "Institutionalizing Democracy in Africa: A Comment on the African Charter on Democracy, Elections and Governance," *African Journal of Legal Studies* 5, no. 2 (2012).

79. Adeniyi Basiru and Olusesan Osunkoya, "Between the Rock and a Hard Place: The Africa Union and Democracy Promotion in Africa," 50.

80. A. R. Mustapha, "Rethinking Africanist Political Science," in *The Study of Africa, Vol.1: Disciplinary and Interdisciplinary Encounters*. ed. P.T Zelesa (Dakar: CODESRIA, 2006).

81. T. Mkandawire, "Maladjusted African Economies and Globalization," *African Development*, 30, no. 1&2 (2005).

82. Kunle Amuwo, "Capitalist Globalization and the Roles of the International Community in Resource Conflicts in Africa," *Africa Development*, XXX, no. 3 &4 (2009), 18.

83. See Landau, *Exorcising the Demons Within: Xenophobia, Violence and Statecraft in Contemporary South Africa.*

84. See Jennifer Keister, "The Illusion of Chaos: Why Ungoverned Spaces Aren't Ungoverned and Why That Matters." *Policy Analysis*, 766 (2014): 1–24; Anne Clunan and Harold Trinkunas, *Ungoverned Spaces: Alternatives to State Authority in an Era of Softened Sovereignty* (Stanford, CA: Stanford University Press, 2010).

85. See Olawale Albert, *Beyond Nigeria's Sambisa: Forests, Insurgency and Counter-Insurgency in Africa* (Ibadan: Ibadan University Press, 2017); Al Chukwuma Okoli, "Boko Haram Insurgency and the Necessity for Trans-territorial Forestland Governance in the Lower Lake Chad Basin," *African Journal on Conflict Resolution*, 19, no. 1 (2019): 37–56.

86. P. Adejoh, "The State, Terrorism and Nigeria's National Security," in *Terrorism and Counter Terrorism War in Nigeria: Essays in Honour of Lieutenant General Tukur Yusuf Buratai*, ed. P. Adejoh and W. Adisa (Lagos: University of Lagos Press, 2018).

87. See D. Rothchild and N. Chazan, eds., *The Precarious Balance: The State and Society in Africa* (Boulder: Westview, 1988).

88. Archie Mafeje, "State and Civil Society in Independent Africa," in *Networking with a View to Promoting Peace: Conflicts in the Horn of Africa*, ed. Henrich Boll Foundation (Addis Ababa: Henrich Boll, 1999), 67–82.

BIBLIOGRAPHY

Adejumobi, S. "Identity, Citizenship and Conflict: The African Experience". In *The Crisis of the State and Regionalism in West Africa*, edited by Alade Fawole & Charles Ukeje. Dakar: CODESRIA, 2005.

Adekanye, B. *Linking Conflict Diagnosis, Conflict Prevention, Conflict Management in Contemporary Africa*. Lagos: Ababa Press Ltd, 2007.

Adepoju, A. and Basiru, A. "The State and Crisis of Citizenship in Contemporary Africa: Revisiting the Globalization Thesis". *African Journal of Democracy & Governance*, no. 2&3 (2019): 202–226.

Ake, C. *Democracy and Development in Africa*. Washington, DC: The Brookings Institution, 1996.

Albert, O. *Beyond Nigeria's Sambisa: Forests, Insurgency and Counter-Insurgency in Africa*. Ibadan: Ibadan University Press, 2017.

Amuwo, K. "Capitalist Globalization and the Roles of the International Community in Resource Conflicts in Africa". *Africa Development* no. 3&4 (2009): 227–266.

Banegas, R. and Marshall-Fratani, R. "Cote d'Ivoire: Negotiating Identity and Citizenship". In *African Guerrillas: Raging against the Machine*, edited by M. Boas and K. C. Dunn. Boulder, CO: Lynne Rienner, 2007.

Basiru, A and Osunkoya, O. "Between the Rock and a Hard Place: The Africa Union and Democracy Promotion in Africa". *Journal of Governance and Development* 16, no. 1 (2020): 49–67.

Basiru, A. "Globalization and the State: Implications for the State of Human Rights in Africa". *Inkanyiso: Humanities and Social Sciences Journal* 7, no. 1 (2015): 53–59.

Basiru, A. "Extra-African Powers and the Crisis of Regionalism in Africa: Background to and Reflections on France's Engagement with Africa". *Africa Review* 8, no. 2 (2016): 96–107.

Basiru, A. et al "Nigeria's Quadrilemma: Globalization, State delegitimization, Religious Fundamentalism and Insecurity". *Journal of International Studies* 12, (2016): 145–160.

Boone, C. and Kriger, N. "*Land Patronage and Elections: Winners and Losers in Zimbabwe and Côte d'Ivoire*". In *Voting in Fear: Electoral Violence in Sub-Saharan Africa*, edited by D. A. Bekoe. Washington DC: United States Institute for Peace Press, 2012.

Chinsinga, B. "Resurrecting the Developmental State in Malawi" In *Reforming the Malawian Public Sector*, edited by R. Tambulasi. Dakar: CODESRIA, 2010.

Clunan, A. and Trinkunas, H. *Ungoverned Spaces: Alternatives to State Authority in an Era of Softened Sovereignty*. Stanford, CA: Stanford University Press, 2010.

Cote, I. and Mitchell, M. I. "Elections and 'Sons of the Soil': Conflict Dynamics in Africa and Asia". *Democratization* 23, no. 4 (2016): 657–677.

Cox, R. "A Perspective on Globalization". In *Globalization: Critical Reflections*, edited by J. Mittelman. New York: Lynne Reinner, 1997.

Dragger, R. "Republican Citizenship". In *Handbook of Citizenship Studies*, edited by E. Isin and B. Turner. London: Sage, 2002.

Ekeh, P. "Colonialism and the Two Publics in Africa: A Theoretical Statement". *Comparative Studies in Society and History* 17, no. 1 (1975): 91–112.

Fund for Peace. *Fragile State Index*. Washington, DC: Fund for Peace (FFP) Publishers, 2020.

Gallie, W. B "Essentially Contested Concepts". In *The Importance of Language*, edited by M. Black. New Jersey: Prentice Hall, 1962.

Glen, P. J. "Institutionalizing Democracy in Africa: A Comment on the African Charter on Democracy, Elections and Governance". *African Journal of Legal Studies*, 5 (153), 2012.

Harrison, G. *The World Bank and Africa: The Construction of Governance States.* London: Routledge, 2004.

Heater, D. *What is Citizenship?*. Cambridge: Polity Press, 1999.

Held, D. and McGrew, A. *The Global Transformations Readers.* Cambridge: Polity, 2003.

Held, D. et al. "People on the Move". In *Global Transformations,* edited by D. Held et al. Cambridge: Polity, 1999.

Herbst, J. and Joseph, R. "Correspondence: Responding to state failure in Africa". *International Security* 22, no. 92 (1997): 175–184.

Ifidon, E. "Citizenship, Statehood and the Problem of Democratization". *Africa Development*21, no. 4 (1996): 93–107.

Jones, A. *Dictionary of Globalization.* Cambridge: Polity Press, 2006.

Kaldor, M. *New and Old Wars: Organized Violence in a Global Era.* London: Polity Press, 1998.

Keister, J. "The Illusion of Chaos: Why Ungoverned Spaces aren't Ungoverned and Why That Matters". *Policy Analysis*, no. 766 (2014): 1–24.

Khan, S. E "Bringing the State Back In: Critique of Neo-liberal Globalization". *African Journal of International Affairs and Development*, 11, no. 1 (1995): 128–144.

Khor, M. *Rethinking Globalization: Critical Issues and Policy Choices.* London: Zed Books, 2001.

Kofman, E. and Youngs, C. *Globalization: Theory and Practice.* London: Pinter, 2001.

Krasner, S. "Compromising Westphalia". In *The Global Transformations Readers,* edited by D. Held and A. McGrew. Cambridge: Polity, 2003.

Kuran, T. "Ethnic Norms and their Transformation through reputational Cascade". *Journal of Legal Studies* 27, no. 2 (1998): 623–659.

Landau, L. "Loving the Alien? Citizenship, Law, and the Future in South Africa's Demonic Society". *African Affairs*, 109, no. 435 (2010): 213–230.

Landau, L. *Exorcising the Demons Within: Xenophobia, Violence and Statecraft in Contemporary South Africa.* Johannesburg: Wits University Press, 2011.

Lumumba-Kasongo, T. "Reconceptualizing the State as the Leading Agent of Development in the Context of Globalization in Africa". *African Journal of Political Science* 7, no. 1 (2002): 79–108.

Mafeje, A. "State and Civil Society in Independent Africa" In *Networking with a View to Promoting Peace: Conflicts in the Horn of Africa,* edited by Henrich Boll Foundation. Addis Ababa: Henrich Boll, 1999.

Mamdani, M. *When Victims Become Killers: Colonialism, Nativism and the Genocide in Rwanda.* Kampala, Fountain Publishers/Oxford, James Currey, 2001.

Mamdani, M. *Citizen and Subject: Contemporary Africa and the Legacy of Late Colonialism.* Princeton: Princeton University Press, 1996.

Mazrui, A. "Identity Politics and the Nation-State under Siege: Towards a Theory of Reverse Evolution". *Social Dynamics* 25, no. 2 (1999): 5–25.

Medard, J. "The Underdeveloped State in Tropical Africa: Political Clientelism or Neo-Patrimonialism". In *Private Patronage and Public Power*, edited by C. Clapham. London: Pinter, 1982.

Mengisteab, K. "Globalization and State-Society Relations in Africa". *African Development* 33, no. 2 (2008): 37–65.

Miller, S. D. *Xenophobia toward Refugees and other forced Migrants*. Ontario: Centre for International Governance Innovation, 2018.

Misago, P. J. "Politics by Other Means? The Political Economy of Xenophobic in Post-Apartheid South Africa". *The Black Scholar* 47, no. 2 (2017): 40–53.

Mkandawire, T. "Maladjusted African Economies and Globalization". *African Development* 30, no. 1 (2005): 1–33.

Mustapha, A. R. "Rethinking Africanist Political Science". In *The Study of Africa, Vol.1: Disciplinary and Interdisciplinary Encounters*, edited by P. T. Zelesa. Dakar: CODESRIA, 2006.

Nabudere, D. "Globalization, the African Post-Colonial State, Post Traditionalism and the New World Order". In *Globalization and the African Post- Colonial State*, edited by D. Nabudere. Harare: AAPS Books, 2001.

Ninsin, K. *Globalization and the Future of Africa*. Harare: AAPS Occasional Paper Series 4, no. 1 (2000).

Nyerere, J. "Spearhead". In *The Ideologies of Developing Nations*, edited by P. Sigmund. New York: Praeger, 1963.

Ohmae, K. "The End of the Nation State" In *The Globalization Reader*, edited by J. Lechner and F. Boli. Oxford: Blackwell, 2004.

Okoli, A. "Boko Haram Insurgency and the Necessity for Trans-Territorial Forestland Governance in the Lower Lake Chad Basin". *African Journal on Conflict Resolution* 19, no. 1 (2019): 37–56.

Opello, W. and Rosow, S. *The Nation-State and Global Order: A Historical Introduction to Contemporary Politics*. London: Lynne Reiner, 2000.

Osaghae, E. "Exiting from the state in Nigeria". *Journal of African Political Science* 4, no. 1 (1999): 83–98.

Osaghae, E. "Revisiting the concepts of State fragility and State building in Africa". In *Fifty Years of Nationhood? State, Society and Politics in Nigeria (1960-2010)*, edited by S. O Akinboye and M. M Fadakinte. Lagos: Concept Publications Limited, 2010.

Robertson, R. *Globalization: Social Theory and Global Culture*. London: Sage Publication, 1993.

Rodney, W. *How Europe Underdeveloped Africa*. Dar-es-Salam: Tanzania Publishing House, 1972.

Rosenau, J. *The Study of World Politics, Volume 2: Globalization and Governance*. London/New York: Routledge, 2006.

Rothchild, D. and Chazan. N. edited *The Precarious Balance: The State and Society in Africa*. Boulder: Westview, 1988.

Strange, S. "The Declining Authority of States". In *The Globalization Reader*, edited by J. Lechner and F. Boli. Oxford: Blackwell, 2004.

Tekena, T. *Peace and Violence in Nigeria*. Ibadan: History Project, 1991.

Thomas, C. and Falola, T. *Secession and Separatist Conflicts in Postcolonial Africa*. Calgary: University of Calgary Press, 2020.

Thomson, A. *An Introduction to African Politics*. London/New York: Routledge, 2000.

Tidwell, A. and Lerche, C. "Globalization and Conflict Resolution". *International Journal of Peace Studies* 9, no. 1 (2004): 47–59.

Tilly, C. "Citizen, Identity and Social History". *International Review of Social History* 40, no. 3, (1996): 1–17.

Udombana, N. J. "Articulating the Right to Democratic Governance in Africa". *Michigan Journal of International Law* 24, no. 4 (2003).

Wulf, H. *Challenging the Weberian Concept of the State: The Future of the Monopoly of Violence*. The Australian Centre for Peace and Conflict Studies Occasional Papers Series. Number 9, December 2007. Available from: http://www.wulf-herbert.de/ACPACS-occpaper9. pdf [Accessed 21 October 2018].

Chapter 2

The Psychology and the Psychosocial Impacts of Xenophobia and Nativism

Kizito N. C. Okeke

There are factors that are catalysts to the resurgence of xenophobia and nativism, and with the violence associated with them in many countries, globally. Certain factors, such as economic and political interests of individuals, groups, and nations, have pushed to the extreme the forces of xenophobia and nativism. Some despicable statements, policies, and ideologies that directly promote these societal ills have worsened the situation in some countries and left dumbfounded those humans who still have decency and integrity. Indeed, any conscionable person would ponder and question, "How could humanity degenerate to such a low level of existence in this era?" Xenophobia and nativism do culminate in violence and exacerbate the culture of violence that is progressively and destructively making its ugly inroad into different segments of societies, globally. Xenophobes and nativists operate on intense irrational fear and are subjected to levels of cognitive distortions which fuel irresponsible actions and violent conflicts.

The 2001 World Conference against racism in Durban, South Africa, under the auspices of the United Nations (UN),[1] was a significant move in addressing issues of racism, slavery, nativism, xenophobia, and other related intolerance. This conference promoted measures toward improving societal cohesion, the respect for people of diverse ethnic and racial backgrounds, and respect for the dignity of the human person and human rights. The sole aim of this conference was the speedy and comprehensive eradication of all forms of racism, racial discrimination, xenophobia, nativism, and related intolerance.[2] The UN describes xenophobia as "attitudes, prejudices and behavior that reject, exclude and often vilify persons, based on the perception that they are outsiders or foreigners to the community, society or national identity."[3] Xenophobia is like nativism in some ways, because both share in the extreme fear or hatred of the out-groups, foreigners, or strangers and, perhaps, with the unhealthy combination of extreme attachment to homeland culture or in-group culture. In some cases, these may appear deceptive to unsuspecting individuals or groups who may unknowingly embrace xenophobia or nativism because it is camouflaged or clothed with the garment of patriotism. Both xenophobia and nativism breed bias, prejudice, disunity, and violence in the society, and in several cases lead to fatalities and wanton destruction of properties.

When xenophobia and nativism are embedded in racism, racism is equipped with the deadliest venoms, and it markedly displays the worst of human cruelties to fellow humans. This maybe the case, in the most recent displays of systemic racism in the United States (USA or US), as orchestrated through the senseless brutality of police officers against African Americans. The event of May 25, 2020, in which a white police officer, using his knee, pinned Mr. George Floyd[4] to the ground for more than nine minutes, is one of the most recent demonstrations of police brutality against an African American that went viral. The police officer remained indifferent to Mr. Floyd's panting and gasping for breath with the words "I can't breathe." This act of cruelty led to the death of Floyd. It is unbelievable that while this officer inflicted severe pain on Floyd's neck and Floyd continuously pleaded to be allowed to breathe some air, his fellow officers stood aloof without any care or empathy; but many Americans and the world could not remain silent. This unimaginable cruelty is an assault to our common humanity and hits all racial groups with utmost shock and disbelief. But the good thing that came out of these police officers' brutality was that they rallied all races together, the white, black, and brown, to mount widespread protests. All races united in our common humanity and chanted recurrently in unison "Black Lives Matter" or "I Can't Breathe." There is no denial of the fact that humans by nature may have a soft spot or preference for their in-group, culture, and the rejection of the possibility of being misrepresented or dominated by the out-group. But how humans respond to these existential issues are significant factors in understanding the violence emanating from xenophobia and nativism. The victims of these evils are not without serious physical and psychological consequences, and among other things, they leave the society much more impoverished and dehumanized.

This chapter examines xenophobia and nativism by reviewing some of the relevant literature. It will discuss the ideological framework and the psychosocial impacts of xenophobia and nativism with a focus on Africans, both those within the continent and in the diaspora. Africans, in general, continue to bear the brunt of these evil forces. I will discuss ways to regain African consciousness in these struggles toward more meaningful and purposeful

participation in international affairs, and global political and economic policies that will give Africa a path to a better future.

BACKGROUNDS AND SIGNIFICANT EXPERIENCES

Generally, xenophobia and nativism have preference for the in-group as
opposed to the out-groups and may claim to protect the in-group from the
out-group. Prior to discussing certain backgrounds and their significant manifestations in the events of the world, I will make some simple differentiations
between xenophobia and nativism. Xenophobia can extend to the cultural
expressions of the out-group that do not pose any harm or threat to the in-group,
and this irrational fear can be sustained by the overly suspiciousness and mistrust of the in-group about the out-group. This irrational and intense fear can
lead to disastrous outcomes. When irrational fear and arbitrariness lead the way,
any slight provocation could ignite violence. This may explain why xenophobia has engendered catastrophic conflicts, such as wars, ethnic cleansing, and
genocides. Nativism can help to rouse xenophobic behavior. Nativism is the
extreme belief in the protection of the interests of native inhabitants at all costs
and against out-groups or foreigners. Policies are made with the sole intention
of protecting such interests. Nativism can develop into xenophobia and may
be a catalyst to xenophobic attacks. In both cases of xenophobia and nativism,
policies may include, and not limited to, strict-immigration measures, systemic
discrimination, and disenfranchisement of the out-groups. It is not uncommon to camouflage them as patriotism. At times, sensitive and decent people
that naturally are opposed to xenophobia and nativism could be deceived into
embracing them when they are camouflaged as patriotism. Although nativism
seems milder than xenophobia, both can lead to the same outcomes, which are
often catastrophic. Therefore, both xenophobia and nativism are dangerous to
societal cohesion, unity, holistic development, and peace. The discussions that
follow will revolve on xenophobia most of the time. I will discuss xenophobia
briefly from psychological perspective on mental disorders.

Xenophobia is classified under anxiety-related disorders, and the Diagnostic
Statistical Manual of Mental Disorders (DSM-V) has rules for a diagnosis of
phobia.[5] Therefore, a diagnosis for phobia would include two or more of the
following symptoms: that a person presents excessive, persistent, and intense
fear when the person is exposed to foreigners or strangers; that the person's
anxiety or fear is disproportionate to any actual danger posed by these
individuals and manifests almost, immediately, when the person is in the
presence of the triggering person; that the person affected goes to extremes
to avoid triggering foreigners or strangers or experiences excessive distress

in their presence; that person's experience of phobia is self-limiting, that is, that the anxiety is triggered by being near strangers or foreigners renders the person unable to function normally; that the person's phobia must last for six months or longer to be diagnosed as such; and that all the other anxiety disorders must be ruled out before a phobia is positively diagnosed, since symptoms of different disorders can appear similar in some cases.[6] There are many symptoms associated with phobia and xenophobia. For now, it suffices to state the criteria for a diagnosis in accordance with the categorical approach, and to include that in extreme and rare cases of xenophobia, a person may display a morbid preoccupation with strangers or foreigners and may even become violent.

THE MINDSET AND RATIONALIZATION

The world has known many horrific events, such that they can never be erased in memories and in the annals of world history, some of which are epochal displays of the evils of xenophobia. These events and their experiences have played roles in shaping countries, continents, the world, and our history at large. In as much as fear, intense fear, or irrational fear is the driving force for xenophobia, another force is pride or claim to superiority over all other races. The feeling and thinking that one is more superior than another and that one's race is more superior than another are factors that nurture xenophobia and other related intolerance against people of different backgrounds. For these reasons, the ancient Greeks and Romans indulged in the superiority claim to downgrade other cultures and their belief systems. This justified the enslavement of others.[7] This approach was introduced into our world and facilitated the continuous process of dehumanization through racism, xenophobia, nativism, and other discriminatory behaviors for centuries. It is important to note that there are factors that can promote xenophobia overtly and covertly, and there are factors that predispose people to xenophobic violence. We have a lot to learn from the Greek society.

The Greek society was male-dominated. It was made up of different classes, and slaves were an essential and normal part of the societal life. These slaves could be acquired through conquest, capture, and trade and were considered as the lowest class in the society. These cultural beliefs and mindset could distort humans' cognitive processes. This was the case in early Greece where great intellectuals showed such cognitive distortions. The reference to another group or foreigners as barbarians by the ancient Greeks is a denigration of inferiority. The likes of Aristotle fell into the net of these cultural beliefs to propose the argument that slaves were demonstrably inferior, a product of their environment and inherited characteristics.[8]

Therefore, Greeks held that they, the Greeks, had the best characteristics, had the purest bloodline, and were born to rule and enslave others. Although the Greeks believed that slaves could regain their freedom, not very many slaves regained their freedom, because the pathways to freedom were uphill tasks in all ramifications. As it is said, evil begets evil; the rationalization and justification of the sentiments that breed these societal evils and the societal evils themselves continued beyond the Greeks.

Like Aristotle's view on slavery, it is surprising that other intellectuals were overwhelmed by cultural beliefs and could not account for basic knowledge in human life as they fell into the same superiority flaw. Among them is Immanuel Kant who is guilty of endorsing the white race as a superior race. His anthropological perspective holds that, unlike other cultures or races, only the white race contains all the incentives and talents, and the highest level of knowledge, and is therefore superior to other races.[9] This view made Kant to be uncritical about colonialism and slavery. Kant may have been overly influenced by the cultural mindset of his people than his intellectual ability. But the fact remains that the Greeks' view continued to spread even among highly educated classes and in political ideologies through modern times. Nazism, which is a form of fascism, embodies extreme hate and discrimination, racial supremacy, anti-Semitism, scientific racism, and weaponized eugenics. The Nazi leadership and Hitler, the master of the Third Reich, unleashed one of the worst human cruelties in history in the unimaginable evil of the Holocaust. We must not forget that the foundation was already laid for evil minds and political bigots to explore. Others improved upon the approach in various ways. Thus, the mindset cannot be ruled out in the pursuit of eugenics. In fact, in 1883, Galton's approach to eugenics, which references "wellborn," is highly indicative of this mindset. He believed that the human race could help direct its future by selectively breeding individuals who have "desired" traits.[10] In accordance with his studies in eugenics, Galton concluded that an elite position in society was due to a good genetic makeup and planned to improve the human race through selective breeding. Although, it never materialized, it eventually took sinister turns in other countries. This rationale behind eugenics with its negative connotations spread to other countries, including the United States.[11] This is especially the case, when social Darwinism and eugenics movements promoted the false notion that there was an evolutionary basis for the inferiority of African Americans. This misleading ideological position favored the European Americans, who erroneously believed that African Americans were a threat in their wheel of progress.[12] The cognitive distortions caused by the ideological frameworks emanating from the false interpretation of Darwin's theory of evolution, natural selection, and eugenics continued to spread its destructive tentacles in the American society and Europe. However, the eugenics movement in the United States slowly lost favor over time and was waning by the start of the Second World War. When the horrors of Nazi Germany became apparent, as well as Hitler's use of eugenic principles to justify the atrocities, eugenics lost all credibility as a field of study or even an ideal that should be pursued.[13] Therefore, once a human being is labeled inferior or undesirable for any reason and it is acceptable or ignored, the boundary will continue to shift until it unleashes a human catastrophe. To take it further, Hitler's approach is rooted in such rationalization, and this rationalization always has ripple effects. The recent political climates in Europe and America are obviously indicative of the worsening situation. All these continue to nurture the mindset for the evils of racism, xenophobia, nativism, prejudice, and other types of discrimination.

All through history, slavery has continued in different forms and created further problems for theslave masters the slaves themselves, and the world at large. After the abolition of slavery, problems arose, such as what to do with newly liberated slaves, whether to absorb them in the society or not? Why should we, the in-group, allow this out-group to mix with our kind? How can they live with us in our communities, states, and even marry our daughters? In England and the United States, the answer to some of the questions that arose was to send free blacks back to Africa. In 1787 and sequel to England's abolishment of slavery, most of the freed slaves that were settled in Sierra Leone by the British government died of disease within two years or died in warfare with local inhabitants. They were a total of 300 former slaves and 70 white prostitutes that the British government relocated to Sierra Leone, West Africa.[14] The death toll of this initial effort did not deter the British government, and in 1792 and thereafter, thousands of freed slaves were continuously sent to Sierra Leone. This same approach was in tandem with the American mindset, to send free black Americans to Africa, although in this case, through colonization. A colony was created in Africa for this purpose, and Liberia is a colony that was created in 1847. About 12,000 freed slaves were relocated to Liberia within a period of 40 years. This move was contrary to the popular black-led "Back to Africa" movements. These movements maintained that the Africans' consciousness toward determining their future and owning their destiny through the establishment of their own homeland was the only feasible way to end slavery and the evils associated with it. Whatever was the intention of the Colonization Society and whether it was supported by some African Americans or not is not the main issue. The main issue is, why were Africans not allowed to be part and parcel of the country their fathers, forefathers, and ancestors built with their sweat and blood? One cannot rule out the issue of racism, xenophobia, and nativism. As history dictates, many abolitionists saw the deportation of black Americans to Liberia as human cruelty because these African Americans were forced to survive in a new environment with new diseases, and without enough preparation.[15] Even after many years of settlement, living and working to build the nations, Africans were still seen as strangers, unqualified citizens by other strangers, who are the European Americans.

Racism, xenophobia, nativism, and related intolerances were gradually fermenting and to explode at intervals and with levels of intensity. Slaves and their descendants continued to bear the brunt with all the trauma, mental, and psychological discomforts. Some of the significant events reminiscent of these include slavery and post-slave era oppressions, African American experiences of racism, the destruction of African culture through the British indirect rule system, and the French policy of assimilation. All these oppressively and systematically aimed at destroying the dignity of the Africans, while at the same time promoting the superiority of the Europeans and Americans. In addition, the African continuous experience of xenophobia in Europe, Asia, Israel, and the Middle East are testaments to the fact that Africans have suffered more of these evils than any other race. The effects continue to be the catalysts of other societal upheavals, such as proxy-wars, wars in Africa that have produced at least two genocides (Biafran and Rwandan genocides). Other significant world events that inform xenophobic violence include, and are not limited to, Native American experience of racism, Armenian genocide in Turkey, and the Holocaust.

THE CULTURE OF VIOLENCE

Xenophobia and nativism breed violence and cause physical and mental injuries. Sequel to the physical and mental agonies of slavery, African Americans, especially, have severally, experienced the explosions, the trauma, and the mental and psychological discomforts caused by racism, xenophobia, and nativism. Almost all segments of the African Americans' life are fractured by these societal ills. Let me limit my discussion to the heinous atrocities of Black Wall Street Massacre or the Tulsa Race Massacre in Greenwood district in Tulsa, Oklahoma, in May 31, 1921.[16] In addition, I will discuss the Tuskegee experiment, officially referred to as "Tuskegee Study of Untreated Syphilis in the Negro Male."[17] Concerning the Black Wall Street Massacre, white mobs, who were supported by city officials with weapons, attacked black residents and businesses and destroyed what was the pinnacle of a successful black race in the United States. They hanged, shot, and burned African Americans alive and looted their properties. This sudden attack had both ground force and air force as if they were at war with the worst adversary of the nation. As the white mobs mounted a ground attack, private aircraft coordinated the bombing of the wealthiest black community in the United States. There were many casualties, thousands were interned in large facilities, and many of them for days. It is described as the single most catastrophic incident in American history due to racism and invariably xenophobia and nativism.[18] All these happened because of a false accusation that a 19-year-old African American assaulted a 17-year-old European American. The mindset of the perpetrators of this evil is indubitably nurtured by supremacist ideology and the rejection and violent attack on an out-group for no justifiable reason. The Tuskegee experiment with black Americans is equally atrocious and more evil-inclined, since it was an evil planned and executed not by mobs but by the intellectual class on whom society reposes its trust. This happened in 1932 when the Public Health system in the United States worked with the Tuskegee Institute to discover a cure for syphilis. The study initially involved 600 African American men; while 399 had syphilis, 201 did not. The study did not have ethical justification and was conducted without the benefit of informed consent by the patients and all participants.[19] Unfortunately, they were intentionally not administered the proper treatment for their illness, even though, penicillin was discovered as a better treatment for the disease in 1948. Ironically, in exchange for taking part in the study, the participants received free medical exams, free meals, and burial insurance. Originally, the study was to last for 6 months, but it went on for about 40 years. Although the study had to be stopped in 1972, in 1973, a class action lawsuit went in favor of the participants and their families. Both incidences demonstrate how extreme the in-group can go against its perceived out-group.

The Native Americans' experiences, too, are unimaginably beyond measure, and I will use the "Wounded Knee Massacre" as a microcosmic unveiling of the Native Americans' experiences. Recently the U.S. Congress apologized to the descendants of Native Americans for this massacre of more than a century ago. The Congress expressed "Deep regret" for these victims. There were about 400 men, women, and children of Chief Big Foot's band of Minneconjou Sioux who were massacred at Wounded Knee, on December 29, 1890.[20] The apology extended to facets of long history of official depredations and ill-conceived policies by the government that undermined the existence and survival of the Native Americans who are original inhabitants of the territory. It acknowledged that the government violated many of the treaties ratified by Congress and other diplomatic agreements it had with the Native Americans and were involved in numerous violent conflicts that undermined their fundamental human rights. All these culminated in their forceful removal from their traditional homelands to government-controlled reservations through an act commonly referred to as "Indian Removal Act."[21] Although all these and more happened to them, the world has not explicitly pronounced these deadly attacks and all that the Native Americans suffered as genocide.

The Armenian genocide by Turkey was acknowledged by the U.S. Congress recently.[22] This genocide occurred during the period of 1915–1923.[23] The UN, 35 years ago, was considering the Armenian massacre as a case for genocide and in a joint letter asked the Turkish ambassador to provide answers within 60 days to some 7 questions that would respond to significant issues in the case such as information and comments about the allegations attributed to Turkey in relation to the tragic events that claimed the lives of about 1.5 million Armenians. The Turkish government was to give account of the whereabouts of Armenians who were subjected to forced internal displacement, detention, extrajudicial killings, and enforced disappearances. But the U.S. Congress had overwhelming evidence to recognize the massacre as genocide and did vote to recognize it overwhelmingly. Another genocidal act waiting to be officially acknowledged by the international community is Nigeria's Biafran civil war that led to the Biafran genocide. This was fueled by hatred for another ethnic group, the Igbo people, who did not share similar cultural beliefs with the other ethnic groups, especially in the northern and western parts of the country. The worldview of the Igbo people is much more democratic and communal, while in the northern and western part of the country, it was much more monarchical and feudal. The British could easily apply their system of indirect rule with other ethnic groups but found it very difficult with the Igbo people. The British colonial mentality prevailed in making it impossible for those likely to oppose their colonialism to ascend to leadership in Nigeria. The British Amalgamation of these diverse ethnic groups was a time bomb waiting to explode, but such future explosion was s to the greater benefits of the British colonial masters. In summary, the northern and western regions of Nigeria erupted in a pogrom as thousands of resident Igbos were slaughtered. The federal government did nothing to stop the carnage, and the worst of it, the British government downplayed the massacre.[24] And this is a genocide whether officially recognized or not. And the British government can never wash off the shameful role it played. Britain's covert interference ensured that weapons and ammunition poured in quietly and lied about everything to the international community. In coordination with the Soviet Ilyushin bombers, they bombed villages, indiscriminately; bombed civilians, men, women, and children; and starved others to death. It is estimated that over two million Igbos were assassinated, and children were over a million.[25] The Armenian and Biafran massacres are genocides in accordance with the UN definition of it, when it said, "Genocide means any of the following acts committed with the intent to destroy, in whole or in part, a national, ethnic, racial or religious group."[26] The UN itemized five areas that genocide could be committed, such as "killing members of the group; causing serious bodily or mental harm to members of the group; . . ."[27] All these could have been avoided, and the British government cannot escape shame and guilt.

It is said that evil begets evil, and likewise hate begets hate; therefore, the claim that the U.S. model of racism influenced the Nazi race law cannot be ignored in the discussions of racism. It may have been an inspiration or a blueprint for Nazi Germany's idea of concentration camps and other racist policies. Whitman[28] argued that Hitler's admiration for the U.S. practices is found in his *Mein Kampf*, throughout the 1930s, and that his most radical lawyers eagerly advocated the use of the U.S. model. We must understand the ideologies and forces that nurture racism to fight against them successfully. Therefore, the UN must do more to fight against ideologies and forces that nurture racism in a timely fashion, to investigate and resolve pending cases of genocide so that they do not linger for decades, and to sanction countries and individuals who are culprits. The label hanging against countries that are guilty of genocide, especially, when recognized by the UN and influential countries in world economy and politics, is a significant step.

The most recent event in South Africa that claimed the lives of migrants and refugees from other African countries is a clear case of xenophobia. South Africa already had existing sentiments and prejudices, especially, among the poor and working class. They have severally protested foreign nationals who, perhaps, further compounded their already poverty-stricken conditions by competing for the few available job positions. What used to be the normal protest-like approaches turned into more violent ones, partly because of social media and partly because of economic factors. Xenophobic attacks in South Africa, amid the looting of businesses and burning of shops and properties, have claimed many lives. In late August 2019, xenophobic violence is reported to have claimed at least 12 lives, while previously, in 2008, it left about 62 people dead.[29] South Africa had been a good target for migrants because of its high level of industrialization in Africa. Many migrants went to South Africa for jobs, to escape political persecutions and war, and for other reasons. Many years of apartheid in South Africa and many years of exploitation by the whites are already factors that would predispose them to fight for their survival at any slight provocation or perceived threat to their economic life.

In Europe, xenophobia is on the rise. Discussions of xenophobia in Europe have attracted more attention in recent times because of the drastic measures taken by some European countries against migrants and nationals of other continents, especially Africa. The history of Europe and America has given contextual and experiential interpretations to xenophobia and racism. Racism exists in these countries, but while the U.S. history implicates that, with the shameful history of racism, the European countries would prefer a different connotation and would not want to be lumped with America's historical racism. Therefore, Europe would settle for xenophobia to distance itself from the U.S. racism. The UN has shown how cheap journalism and tabloid journalists looking for cheap stories have continuously, in subtle ways, increased racism and xenophobia in Europe.[30] Political ideologies hardly die, and so after the Second World War in 1945, although fascism tore Europe apart in the 1930s, the remnants of extreme right parties resurfaced in the margins of politics. The new manifestations of racism, xenophobia, and nativism in Europe are in the name of patriotism, right-wing populist parties, and the denial of the evils of the past, such as Holocaust denial. Three factors can attest to the huge success of these societal evils in Europe: The first is the fact that Europe has introduced new legislation to enforce tolerance, which was initially seen to be part and parcel of the European simple and inclusive way of life. Secondly, it is unbelievable that this extreme right group that was once unacceptable in the European social and political life is rising to mainstream political participation with increasing memberships and self-confidence to reach any extremes. Lastly, there are more racist campaigns and more racist politicians among the current 785 members of the European Parliament.[31] In addition, coded political expressions have camouflaged these evils as patriotism. Before these evils eat deeper into Europe, the European Union must put in place the laws that help to root out racism and related intolerances and also find better ways to enforce those laws.

Asians and Asian countries are not left out. The recent Covid-19 pandemic exposed how Asians suffered xenophobic violence in both Europe and the United States.[32] While Asians in the diaspora suffered these attacks in Europe and America, nationals of other countries in Asian countries were also subjected to xenophobic assaults. Africans have suffered some xenophobic attacks in Asia. For example, Africans were unfairly treated against international laws and for no justifiable reasons in China. Africans in certain places in China were evicted from apartments where they are legal residents and in hotels where they legally lodged simply because they are Africans. In some places, the law enforcement officers extended their unlawful treatment with a seizure of their international passports which is completely against international law. The Chinese law enforcement officers made matters even worse when they quarantined Africans beyond the 14 days that they quarantined Chinese citizens. In some cases, they facilitated a forced treatment for coronavirus on Africans who were neither sick nor requested any treatment or vaccination.[33] It took the intervention of the Nigerian diplomat, Razaq Lawal, to retrieve Nigerian passports but with severe criticism of Chinese officials in the maltreatment of Nigerians in Guangzhou. He reiterated that Chinese citizens in Nigeria are not discriminated against but that they receive the same treatment as Nigerians.

The worst in the spread of racism, xenophobia, and nativism globally is that such a mindset and ideologies have crept into political and religious arenas, thus making political dialogue a hostile engagement and religious dialogue and advocacy are often charged with sentiments and political undertones.

Unfortunately, the poor on both sides are always those who suffer the brunt of these societal upheavals.

CAUSES, THEORIES, AND THE
PSYCHOSOCIAL IMPACTS

There are so many factors that can contribute to xenophobia and nativism, and my discussions of some of the significant violent events associated with these evils already implicate some factors. It is understood that fear or hatred of out-groups, foreigners, or strangers are foundational factors in the activities of xenophobes and nativists. But this fear, from the evolutionary perspective, can be construed as part of humans' survivalist instincts. This is in accordance with the evolutionary idea that humans are better prepared, biologically, to fear certain stimuli more than other animals, and this helped early humans to survive in their environment.[34] Imagine what would have happened if the Native Americans acted on their initial fear and instinct about the European Americans' presence in their land and denied them any support to live in the area. They must have had their fears and anxiety, in line with the evolutionary perspective. Significant steps in this experience are the ability to differentiate between irrational and rational fear and the ability to make a responsible decision. However, when the irrational fear overwhelms the rational thought process and a responsible decision is impeded, then the irrational fear becomes the determinant factor in decision-making, which is dangerous and can lead to catastrophic outcomes. Human survival does involve ability to distinguish friends from enemies. It seemed that a primitive method of detecting coalitions and alliances was shared appearances.[35] This means that humans developed something we can describe as a neurocognitive machinery that helped to process phenotypic features as a means of alliance detection. Therefore, it suffices to state the obvious that humans are more likely to be interested in their in-group than the out-group, but irrational fear is a dangerous thing. In the discussion of the causes of xenophobia and nativism, we must acknowledge that there are many factors implicated. For lack of enough space in this chapter, I will limit my discussion to the following factors: economic interest, political interest, racism, feeling of insecurity, and sociocultural factors.

Many significant events in our world and the policies of nations are overly influenced by the economy or economic gains and interests. Economic interests can force some governments to sacrifice integrity, fairness, and justice, and one can say that in the world today, economic interest is a greater driving force in many decisions at the local, national, and international levels. When nationals of other countries are needed and they help to build and promote the economy of the private and public sectors, these strangers are likely to be tolerated and at times celebrated. But when these dynamics change and they begin to enjoy the dividends of the flourishing economy, and begin to influence the demand and supply chain, the initial feelings of those who claim to be rightful citizens may change. Those who consider themselves as rightful citizens and who have to compete in the capitalist market economy will begin to develop some negative and dangerous sentiments. Usually, since they have had it easier than the strangers all along and were not exposed to the difficult experiences of hard life that the strangers may have had initially, they may be overwhelmed and begin to see the strangers as the architect of their hardships or problems. They can become disgruntled and vulnerable to xenophobic violence with the slightest provocation or incentivization. This situation could even be made worse when politicians who are interested in political powers cease such opportunity to exploit their vulnerability to rally their support with xenophobic campaigns, utterances, and hate speeches. These simply whip up the existing sentiments to see strangers as the architect of economic hardships. Unfortunately, this political strategy has increased in Europe and America. The tone of political campaigns and anti-migrant speeches and policies can ginger up intolerant and violent behavior against nationals of other countries. This strategy cannot be ruled out in the growing sentiments, intolerant and violent attacks on immigrants in South Africa, Europe, and the United States. It seemed to be the catalyst in one of the earliest and severest xenophobic attacks in London, the *Evil May Day*, of 1517.

Racism is a strong factor, and when we discuss the African experience of xenophobia and nativism in Europe, America, and Asia, it is much severer than the experience of other immigrant nationals. The background of slavery and the fact that Africans cannot easily blend within European American communities subject Africans to all sorts of discriminations and oppressions. When Africans suffer xenophobic attacks in other continents, racism cannot be ruled out. Generally, racism is the foundation of the worst kind of xenophobia, nativism, and all sorts of discriminations. Racism can be construed based on the assumption that the differences among groups are biologically based, that one's own race is superior, and with the view that the practices that formalize the domination of one racial group over another racial group are justifiable.[36] It is made up of beliefs, attitudes, institutional arrangements, and acts that tend to denigrate others who have different phenotypic characteristics.[37] Different forms of racism in the modern world, such as symbolic racism and aversive racism, are xenophobic behaviors waiting for a violent explosion.[38] These are modern forms of racism where, for example, racism is intended but camouflaged and nonracial reasons are used as the yardstick for attitudes that are against other racial groups. Modern racists deny the oppressive backgrounds that subjugate other racial groups and view responsibility for success or failure as residing within the individual.

Lastly, I would like to discuss insecurity and sociocultural factors. In line with the evolutionary perspective that I have discussed, the feeling of insecurity is a factor that can cause the rejection of out-groups and violence against them. Culturally, people from certain cultures seem to be more psychologically predisposed or vulnerable to a feeling of insecurity. Individuals from such cultures may be overly suspicious of the out-groups, and this will diminish the level of relationship between individuals from the in-group and out-group. Such over-suspiciousness seems to facilitate a non-tolerant attitude toward strangers. Other social-cultural factors include the following: the fear that the strangers or the out-groups may negatively influence the culture of the in-group, the fear that strangers may reduce the in-group or the natives to a minority status in their own land, the fear that the religion of strangers may become the major religion, the fear that the demography of the area may change to the disadvantage of the in-groups or natives, the fear that strangers may wield more power in the society than the in-groups or natives, and the fear that strangers may take over their country. Therefore, nationalism and patriotism can directly or indirectly whip up sentiments against strangers or out-groups. The experiences of these societal evils generally have some negative impacts on the physical and mental well-being of all, especially the victims.

THEORIES THAT EXPLAIN XENOPHOBIA, NATIVISM, AND OTHER RELATED INTOLERANCE

All the factors that are associated with xenophobia and other kinds of discrimination can be understood from the perspectives of scapegoat theory, power theory, and power-conflict theory. In various ways they emphasize the forces I have discussed that engender xenophobia, nativism, and other related intolerances. There are also other theories, but for the limited space I have, I will limit my discussions to these three theories. Scapegoat theory, from the perspective of social psychology, relates to prejudice and all kinds of discrimination through which people tend to express dissatisfaction, frustration, and hostility for failure to meet their life's needs.[39] When people find themselves in any situation that hinders the achievement of their intended goals, they become psychologically predisposed to confront whatever is considered the obstacle. In certain cases, the obstacle may be wrongly construed, and foreigners are blamed for such frustration and difficult experiences. The foreigners are seen as responsible for the failure to meet their life's needs, and they are made to suffer the consequences in various ways, such as excessive promotion of native rights and privileges to the detriment of strangers. Foreigners become the scapegoat and may be subjected to xenophobic violence. The main factors that are responsible for their predicament, such as unemployment, poverty, and failed government policies, are overlooked. Foreigners are blamed for all the societal evils and suffer the consequences. Political bigots can make sentimental insinuations that label foreigners as such. This may explain the recent rise in supremacist groups and xenophobic behaviors in America. Probably, the whites have started to experience unemployment, poverty, and homelessness, which have always been part and parcel of the African American life. These experiences were blamed on foreigners by some misguided minds, which led to increased tension in the American society and xenophobic attacks on those perceived to be foreigners. This mentality, in the case of Germany, fostered the Holocaust, as the Germans used the Jews as scapegoats for all their country's problems and did the unthinkable to them.

Power is an important construct in psychology, other social sciences, and in human relationships in general. Power theory gives the perspective that the relationship between groups is a function of their competitive positions, and power is needed for control. Whoever threatens this power will receive stiff opposition, and an actual offender or even a suspect becomes a subject of hate and, possibly, violence.[40] Therefore, if a group feels its power is threatened by another group, the former feels insecure and burdened with uncertainties about the future. Their resentment and animosity may not be because of the competition but on the perceived threat to that hold on power. In accordance with this theory, when the in-group feels that its power is threatened, it can unleash its aggression and animosity on the out-group and may disguise the main intention with other factors. The struggle to possess power at all costs can promote xenophobia and nativism. Interestingly, this made a big show during Barack Obama's presidency in the United States.

Lastly, the power-conflict theory is in certain ways like the power theory. However, the former tends to neutralize the out-groups, which the in-group or the dominant group perceives as a threat to its position of power, with all the rights and privileges associated with it. Power is used to protect and enhance the in-group interest, or in certain cases, the dominant group's interest.[41] The group that feels threatened would employ various mechanisms, such as racism, xenophobia, stigmatization, prejudice, hate speech, and so on, to arouse sentiments against the other group or groups. The outcomes may be beneficial in keeping the intended status quo and serve to relieve tensions, too. Tensions and conflicts can arise in the society because of the uneven distribution of resources, wealth, and power. The ruling class or wealthy class makes use of these conflicts and tensions and may create them when the society is calm, as a way to keep holding on to power and to keep the society in check.[42] This theory may explain why politicians can go too low in whipping up sentiments and causing conflicts among groups, with the sole purpose of holding on to power. These strategies have led to xenophobic and other related intolerance. The recent End Special Anti-Robbery Squad (SARS) protests in Nigeria encapsulate this theory. The End SARS protest was an unprecedented clarion call to Nigerian government by Nigerians to end police brutality and extrajudicial killings by the police. The political powers, instead of focusing on the legitimate and genuine demands of the protesters who were well-organized, nonviolent, and purposeful, chose to use force by deploying the Nigerian military who shot at them at Lagos Lekki gate.[43] The Nigerian youth came out en masse to protest the failure of the political leaders in almost all areas of life. It is a failed state epitomized in deep-rooted corruption that has crippled the present regime and the advancement of this country. Nigeria is endowed with very rich mineral resources which had positioned her to be numbered among the richest countries in the world, but unfortunately that is not the case. The protest should be one of the best organized protests in the world: nonviolent, peaceful, vocal, cleaned up each day, and the youth loudly projected all their demands to the Nigerian government. It was no longer "business as usual" they insisted, but the corrupt leaders failed to read the writing on the wall. Those that enjoyed the oppressive power decided to use hoodlums to stir up crises and violent activities and to whip up ethnic sentiments and conflicts. Some mischievous voices used xenophobic threats by giving the Igbos an ultimatum to leave Lagos and go back home. The response from the government of Nigeria was the deployment of the military, which, unfortunately, worsened the situation since unarmed and innocent civilians were killed. These killings by the Nigerian military have elicited an empathetic outrage from people across the world and heightened the consciousness of the international community with a call for justice against such criminality. Thus, the UN human rights experts have requested an independent and credible investigation on what the UN considers a huge violation of human rights.[44] Unfortunately, these killings by the military skyrocketed conflict and violence across the country, and it is indeed a turning point in Nigeria's history of oppressive regimes. The usual colonial tactics of whipping up ethnic sentiments as a camouflage was an abysmal failure. It rather united the Igbos and the Yorubas, as some prominent Yorubas vehemently opposed these mischievous voices that wanted to change the correct narrative.[45] Thanks to technological advancement and social media, the culprits could not be hidden from the eyes of the world when captured on videos. These three theories are insightful in understanding the root causes of xenophobia and other related intolerances.

THE PSYCHOSOCIAL IMPACTS

The experiences of the violence emanating from xenophobia and nativism are generally emotionally discomforting, and the level of severity varies. There is no doubt that victims can be exposed to traumatic experiences that can develop to Post-traumatic Stress Disorder (PTSD). The experiences of the victims that I have already discussed are factors often associated with PTSD. PTSD is generally marked by frequent experiencing of a traumatic event through memories, images, nightmares, and other ways that remind victims about the event.[46] Some of the victims of xenophobic attacks cannot live without the painful experience of their new detested world that leaves them with painful memories. Before such a painful experience develops into PTSD, victims may have suffered from Acute Stress Disorder (ASD) which involves distressing memories, dreams, and negative mood. Other symptoms include dissociation, when victims have feelings of detachment from reality or no longer feel the usual connectedness to others and thereby try to avoid people. These symptoms associated with ASD usually occur immediately following the traumatic event and may last between three days and a month.[47]

PTSD will further expose these victims to depressive disorders, anxiety-related disorders, and suicidal ideation and behavior, and they may take false-refuge in substance use. They may become addicted to the use of substances, which may lead to substance use disorder. Mental disorders, such as anxiety-related disorders, are highly comorbid, that is, they are associated with other mental disorders in a person. Anxiety-related disorders and depression are often comorbid, while anxiety-related disorders and substance use disorders may also be comorbid. The former, anxiety-related disorders and depression, shares some symptoms of mania, irritability, restlessness, guilt, poor self-concept, nervousness, and withdrawal. This comorbidity is sometimes referred to as negative affectivity.[48] Unfortunately, people who suffer from anxiety-related disorders are at risk of suicide. When the victims' depression and mania become so severe and interfere with their daily functioning, they may have a depressive disorder or a bipolar disorder, which are collectively referred to as mood disorders. These troubling experiences can lead to cognitive distortions or negative thought patterns. Thus, victims begin to develop a negative cognitive triad: they have overly distorted and pessimistic views about themselves, about the surrounding world, and about their future. It is more likely that these victims will view their events in negative ways and have catastrophic thoughts and interpretations about them. In some cases, these are automatic thoughts because they are constantly repeated over the course of a day.[49]

The problems of hopelessness and learned helplessness may develop because of extreme physical and mental distress. In accordance with hopelessness theory, these victims may likely believe that the traumatic event will last a long time and will affect most areas of their life. Victims develop a feeling of hopelessness because of the abuse and exploitation they have suffered and may further engender a feeling of low self-esteem. The psychological harm is further worsened through learned helplessness when the victims believe that no matter what they do, their efforts cannot change the situation.[50] The PTSDs, the high levels of comorbidity of mental disorders among these victims, and the externalization of the associated symptoms will require an integrated approach of treatment that takes into cognizance all segments of the life of the victims. This trauma-informed approach is very important in enhancing a holistic process of recovery because it systematically involves significant areas of the victims' life, which include, but are not limited to, law enforcement, health care, education, family, culture, and the future. Both the group and individual counseling must be sensitive to the history, the cultural backgrounds, and the beliefs of the victims. Since anxiety-related and depressive disorders make the victims vulnerable to low self-esteem and suicidal ideation and behavior, therapies should be geared toward restoring self-esteem, empowerment, and a true reconnection of the victims to themselves, to the society, and to the world.

Any society will triumph if there is unity of purpose, societal cohesion, security, and peace, and these are eroded continuously by the evils of racism, xenophobia, and nativism. The most recent experience of Black Lives Matter protests in the United States that went viral and that received unprecedented support from all nooks and crannies of the world is a great testament to the war against the evils of racism, xenophobia, prejudice, and all kinds of discrimination. All breed hostility against people of different backgrounds. The seed of hatred, animosity, and violence that they sow and nurture continue to do harm to the society and makes it an unhealthy environment for mental well-being.

Individuals and groups may suffer from an increasing poverty rate when they are denied social and economic opportunities or easy access to the goods of society. The implicit bias against other nationals or out-groups would put them in disadvantaged positions in the social and economic life of the state. These situations jeopardize the congenial environment that should facilitate the full contribution of their talents to the growth of the economy and social life.

The out-group often suffers isolationism. This happens when the members of the out-group isolate themselves from the community and deny themselves the social life as a coping measure to avoid confrontation, hostility, hate speeches, and fatalities. When all people are not given equal opportunity in the economic and political life of the society where they live, the society cannot harness all the talents for the betterment of the society. In this kind of environment, social injustices prevail. And this situation often leads to more disastrous outcomes. It can be the catalyst for hate crimes, war, genocide, and crimes against humanity. Even though not everyone who is racist or xenophobic may commit these crimes, one cannot rule out the fact that even covert racism or xenophobia can have insidious effects on both the individual and society at large.

Clues to combating xenophobia include a good effort to widen one's knowledge on areas that one is susceptible to irrational beliefs about the out-groups or unsubstantiated irritations about people of different backgrounds. An openness to understand other people, cultures, and the unknown will go a long way to help one to face one's fears and forestall irrationalities and cognitive distortions. One must confront sources of those fears and be well-informed about them and with the understanding that knowledge is good, but half knowledge is dangerous. Half knowledge about certain things may be the source of irrational fears. An effort to replace negative emotions about strangers and fears about strangers with positive emotions about them is also helpful. Lastly, and very importantly, laws should be enacted at all levels, local, state, national, and international levels, and properly enforced to combat these evils.

Africa's Purposeful Economic Plan, Identity, and Solidarity

Africans have suffered more of the brunt of these societal evils, and it is disheartening to keep seeing such denigration in different forms across the globe. The first solution will be for Africans (leaders) to fix African countries economically. No African should be happy with the slow or little progress achieved in the African continent. And as I blame African leaders and Africans in general for the low level of governance and low technological development, I am not oblivious of the huge obstacles that were heaped on Africa's road to progress. These obstacles are colonialism that Africans have not recovered from, neocolonialism that has replaced the former, racism that remains a deadly sword against Africans, and all the political, social, and economic ideologies that keep Africa in constant check of higher technological advancement by the neocolonial tools of domination and oppression. Africa's progress is a matter of time, but the journey must continue with determination. The first step is for Africans to be extra conscious of the forces of colonialism and neocolonialism and to keep them seriously in check in their engagements at the local, national, and international affairs and policies. Africa must assume the level of equality due to sovereign nations in accordance with the democratic principles often chanted and promoted by Europe and America. If the neocolonial mentality still exists in different forms overtly, and in some cases, covertly, Africans must oppose any structure that seems to suggest such evils. By implication, African leaders must demand an exemplary practice of democracy at the Security Council with a good membership or equal representation of the African continent. The present structure still represents, for the most part, the structure of colonialism and neocolonialism. The current structure of the Security Council of the UN does not look like a structure that will serve better the interest of the African nations. It currently maintains five permanent members, China, France, Russian Federation, the United Kingdom, and the United States, and these five countries have veto powers. Some continents are overly represented, while Africa has no representation in the permanent membership. This does not seem to be a structure that will fight hard for the liberation of the African nations, especially where countries, such as the United Kingdom, France, and the United States, who had played major roles in colonialism and slavery remain very influential as permanent members. The United Nations (UN) was founded on October 24, 1945, when some African countries had not gained independence. How can such a structure represent the interest of African countries? The ideal situation should be to improve the body with the permanent membership of African countries and make it much more democratic. Africans cannot afford to allow the most influential colonial masters and slave masters to exclude their participation in the very important organ of the UN. African leaders must deal with other international bodies with heightened consciousness and purposefulness. Dealings with other bodies, such as the World bank and the IMF (the International Monetary Fund), should be with conscientious alertness and diligence. Africans have the intellectual capabilities to plan African economies and policies, and her leaders must tap from these human resources. To fix Africa is tantamount to reducing the brunt of these societal evils that mostly affect Africans. Amid all that the international bodies do in the name of assistance to Africa, what is most important to them is the raw material in Africa, and for the raw material, they would prefer to leave Africa less technologically developed.

Africa's natural resources make Africa irresistible to all other nations, and Africa must use its natural resources as a powerful bargaining power by controlling these resources and not to accept the economic dictatorship of the European, American, and Asian trades. Other countries are interested in keeping Africa less technologically developed because of the untamed selfish desire for African raw materials. African countries can put an enviable economic plan through unified purpose and policy. The idea is to have an independent African economy. African countries, or preferably the anglophone and francophone countries, can unite to fully fund one or two separate banks (a unified bank) that are fully dedicated to giving loans for technological development and in the building of manufacturing industries. Africa has to operate under a unified currency and to demand and insist on gold payment for her raw materials.[51] This is because the building of industries to improve the manufacturing economic sector will be the most effective boost to a rising Africa. Imagine what economic impact it would have made if France should return the money it has oppressively deprived of the francophone countries in the name of colonial tax or for the benefit of colonialism, or for a safe keep in its central bank in France. It would transform these francophones' economies in huge measures. This may not happen soon and the same with compensations and reparations for Africans and African countries; however, African leaders can build up support from within. African countries can pull resources together to support each other in stepping up manufacturing industries within for the benefits of all Africans.

CONCLUSION

All forms of discrimination, racism, xenophobia, nativism, and other related intolerance are harmful to humans and the society. Unfortunately, Africans have suffered the brunt of these evils from the slave era to date. Africa is still overwhelmed by the forces of colonialism and the new forces of neocolonialism. With less technological advancement, it struggles to overcome poverty and Africans scramble for jobs both within and beyond the continent, and these situations predispose Africans to xenophobic violence and all sorts of discrimination. Xenophobia and other forms of discrimination leave the world more impoverished and at a loss in our common humanity. Efforts to combat these menaces must begin from the ideological mindset that breeds all forms of discrimination, bias, and prejudice about people of different backgrounds or the out-groups. All ideologies that promote these vices do not die but continue to bear their destructive fruit through the ages. From the ancient Greek denigration of others as barbarians to Aristotle's belief that slaves are demonstrably inferior, from Galton's ideology of *desired traits* or *well born* in his eugenics, to social Darwinism and eugenics, all promoted the mindset that created a culture of violence to the out-groups and led to catastrophes in history, such as slavery, Holocaust, and others. Africans are still suffering the brunt of these evils more than any other race. But Africa has what it takes to overcome and rise to prominence in the world economy and politics, if she focuses on her natural resources and fully controls them for a greater turn of her destiny. Widespread unemployment and poverty, which are responsible for the migration of large populations of Africans within and without, and which expose them to racial and xenophobic violence, could be brought to the barest minimum through a purposeful focus on Africa's raw materials. The raw materials in Africa make Africa almost irresistible to other countries, and Africa must use this power to triumph and win her destiny.

NOTES

1. "World Conference against Racism, Racial Discrimination, Xenophobia and Related Intolerance," *United Nations*, 31 August–7 September 2001.

2. Ibid.

3. International Migration, Racism, Discrimination and Xenophobia. A publication prepared by: International Labour Office (ILO), International Organization for Migration (IOM), *Office of the United Nations High Commissioner for Human Rights* (OHCHR), 2001. Retrieved online July 3, 2014 at www.unesco.org/most/migration/imrdx.pdf.

4. "Editorial: A very abbreviated history of police officers killing Black people," *Los Angeles Times*, (2020, June 4).

5. American Psychiatric Association. *Diagnostic and Statistical Manual of Mental Disorders*, 5th ed. (Arlington, VA: Author, 2013).

6. Ibid.

7. Cartwright, Mark. "Ancient Greek Society." Ancient History Encyclopedia. Last modified May 15, 2018. https://www.ancient.eu/article/483/.

8. Ibid.

9. Kant, Immanuel. *Anthropology from a Pragmatic View*, trans. Mary Gregor (The Hague: Martinus Nijhoff, [1798] 1974).

10. Galton, F. *Hereditary Genius: An Inquiry into Its Laws and Consequences* (London: Macmillan, 1869).

11. Norrgard, K. "Human Testing, the Eugenics Movement, and IRBs." *Nature Education* 1, no. 1 (2008): 170.

12. Hall, Gordon Nagayama, *Multicultural Psychology*, 2nd ed. (Boston: Pearson, Prentice Hall, 2010), 69–91; Jones, James, M. *Prejudice and Racism*, 2nd ed. (New York: McGraw-Hall).

13. Grodin, M. A., Miller, E. L., and Kelly, J. I. "The Nazi Physicians as Leaders in Eugenics and 'Euthanasia': Lessons for Today." *American Journal of Public Health* 108, no. 1 (2018): 53–57. doi:10.2105/AJPH.2017.304120.

14. "Death on the Grain Coast," The Guardian News, August 30, 2005. https://www.theguardian.com/uk/2005/aug/31/race.bookextracts.

15. "Founding of Liberia, 1847," The US Department of State. https://history.state.gov/milestones/1830-1860/liberia (October 29, 2020).

16. "What to Know About the Tulsa Greenwood Massacre," *New York Times* (Maggie Astor June 20, 2020). https://www.nytimes.com/2020/06/20/us/tulsa-greenwood-massacre.html.

17. "U.S. Public Health Service Syphilis Study at Tuskegee," National Center for HIV/AIDS, Viral Hepatitis, STD, and TB Prevention , Centers for Disease Control and Prevention (US), March 2, 2020.

18. Ellsworth, Scott, *Death in a Promised Land* (Louisiana State University Press, 1992), pp. 47–48. Retrieved October 10, 2020.

19. Ibid.

20. Phil Brasher, "Congress Apologizes to Wounded Knee Victims." *NPR News*, October 25, 1990.

21. "Indian Removal Act: Primary Documents in American History." *Library of Congress.* https://guides.loc.gov/indian-removal-act.

22. Humeyra Pamuk, "U.S. Senate Passes Resolution Recognizing Armenian Genocide, Angering Turkey." *Reuters News*, December 12, 2019. https://www.reuters.com/article/us-usa-turkey-armenia/u-s-senate-passes-resolution-recognizing-armenian-genocide-angering-turkey-idUSKBN1YG2DZ.

23. "Amid Global Pandemic, US Congress Pivots with ANCA to Online Calls for Armenian Genocide Justice." *The Armenian Weekly*, May 20, 2020. https://armenianweekly.com/2020/05/20/amid-global-pandemic-us-congress-pivots-with-anca-to-online-calls-for-armenian-genocide-justice/.

24. Frederick Forsyth, "Buried for 50 years: Britain's Shameful Role in the Biafran War." *The Guardian News*, January 21, 2020. https://www.theguardian.com/commentisfree/2020/jan/21/buried-50-years-britain-shamesful-role-biafran-war-frederick-forsyth.

25. Ibid.

26. "The Genocide Convention," The Office on Genocide Prevention and the Responsibility to Protect (United Nations, December 9, 1948). https://www.un.org/en/genocideprevention/genocide-convention.shtml.

27. Ibid.

28. James Q. Whitman, *Hitler's American Model: The United States and the Making of Nazi Race Law* (Princeton: Princeton University Press, 2017).

29. South Africa: Widespread Xenophobic Violence, Human Rights Watch, September 17, 2020. https://www.hrw.org/news/2020/09/17/south-africa-widespread-xenophobic-violence#.

30. In the Wake of Xenophobia: The New Racism in Europe. Retrieved October 9, 2020. https://www.un.org/en/chronicle/article/wake-xenophobia-new-racism-europe.

31. Isil Gachet, Combating Racism and Racial Discrimination in Europe. UN News, retrieved October 12, 2020. https://www.un.org/en/chronicle/article/combating-racism-and-racial-discrimination-europe.

32. Sabrina Tavernise and Richard A. Oppel, *Spit On, Yelled At, Attacked: Chinese-Americans Fear for Their Safety* (New York Times, 2020).

33. Jenni Marsh, Shawn Deng, and Nectar Gan, "Africans in Guangzhou Are on Edge, After Many Are Left Homeless Amid Rising Xenophobia as China Fights a Second Wave of Coronavirus." *CNN News*, April 12, 2020. https://www.cnn.com/2020/04/10/china/africans-guangzhou-china-coronavirus-hnk-intl/index.html; Hangwei Li, "Mistreatment of Africans in Guangzhou threatens China's Coronavirus Diplomacy." *Conversation News*, April 17, 2020. https://theconversation.com/mistreatment-of-africans-in-guangzhou-threatens-chinas-coronavirus-diplomacy-136348.

34. Christopher Kearny and Timothy Trull, *Abnormal Psychology and Life*, 2nd ed. (Canada: Cengage Learning, 2015), pp. 99–138.

35. Leda Cosmides, John Tooby, and Robert Kurzban, "Perceptions of Race." *Trends in Cognitive Sciences* 7 (2003): 173–179.

36. Ibid., Jones 1997.

37. R. Clark, N. B. Anderson, V. R. Clark, and D. R. Williams, "Racism as a Stressor for African Americans: A Biosocial Model." *American Psychologist*, 54 (1999): 805–816.

38. David O. Sears, "Symbolic Racism." In P. A. Katz and D. A. Taylor (Eds.), *Perspectives in Social Psychology. Eliminating Racism: Profiles in Controversy* (Plenum Press, 1988), pp. 53–84.

39. Elliott D. Hammer, "Scapegoat Theory." In Roy Baumeister and Kathleen Vohs (Eds.), *Encyclopedia of Social Psychology* (SAGE Publications, 2007).

40. Elliott D. Hammer, "Scapegoat Theory." In Roy Baumeister and Kathleen Vohs (Eds.), *Encyclopedia of Social Psychology* (SAGE Publications, 2007).

41. John. C. Turner, "Explaining the Nature of Power: A Three-Process Theory." *European Journal of Social Psychology*, 35, no. 1 (2005): 1–22.

42. Ibid.

43. *Azu Ishiekwene*Nigeria: "#EndSARS - Sanwo-Olu's Cross and the Meaning of Lekki Toll Gate," *All Africa News*, October 23, 2020.

44. United Nations, Human Rights, "UN Human Rights Experts Demand Nigeria Investigate Shooting of Peaceful Protestors by Soldiers," United Nations, November 3, 2020.

45. Ben Ezeamalu, "#EndSARS: We're 'back to Abacha' Days, Soyinka Says," *Premium Times*, October 21, 2020. https://www.premiumtimesng.com/news/headlines/422124-endsars-were-back-to-abacha-days-soyinka-says.html.

46. Op. cit., Kearney and Trull, 2018, pp. 99–140.

47. Ibid.

48. Ibid.

49. Aaron T. Beck and David J. A. Dozois, "Cognitive Theory and Therapy: Past, Present, and Future." In S. Bloch, S. A. Green, and J. Holmes (Eds.), *Psychiatry: Past, Present, and Prospect* (Oxford University Press, 2014), pp. 366–382.

50. Op. cit., Kearney and Trull, 2018.

51. Ellen Brown, *Why Qaddafi Had to Go: African Gold, Oil and the Challenge to Monetary Imperialism* (The Ecologist, March 14, 2016).

BIBLIOGRAPHY

American Psychiatric Association. *Diagnostic and Statistical Manual of Mental Disorders* (5th edition). Arlington, VA, 2013.

Amid Global Pandemic. US Congress pivots with ANCA to online calls for Armenian Genocide Justice. *The Armenian Weekly,* May 20, 2020. https://armenianweekly.com/2020/05/20/amid-global-pandemic-us-congress-pivots-with-anca-to-online-calls-for-armenian-genocide-justice/

Asser, Martin. "The Muammar Gaddafi story." *BBC News*, October 21, 2011. https://www.bbc.com/news/world-africa-12688033

Astor, Maggie. "What to know about the Tulsa Greenwood Massacre." *New York Times*, June 20, 2020. https://www.nytimes.com/2020/06/20/us/tulsa-greenwood-massacre.html

Beck, Aaron T., & David J. A. Dozois. Cognitive theory and therapy: Past, present, and future. In S. Bloch, S. A. Green, & J. Holmes (eds.), *Psychiatry: Past, Present, and Prospect* (pp. 366–382). Oxford University Press, 2014.

Brown, Ellen. "Why Qaddafi had to go: African gold, oil and the challenge to monetary imperialism." *The Ecologist*, March 14, 2016.

Cartwright, Mark. "Ancient Greek society." *Ancient History Encyclopedia*. Last modified May 15, 2018. https://www.ancient.eu/article/483/.

Clark, R., N. B Anderson, V. R. Clark., & D. R. Williams. Racism as a stressor for African Americans: A biosocial model. *American Psychologist* 54(1999): 805–816.

Cosmides, Leda, John Tooby, & Robert Kurzban. Perceptions of race. *Trends in Cognitive Sciences* 7(2003): 173–179.

Death on the Grain Coast. *The Guardian News*, August 30, 2005. https://www.theguardian.com/uk/2005/aug/31/race.bookextracts

Ellsworth, Scott. *Death in a Promised Land*. Louisiana: State University Press, 1992, pp. 47–48.

Ezeamalu, Ben. "#EndSARS: We're 'back to Abacha' days, Soyinka says." *Premium Times,* October 21, 2020. https://www.premiumtimesng.com/news/headlines/422124-endsars-were-back-to-abacha-days-soyinka-says.html

Ford, Glyn. "In the wake of xenophobia: The New Racism in Europe." *UN Chronicle,* October 09, 2020. https://www.un.org/en/chronicle/article/wake-xenophobia-new-racism-europe

Forsyth, Frederick. "Buried for 50 years: Britain's shameful role in the Biafran war." *The Guardian News,* January 21, 2020. https://www.theguardian.com/commentisfree/2020/jan/21/buried-50-years-britain-shamesful-role-biafran-war-frederick-forsyth

Founding of Liberia, 1847. *The US Department of State.* https://history.state.gov/milestones/1830- 1860/liberia (October 29, 2020).

Gachet, Isil. "Combating racism and racial discrimination in Europe." *UN Chronicle*, retrieved October 12, 2020. https://www.un.org/en/chronicle/article/combating-racism-and-racial-discrimination-europe

Galton, Francis. *Hereditary Genius: An Inquiry into Its Laws and Consequences.* London: Macmillan, 1869.

Grodin, M. A., E. L. Miller, & J. I. Kelly. The Nazi physicians as leaders in Eugenics and Euthanasia: Lessons for today. *The American Journal of Public Health*, 108, no. 1(2018): 53–57. doi:10.2105/AJPH.2017.304120

Hall, Gordon Nagayama. *Multicultural Psychology* (2nd edition). Boston: Pearson, Prentice Hall, 2010, pp. 69–91.

Hammer, Elliott D. "Scapegoat theory". In Baumeister, Roy & Vohs, Kathleen (eds.), *Encyclopedia of Social Psychology*. SAGE Publications, 2007.

"Indian Removal Act: Primary Documents in American History." Library of Congress. https://guides.loc.gov/indian-removal-act

"International Migration, Racism, Discrimination and Xenophobia. A publication prepared by: International Labour Office (ILO), International Organization for Migration (IOM), Office of the United Nations High Commissioner for Human

Rights (OHCHR). (2001). Retrieved online July 3, 2014 at www.unesco.org/most /migration/imrdx.pdf.

Ishiekwene, Azu. Nigeria: #EndSARS - Sanwo-Olu's cross and the meaning of Lekki Toll Gate. *All Africa News*, October 23, 2020. https://allafrica.com/stories /202010230267.html

James Q. Whitman. *Hitler's American Model: The United States and the Making of Nazi Race Law*. New Jersey: Princeton University Press, 2017.

Jenni, Marsh, Shawn Deng & Nectar Gan. "Africans in Guangzhou are on edge, after many are left homeless amid rising xenophobia as China fights a second wave of coronavirus." *CNN News*, April 12, 2020. https://www.cnn.com/2020/04/10/china /africans-guangzhou-china-coronavirus-hnk-intl/index.html

Jones, James, M. *Prejudice and Racism* (2nd edition). New York: McGraw-Hall, 1977.

Kant, Immanuel. *Anthropology from a Pragmatic View* (trans by Mary Gregor). The Hague: Martinus Nijhoff, [1798] 1974.

Kearny, Christopher & Timothy Trull. *Abnormal Psychology and Life* (3rd edition). Canada: Cengage Learning, 2018, pp. 99–138.

Li, Hangwei. "Mistreatment of Africans in Guangzhou threatens China's coronavirus diplomacy." *Conversation News*, April 17, 2020. https://theconversation.com /mistreatment-of-africans-in-guangzhou-threatens-chinas-coronavirus-diplomacy -136348

Los Angeles Times. "Editorial: A very abbreviated history of police officers killing black people." *Los Angeles Times*, (2020, June 4). From: https://www.latimes.com /opinion/story/2020-06-04/police-killings-black-victims

Norrgard, Karen. Human testing, the eugenics movement, and IRBs. *Nature Education* 1, no. 1(2008): 170.

Pamuk, Humeyra. "U.S. senate passes resolution recognizing Armenian genocide, angering Turkey." *Reuters News*, December 12, 2019. https://www.reuters.com/ article/us-usa-turkey-armenia/u-s-senate-passes-resolution-recognizing-armenian -genocide-angering-turkey-idUSKBN1YG2DZ

Phil Brasher. "Congress apologizes to wounded knee victims." *NPR News*, October 25, 1990.

Sears, O. David. "Symbolic racism." In P. A. Katz & D. A. Taylor (eds.), *Eliminating Racism: Perspectives in Social Psychology* (pp. 53–84). Plenum Press, 1988.

South Africa: Widespread Xenophobic Violence, Human Rights Watch, September 17, 2020. https://www.hrw.org/news/2020/09/17/south-africa-widespread-xeno-phobic-violence#

Tavernise, Sabrina & Richard A. Oppel. "Spit on, yelled at, attacked: Chinese-Americans fear for their safety." *New York Times*, March 23, 2020.

The Genocide Convention. The office on genocide prevention and the responsibility to protect. *United Nations*, December 9, 1948. https://www.un.org/en/ genocideprevention/genocide-convention.shtml

Turner, John. C. Explaining the nature of power: A three-process theory. *European Journal of Social Psychology* 35, no. 1 (2005): 1–22.

United Nations, Human Rights. "UN human rights experts demand Nigeria investigate shooting of peaceful protestors by soldiers." *United Nations*, November 3, 2020. https://www.ohchr.org/EN/NewsEvents/Pages/DisplayNews.aspx?NewsID =26468&LangID=E

U.S. Public Health Service Syphilis Study at Tuskegee, National Center for HIV/ AIDS. Viral Hepatitis, STD, and TB Prevention, Center for Diseases Control and Prevention, US, March 2, 2020.

Wilson, Derek. "Evil May Day." *History Today Magazine*, vol. 67 Issue 6 June 2017. https://www.historytoday.com/archive/feature/evil-may-day-1517

World Conference against Racism, Racial Discrimination, Xenophobia and Related Intolerance. *United Nations*, August 27, 2001. https://www.un.org/press/en/2001/ rd918.doc.htm

Chapter 3

Xenophobia and the Legacy of Apartheid in South Africa

The Continued Process of Creating Subalterns in Africa

Robert Maseko

COLONIALITY AND ITS EFFECTS IN SOUTH AFRICA

The prevalence of the phenomenon currently known as xenophobia in South Africa cannot be fully accounted for outside the complexities of the continuing colonial experience and relations among the people of South Africa. What remains problematic today in South Africa is the economic inequality between blacks and whites and poverty within black communities: a situation which explains why incidents of violent xenophobia are common only in black communities. There has been an increase in tensions between white and black South Africans and between black South Africans and black Africans from other African nations. Tensions between black South Africans and blacks from other African nations have resulted in xenophobic violence of unimaginable proportions. It is a pity that the beneficiaries of the oppressive apartheid system still arrogantly refuse to acknowledge the source of their wealth and privilege.[1] One of the fallacies of modern politics is that the removal of juridical colonial administrations in Africa amounted to decolonization.[2] While direct colonialism is long gone, coloniality still influences our modern political economy, imagination, and knowledge systems. South Africa is still entangled in the past, and it is this "past" which still influences and shapes the future of the country. The citizen-subject binary, as predicted by Mahmood Mamdani, is a lived reality of being black and African.[3] But how did South Africa end up in such a situation, where black-on-black violence became the order of the day? Why are black African nationals targeted in xenophobic violence, while

65

other racial groups of lighter skin are not victims of native rage? These are critical questions which this chapter seeks to address.

This chapter seeks to explore and explain the processes that underpin the reproduction of colonial subalternity and the identity and experience of a people generally classified and categorized as "non-Western" subjects within the current modern world system. The main thrust of this paper is the continued coloniality and apartheid divisions which promote the insider-outsider mentality on citizens, the creation of superior and inferior people, and the influences on national policy. The presence of the white-controlled media industry, a substantive influential white population, whiteness, and black elites educated in Westernized universities, has actually necessitated the sustenance of coloniality and continued divisions in South Africa. To answer the questions earlier, let me perhaps dwell deeper on the project of colonialism, and what it did to the native population, and more so, the failed nationalist project of the African National Congress (ANC) government after the end of apartheid. In doing so, I introduce the concept of coloniality as a starting point in the analysis of black-on-black violence and marginalization.

The project of Western modernity can be traced back to the conquest of the present-day Americas in 1492,[4] while in South Africa it dates back to the arrival of the first European settlers in the Cape in 1652, and other colonial encounters along the African coast. Coloniality is a global power structure cascading in and through ongoing processes of colonialism, but surviving the postindependence decolonization project, and continuing to underpin asymmetrical power relations between the "Global North" and the "Global South." In the end, it involves sustaining a hierarchical modern capitalist world order with "race" as a fundamental organizing principle. Maldonado-Torres had this to say on coloniality:

> Coloniality is different from colonialism. Colonialism denotes a political and economic relation in which the sovereignty of a nation or a people rests on the power of another nation, which makes such nations an empire. Coloniality, instead, refers to long-standing patterns of power that emerged as a result of colonialism, but that define culture, labour, intersubjective relations, and knowledge production well beyond the strict limits of colonial administrations. Thus coloniality survives colonialism.[5]

The Western project of modernity is underpinned by the logic of coloniality as an unwritten and hidden agenda and, as argued by Walter Mignolo,[6] there is in fact no modernity without coloniality: "Coloniality, in other words, is constitutive of modernity." In South Africa, colonialism and apartheid were all projects of modernity which sought to maintain the status quo of the superiority of the North over the South. Postapartheid entanglements arose through surviving coloniality embedded in institutions which were inherited from colonial administrations.

The specific entry point for this chapter is the coloniality of "being" as introduced by Nelson Maldonado-Torres. According to Maldonado-Torres, coloniality of being becomes a useful tool in analyzing oppressed people, whose ontological density and humanity have been stripped off. In describing the classification of the world population based on color lines, he argues that those who are lighter in complexion (for instance, Asians and Indians) are seen as closer to the white man and, therefore, closer to humanity, while those who are darker (black people) are further and far from humanity: "The 'Lighter' one's skin is, the closer to full humanity one is, and vice versa. As the Conquerors took on the role of mapping the world, they kept reproducing this vision of things. The whole world was practically seen in the light of this logic. This is the beginning of 'global coloniality.'"[7]

The statement above is relevant in the context of the history of South Africa, where people were classified according to their pigmentation, such that race became socially constructed: white people at the top of the human hierarchy, followed by Indians and coloreds, and then, languishing at the bottom of the hierarchy, were the blacks, who are, ironically, the natives of the country. In South Africa, xenophobic violence is unleashed on dark-skinned African nationals, and, ironically, while this happens, the perpetrators (black South Africans) view themselves as light-skinned. During colonialism, extreme violence was used to convert the black South Africans into Christianity, as they were believed to be barbaric and worshiping a devilish god. In this respect, Maldonado-Torres had this to say:

> Hellish existence in the colonial world carries with it both the radical and the gendered aspects of the naturalization of the non-ethics of war. Indeed, coloniality of Being, primarily refers to the normalisation of extraordinary events that take place in war. While in war there is murder and rape, in the hell of the colonial world murder and rape become day to day occurrences and menaces. "Killability" and "rapeability" are inscribed into the images of the colonial bodies.[8]

The coloniality of being allows some people to be reduced to a level of nonbeing (treated less than human beings), and once some groups are characterized as less than humans, it justifies torture, exclusion, and expropriation. This is a form of racism that has its roots in the colonial past; thus, Frantz Fanon[9] writes about the line of the human that divides humanity; those who are located below the line are labeled as subhuman or nonhuman. Boaventura de Sousa Santos[10] writes about an abyssal line, which divides the zone of nonbeing from the zone of being. Ramón Grosfoguel's definition of racism is critical to reflect in this chapter, as it sheds light into the postapartheid xenophobia: that it has its roots in racial practices of the past. He states that

> racism is a global hierarchy of superiority and inferiority along the line of the human that have been politically, culturally and economically produced and reproduced for centuries by the institutions of the "capitalist/patriarchal western-centric/Christian-centric modern/colonial world-system." . . . This definition of racism allows us to conceive of diverse forms of racism, evading the reductionisms of many existing definitions. Depending on the different colonial histories in diverse regions of the world, the hierarchy of superiority/inferiority along the lines of the human race can be constructed through diverse racial markers. Racism can be marked by color, ethnicity, language, culture and/or religion.[11]

For Ramón Grosfoguel,[12] those located above the line of the human enjoy privileges associated with being human, such as access to human rights, civil rights, women rights, labor rights, the rights to epistemologies and spiritualities, and the right to identities. It is evidently clear from the definition above that racism has different markers. Xenophobic violence experienced in South Africa is, without doubt, being motivated by the ongoing processes of coloniality. African nationals in South Africa are attacked, discriminated against, and killed simply because of the color of their skin, language, culture, and ethnicity.

The concept of "coloniality of being" helps in understanding how black identity and subjectivity were produced in the creation of a population considered less human. In South Africa, white subjectivity was created in order to supervise black subjectivity. Besides forced conversion to Christianity, manual labor was articulated as one of the means by which to civilize black people, and this involved drawing them into the evolving capitalist system as providers of cheap labor. This is why the mining industry coerced labor from all over the region of Southern Africa. Coloniality, as a present condition, has seen the massacre of people in Marikana in South Africa and the continued inhuman treatment of foreign nationals by state institutions and communities. Postapartheid South Africa still resembles the past and the only difference being the fact that the perpetrator is the black political leadership against other blacks.

Coloniality explains why most decolonial projects have failed in many African countries. Africa has never been given the opportunity to fully change the colonial institutions as a result of continued interference from the global superpowers. Mental colonization became the hardest obstacle to decolonize; it corrupted people's mentality, consciousness, souls, and imagination.[13]

In South Africa, colonialism set tribes against tribes and ethnic groups against ethnic groups. However, postapartheid South Africa saw the victims of colonialism becoming the perpetrators of violence, and this time, the enemy became a black African foreign national. Violent attacks on foreign nationals are rampant in former homelands, formerly known as Bantustans.[14] Colonialism and apartheid still shape and influence social policy, labor, capital, and subjectivity. The worst affected by coloniality are the political elite trapped in what Frantz Fanon[15] calls the pitfalls of national consciousness and what William Du Bois[16] calls double consciousness: a process where those fighting colonialism aspire to be the new oppressor of their own people. Some have argued that those who fought colonialism, desired the life of their enemy, and they wished to be oppressors themselves. However, Frantz Fanon suggests an overhaul of the whole oppressive structure when he contends, "To tell the truth, the proof of success lies in a whole social structure being changed from the bottom up."[17] Africa should invest in ways that ensure reimagining the future of its people, a future which is driven by humanity needs, and a future which includes everyone. Otherwise, black Africans will continue to live in poverty, they will continue to die from diseases, and they will continue killing each other with impunity. On the contrary, calls for the intensification of border controls have resurfaced in South Africa, with some groups advocating mass deportation of foreign nationals.

ERECTING FENCES AND BUILDING WALLS

The phenomenon of closing and tightening border security is not peculiar to South Africa only, but rather, it has been a global phenomenon motivated by the ideas of invasion, terrorism, and aliens. From the Great Wall of China to the Berlin Wall, walls have been part of the protection of ancient empires. When the Berlin Wall collapsed, some people even envisioned a "borderless and deterritorialized world"[18] and "a Europe without walls, without fences, and without borders."[19] The fall of the Berlin Wall gave hope that the world is finally opening up to the idea of a global village. However, the excitement didn't last, as more countries started walling themselves.[20] It has been a common phenomenon in developed nations in North America, Eastern Europe, and the Middle East. Research shows that international borders are becoming a stumbling block in achieving global peace and attainment of human rights for all. Though Burcu Koca[21] argues that borders are a source of peace building, they can be a source of conflict, as well as a source of producing and reproducing difference. However, each country has a duty to protect its own borders from illegal smuggling of goods and weapons, human trafficking, and drug trafficking.[22] In Kenya, a border wall and a fence has been proposed after several cross-border terrorist attacks, mainly from war-torn Somalia.[23] In Europe, more countries are building walls instead of protecting refugees, and this has led to mass death of refugees along the borders.[24] However, David Makovsky[25] is of the opinion that in the context of war between Israel and Palestine, a properly built border wall can promote peace, while a poorly built border wall can escalate tensions. He even goes on to ask the U.S. government to support the construction of a wall. In Africa, borders and fences are becoming a stumbling block in the achievement of Pan-Africanist goals and the project of decolonization, because of xenophobia and nativism.

In South Africa, many people believe that the country's borders are porous, and this is the reason the country has illegal immigrants and rampant problems of human trafficking.[26] However, some believe that the current global refugee crisis cannot be mediated by the building of walls and the erecting of fences.[27] Migration and illegal border crossing have become a global problem as more people migrate to seek better economic opportunities and refuge.

Africa remains closed to itself, but open to the rest of the world; it has become difficult for Africans to move freely between African borders, while citizens of China, Europe, and America continue to have unlimited access to the continent. Xenophobia in the continent is affecting intracontinental relations, as black Africans continue to marginalize each other. In South Africa, xenophobia has found its way in national politics, and the country has seen the enactment of policies believed to be motivated by hatred of other Africans, under the guise of "South Africa First," "local empowerment," "patriotism/proudly South African," and "#PutSouthAfricansFirst" slogans.

The recent erection of a border fence between South Africa and Zimbabwe[28] has led some to believe that xenophobia, and nothing else, was the motive behind such acts, though it was justified as a means of protecting South African citizens from the recent coronavirus outbreak, despite the fact that the virus was brought into the country through national airports by travelers from countries such as Italy and the United States. One wonders why the South African government did not erect new fences on the borders near the ports of entry with neighboring countries such as Swaziland, Lesotho, Namibia, and Botswana. In other words, the perceived threat was only coming from the North. The fence, which cost about R39 million (more than US$2 million), was deemed to be ineffective, as more people continued to cross. It is believed the fence was cut open several times by people, taking with them goods to be consumed in Zimbabwe during the coronavirus lockdown.[29] More so, the announcements by the government that foreign nationals would not be legible for state food aid and that all companies in the hospitality industry would be required to employ South Africans in order to qualify for government subsidy during and after the Covid-19 pandemic have been argued by some as xenophobic initiatives by the state.[30]

On September 23, 2020 a group of protesters under the banner "#PutSouthAfricansFirst" marched to the Nigerian and Zimbabwean embassies against what they called "atrocities" committed by foreigners in the country, and they called for the deportation of all undocumented migrants, accusing them of crimes such as drug abuse, human trafficking, violence against women, and service delivery failures.[31] They carried placards with their grievances printed on them:

"WE DEMAND DAILY RAIDS IN CITIES BY SOLDIERS,"
"WE WANT OUR COUNTRY BACK,"
"DEPORT ALL ILLEGAL FOREIGNERS BLACK AND WHITE"
"WE DEMAND LAW & ORDER & IMMIGRATION CONTROL IN SOUTH
  AFRICA,"
FIRE FOREIGNERS IN GOVERNMENT DEPARTMENTS,
"@ DHA SELLING OUR PASSPORTS TO THE NIGERIANS"[32]

On September 26, 2020, the Independent Online news announced that the Gauteng provincial government had come up with a draft proposal (Gauteng Economic Development Bill), in an attempt to limit foreign nationals from doing business in townships in the province. It was reported that only foreign nationals who are permanent residents in the country will be allowed to do business (business licenses were not issued to foreign nationals with work permits and temporary residence permits), as a means of revitalizing the economy.[33]

A brief historical overview of the developments of xenophobic attitudes points to a constant, and yet unattended, problem. In June 2008, a Mozambican national, Ernesto Nhamuave, was stabbed and set alight in front of media cameras in Ramaphosa informal settlement.[34] Again, in broad daylight before dozens of spectators, a Mozambican national, Emmanuel Sithole, was stabbed and killed on April 18, 2015 in Alexandra Township.[35] Similarly, in 2015 and 2019, waves of xenophobic violence left many killed, injured, and homeless.

The killers of Sithole and Nhamuave did so with an understanding that society had approved of their actions. The killings were simply a result of hatred of black foreigners. The men and women who attack black foreign nationals are, in other words, enacting a colonial logic traceable to the structure of colonialism and apartheid. The government of South Africa denies the fact that the attacks on black foreign nationals are xenophobic, opting for a rhetoric that the attacks were acts of criminality.[36] It is estimated that from the period of 2008 to 2015, more than 350 people were killed in xenophobic attacks in South Africa.[37]

In the 2008 xenophobic attacks, out of 62 people killed, 22 of them were South African nationals. In a Tweet message (through the ANC Parliament Twitter handle) by the then minister of defense, Nosiviwe Mapisa-Nqakula, on September 10, 2019, out of 12 people killed in xenophobic violence, 2 were foreigners and 10 (83%) were South Africans.[38] It appears the South Africans killed were mistaken for foreign nationals. In some cases foreign nationals fought back and killed the attackers, the South Africans. Scholars, such as Van Muster, point to the failure of national politics; when politics fails, there is always a mobilization of politics of insecurity.[39] This has become more pronounced in European politics in countries such as Germany, France, and England, where Muslims have become the "other" in the era of terrorism. Van Muster defines politics of insecurity as the politicization of one's self and that the "self" is dependent on the elimination of the dangerous other. For Slavoj Žižek, this is populism resulting from the lack of political reasoning by the "enlightened liberal-technocratic elite."[40] In this chapter, it will also be important to examine the role of colonialism and apartheid in the failure of postapartheid South Africa.

THE LEGACY OF APARTHEID IN SOUTH AFRICA

The Southern African story has always been a history of migration and move-ment across the region and the African continent at large. The mining industry of South Africa is a story of migrant labor and coerced labor from across the Southern African region. Foreign nationals have played a pivotal role in the creation of a modern South Africa; their involvement in economic develop-ment, politics, liberation movements, and labor movements is undisputed. The country has a relatively strong and stable economy in the Southern African region and in the African continent; the country has relatively strong state institutions and strong social spending regimes. For these reasons, the country has been more attractive to migrants around the continent, who are otherwise looking for better economic opportunities or political refuge.[41] However, the country is currently experiencing numerous economic challenges; these include high unemployment rates, increasingly dwindling economic oppor-tunities, an ever-increasing housing backlog, and a bulging informal housing problem. Also, there has been an increase in the number of broken families, with mothers having to face the brunt of being sole providers. As such, the state is increasingly under pressure to meet its obligation of providing social and health care services to the millions of unemployed citizens, as well as education and support and security to millions of women and children.[42] In this context, foreign nationals who arrive in the country find an already overstretched system and are seen as invaders and automatically assume the status of "being unwanted." Media in South Africa has constantly played a sig-nificant role in promoting and in fighting xenophobia. Foreign nationals have lived in the periphery, marginalized by state institutions and communities;

they have become subalterns, the unwanted, and the derelicts. Similarly, during the days of colonialism and apartheid, the state created a system that pushed black people into becoming subalterns; the process of othering foreign nationals in postapartheid South Africa is so intense that it has permeated the upper echelons of state institutions.

The media, which remains predominantly white-owned, in the case of South Africa, has constantly referred to foreign African nationals as "floods of foreigners" or "hordes of foreigners."[43] Surprisingly, the focus of the media has only been on black foreign migrants, despite the fact that there are so many foreign white migrants in the country. Scholars such as Michael Neocosmos, Grace Idahosa, Louise Vincent, and Nahla Valji[44] have argued that national projects designed to build national consciousness among South African citizens have accelerated the divisions between locals and foreign nationals. As a result, black African foreign nationals are now perceived as terrorists and as invaders seeking to destroy the social fabric. During the coronavirus pandemic lockdowns, social media was awash with people calling for the removal of foreign nationals from the mainstream economy.

Prior to 1994, black South Africans were not part of the citizenry of the country, because the apartheid system excluded them. In other words, black South Africans became foreigners on their own land. Since the apartheid legacy was centered on the victimization of the black population, soon after democracy, South Africans adopted the enemy's methods of "victimization and violence," and their targets became black African immigrants. During apartheid, the state created its own citizens and subjects, and in a neo-apartheid South Africa, the state continues to fulfill this role. The native population was categorized as aliens or native foreigners,[45] and their culture was thought to be stagnant. The question of nativity is always problematic as it is always premised on the idea of frozen cultures and identities.[46] South African nationalism continues to uphold cultures and identities created by the colonial and apartheid regimes.

With the scarcity of jobs, widespread poverty, poor sanitation, illiteracy, and lack of housing and other services, black foreign migrants have become a "legitimate" target, seen as usurpers of what is entitled to those historically oppressed by apartheid. In light of the discrimination of black people by the colonial and apartheid regimes, one expects black South Africans to be more sympathetic to African migrants; however, the opposite is happening in postapartheid South Africa.[47] Michael Neocosmos argues that poverty results in powerlessness, and the powerless vent their anger on the weak. Current government institutions are xenophobic in themselves; these include the ministry of home affairs, the parliament, the police department, the media, and the judiciary; they all have labeled foreigners as a threat to national security.[48] As a result, the powerless now believe that the influx of foreign nationals is the cause of all the economic and social challenges they are facing. One draws from Boaventura Santos's concept of abyssal thinking to understand the rage and hate of foreigners prevalent in South Africa's informal settlements.[49]

Because of lack of unity among South Africans, Ivor Chipkin[50] asks a theoretical question: Do South Africans exist? Also, because of confusion of identity in Africa, Sabelo Ndlovu-Gatsheni[51] asks an important question: Do Africans Exist? Answers to these questions can be drawn from the systems the apartheid structures employed to destroy the African and the South African identity in Mahmood Mamdani's *Define and Rule: Native as Political Identity*.[52] Creating a common African identity would require a conscious reflection on what really binds Africans together in the continent, the shared history, and struggles for liberation, and colonialism should be the starting point. South Africa is part of Africa, and the country has a common shared history with other African countries. A good number of South Africa's political struggle icons were accommodated by African states during the fight against apartheid. Thus, Pan-Africanism becomes a binding force and an antidote to colonially engineered division, which has resulted in xenophobic violence.

FAILED NATIONALISM IN SOUTH AFRICA

There are numerous legacies of apartheid in South Africa. There is a political legacy, social and economic legacy, spatial legacy, brutality, broken families, unemployment, forced labor, and ethnic and tribal divisions. Land expropriation and nationalism are also some of the many legacies of apartheid. Apartheid promoted nationalism on exclusive terms—whites on one side and blacks and the people of color on the other side. This form of nationalism was based on dividing the population based on color, ethnicity, and religion. Thus, Mahmood Mamdani describes this as a "define and rule" strategy, and in doing so, the concept of "citizens and subjects" was created.[53] Postapartheid nationalism was intentionally inclusive in nature, but it faced resistance from xenophobia, nativism, ethnicity, and tribalism and then retained most of the apartheid nationalistic traits. In a postapartheid scenario, it is difficult to differentiate between black South Africans and black Africans; as mentioned in the previous section of this chapter, during xenophobic attacks many South Africans were killed after being mistaken for foreign nationals. For example, out of 62 people killed in 2008 xenophobic attacks, 22 were South African nationals.[54] It is evidently clear that the country has a long history of contested identity and citizenship.[55] Contrary to the "first" (apartheid nationalism), the "second" (postapartheid nationalism) is less prone to include and tends to exclude populations. Consequently, alienation, xenophobia, and its political instrumentalization are its curse.

The rise of South African nationalism such as the radical socioeconomic transformation and the ANC government pronouncing itself as a National Democratic Revolution coincided with the decline of African nationalism projects in South Africa. The preexisting national projects made it difficult for South African nationalism to take off. One of the biggest mistakes by former liberation movements in Africa was to allow themselves to be dictated by colonial institutions and colonial modernity, which diluted liberation movements and turned them into emancipatory movements, thereby celebrating democracy rather than freedom. In the end liberal democracy won the day rather than decolonization and freedom.[56] Some recent nationalist projects in South Africa tend to exclude populations, alienate, and promote xenophobia.[57] As a result, all the old practices of apartheid institutions were retained; black people began to discriminate one another because of the failed promises of emancipation and democracy. Angry black South Africans began to vent their anger on other poor African migrants seen as threats to national resources. There is a racial logic to this because black Africans from other African nations are believed to be dark-skinned, and derogatory names such as *amakwerekwere* (meaning those who cannot articulate the local language) are used to call them,[58] while, on one hand, black South Africans view themselves as light-skinned, perpetuating the presumption that they (black South Africans) are closer to humanity and whiteness. Their ontological density is not questioned as compared to that of other African nations, who are mainly discriminated against based on their looks, culture, and language. Writers such as Adjai and Lazaridis have argued that South Africa is stuck on color racism, and this is the reason black African nationals are targeted in poor communities. They further argue that South Africa needs to move toward an understanding of difference, diversity, and cultural pluralism.[59]

The entanglements of postapartheid South African identity can be traced back to colonialism and apartheid, which sought to create the black identity as that of divided people. Colonialism divided and regrouped black people according to their language and cultures, while at the same time creating borders that cut across communities,[60] and this is the case in present-day South Africa where certain groups of people find themselves suddenly cut out from their communities. Now the pertinent question is, who is "South African" in present-day South Africa? a country characterized by various ethnic and racial groups that shared the same struggles of colonialism and apartheid. The processes of Anglicanization, Afrikanerization, and Africanization attempted to engage the question of identity and the imaginations of the nation, which was and is still multiracial and multicultural in its composition.[61] In a nutshell, South African nationalism is so conflicted and contested along race, religion, ethnicity, culture, and language. The politics of nation-building driven by the elite ANC government could not solve these entanglements, but rather used the politics of exclusion as a method of campaign and a political tool to win votes.

However, some argue that the globalization of economies around the world has rendered the nation-state irrelevant as more people move around, following capital. This has also triggered international labor migration, because of improved transport and communication systems. Thus, nationalism strengthens national identities and local cultures, while, on the other hand, it promotes strong feelings of hatred of foreign nationals.[62] In South Africa, under the pretext of the spirit of Pan-Africanism, nationalism has degenerated to nativism and xenophobia. The language of reform does not advocate for total decolonization and change of the inherited colonial institutions; it does not seek to challenge coloniality either.[63] This has resulted in failed nationalist projects in Africa. New forms of racism have found their way into neo-apartheid South Africa; the new forms of racism are based on discrimination of people based on their nationality rather than the color of their skin.[64] Frantz Fanon puts the blame squarely on the postcolonial bourgeoisie, as he argues that they fell into the pitfalls of consciousness. The African bourgeoisie do not engage in production; rather they use the opportunity to loot public resources and hide their loot in foreign banks. There is no spirit of Pan-Africanism in South Africa in a political space run by African elites and the middle class.[65] Currently there is a serious struggle to form new African identities, which will move beyond the confines of race, tribe, ethnicity, gender, class, language, culture, and religion.[66] Being a foreigner in South Africa has become an unpleasant position and an embarrassment to the African Union's mission of uniting nations of the continent.

BEING A FOREIGNER

There is a high possibility of death, discrimination, hunger, and marginalization for foreign nationals in South Africa. This is a racial category associated with being alien, unwanted, very dark-skinned, thief, drug trafficker, human trafficker, rapist, and all forms of crime one can imagine. Being a foreigner is being black in South Africa; this is a product of colonialism, apartheid, disposition, forced labor, and expropriation. Describing the black condition, Lewis Gordon gives a clear description of what it means to be black in postcolonial Africa:

> It means living with the possibility of one's arbitrary death as a legitimate feature of a system. It also means witnessing concrete instances of arbitrary death and

social practices that demonstrate that one group of people's lives are less valuable than others' to the point of them not being considered to be really people at all.[67]

In South Africa, only blacks kill each other in xenophobic attacks, and it appears black people from other African nations have become a "problem" in South African communities. They are called "problem" people mainly because they are perceived as invaders, *makwerekwere*, criminals, drug dealers, and looters of resources. Though William Du Bois calls foreign nationals "problem people," he reminds us to feel for them and to put ourselves in their shoes by asking this critical question: "How does it feel to be a problem?"[68] This is a philosophical question that requires an in-depth understanding of subjects in their original environment. Foreign nationals in South Africa are already in the category of people viewed as socially problematic and whose demands are unreasonable. However, Steve Biko reminds us that black people do not have a problem at all, and the problem is solely with the oppressor, as he says, "The problem is white racism and it rests squarely on the laps of the white society."[69]

The black man wishes for joy and freedom, he wishes for liberation, but in this capitalist modernity, the joy and liberation may not be coming soon, rather it is a lifetime struggle of poverty and misery. A black foreigner in South Africa is rendered invisible and survives on the margins of society. Despite the rhetoric that Africa belongs to Africans, black foreign nationals from other African nations are viewed with skepticism. Lewis Gordon supports these observations when he writes,

> I look into the lived-reality of the people hidden in plain sight—people who are submerged and, as a consequence, supposedly "do not exist." It has always struck me as odd that people could be invisible while standing right before us.[70]

Current institutions in South Africa continue to perpetuate the misconception that foreign nationals are an unwanted group in society. The post-Covid-19 scenario looks bleak for foreign nationals as discrimination continues in institutions such as places of work, and communities, mainly because of the collapsed economy, due to the pandemic.

THE WORLD WITHOUT OTHERS

The world is increasingly closing out on "others"; different nations and societies are increasingly becoming intolerant of people from other cultures. According to Sabelo Ndlovu-Gatsheni, the idea of the world without others was the main driving force behind the invasion and plundering of other nations by the colonizers; this was the beginning of racism, xenophobia, Islamophobia, anti-Semitism, tribalism, ethnicity, and many more isms.[71] This assertion is critical in this chapter; it helps one understand the reasons for the continued emulation of the colonial model of the world by Africa. In a colonizer's model of a "one world," it is where racists believe that the world must be occupied by people of their own race, where tribalists believe that only people of their tribe must exist, where patriarchs believe only men should exist, and where Islamophobes believe only their religion must exist. In short, the world is increasingly intolerant of difference, the very idea of a universal world is flawed, and instead, a pluriversal world where difference defines who we are should be promoted. On the paradigm of one world, this is what Ndlovu-Gatsheni writes,

> At one level is the "paradigm of the One," which is predicated on a strong belief in singularities of one God, one state, one knowledge, one nation, one culture, one language, one identity, one sexual orientation, one religion, one way of knowing, one economic system, one political system, one moral order, one wife, one husband, and in rigid ideas of bounded sovereignties and citizenship.[72]

The statement above points out to the source of hatred for another human being around the world. The abyssal form of thinking can also be understood from the perspective of the "pyramid of hate"[73] and how it functions. Genocidal actions start from minor forms of hatred, and such actions are sometimes considered normal by society. Such beliefs begin with the collective thinking of the colonizers' model of the world: a world without others. Anyone who does not fit into the collective belief system becomes a target and an enemy of the "people." These belief systems start as general negative comments and jokes about certain groups of people, then degenerate into different forms of discrimination and exclusion, and finally degenerate into acts of killings and genocide.[74] Perpetrators usually justify hate as "love." For one to hate, one needs the "other" in order to create "us" in relation to "others."[75] Sara Ahmed argues that violence against other humans is a way of sealing the fate of other identities. Killings and hate have become normalized in the zone of nonbeing. Being black in the context of the zone of nonbeing is being an irrational subject, and life becomes a day-to-day struggle for survival.

Sabelo Ndlovu-Gatsheni writes about a world without others, the birth of a Cartesian Subject: a philosophy promulgated by Rene Descartes.[76] The cogito, ergo sum (I Think, Therefore I Am) became a philosophical springboard to justify invasion in the colonies as the natives were viewed as people without land, knowledge, development, history, and religion.[77] Armed with this philosophy, Europeans began to conquer the world as they assumed the position of an all-knowing being and accorded themselves with ontological density, while doubting the humanity of others. Western philosophy has a tendency of replacing God as the foundation of knowledge with the Western subject as the all-knowing subject.[78] According to Ramón Grosfoguel, All the attributes of God are extrapolated to western man. . . . Universal truth beyond spatial and temporal limits, privileges access to the laws of the universe, and grants the capacity to produce scientific knowledge and theory placed in the mind of a western man.[79]

In this line of thinking, the mind is now separated from the body. But can the mind really be separated from the body? On the contrary, the two are interdependent; one cannot exist without the other, and thought is the product of both. With this assertion, the world becomes a space where difference cannot be tolerated; thus in South Africa today, xenophobia is premised on the idea of intolerance to diversity and pluriversality.

Hate has been normalized in society, and this is how differences are constructed; this in turn could lead to genocide. There are many ways of dehumanizing human beings; perpetuating of violence against a category of people is one of the dehumanizing methods. The colonial system, through the abyssal thinking, produced its own victims: victims who are more than willing to harm others. Increasing dehumanization and brutalization reproduces more brutes. This is how the apartheid regime produced brutes that we see today. To think in this way is to understand xenophobia in South Africa; it is to understand the normalization of the abnormal. The extent and the willingness to see people harmed because of who they are or which group they belong to is alarming. Such a situation is not a coincidence in South Africa, as the dominant groups (black nationalists), who are a product of a colonial system, are responsible for leading the violence or hate toward other groups in society. These groups of black nationalists were trained by colonialists to be more brutal than their colonial masters, hence Frantz Fanon writes about the "pitfalls of national consciousness."[80] Genocidal ideas always come with the denial of other people's humanity. The creation of the zone of nonbeing is based on genocidal ideology. However, one may ask why death, as a way of life in the zone of nonbeing, is not adequately reported in the mainstream media in South Africa. This is because the colonial system made natives invisible in the South African space. More so, the media is predominantly white-owned and usually conforms to the standards and norms of the global colonial modernity. The white-owned media industry has often portrayed foreign nationals as guilty of certain crimes in the county, and in doing so they have contributed immensely to the creation of divisions in the general population.[81] Some black South Africans are adamant that foreign nationals "should remain in their own countries and try to sort out the problems of these respective countries, rather than fleeing them," because South Africa has "too many problems of its own," and in any case "cannot be expected to solve all the problems of Africa."[82]

This is one example of the influence of the white-owned media in perpetuating attitudes and perceptions about foreign nationals on the local population.[83] The same media played a role in spreading information about the South Africa-Zimbabwe border, making the public believe that it was porous, and this resulted in the erection of a new (but ineffective) border fence.

CONCLUSION

As argued extensively in this chapter, foreign nationals in nations around the world have to deal with all forms of injustices, and these include violent attacks, discrimination, diseases, death, hunger, and not to mention the psychological effect of such injustices. The death of foreign nationals in xenophobic attacks in the zone of nonbeing is not exceptional. The situation calls for the problematization of the existence of this zone, and how it is reproduced and regulated. The current postapartheid situation in South Africa was inherited from the colonial and apartheid regimes. Problematizing the existence of this zone allows one to judge those who are responsible for its creation and to imagine new ways of being, new humanity, and ways of thinking which do not promote discrimination, but to embrace diversity, Pan-Africanism, and pluriversality. This means tackling coloniality head-on. In dealing with xenophobia, xenophobic violence, race, and racism, South Africa needs to adopt a post-abyssal way of thinking, and a critical decolonial theory, as a remedy to all forms of discrimination.

This chapter reflects on the ills of imagination of the South African system, a system which tends to exclude those on the periphery of the economy, who are, in this case, the poor majority. It is a discriminatory and unsustainable system which promotes black-on-black violence. The poor majority are deliberately driven into a situation where they have to fight for resources, while the minority enjoy the benefits inherited from the apartheid system, a system whose legacy is still present in current government institutions. The first process to regain the humanity status of marginalized groups such as foreigners requires mediation on what it means to be human in the first place.[84] Lewis Gordon refers to the situation of human beings treated as less human, as "death-bound subjectivity." He argues that in dealing with "death-bound subjectivity," it requires the suspension of ethics. The situation of foreigners in South Africa can be described as "death-bound subjectivity," since society normalizes death and suspends ethical issues in the process.

The biggest challenge that South Africa has is to translate nativism into nationalism and Pan-Africanism, as well as dealing with racial divisions, ethnic divisions, religious divisions, tribal divisions, and national divisions. The struggle now is to create a broader African identity, which will accommodate all identities, in order to eliminate xenophobia and racism and all types of isms associated with the pitfalls of consciousness. South Africa needs to move beyond the entrapments of bordered nationalism and nativism into Pan-Africanism and transmodernity. Modernity has created more problems in the world, and it has failed to save the world from social, economic, and environmental destruction. Xenophobia in South Africa remains strongly embedded in government and private institutions, and the media has done little but to promote it in many ways discussed in this chapter. With the spread of the coronavirus in African nations, which has almost collapsed the economies of some countries, it is highly likely that more nations will experience waves of xenophobic violence.

NOTES

1. Gobodo-Madikizela Pumla. "Remembering the past: Nostalgia, traumatic memory, and the legacy of apartheid." *Peace and Conflict: Journal of Peace Psychology* 18, no. 3 (2012): 252.

2. Ramón Grosfoguel. "The epistemic decolonial turn: Beyond political-economy paradigms." *Cultural Studies* 21, no. 2–3 (2007): 211–223.

3. Mahmood Mamdani. *Define and Rule: Native as Political Identity.* Harvard University Press, 2012.

4. Grosfoguel, "The epistemic decolonial turn," 211–223; Bernard Magubane. *Race and the Construction of the Dispensable Other.* Unisa Press, 2007; Walter Mignolo. *The Darker Side of Western Modernity: Global Futures Decolonial Options.* Duke University Press, 2011.

5. Maldonado-Torres Nelson. "On the coloniality of being: Contributions to the development of a concept." *Cultural Studies* 21, no. 2–3 (2007): 243.

6. Mignolo, *The Darker Side of Western Modernity,* 2.

7. Maldonado-Torres, "On coloniality of being," 244.

8. Maldonado-Torres, "On coloniality of being," 255.

9. Frantz Fanon. "The Wretched of the Earth London." (1963).

10. Boaventura de Sousa Santos. "Beyond abyssal thinking: From global lines to ecologies of knowledge." *Binghamton University Review* 30, no. 1 (2007): 45–89.

11. Grosfoguel Ramón. "What is racism?" *Journal of World-Systems Research* 22, no. 1 (2016): 10.

12. Grosfoguel, "What is racism?," 2016.

13. J. Ndlovu-Gatsheni Sabelo. *Coloniality of Power in Postcolonial Africa.* African Books Collective, 2013.

14. Michael Noble and Gemma Wright. "Using indicators of multiple deprivations to demonstrate the spatial legacy of apartheid in South Africa." *Social Indicators Research* 112, no. 1 (2013): 187–201.

15. Fanon, "The wretched of the earth." (1963).

16. Edward Du Bois William. *The Souls of Black Folk.* Oxford University Press, 2008.

17. Fanon, "The wretched of the earth." 27.

18. Burcu Toğral Koca. "Bordering practices across Europe: The rise of 'walls' and 'fences.'" *Migration Letters* 16, no. 2 (2019): 183–194.

19. Dimitris Skleparis. "'A Europe without walls, without fences, without borders': A desecuritisation of migration doomed to fail." *Political Studies* 66, no. 4 (2018): 985–1001.

20. Elisabeth Vallet and Charles-Philippe David. "Good fences for good neighbours? States, couples and walls." In *Building Sustainable Couples in International Relations*, pp. 66–87. Palgrave Macmillan, London, 2014.

21. Burcu Toğral Koca, "Bordering practices across Europe."

22. Gideon Biger. "Walls, fences and international borders." *Studiaz Geografii Polityczneji Historycznej* 2 (2013): 87–108.

23. Brendon Cannon. "Terrorists, geopolitics and Kenya's proposed border wall with Somalia." *Contemporary Voices: St Andrews Journal of International Relations* 7, no. 2 (2016).

24. Burcu Toğral Koca. "Bordering Practices across Europe," 2019.

25. David Makovsky. "How to build a fence." *Foreign Affairs* (2004): 50–64.

26. Belinda Dodson. "Porous borders: Gender and migration in Southern Africa." *South African Geographical Journal* 82, no. 1 (2000): 40–46.

27. Biger, "Walls, fences and international borders," 2013.

28. Samantha Graham-Mare. "Beitbridge border fence reveals true incompetence of DPWI." *DA News Website*, 24 April 2020. https://www.da.org.za/2020/04/beitbridge-border-fence-reveals-true-incompetence-of-dpwi; Chris Muronzi. "Zimbabwe unfazed by South Africa plan to erect border fence." *Aljazeera News*, 21 March 2020. https://www.aljazeera.com/news/2020/3/21/zimbabwe-unfazed-by-south-africa-plan-to-erect-border-fence

29. Jason Felix. "Beitbridge fiasco: Contractors agree to pay any amount ordered against them." *News24*, 16 October 2020, https://www.news24.com/news24/southafrica/news/beitbridge-fiasco-contractors-agree-to-pay-any-amount-ordered-against-them-20201016

30. Naledi Sishange. "'There is going to be a new way of doing things': Mboweni on business after lockdown." *TimesLive*, 24 April 2020. https://www.timeslive.co.za/politics/2020-04-24-there-is-going-to-be-a-new-way-of-doing-things-mboweni-on-business-after-lockdown/; Michael Cohen and Prinesha Naidoo. "South Africa must put locals first post virus, Mboweni say." *Bloomberg News*, 24 April 2020. https://www.bloomberg.com/news/articles/2020-04-24/south-africa-must-put-locals-first-post-virus-mboweni-says

31. Greg Nicolson. "Protest against foreign nationals a signal that violence may follow, say experts." *Daily Maverick.* 24 September 2020. https://www.dailymaverick

.co.za/article/2020-09-24-protest-against-foreign-nationals-a-signal-that-violence
-may-follow-say-experts

32. Abigail Javier. "Gallery: Put South Africans first march heads to Nigerian embassy." *Eyewitness News*, 23 September 2020. https://ewn.co.za/2020/09/23/gallery-putsouthafricafirst-march-heads-to-nigerian-embassy

33. Loyiso Sidimba. "New law to bar foreigners doing business in Gauteng Townships." *IOL News Online*, 26 September 2020. https://www.iol.co.za/news/politics/new-law-to-bar-foreigners-doing-business-in-gauteng-townships-f7feb3a0-6c9a-48d0-abf5-36276bbe52f7

34. Sibongile Khumalo. "No justice for burning man." *Mail & Guardian*, 30 July 2010. https://mg.co.za/article/2010-07-30-no-justice-for-burning-man/; Beauregard Tromp. "SA's xenophobia shame: 'burning man' case shut." *TimesLive*, 15 February 2015. https://www.timeslive.co.za/sunday-times/lifestyle/2015-02-15-sas-xenophobia-shame-burning-man-case-shut/

35. Times*Live*. "Government says Sithole was not a victim of xenophobia as it releases names of those killed." 28 April 2015, http://www.timeslive.co.za/local/2015/04/28/Government-says-Sithole-was-not-a-victim-of-xenophobia-as-it-releases-names-of-those-killed1; eNCA News. "Sithole killers sentenced." 1 February 2016, https://www.enca.com/south-africa/sithole-killers-sentenced; Wisani Sithole. "Makhubele, family members lose faith in SA justice system." *SABC News*, 4 May 2015. http://www.sabc.co.za/news/a/9179f60048404abfb073ff4d1170398b/Sithole undefinedfamilyundefinedmembersundefinedloseundefinedfaithundefinedinundefin edSAundefinedjusticeundefinedsystem-20150405.

36. Times Live, "Sithole was not a victim of xenophobia," 2015.

37. James Hall. "Anti-foreigner violence exposes festering conflict in South Africa:: Southern Africa-issue in focus." *Africa Conflict Monitor* 2015, no. May 2015 (2015): 71–77.

38. Tom Head. "Revealed: 83% of lives lost to xenophobic protests were South Africans." *The South African*, 10 September 2019. https://www.thesouthafrican.com/news/xenophobic-violence-south-african-how-many-killed-death-toll/

39. RensVan Munster. "The desecuritisation of illegal migration: The case for a European belonging without community." (2004).

40. Slavoj Žižek. "Against the populist temptation." *Critical inquiry* 32, no. 3 (2006): 551–574.

41. Debbie Budlender and Francie Lund. "South Africa: A legacy of family disruption." *Development and Change* 42, no. 4 (2011): 925–946.

42. Budlender and Lund, "South Africa," 2011; Michael Noble and Gemma Wright. "Using indicators of multiple deprivation to demonstrate the spatial legacy of apartheid in South Africa." *Social Indicators Research* 112, no. 1 (2013): 187–201.

43. Morgan Ndlovu. "Manufacturing black-on-black violence in Africa: A decolonial perspective on Mfecane and Afrophobia/xenophobia in South Africa." *International Journal of African Renaissance Studies-Multi-, Inter-and Transdisciplinarity* 12, no. 2 (2017): 97–109.

44. Michael Neocosmos. "The politics of fear and the fear of politics: Reflections on xenophobic violence in South Africa." *Journal of Asian and African studies*

43, no. 6 (2008): 586–594; Michael Neocosmos. *From Foreign Natives to Native Foreigners. Explaining Xenophobia in Post-apartheid South Africa: Explaining Xenophobia in Post-apartheid South Africa: Citizenship and Nationalism, Identity and Politics.* African Books Collective, 2010; Grace Idahosa and D. Vincent. "Xenophobia, sovereign power and the limits of citizenship." *Africa Review* 6, no. 2 (2014): 94–104; Nahla Valji. "Creating the nation: The rise of violent xenophobia in the new South Africa." *Unpublished Master's Thesis, York University* (2003).

45. Neocosmos, "The politics of fear and the fear of politics," 2008.

46. Francis, B. Nyamnjoh. "Racism, ethnicity and the media in Africa: Reflections inspired by studies of xenophobia in Cameroon and South Africa." *Africa Spectrum* 45, no. 1 (2010): 57–93.

47. Adjai Carol and Gabriella Lazaridis. "Migration, xenophobia and new racism in post-apartheid South Africa." *International Journal of Social Science Studies* 1 (2013): 192.

48. Neocosmos, "The politics of fear and the fear of politics," 2008.

49. Santos, "Beyond abyssal thinking," 2007.

50. Chipkin Ivor. *Do South Africans Exist?: Nationalism, Democracy and the Identity of "the People."* Wits University Press, 2007.

51. J. Ndlovu-Gatsheni Sabelo. "Do 'Africans' exist? Genealogies and paradoxes of African identities and the discourses of nativism and xenophobia." *African Identities* 8, no. 3 (2010): 281–295.

52. Mamdani, "Define and rule," 2012.

53. Mamdani, "Citizens and subjects," 2017.

54. Annsilla Nyar. "What happened? A narrative of the May 2008 xenophobic violence." (2011).

55. Sabelo J. Ndlovu-Gatsheni. *Coloniality of Power in Postcolonial Africa.* African Books Collective, 2013.

56. Ndlovu-Gatsheni, *Coloniality of Power in Postcolonial Africa,* 2013.

57. Dirk Kohnert. "New nationalism and development in Africa." *Africa Spectrum* 44, no. 1 (2009): 111–123.

58. Nyamnjoh, "Racism, ethnicity and the media in Africa," 2010.

59. Adjai and Lazaridis, "Migration, xenophobia and new racism,"2013.

60. Norbert Kersting. "New nationalism and xenophobia in Africa–A new inclination?." *Africa Spectrum* 44, no. 1 (2009): 7–18.

61. Ndlovu-Gatsheni, "Coloniality of power in postcolonial Africa," 2013.

62. Kersting, "New nationalism and xenophobia," 2009.

63. Ndlovu-Gatsheni, "Coloniality of power in postcolonial Africa," 2013.

64. Adjai and Lazaridis "Migration, xenophobia and new racism," 2013.

65. Kersting, "New nationalism and xenophobia," 2009.

66. Ndlovu-Gatsheni, "Do 'Africans' exist?," 2010.

67. Gordon, "Through the hellish zone of nonbeing," 11.

68. Du Bois, "The souls of black folk," 4.

69. Biko, "I write what I like," 25.

70. Gordon, "Through the hellish zone of nonbeing," 7.

71. J. Ndlovu-Gatsheni Sabelo. "A world without others? Specter of difference and toxic identitarian politics." *International Journal of Critical Diversity Studies* 1, no. 1 (2018): 80–96.

72. Ndlovu-Gatsheni, "A world without others?," 81.

73. Anti-Defamation League. "Anti-Defamation League state hate crime statutory provisions." *Retrieved March* 24 (2005): 2006.

74. Anti-Defamation League, "Anti-Defamation League state hate crime statutory provisions."

75. Ahmed Sara. "The organisation of hate." *Law and Critique* 12, no. 3 (2001): 345–365.

76. Ndlovu-Gatsheni, "A world without others?," 2018.

77. Maldonado-Torres, "On coloniality of being," 2007.

78. Ramón Grosfoguel. "A decolonial approach to political-economy: Transmodernity, border thinking and global coloniality." *Kult* 6, no. 1 (2009): 10–38.

79. Grosfoguel, "A decolonial approach to political-economy," 15.

80. Fanon, *The Wretched of the Earth*, 1963.

81. Nyamnjoh, "Racism, ethnicity and the media in Africa," 2010.

82. Nyamnjoh, "Racism, ethnicity and the media in Africa," 66.

83. Nyamnjoh, "Racism, ethnicity and the media in Africa," 2010.

84. Gordon, "Through the hellish zone of nonbeing," 2007.

BIBLIOGRAPHY

Adjai, Carol, and Gabriella Lazaridis. "Migration, xenophobia and new racism in post-apartheid South Africa." *International Journal of Social Science Studies* 1 (2013): 192.

Ahmed, Sara. "The organisation of hate." *Law and Critique* 12, no. 3 (2001): 345–365.

Biger, Gideon. "Walls, fences and international borders." *Studia z Geografii Politycznej Historycznej* 2 (2013): 87–108.

Budlender, Debbie, and Francie Lund. "South Africa: A legacy of family disruption." *Development and Change* 42, no. 4 (2011): 925–946.

Burnett, John. "$11 Billion and counting: Trump's border wall would be the world's most costly." *NPR News,* 19 January 2020. https://www.npr.org/2020/01/19/797319968/-11-billion-and-counting-trumps-border-wall-would-be-the-world-s-most-costly

Cannon, Brendon. "Terrorists, geopolitics and Kenya's proposed border wall with Somalia." *Contemporary Voices: St Andrews Journal of International Relations* 7, no. 2 (2016): 23–37.

Chipkin, Ivor. *Do South Africans Exist?: Nationalism, Democracy and the Identity of 'the People'.* Wits University Press, 2007.

Cohen, Michael, and Prinesha Naidoo. "South Africa must put locals first post virus, Mboweni say." *Bloomberg News,* 24 April 2020. https://www.bloomberg.com/news/articles/2020-04-24/south-africa-must-put-locals-first-post-virus-mboweni-says de Sousa Santos, Boaventura. "Beyond abyssal thinking: From global lines to ecologies of knowledges." *Review (Fernand Braudel Center)* (2007): 45–89.

Dodson, Belinda. "Porous borders: Gender and migration in Southern Africa." *South African Geographical Journal* 82, no. 1 (2000): 40–46.

Du Bois, William Edward Burghardt. *The Souls of Black Folk.* Oxford University Press, 2008.

eNCA News. "Sithole killers sentenced." *eNCA News*, 1 February 2016, https://www.enca.com/south-africa/sithole-killers-sentenced

Fanon, F. "Black Skin/White Masks, trans. Charles Lam Markmann, New York: Grove (2004)." *The Wretched of the Earth* (1967).

Fanon, Frantz. "The wretched of the earth London." (1963).

Felix, Jason. "Beitbridge fiasco: Contractors agree to pay any amount ordered against them." *News24*, 16 October 2020, https://www.news24.com/news24/southafrica/news/beitbridge-fiasco-contractors-agree-to-pay-any-amount-ordered-against-them-20201016

Gobodo-Madikizela, Pumla. "Remembering the past: Nostalgia, traumatic memory, and the legacy of apartheid." *Peace and Conflict: Journal of Peace Psychology* 18, no. 3 (2012): 252.

Gordon, L. "Through the Hellish zone of nonbeing thinking through fanon, disaster, and the damned of the earth. Temple University." *Human Architecture, Special Double-issue: Journal of the Sociology of Self-knowledge* 5 (2007): 5–12.

Graham-Mare, Samantha. "Beitbridge border fence reveals true incompetence of DPWI." *DA News Website*, 24 April 2020. https://www.da.org.za/2020/04/beitbridge-border-fence-reveals-true-incompetence-of-dpwi

Grosfoguel, Ramón. "A decolonial approach to political-economy: Transmodernity, border thinking and global coloniality." *Kult* 6, no. 1 (2009): 10–38.

Grosfoguel, Ramón. "The epistemic decolonial turn: Beyond political-economy paradigms." *Cultural Studies* 21, no. 2–3 (2007): 211–223.

Grosfoguel, Ramón. "What is racism?" *Journal of World-Systems Research* 22, no. 1 (2016): 9–15.

Hall, James. "Anti-foreigner violence exposes festering conflict in South Africa: Southern Africa-issue in focus." *Africa Conflict Monitor* 2015, no. May 2015 (2015): 71–77.

Head, Tom. "Revealed: 83% of lives lost to xenophobic protests were South Africans." *The South African*, 10 September 2019. https://www.thesouthafrican.com/news/xenophobic-violence-south-african-how-many-killed-death-toll/

Idahosa, Grace, and Louise D. Vincent. "Xenophobia, sovereign power and the limits of citizenship." *Africa Review* 6, no. 2 (2014): 94–104.

Javier, Abigail. "Gallery: Put South Africans first march heads to Nigerian embassy." *Eyewitness News*, 23 September 2020. https://ewn.co.za/2020/09/23/gallery-put-southafricafirst-march-heads-to-nigerian-embassy

Kersting, Norbert. "New nationalism and xenophobia in Africa–A new inclination?." *Africa Spectrum* 44, no. 1 (2009): 7–18.

Koca, Burcu Toğral. "Bordering practices across Europe: The rise of "walls" and "fences"." *Migration Letters* 16, no. 2 (2019): 183–194.

Kohnert, Dirk. "New nationalism and development in Africa." *Africa Spectrum* 44, no. 1 (2009): 111–123.

Khumalo, Sibongile. "No justice for burning man." *Mail &Guadian*, 30 July 2010. https://mg.co.za/article/2010-07-30-no-justice-for-burning-man/

League, Anti-Defamation. "Anti Defamation League state hate crime statutory provisions." *Retrieved March* 24 (2005): 2006.

Magubane, Bernard. *Race and the Construction of the Dispensable Other.* Unisa Press, 2007.

Makhubele, Wisani. "Sithole family members lose faith in SA justice system." *SABC News,* 4 May 2015. http://www.sabc.co.za/news/a/9179f60048404abfb073ff4 d1170398b/Sitholeundefinedfamilyundefinedmembersundefinedloseundefinedfai thundefinedinundefinedSAundefinedjusticeundefinedsystem-20150405

Makovsky, David. "How to build a fence." *Foreign Affairs* (2004): 50–64.

Maldonado-Torres, Nelson. *Against War: Views from the Underside of Modernity.* Duke University Press, 2008.

Maldonado-Torres, Nelson. "On the coloniality of being: Contributions to the development of a concept." *Cultural studies* 21, no. 2–3 (2007): 240–270.

Mamdani, Mahmood. *Citizen and Subject: Contemporary Africa and the Legacy of Late Colonialism.* Princeton University Press, 2018.

Mamdani, Mahmood. *Define and Rule: Native as Political Identity.* Harvard University Press, 2012.

Mignolo, Walter. *The Darker Side of Western Modernity: Global Futures, Decolonial Options.* Duke University Press, 2011.

Minca, Claudio, and Alexandra Rijke. "Walls! Walls! Walls." *Society and Space* 4 (2017).

Muronzi, Chris. "Zimbabwe unfazed by South Africa plan to erect border fence." *Aljazeera News*, 21 March 2020. https://www.aljazeera.com/news/2020/3/21/ zimbabwe-unfazed-by-south-africa-plan-to-erect-border-fence

Ndlovu, Morgan. "Manufacturing black-on-black violence in Africa: A decolonial perspective on Mfecane and Afrophobia/xenophobia in South Africa." *International Journal of African Renaissance Studies-Multi-, Inter-and Transdisciplinarity* 12, no. 2 (2017): 97–109.

Ndlovu-Gatsheni, Sabelo J. "A world without others? Specter of difference and toxic identitarian politics." *International Journal of Critical Diversity Studies* 1, no. 1 (2018): 80–96.

Ndlovu-Gatsheni, Sabelo J. *Coloniality of Power in Postcolonial Africa.* African Books Collective, 2013.

Ndlovu-Gatsheni, Sabelo J. "Do 'Africans' exist? Genealogies and paradoxes of African identities and the discourses of nativism and xenophobia." *African identities* 8, no. 3 (2010): 281–295.

Neocosmos, Michael. *From Foreign Natives to Native Foreigners. Explaining Xenophobia in Post-apartheid South Africa: Explaining Xenophobia in Post-apartheid South Africa: Citizenship and Nationalism, Identity and Politics.* African Books Collective, 2010.

Neocosmos, Michael. "The politics of fear and the fear of politics: Reflections on xenophobic violence in South Africa." *Journal of Asian and African Studies* 43, no. 6 (2008): 586–594.

Nicolson, Greg. "Protest against foreign nationals a signal that violence may follow, say experts." *Daily Maverick,* 24 September 2020. https://www.dailymaverick .co.za/article/2020-09-24-protest-against-foreign-nationals-a-signal-that-violence -may-follow-say-experts

Noble, Michael, and Gemma Wright. "Using indicators of multiple deprivation to demonstrate the spatial legacy of apartheid in South Africa." *Social Indicators Research* 112, no. 1 (2013): 187–201.

Nyamnjoh, Francis B. "Racism, ethnicity and the media in Africa: Reflections inspired by studies of xenophobia in Cameroon and South Africa." *Africa Spectrum* 45, no. 1 (2010): 57–93.

Nyar, Annsilla. "What happened? A narrative of the May 2008 xenophobic violence." (2011).

Sidimba, Loyiso. "New law to bar foreigners doing business in Gauteng Townships." *IOL News Online,* 26 September 2020. https://www.iol.co.za/news/politics/new -law-to-bar-foreigners-doing-business-in-gauteng-townships-f7feb3a0-6c9a-48d0 -abf5-36276bbe52f7

Sishange, Naledi. "'There is going to be a new way of doing things': Mboweni on business after lockdown." *TimesLive,* 24 April 2020. https://www.timeslive.co.za/ politics/2020-04-24-there-is-going-to-be-a-new-way-of-doing-things-mboweni-on -business-after-lockdown/

Skleparis, Dimitris. "'A Europe without walls, without fences, without borders': A desecuritisation of migration doomed to fail." *Political Studies* 66, no. 4 (2018): 985–1001.

Steve, Biko. *I Write What I Like: A Selection of His Writings.* Heinemann, 1978.

TimesLive. "Government says Sithole was not a victim of xenophobia as it releases names of those killed." *TimesLive,* 28 April 2015. http://www.timeslive.co.za/ local/2015/04/28/Government-says-Sithole-was-not-a-victim-of-xenophobia-as-it -releases-names-of-those-killed1

Tromp, Beauregard. "SA's xenophobia shame: 'burning man' case shut." *TimesLive,* 15 February 2015. https://www.timeslive.co.za/sunday-times/lifestyle/2015-02-15 -sas-xenophobia-shame-burning-man-case-shut/

Valji, Nahla. "Creating the nation: The rise of violent xenophobia in the new South Africa." *Unpublished Masters Thesis, York University* (2003).

Vallet, Elisabeth, and Charles-Philippe David. "Good fences for good neighbours? States, couples and walls." In *Building Sustainable Couples in International Relations,* pp. 66–87. Palgrave Macmillan, London, 2014.

Van Munster, Rens. "The desecuritisation of illegal migration: The case for a European belonging without community." (2004).

Žižek, Slavoj. "Against the populist temptation." *Critical Inquiry* 32, no. 3 (2006): 551–574.

Chapter 4

Xenophobia or Afrophobia?

A Policy Perspectives

Seun Bamidele

Nativity remains one of the most significant and valuable identities of the individual in any given human society.[1] Place of birth establishes an individual as a subject or national of a sovereign state for easy identification and for the protection of various human rights. Knowledge of a person's place of birth affords the state jurisdiction over the person and grants the person protection against other states.[2] Nativity has arguably played a more vital role in the religious, cultural, social, economic, and political development of human societies than any other means of legal identification.[3] In Africa, it offers religious, cultural, social, political and economic solidarity, and identification. As a result, it is essential that individuals continue to be identified as citizens of certain states. Governments set up mechanisms of legal identification to ensure long-standing social, economic, and political relations between states and between the state and the individual, and to monitor numbers of citizens and foreign migrants respectively.[4] Nativity in Africa plays an important role in both ideas and in governance today because it feeds into the Pan-Africanism construct. This occurs within a governance and nativity framework of advocacy for a political union of all the states of Africa. It is argued that nativity, governance, and Pan-Africanism hold the key to African countries' development.

Within the context of South Africa, the importance of Pan-Africanism cannot be underestimated. Beyond nativity only, Pan-Africanism entails deep-rooted politics that promote the political union of all the indigenous inhabitants of the African region, both African natives and African foreign migrants in any particular country.[5] The success or failure of governance in South Africa is linked with two fundamental factors: the dominant power of the formal actor (the State), and the activities of the informal actors (black natives) in endorsing Pan-Africanism prospects. While studies have focused on the supposed overarching reach of the State as the all-deciding formal actor, it is important to note that informal actors (black natives) also play vital roles in governance and its associated politics.

Politics, here, means power relations and the curtailing and/or promoting of xenophobia beyond the confines of the State. One such instance exists between the black natives and the African migrants in South Africa. For long, African migrants have suffered from a "trajectory of xenophobia with the black natives."[6] Since the end of apartheid, black political leaders across party divides in South Africa have tapped into existing anti-African sentiment and created an atmosphere of hostility toward African migrants, causing black natives to turn to violence.[7] Frequent rounds of devastating xenophobic attacks have occurred between black natives and African migrants over control of resources (jobs and businesses) and the "nativity" and "migrant" dichotomy.[8] Although these attacks occur only intermittently, the consequences are enormous in terms of destruction of property and businesses belonging to African migrants, and, in many cases, their forced relocation either to their own homelands or to other parts of South Africa.[9] To resolve xenophobic attacks on African migrants, various peace processes have been put in place. However, peaceful coexistence between foreign nationals and South Africans remains fleeting and tentative in South African society. Why is this so? What accounts for the intractable xenophobic attacks from black South African natives against African migrants? This study interrogates these questions.

STUDY AREA AND METHODOLOGY

Fieldwork for the study was carried out between August and September 2018 in South Africa. Fieldwork took place in Pretoria, Durban, and Johannesburg, where many African migrants dwell. Interviews were conducted with both African migrants and black South African natives. Durban and Johannesburg were volatile areas during the xenophobic attacks and have much in common. Most African migrant leaders reside in these cities, as do a huge proportion of the country's black leaders and elites.

The study combined descriptive and interpretative methods of data collection and content analysis, making use of both primary and secondary data. While the primary data was generated through interviews and focus group discussions, secondary data was sourced from relevant journals, texts, newspapers, magazines, archival materials, declassified reports, unpublished theses, dissertations, and internet and conference papers. In-depth interviews were employed for primary data collection with the relevant respondents. Three categories of people were interviewed: (a) African migrants; (b) members of the public, including black traditional rulers, chiefs, the elderly, and the young; and (c) black state officials who are tasked with policy formulation to address the xenophobic attacks in these localities. The data was analyzed qualitatively.

SETTING THE FRAMEWORK

Some of the reasons for the xenophobic attacks have been said to include inconsistent state policies and the fragmented agendas of the South African state; the presence of "spoilers" among various interested parties; the nature and dynamics of post-xenophobic-attack peace bargaining; the socioeconomic and political opportunities offered by xenophobic attacks, especially over available resources; and the inadequacy of external support.[10] Xenophobic attacks may involve African migrants making use of black natives' available resources as economic opportunities, violations of state reform legislation, access to available resources for development, and natives and migrants demanding rights, both as groups and as individuals.[11] This is an indication of the lack of understanding on all sides about immigration policies and laws and the various Pan-Africanist agreements that have been made.

Perhaps there is no better example of intractable xenophobic attacks than in South Africa, where attacks are associated with economic rights, available resources in communities, social status, property ownership, and rights to State resources such as grants have become a recurring theme that never seems to quite go away. Xenophobic attacks have made livelihoods and settlement quite problematic for both sides of the conflict, as African migrants and South African black natives continue to coexist in at best an uneasy, short-lived truce.

XENOPHOBIA: BLACK NATIVES
AND AFRICAN MIGRANTS

Xenophobia or Afrophobia has deep roots in South Africa, being linked to apartheid and colonialism.[12] Unfortunately, African National Congress (ANC) politicians in the neo-apartheid era have not only failed to confront xenophobia but used it to the detriment of Pan-Africanism. The failure of public services continues to be a vital sticking point of policy relevance in developing countries, South Africa included. In the case of South Africa, it contributes to anti-African migrant sentiment.

Notwithstanding the ANC's lip service to Pan-Africanism, the legacy of the country's exceptionalism remains in what scholars such as Tshepo Madlingozi refer to as the "neo-apartheid" period.[13] Government policies entail a mechanism of meshing the rights, responsibilities, and duties that govern the lives of natives and African migrants and their assets. For this reason, xenophobia cannot be discussed meaningfully without due attention to policies and the government's mandate to protect natives and migrants across the various political divisions, from the Africanists and Pan-Africanists nonmainstream political groups to the traditional, mainstream, and even far-right political grouping in South Africa.

For some time, African migrants have battled for recognition of their rights to resources (properties, assets, funds, etc.) in South Africa, along with compensation for property that has been destroyed by black natives during xenophobic attacks.[14] The push began after apartheid, when black natives assumed political office; only a few years later, xenophobic attacks became common.[15] However, violence over resources (jobs and businesses) became intense in 2008, leaving many African migrants with no home or means of livelihood.[16] The 2008 xenophobic attacks led various Africans to call on South African politicians to end the violence and to find a lasting solution to the problem.[17]

Black natives and African migrants have been neighbors in South Africa ever since the creation of the Union of South Africa on May 31, 1910, eight years after the end of the Second Boer War and after four years of negotiation by an act of the British Parliament (the South Africa Act 1909). In 1994, after apartheid ended, unemployment was high.[18] While many black natives rose to the middle class and a select few to the ranks of the elite, the overall unemployment rate of black native people worsened between 1994 and 2003 by official metrics and significantly so when expanded definitions are used.[19] Poverty among whites, which was previously rare, also increased.[20]

The current government has struggled to achieve the monetary and fiscal discipline necessary to ensure both economic growth and the redistribution of wealth required for lasting peace. In 2008, xenophobic attacks left over 60 people dead.[21] The Centre on Housing Rights and Evictions estimated that over 100,000 people were driven from their homes.[22] The targets were mainly African migrants seeking asylum.[23] In a 2006 survey, the South African Migration Project concluded that South Africans were more opposed to African migrants than to any other national group.[24] In 2008, the UN High Commissioner for Refugees reported that over 200,000 African migrants had applied for asylum in South Africa, almost four times as many as the year before.[25] These African migrants were from Zimbabwe, Burundi, the Democratic Republic of the Congo, Rwanda, Eritrea, Ethiopia, and Somalia.[26] Competition over jobs, business opportunities, public services, and housing led to tension between black natives and these African migrants.[27] While xenophobia in South Africa is still a problem, recent violence has not been as widespread as initially feared.[28]

As South Africa continues to grapple with xenophobia, one of the proposed solutions has been to pass legislation, such as the pending Hate Crimes and Hate Speech Bill, which would uphold South Africa's ban on xenophobia.[29] All along, black natives' relationships with African migrants have been acrimonious, with the two groups taking an adversarial stance. Tensions are exacerbated by a lack of service delivery by the State regarding the provision of roads, water, employment, business opportunities, and housing, which has fueled accusations that what little services there are go to migrants. The result has been a series of high-intensity xenophobic attacks and destruction of property, forced displacement, relocations, and long legal cases.[30] All of this occurs amid the ongoing hardships experienced by African migrants in establishing jobs and businesses and acquiring accommodation. It has led to a widening gap between the two main parties wanting to secure these amenities.

It has been noted that xenophobic attacks significantly increased after the election of the black majority government in 1994.[31] In 2018, there were more than 500 xenophobic attacks against African migrants in South Africa.[32] In its attempts to overcome the divides of the past and build new forms of social cohesion, the ANC government embarked on aggressive and inclusive policies. One unanticipated by-product of this project has been a growth in intolerance toward African migrants.[33]

Xenophobic attacks against African migrants have become almost an accepted part of South African society, with communities divided by hostility and suspicion. After a first wave of xenophobic attacks in 2007/2008, a second wave swept through the country in 2015.[34] The riots and attacks in Johannesburg were similar in nature and origin to the 2007/2008 attacks and occurred against a background of competition for jobs, business opportunities, public services, and housing. In 2019, xenophobic attacks broke out again, targeting African migrants in Sydenham, Jadhu Place, and Overport in Durban.[35] Around 100 people attacked businesses owned by foreign nationals, resulting in around 50 people seeking shelter at a local police station[36] and many deaths.[37] South Africa's general election was blamed for contributing to xenophobic feelings, since during this time the ANC was committed to cracking down on undocumented African migrants involved in criminal activities.[38] The attacks on African migrants were criticized by both the South African government and all political parties, amid calls to ensure that xenophobic sentiment was not exploited for electoral purposes.[39]

Why were African people so at loggerheads with each other? Available studies and my fieldwork revealed that the black natives and African migrants have a long history of animosity that devolves down to competition over jobs, business opportunities, public services, and housing, along with an internal and cultural native-migrant dichotomy.

COMPETITION AND OWNERSHIP

Nearly all the literature on the xenophobia between black natives and African migrants in South Africa identifies competition over jobs, business opportunities, public services, and housing as major factors in the adversarial relations between the two groups. Competition over jobs, business opportunities, public services, and housing has to do with the differential narration of nativity and legal legislation of the two groups. In 2019, the Gauteng provincial government controversially proposed the Gauteng Township Economic Development Bill which seeks to prevent businesses operated by African migrants without black South African native employees from operating in the province's informal economy.[40] While those who are in support of the bill state that it will reduce xenophobia by clearing up regulatory regimes that African migrants are accused of violating, detractors of the bill state that its explicit targeting of African migrants is xenophobic and legitimizes xenophobia.

As is the case for many migrant groups all over the world, neither the black natives nor African migrants have the overall power over jobs, business opportunities, public services, and housing in whatever location the contestation occurs. It has been stated that African migrant business owners cannot expect to coexist peacefully with native business owners unless they share their trade secrets with them. In addition, South African black natives maintain that African migrant business owners have an advantage over them owing to the marginalization of native South Africans that started during apartheid. According to a 37-year-old respondent in Durban, the argument is that "African migrants cannot barricade themselves and refuse to share their practices with native business owners. The position has been met with widespread criticism."[41]

An inquiry by the Competition Commission, the country's antitrust regulator, indicated that a difference in performance between African migrants and native business owners has created a perception that African migrants are more successful than black natives.[42] While there is nothing wrong with examining the dynamics of competition, "the insinuation that African migrant business owners were to blame for the decline of black native-owned small business was worrying," stated by another respondent (47 years) in Durban.[43] The respondent further stated that "until recently, business ownership was often based on nativity and the decisions of the Department of South African Small Business Development, so that many black natives regarded themselves as the legitimate owners of whatever businesses arose in townships."[44] Ascription of ownership through the department makes the African migrants, according to the South African "black natives" in Johannesburg (54 years), "mere migrants who must pay compensation and accord recognition of their migrant status as a condition for continuing to live and do business on the land given to them."[45] Directly related to the jobs, business opportunities, public services, and housing rights issue is the issue of nativity and migration. Black native South Africans see themselves as the real owners of the jobs, business opportunities, public services, and housing, and regard other Africans as interlopers on their land. The concept of nativity/migration has implications for jobs, business opportunities, public services, and housing. Nativity confers certain rights and privileges that migrants do not have.

To refer to someone as a migrant within the world context means such a person cannot be treated equally with the natives and that there must be special recognition and compensation for both natives and migrants respectively. In South Africa, the 2007/2008 xenophobic attacks broke out partly in protest against relocation, resettlement without compensation and recognition, and the native/migrant dichotomy. The central question then is who owns the jobs, business opportunities, public services, and housing? This has been the main cause of xenophobic attacks between the black natives and the African migrants. The question remains unanswered as the black natives and African migrants claim ownership of the jobs, business opportunities, public services, and housing. In the words of a respondent from the South African natives' group in Durban (48 years),

> South Africa is not under the control of any African migrants. We believe that the current State was created as a result of our agitations to the apartheid government. The ownership of the jobs, business opportunities; public services and housing belong to us. The State will belong to all black natives. The State was established through post-apartheid declarations to vest all our jobs, business opportunities, public services and housing under the control of the black natives. The black natives are the owners of everything, not African migrants. No, they are migrants in the State. By the law, they are tenants and everything belongs to us.[46]

All the African migrants disagreed with the notions of the black South African natives. In the words of a respondent, a businessman (64 years) from one of the African countries,

> We are not in competition with them and the xenophobic attacks are not deliberate. We "African migrants" are claiming compensation from the South African government over the destruction of our jobs, business opportunities, public services and housing under attacks of the black natives. Long ago, we have been here before apartheid and we have rights over our jobs, business opportunities, public services and housing. The State is just an abstract geographical location and State black natives must also respect our rights in

the country. Because of their position in government, they now said the whole jobs, business opportunities, public services and housing belongs to them, not migrants. The jobs, business opportunities, public services and housing belong to us. They are natives and we are migrants. That is the truth. We also need compensation and recognition.[47]

What we see here is South African black natives and African migrants laying equal claim to ownership of the jobs, business opportunities, public services, and housing. All the respondents from the black native and African migrants' groups held passionately to their claims. While black natives lay claim to original ownership through nativity, the African migrants see themselves as the natural natives of the locality stretching back to the time of their immigration into South Africa.

The implication is that peace between the groups is still a long way off. The competition for ownership of jobs, business opportunities, public services, and housing is a major source of xenophobic attacks. The inability of South African black natives to establish a clear-cut boundary between themselves and African migrants has further compounded the problem.

POLITICS OVER RESOURCES

The notion of discrimination and competition for ownership of jobs, business opportunities, public services, and housing fueling xenophobic attacks by black South African natives against African migrants in South Africa has attracted huge representations in the literature. The case of black South African natives versus African migrants operates within the framework of "the resource curse." The 2019 wave of xenophobic attacks occurred because of discrimination and competition over available resources in terms of jobs, business opportunities, public services, and housing, as well as forced displacement without compensation for the families of African migrants after the destruction of their properties and businesses. Most studies have yet to interrogate the politics of discrimination and competition for ownership of resources between the black South African natives and African migrants in the country.[48] Since 1994, African migrants from Somalia, Mozambique, Zimbabwe, Nigeria, and the Democratic Republic of Congo have been filing lawsuits seeking to compel the South African government to prosecute the perpetrators of xenophobic attacks and to recognize their legal rights to their jobs, businesses, public services, and housing.[49] Currently, the South African government still categorizes the complainants as African migrants, without considering Pan-Africanism, and thus denying African migrants their rights and effectively rejecting the deeply rooted and widely promoted political union of all the indigenous inhabitants of Africa. The only aspects of society that might give black South African natives an advantageous position are those that are controlled by white South African natives, because of their supportive attitude toward African migrants in the country. In effect, African migrants have been deprived of their right to own their businesses and various other things they are entitled to by the State.

For the black South African native government to have any leverage on the continent, they must see African migrants as part of the political union of all indigenous inhabitants in their land. The only thing that could give them the much-needed African country recognition is the recognition of Pan-Africanism, because it speaks to the unity of all the indigenous inhabitants of Africa. This explains why Pan-Africanism has to be fought for in Africa. A respondent in Durban (57 years) pointed out that "the only way there will be peace in South Africa is for the same gestures that apply to South Africans to also be extended to migrants; i.e., granting compensation for destroyed lives and properties in the country."[50]

XENOPHOBIC BITTERNESS: PROTESTS AGAINST THE STATE

According to 51-year-old respondent in Johannesburg , "Of all the xenophobic attacks and skirmishes between the black South African natives and African migrants, the 2019 attacks appear to be the most upsetting in terms of intensity, scale and destruction of property and casualties recorded."[51] The use of soft weapons by the national security forces was required to quell the South African natives in these xenophobic uprisings. This incident provoked bitter declarations by the black South African natives that the State did not recognize their nativity and their preeminent right to jobs, business opportunities, public services, and housing. They swore to continue with violent protests against African migrants for the continuous forced displacements, marginalization, relocation without compensation, deprivation, and exclusion that they experienced in their own country. According to a respondent in Johannesburg (59 years), "Black South African natives are peace-loving people but the South African authorities are not ready to listen to them."[52] She further stated that "their bitterness was palpable and makes them prone to continuous acts of aggression against African migrants."[53]

According to another respondent in Durban (44 years), "The xenophobic attacks really date back to 1994, when incidents involving nativity began to gather pace".[54] Available data showed that within two months in that year, at least 67 people died in what were identified as xenophobic attacks.[55] In 2000, seven African migrants were killed on the Cape Flats over five weeks in what police described as xenophobic attacks, possibly motivated by the fear that African migrants would claim property belonging to locals.[56] In 2008, a series of attacks left 62 people dead, 21 of them black South African natives. The attacks were motivated by xenophobia.[57] In total, 1,400 suspects were arrested in connection with the attacks.

Nine months after the attacks, 128 individuals had been convicted and 30 had been found not guilty in 105 concluded court cases.[58] Altogether, 208 cases had been withdrawn and 156 were still being heard.[59] One year after the attacks, prosecutors said that 138 people had been convicted, 182 cases had been withdrawn because witnesses or complainants had left the country, 51 cases were underway or ready for trial, and 82 had been referred for further investigation.[60]

In 2009, a community of 1,500–2,500 Zimbabwean farm workers was forcibly evicted from their homes in the informal settlements of De Doorns, a grape-farming town in the Western Cape. No persons were physically assaulted but homes were trashed and looted, leading to the biggest forced displacement of African migrants since 2008.[61] At the time, State officials and national security agencies accused black South African natives of seizing property and xenophobic attacks against the African migrants and of destroying their properties in various locations in the country.[62]

Although these claims could not be verified, it was obvious that the xenophobic attacks resulted in destruction of businesses, public services, and housing and resulted in forced displacements. The scars of black South African natives' activities are still visible in South Africa. After many years of aggression and enmity, a modicum of peace gradually returned. The peace process comprised a complex series of interactions between various actors and institutions, including government authorities, black South African native leaders, the youth, and African migrants.

THE GOVERNMENT

The continuation of the hostility could be blamed on the inability of the government to respond appropriately to the plight of African migrants in South Africa. The government did not come to the aid of African migrants until 2015, one year after that wave of high-intensity xenophobic attacks began. African migrants therefore had to resort to self-defense for the preservation of their lives and property. Eventually, the State responded using national security forces in a violent way, which helped to reduce the deadly hostilities. In that wave of attacks, government success was aided by the fact that the black South African natives had simply become weary. The stability allowed the

State to establish policies and a commission to look into the conflict between black South African natives and African migrants in matters to do with jobs, business opportunities, public services, and housing. The commission collected reports from all the parties and actors and submitted its findings to the government, which were never made public.

This government action resulted in temporary relief and not permanent peace. Black South African natives remained in their territories and fear of resumed attacks among migrants was palpable. As competition continued in terms of access to jobs, business opportunities, public services, and housing, South African politicians decided to step in by forming alliances across the lines, with support from several political parties. On July 5, 2015, the Economic Freedom Fighters (EFF) pleaded with Johannesburg residents for peace and invited both parties to a peace and bargaining dialogue.[63] The black South African natives were led by several politicians, supported by indigenous chiefs from the various settlements. At this dialogue, all agreed to cease warring and embrace peace. Attacks ceased for a certain duration.

The success of the initiative became a tool in the hands of a few political parties, enabling them to secure the country. They subsequently built up a network of informants through a bottom-up approach, obtaining regular firsthand information about impending breaches of the peace, which they always quickly addressed through public announcements. Part of the method was to invite representatives and activists of black South African natives and African migrants to dialogues. In this way, the political approach proved far more successful than the use of national security forces in building peace in the country. The EFF said, "We call on our fellow South Africans to stop the violence against other poor people in our communities." A respondent in Johannesburg (41 years) said, "Xenophobic attacks will never resolve the problems our country faces because they were never caused by foreign nationals in the first place."[64] In this way the EFF turned the xenophobic attacks into a means for their own political ends—to draw attention to the failures of the governing party to provide adequate services, jobs, and housing. Thus they gained political leverage from the attacks.

The success of the approach used by the EFF and other political parties hinged on the support of the black South African natives, in particular. The government realized the value of those representatives in securing peace and developed government policies through constant dialogue and recognition of the black South African natives. Government actions regarding the conflict were very important because they helped to manage the situation. They were effective because they were informed by the input directives of the black South African natives, political leaders, and African migrants who called for peaceful dialogue.

POLICY PERSPECTIVES ON XENOPHOBIA

In policy debates about these attacks, the blame is typically placed on black South African natives. However, much responsibility for the current situation lies with the post-apartheid government's failure to successfully decolonize South Africa. One major flaw in the peace arrangement spearheaded by the post-apartheid government was the lack of consideration of migrants in their immigration policies and their very unfavorable actions regarding jobs and businesses, along with lack of provision for relocation and compensation for thousands of African migrants who lost property through violent attacks. African migrants have protested their right to own property and to engage in businesses and government's apparent mixed messaging when it comes to their position in South Africa. In another personal communication with a respondent in Johannesburg (67 years), during the 2019 protest, for instance, politicians declared to cheering crowds, "Everyone just arrives in our townships and rural areas and sets up businesses without licenses and permits. We are going to bring this to an end. And those who are operating illegally, wherever they come from, must now know."[65]

Other party leaders, such as those of the Democratic Alliance and the Congress of the People (Cope), have also contributed to an atmosphere that promotes xenophobic attacks. In addition to another respondent in Durban (53 years), "they have made similar claims that African migrants are flooding the country and undermining its security and prosperity, even though African migrants make up about 1.6 million of South Africa's 55 million people."[66] Also, the health minister claimed South Africa needed to reexamine its immigration policies, saying, "Our hospitals are full, we cannot control African migrants because overcrowding and infection control starts failing."[67]

After apartheid ended, many black South African native youths became idle. Having received unfulfilled promises from the post-apartheid government with regard to jobs and prosperity, and with weapons like cutlasses and guns flooding society, many townships became centers of crime. Cases of killings and armed robberies were common, and still are. Townships changed for the worse. The national security forces, government, and African migrants themselves were overwhelmed with almost daily incidents of harassment and killings. Eventually policies and programs were developed to attempt to stem the growing tide of criminality. In support of the claim, one respondent in Durban (62 years) stated that "the ANC also appointed a few fairly ruthless leaders in the police and security forces who were feared by everybody, including black South African natives."[68] Black South African native leaders met with the national security forces and issued orders to their youth leaders to put a stop to criminality in any locality. The personalities of the black

South African native leaders became a force to be reckoned. The rate of crime is still prevalent in the affected townships without a sigh of relief.

In recognition of the case of the black South African natives, the government appears to have entrusted the security of certain townships to local black South African native leaders. The implication here is that the black South African natives had the townships under their control. All acts of crimes or anything capable of breaching the peace were noted and responded to by them. In this way, they could carry out violent acts against the African migrants with a cloak of semi-legitimacy. They also worked together with national security forces.

To this day, when national security forces suspect any breach of peace, they move in to apprehend or neutralize activities, always in favor of black South African natives. State officials and black South African natives place much trust in them. Virtually all respondents attested to the indulgence of the black South African natives when it comes to acts of violence committed by security forces against migrants.

NATIVITY AND PAN-AFRICANISM: WHAT KIND OF PEACE IN SOUTH AFRICA?

Based on the fieldwork, I conclude that there is currently a relative peace in many South African black locations. However, the question is what kind of relative peace? Based on the discussion so far, one can conclude that it is a speculative peace. Two factors indicate this. The first is that the peace in many townships is sustained by the post-apartheid government and security forces. How long can peace that is supervised really last? What happens in the case of the death of the black South African native leaders in the ANC who reached the peace agreement with the African migrants? When hostility and xenophobic attacks begin rising, what action will be undertaken that promotes a lasting solution? Research findings show that the kind of peace being supervised by the post-apartheid black native government may not last long. Secondly, the politics of discrimination and the ongoing competition over jobs, business opportunities, public services, and housing between black South African natives and African migrants that is responsible for the hostility has yet to be addressed. As indicated in respondents' comments, both groups lay claim to jobs, business opportunities, public services, and housing. Neither group is ready to let go. In the words of a respondent in Johannesburg (56 years),

All African migrants who are within South Africa and have skills but are not documented must be documented and retained. Those without skills but are looking for jobs—the government must assist them to return to their original countries. Noticeably, business leaders are also complicit in stoking Afrophobic sentiment. Several South African black employers, such as farm owners, routinely exploit undocumented migrants with low pay and poor working conditions. These practices often undermine existing labour laws and increase tensions between natives and African migrants.[69]

In the same vein, another black South African native (48 years) from Zululand said,

> Economic drivers of native-led attacks against African migrants are inextricable from South Africa's anti-black history. Before apartheid's end, black South Africans were not natives of the country but segregated into homelands or Bantustans. While denying black natives' nativity, the apartheid government promoted immigration from white countries. The ruling white settler minority saw their country as separate from the African continent.[70]

The implication of all of this is that hostilities are not over. All indications point to a state of simmering resentment and an uneasy coexistence. The issue now is the conflict of interest between black South African natives and African migrants. What obtains at the moment is therefore a relative peace.

Several issues emerge from the study. The first is that the current cessation of hostilities may simply be a result of xenophobia-weariness. The second is the role of black South African native leaders in stoking discrimination and resentment regarding access to jobs, business opportunities, public services, and housing. The third is the place of post-apartheid government policies in maintaining peace in the country.

CONCLUSION

This chapter has examined relations between black South African natives and African migrants in South Africa. The black South African natives and African migrants have long been at war, with scant regard for the principles of Pan-Africanism, which are rarely mentioned by national, provincial, or local leaders. The adversarial relations are based on discrimination and competition over jobs, business opportunities, public services, and housing, along with a deep-seated nativity-migrant dichotomy. A combination of these issues often triggers xenophobic attacks. A cessation of the xenophobic attacks must involve the interplay of the post-apartheid government, local black native leaders, and the African migrants. A major lacuna exists in the ineffective peace process of the government action, and the tendency of black South African native leaders who have received anti-xenophobic training to meet social problems with violent protests. The leadership lacunae led to an unprecedented rise in crime shortly after the first xenophobic attacks. It got to a point that some African migrants could not cope, and had to flee

Since 2019 there has been peace. However, this author submits that the current peace in the country is relative and likely to be short-lived. This conclusion is based on two facts. The first is that competition over jobs, business opportunities, public services, and housing show no signs of abating as numbers increase and resources dwindle. This competition has yet to be resolved. All parties lay claim to rights of ownership of jobs, business opportunities, public services, and housing. The second reason is that any peace that is "superintended" by a government cannot be a permanent peace; it needs to be a state that wells up from below through the relative adequacy of resources for all.

NOTES

1. Michael Neocosmos, *From "Foreign Natives" to "Native Foreigners": Explaining Xenophobia in Post-Apartheid South Africa* (Dakar, Senegal: CODESRIA, 2008), 1–160.

2. Anthony P. Cohen, "Boundaries of Consciousness, Consciousness of Boundaries: Critical Questions for Anthropology", in *The Anthropology of Ethnicity: Beyond "Ethnic Groups and Boundaries*, eds. Hans Vermeulen and Cora Govers (Amsterdam: Het Spinhuis Publishers, 1996), 60.

3. Richard Handler, "Is 'Identity' a Useful Cross-Cultural Concept?", in *Commemorations—The Politics of National Identity*, ed. John R. Gillis (Princeton, NJ: Princeton University Press, 1994), 27–40; Brackette F. Williams, "A Class Act: Anthropology and the Race to Nation across Ethnic Terrain", *Annual Review of Anthropology*, 18 (1989): 401–444.

4. Ernest Gellner, *Nations and Nationalism* (London: Basil Blackwell, 1983), 55.

5. Steven Gordon, "A Violent Minority? A Quantitative Analysis of Those Engaged in Anti-immigrant Violence in South Africa", *South African Geographical Journal* 101, no. 2 (2019a): 269–283.

6. Steven Gordon, "The Popularity of State Discourses on Anti-immigrant Violence in South Africa", *The Round Table: The Commonwealth Journal of International Affairs* 108, no. 5 (2019b): 567–578.

7. DW, "South Africa's Politicians Feed Anti-foreigner Violence". Retrieved May 11, 2019, from https://www.dw.com/en/south-africas-politicians-feed-anti-foreignerviolence/a-48157900.

8. Philippa Kerr, Kevin Durrheim, and John Dixon, "Xenophobic Violence and Struggle Discourse", *Journal of Asian and African Studies* 54, no. 7 (2019): 995–1011; Shoghik Hovhannisyan, Christopher F. Baum, Helidah Refiloe Ogude, and

A. Sarkar, ed., *Mixed Migration, Forced Displacement and Job Outcomes in South Africa* (Washington, DC: World Bank, 2018).

9. Steven Gordon, "A Violent Minority? A Quantitative Analysis of Those Engaged in Anti-immigrant Violence in South Africa", *South African Geographical Journal* 101, no. 2 (2019a): 269–283.

10. Cedric de Coning, "The Coherence Dilemma in Peacebuilding and Post-conflict Reconstruction Systems", *African Journal on Conflict Resolution* 8, no. 3 (2008): 85–110; Stephen John Stedman, "Spoiler Problems in Peace Processes", *International Security* 22, no. 2 (1997): 5–53; Pierre Du Toit, "Why Post-Settlement Settlements?", *Journal of Democracy* 14, no. 3 (2003): 104–118; Paul Collier, "Doing Well Out of War: An Economic Perspective", in *Greed and Grievance: Economic Agendas in Civil War*, eds. Mats R. Berdal and David Malone (Boulder, CO: Lynne Rienner, 2000), 91–111; Simon Chesterman, *You, the People: The United Nations, Transitional Administration, and State-Building* (Oxford: Oxford University Press, 2004), 1–330; Francis Fukuyama, *State-Building: Governance and World Order in the 21st Century* (Ithaca, NY: Cornell University Press, 2004), 1–160.

11. Silindile Mlilo and Jean Pierre Misago, *Xenophobic Violence in South Africa: 1994–2018 an Overview* (Johannesburg: Xenowatch, 2019), 1–7.

12. Laurence Piper and Andrew Charman, "Xenophobia, Price Competition and Violence in the Spaza Sector in South Africa", *African Human Mobility Review* 2, no. 1 (2016): 332–362.

13. Tshepo Madlingozi, "Social Justice in a Time of Neo-apartheid Constitutionalism: Critiquing the Anti-black Economy of Recognition, Incorporation and Distribution", *Stellenbosch Law Review* 1 (2017): 123–147.

14. Loren B. Landau, "Introducing the Demons", in *Exorcising the Demons Within Xenophobia, Violence and Statecraft in Contemporary South Africa*, ed. Loren B. Landau (Johannesburg: Wits University Press, 2011), 1–25.

15. Francis Nyamnjoh, *Insiders and Outsiders: Citizenship and Xenophobia in Contemporary Southern Africa* (Dakar, Senegal: CODESRIA, and London: Zed Books, 2006), 1–273.

16. UN High Commissioner for Refugees (UNHCR), *Protection from Xenophobia: An Evaluation of UNHCR's Regional Office for Southern Africa's Xenophobia Related Programmes*, February 2015, available at: https://www.refworld.org/docid /55d2e1be4.html [accessed 8 November 2020].

17. Aare Afe Babalola, "Xenophobia Attacks of Nigerians in South Africa", *Vanguard News*, 2017, from https://www.vanguardngr.com/2017/03/ xenophobiaattacks-nigerians-south-africa/.

18. Belinda Dodson, "Locating Xenophobia: Debate, Discourse, and Everyday Experience in Cape Town, South Africa", *Africa Today* 56, no. 3 (2010): 2–22.

19. Christopher Claassen, "Explaining South African Xenophobia", *Afrobarometer Working Paper* No. 173 (2017): 1–22.

20. Dewa Mavhinga, "South Africa Launches Plan to Combat Xenophobia and Racism: Crucial Step in South Africa's Path to Justice and Equality", *Human Rights Watch*, 2019. Retrieved May 12, 2019, from https://www.hrw.org/news/2019/03/25/ south-africalaunches-plan-combat-xenophobia-and-racism.

21. Mavhinga, "South Africa Launches Plan to Combat Xenophobia and Racism: Crucial Step in South Africa's Path to Justice and Equality".

22. Claassen, *Explaining South African Xenophobia*, 3.

23. Jonny Steinberg, "Xenophobia and Collective Violence in South Africa: A Note of Skepticism About the Scapegoat", *African Studies Review* 61, no. 3 (2018): 119–134.

24. Adrian Hadland, ed., *Violence and Xenophobia in South Africa: Developing Consensus, Moving to Action* (Pretoria: Human Sciences Research Council, 2008), 1–56.

25. Hadland, ed., *Violence and Xenophobia in South Africa: Developing Consensus, Moving to Action*, 27–28.

26. Olusola Ogunnubi and Lere Amusan, "Nigeria's Attitude Towards South Africa's Perceived Xenophobia: Exploring a Shared Hegemonic Power for Africa's Development", in *The Political Economy of Xenophobia in Africa*, ed. Adeoye O. Akinola (Switzerland: Springer International Publishing, 2018), 53–67.

27. Ogunnubi and Amusan, *Nigeria's Attitude Towards South Africa's Perceived Xenophobia: Exploring a Shared Hegemonic Power for Africa's Development*, 56 .

28. Jonathan Crush, "The Dark Side of Democracy: Migration, Xenophobia and Human Rights in South in South Africa", *International Migration* 38, no. 6 (2000): 103–131.

29. Francis Nyamnjoh, *Insiders and Outsiders: Citizenship and Xenophobia in Contemporary Southern Africa*, 265.

30. Neocosmos, *From "Foreign Natives" to "Native Foreigners": Explaining Xenophobia in Post-Apartheid South Africa*, 87.

31. DW, "South Africa's Politicians Feed Anti-foreigner Violence", May 11, 2019, from https://www.dw.com/en/south-africas-politicians-feed-anti-foreignerviolence /a-48157900; UN High Commissioner for Refugees (UNHCR), *Protection from Xenophobia: An Evaluation of UNHCR's Regional Office for Southern Africa's Xenophobia Related Programmes*.

32. Ogunnubi and Amusan, *Nigeria's Attitude towards South Africa's perceived Xenophobia: Exploring a shared Hegemonic Power for Africa's Development*, 54.

33. DW, "South Africa's Politicians feed Anti-foreigner Violence."

34. Ibid.

35. Ibid.

36. Ibid.

37. Ibid.

38. Ibid.

39. Ibid.

40. Mavhinga, "South Africa Launches Plan to Combat Xenophobia and Racism: Crucial Step in South Africa's Path to Justice and Equality".

41. Personal communication, (name withheld, Male) in Durban (37years), South Africa, August–September, 2018.

42. Mavhinga, "South Africa Launches Plan to Combat Xenophobia and Racism: Crucial Step in South Africa's Path to Justice and Equality".

43. Personal communication, (name withheld, Male) in Durban (47years), South Africa, August–September, 2018.

44. Ibid.

45. Personal communication, (name withheld, Male) in Johannesburg (54years), South Africa, August–September, 2018.

46. Personal communication, (name withheld, Male) in Durban (48years), South Africa, August–September, 2018.

47. Personal communication, (name withheld, Male, businessman) in Durban (64years), South Africa, August–September, 2018.

48. Suren Pillay, "Dangerous Ordinary Discourse: Preliminary Reflections on Xenophobia, Violence and the Public Sphere in South Africa", Paper prepared for Governing the African Public Sphere, the 12th general assembly of CODESRIA. Yaounde, Cameroon, 7–11 December, 2008.

49. Francis B. Nyamnjoh, "Exorcising the Demons within: Xenophobia, Violence and Statecraft in Contemporary South Africa", *Journal of Contemporary African Studies* 32, no. 3 (2014): 397–401.

50. Personal communication, (name withheld, Male) in Durban (57years), South Africa, August–September, 2018.

51. Personal communication, (name withheld, Male) in Durban (51years), South Africa, August–September, 2018 .

52. Personal communication, (name withheld, Female) in Durban (59years), South Africa, August–September, 2018.

53. Ibid.

54. Personal communication, (name withheld, Male) in Durban (44years), South Africa, August–September, 2018.

55. Dewa Mavhinga, "South Africa Launches Plan to Combat Xenophobia and Racism: Crucial Step in South Africa's Path to Justice and Equality".

56. Philippa Kerr., Kevin Durrheim, and John Dixon, "Xenophobic Violence and Struggle Discourse", *Journal of Asian and African Studies* 54, no. 7 (2019): 995–1011.

57. Kerr., Durrheim, and Dixon, "Xenophobic Violence and Struggle Discourse".

58. Ibid.

59. Ibid.

60. Jonny Steinberg, "Xenophobia and Collective Violence in South Africa", 119–134.

61. Ibid.

62. Ibid.

63. Steven Gordon, "Waiting for the Barbarians: A Public Opinion Analysis of South African Attitudes Towards International Migrants", *Ethnic and Racial Studies* 40, no. 10 (2017): 1700–1719.

64. Personal communication, (name withheld, Male) in Johannesburg (41years), South Africa, August–September, 2018.

65. Personal communication, (name withheld, Male) in Johannesburg (67years), South Africa, August–September, 2018.

66. Personal communication, (name withheld, Male) in Durban (53years), South Africa, August–September, 2018.

67. Thabile Mbhele, *Foreign Nationals Are Burdening SA Health System: Motsoaledi*, 14 November 2018 https://www.sabcnews.com/sabcnews/foreign -nationals-are-burdening-sa-health-system-motsoaledi/.

68. Personal communication, (name withheld, Male) in Durban (62years), South Africa, August–September, 2018.

69. Personal communication, (name withheld, Male) in Johannesburg (56years), South Africa, August–September, 2018.

70. Personal communication, (name withheld, Male) in Durban (48years), South Africa, August–September, 2018.

BIBLIOGRAPHY

Babalola, Aare Afe, "Xenophobia Attacks of Nigerians in South Africa", *Vanguard News*, 2017, from https://www.vanguardngr.com/2017/03/xenophobiaattacks -nigerians-south-africa/.

Chesterman, Simon, *You, the People: The United Nations, Transitional Administration, and State-Building* (Oxford: Oxford University Press, 2004), 1–330.

Claassen, Christopher, "Explaining South African Xenophobia", *Afrobarometer Working Paper* No. 173 (2017): 1–22.

Cohen, Abner, *Two-Dimensional Man—An Essay on the Anthropology of Power and Symbolism in Complex Society* (Berkeley, CA: University of California, 1976), 41.

Cohen, Anthony P., "Boundaries of Consciousness, Consciousness of Boundaries: Critical Questions for Anthropology", in *The Anthropology of Ethnicity: Beyond "Ethnic Groups and Boundaries,* eds. Hans Vermeulen and Cora Govers (Amsterdam: Het Spinhuis Publishers, 1996), 60.

Collier, Paul, *Breaking the Conflict Trap: Civil War and Development Policy* (Oxford/New York: Oxford University Press/World Bank, 2003), 117–186.

Collier, Paul, "Doing Well Out of War: An Economic Perspective", in *Greed and Grievance: Economic Agendas in Civil War*, eds., Mats R. Berdal and David Malone (Boulder, CO: Lynne Rienner, 2000), 91–111.

Crush, Jonathan, "The Dark Side of Democracy: Migration, Xenophobia and Human Rights in South in South Africa", *International Migration* 38, no. 6 (2000): 103–131.

Dahrendorf, Nicola, *A Review of Peace Operations: A Case for Change* (London: King's College London, Conflict Security & Development Group, 2003), 1–384.

de Coning, Cedric, "The Coherence Dilemma in Peacebuilding and Post-conflict Reconstruction Systems", *African Journal on Conflict Resolution* 8, no. 3 (2008): 85–110.

Dodson, Belinda, "Locating Xenophobia: Debate, Discourse, and Everyday Experience in Cape Town, South Africa", *Africa Today* 56, no. 3 (2010): 2–22.

Du Toit, Pierre, "Why Post-Settlement Settlements?", *Journal of Democracy* 14, no. 3 (2003): 104–118.

DW, "South Africa's Politicians Feed Anti-foreigner Violence". Retrieved May 11, 2019, from https://www.dw.com/en/south-africas-politicians-feed-anti -foreignerviolence/a-48157900.

Fukuyama, Francis, *State-Building: Governance and World Order in the 21st Century* (Ithaca, NY: Cornell University Press, 2004), 1–160.

Gellner, Ernest, *Nations and Nationalism* (London: Basil Blackwell, 1983), 55.

Gordon, Steven, "A Violent Minority? A Quantitative Analysis of Those Engaged in Anti-immigrant Violence in South Africa", *South African Geographical Journal* 101, no. 2, (2019a): 269–283.

Gordon, Steven, "The Popularity of State Discourses on Anti-immigrant Violence in South Africa", *The Round Table: The Commonwealth Journal of International Affairs* 108, no. 5 (2019b): 567–578.

Gordon, Steven, "Waiting for the Barbarians: A Public Opinion Analysis of South African Attitudes Towards International Migrants", *Ethnic and Racial Studies* 40, no. 10 (2017): 1700–1719.

Hadland, Adrian, ed., *Violence and Xenophobia in South Africa: Developing Consensus, Moving to Action* (Pretoria: Human Sciences Research Council, 2008), 1–56.

Handler, Richard, "Is 'Identity' a Useful Cross-Cultural Concept?", in *Commemorations—The Politics of National Identity*, ed. John R. Gillis (Princeton, NJ: Princeton University Press, 1994), 27–40.

Harris, Bronwyn, *A Foreign Experience: Violence, Crime and Xenophobia during South Africa's Transition* (Johannesburg: Centre for the Study of Violence and Reconciliation, 2001), 1–96.

Harris, Bronwyn, "Xenophobia: A New Pathology for a New South Africa", in *Psychopathology and Social Prejudice*, eds. Derek Hook and Gillian Eagle (Cape Town: University of Cape Town Press, 2002), 169–184.

Hovhannisyan, Shoghik, Christopher F. Baum, Helidah Refiloe Ogude, and A. Sarkar, eds., *Mixed Migration, Forced Displacement and Job Outcomes in South Africa*. Washington, DC: World Bank, 2018.

Kerr, Philippa, Kevin Durrheim, and John Dixon, "Xenophobic Violence and Struggle Discourse", *Journal of Asian and African Studies* 54, no. 7 (2019): 995–1011.

Landau, Loren B., "Introducing the Demons", in *Exorcising the Demons Within Xenophobia, Violence and Statecraft in Contemporary South Africa*, ed. Loren B. Landau (Johannesburg: Wits University Press, 2011), 1–25.

Landau, Loren B., Kaajal Ramjathan-Keogh, and Gayatri Singh, *Xenophobia in South Africa and Problems Related to It* (Johannesburg: University of the Witwatersrand, Forced Migration Studies Programme, 2005), 1–42.

Madlingozi, Tshepo "Social Justice in a Time of Neo-apartheid Constitutionalism: Critiquing the Anti-black Economy of Recognition, Incorporation and Distribution", *Stellenbosch Law Review* 1 (2017): 123–147.

Mavhinga, Dewa, "South Africa Launches Plan to Combat Xenophobia and Racism: Crucial Step in South Africa's Path to Justice and Equality", *Human Rights Watch*, 2019 Retrieved May 12, 2019, from https://www.hrw.org/news/2019/03/25/south -africalaunches-plan-combat-xenophobia-and-racism.

Mlilo, Silindile and Jean Pierre Misago, *Xenophobic Violence in South Africa: 1994–2018 an Overview* (Johannesburg: Xenowatch, 2019), 1–7.

Neocosmos, Michael, *From "Foreign Natives" to "Native Foreigners": Explaining Xenophobia in Post-Apartheid South Africa* (Dakar, Senegal: CODESRIA, 2008), 1–160.

Nyamnjoh, Francis B., "Exorcising the Demons Within: Xenophobia, Violence and Statecraft in Contemporary South Africa", *Journal of Contemporary African Studies* 32, no. 3 (2014): 397–401.

Nyamnjoh, Francis B., *Insiders and Outsiders: Citizenship and Xenophobia in Contemporary Southern Africa* (Dakar, Senegal: CODESRIA, and London: Zed Books, 2006), 1–273.

Ogunnubi, Olusola and Lere Amusan, "Nigeria's Attitude Towards South Africa's Perceived Xenophobia: Exploring a Shared Hegemonic Power for Africa's Development", in *The Political Economy of Xenophobia in Africa*, ed. Adeoye O. Akinola (Switzerland: Springer International Publishing, 2018), 53–67.

Pillay, Suren, "Dangerous Ordinary Discourse: Preliminary Reflections on Xenophobia, Violence and the Public Sphere in South Africa", Paper prepared for Governing the African Public Sphere, the 12th general assembly of CODESRIA. Yaounde, Cameroon, 7–11 December, 2008.

Piper, Laurence and Andrew Charman, "Xenophobia, Price Competition and Violence in the Spaza Sector in South Africa", *African Human Mobility Review* 2, no. 1 (2016): 332–362.

Sharp, John, "Fortress SA": Xenophobic Violence in South Africa", *Anthropology Today* 24, no. 4 (2008): 1–3.

Stedman, Stephen John, "Spoiler Problems in Peace Processes", *International Security* 22, no. 2 (1997): 5–53.

Stedman, Stephen John, Elizabeth M. Cousens, and Donald Rothchild, eds., *Ending Civil Wars: The Implementation of Peace Agreements* (Boulder, CO: Lynne Rienner, 2002), 1–775.

Steinberg, Jonny, "Xenophobia and Collective Violence in South Africa: A Note of Skepticism About the Scapegoat", *African Studies Review* 61, no. 3 (2018): 119–134.

UN High Commissioner for Refugees (UNHCR), *Protection from Xenophobia: An Evaluation of UNHCR's Regional Office for Southern Africa's Xenophobia Related Programmes*, February 2015, available at: https://www.refworld.org/docid/55d2e1be4.html [accessed 8 November 2020].

Valji, Nahla, *Creating the Nation: The Rise of Violent Xenophobia in the New South Africa* (Unpublished Master Thesis, York University, 2003).

Williams, Brackette F., "A Class Act: Anthropology and the Race to Nation Across Ethnic Terrain", *Annual Review of Anthropology* 18 (1989): 401–444.

Chapter 5

#NigeriaMustFall

Exploring the Contours of New Media, Agenda Setting, and Communication Imperatives

Janet Abosede Ogundairo, Victor Onyilor Achem, and Feyisitan Ijimakinwa

Communication is an essential and strategic component of human existence, and has continued to take up different dimensions and shapes, in various societies across the globe. The dynamism of communication is clearly under-scored by the growth and changes that have attended this important element of the human race.[1] Different channels, mediums, and tools are used for mass communication, and these are consistently improved upon to reflect changes in technology and taste. The traditional media of television, radio, and printed publications dominated the communication arena, for many years.[2] Societies were influenced and the human race, including different stakeholders and influencers, were consistently controlled, albeit remotely, by the press. The power and influence of the press is summed up in its description as the "Fourth Estate of the Realm" by Edmund Burke in 1787. According to Burke, the Fourth Estate comprises all that reports news. The term is used to accentuate the freedom of the press and reinforced by its strategic role in setting agendas and directing the pulse of the society.

The influence and exclusivity of the press as agenda setters and public inflencers changed with the advancement of information technology. The growth of this subset of technology resulted in the evolution of new media and revolutionised mass communication. The new media ride on the back of technology and have reined in many people, as the gathering, production, and disemminatiuon of news have become liberalized and open to all. In the world of new media, especially the social media, ethical considerations amount for little as people, with the click of a button, can reach more people with their "own news." In the same vein, more people now receive information including news from more diverse and variegated sources. The reach as well as the rapidity of information disemmination have made the new media, as evidenced by the social media, the greatest influencer of the Modern Age.[3]

The use of hashtags (#) across social media platforms, especially on Twitter, in driving a subject or conversation in the cyberspace, which is described as the last frontier to be conquered, is an important development that has given a different texture to agenda setting.

THE ORIGINS OF THE HASHTAG #NIGERIAMUSTFALL

The hashtag #NigeriaMustFall trended on social media, especially among South Africans, between April and June 2020. It sprang from the resentment of black South African youths against perceived overbearing socioeconomic influence of Nigerian migrants in South Africa. This anti-Nigerian feeling was spread and promoted on Twitter through the hashtag #NigeriaMustFall, and this triggered xenophobic attacks against Nigerians in South Africa.[4] What began as a cyber protest soon degenerated into physical xenophobic attacks on Nigerians: a repeat of previous xenophobic attacks against Nigerians in the country. On another hand and during the same period, the hashtag #NigeriaMustFall was appropriated by aggrieved members of the Igbo ethnic group in Nigeria to drive their opposition to the federal government of Nigeria. The Igbo, Nigeria's third largest ethnic group, have consistently decried decades of alleged marginalization and unfair treatment by successive governments in the country. In order to redress this, they had clamored for the country's return to true federalism with a regional system of government instead of the present unitary system of 36 states.

This chapter adopts the Group Conflict theory to cogently explain the dynamics of new media and how it served as a vehicle that drove the xenophobic attacks against Nigerians in South Africa, as well the secessionist agitations of the Igbo ethnic nationality in Nigeria. The Group Conflict theory is also used to deconstruct perceptions attached to xenophobia and secession-inciting tweets using the hashtag #NigeriaMustFall.

Group Conflict theory as a perspective is used to examine the social dynamics and constructed perceptions attached to the Igbo agitations for secession and the violent attacks on Nigerian migrants in South Africa, structured within the social media space. The hashtag #NigeriaMustFall which trended on Twitter was adopted as a case study to underscore the relevance of Group Conflict theory in exploring the contours of new media and its connection with the discourse of conflict as reflected in xenophobia and secession. It is important to note that Nigeria has a history of violence arising from ethno-religious differences and conflicts, nepotism, political marginalization, resource control, and manipulations. These have stoked the embers of discontentment and anger in different groups and sections that repudiate the present political system and structure in the country. This, however, does not leap off the main focus of xenophobic violence and events that have mostly played out in South Africa and have resulted in the deaths of Nigerians, as well as the looting and destruction of their valuables.

RESEARCH METHODOLOGY

This study is exploratory in design and utilized NVIVO 12 to develop a thematic and textual analysis using the Twitter data set. Samples from this study were sourced from the Twitter database between April and June 2020. The Twitter data set is a pool of knowledge that houses different views, narratives, and opinions of individuals and groups and, when tapped into, helps in understanding the patterns, perspectives, and dynamics of xenophobia and could be used for further conceptualization and analysis

In this study, participants were purposively selected using the following criteria:

i. Must be a resident of Nigeria or South Africa, and
ii. Must be active on Twitter with the hashtag #NigeriaMustFall during the peak period of this online movement (April–June 2020).

Those without these qualifications were excluded from the study. In achieving this, 150 tweets were randomly selected using Ncapture for NVIVO which eventually formed the central setting for this study from which respondents' tweets were carefully selected. These were further deconstructed while similar expressions were collapsed to form themes that helped the study draw valid assumptions that could contribute to the body of knowledge and expand the frontiers of academic knowledge. These themes were textually and thematically analyzed in line with the focus of this chapter. The authors analyzed the data and viewed it together to eliminate contradictions. The online sample areas for this study, South Africa and Nigeria, were purposively selected given the repeated occurrence of xenophobic attacks against some nationals of African countries, especially Nigerians, Zimbabweans, and Mozambicans.

FINDINGS FROM THE STUDY

Construction of the Hashtag #NigeriaMustFall

The analysis of the hashtag #NigeriaMustFall revealed that it was constructed from two main perspectives (Nigerians and Non-Nigerians) with the narratives attached to the hashtag differing between the two groups.

Nigerians' Construction of the Hashtag #NigeriaMustFall

The hashtag #NigeriaMustFall was used by and trended among members of the Igbo ethnic group. The Igbo are the third largest ethnic group in Nigeria, and they are mostly from and resident in the five states in the southeastern part of the country. However, an insignificant number of tweets and retweets with the hashtag #NigeriaMustFall were also traced to twitter users who are Yoruba, another ethnic group in Nigeria. The insiders' (Nigerians) construction of the hashtag is a reflection of the conflictual undercurrents in the polity, especially as concerning discontentment of some of the federating units in the country. Some of the grievances of the affected groups include, and not limited to, sociopolitical marginalization, oppression, intimidation, and nepotism within the Nigeria state. This was the reason for the call for the dissolution of the Nigerian state using the hashtag #NigeriaMustFall. Aside these, there were allegations of undue political advantage and hegemony enjoyed by the predominantly Muslim Hausa/Fulani ethnic groups. Those who clamored for secession also accused the Nigerian government of not promoting equal access to economic resources.[5]

A substantial number of tweets supporting the breakup of Nigeria believed to have emanated from twitter users who are Igbo also carried the hashtag #IPOB. The group Indigenous People of Biafra (IPOB) had been in the forefront of the agitations for the breakaway of the Igbo ethnic group from Nigeria. IPOB itself is a breakaway from the Movement for the Actualization of the Sovereign State of Biafra (MASSOB), a group founded by Ralph Uwazuruike in 1999. MASSOB opposes the Nigerian government and advocates self-determination for the Igbo and the creation of Biafra, the rebel state proclaimed by the Igbo during the Nigerian Civil War of 1967 and 1970. The group creatively and strategically uses mediums such as Radio Biafra and Biafra online TV to promote the Biafran cause.[6]

IPOB is the most popular, radical, and controversial of all the groups that clamor for the actualization of Biafra. Rooted in the continuation of the secessionist attempt that led to the Nigerian Civil War and loss of over three million Igbo lives,[7,8] IPOB, under the leadership of Nnamdi Kanu, calls out the federal government of Nigeria. The group has been accused of inciting violence and promoting anarchy in the country, especially with its continued call for the breakaway and proclamation of Biafra Republic from Nigeria.[9]

Supporting the IPOB Agenda, a Twitter User Retweeted

Is this the type of #Nigeria you wanna be in? A blood-thirsty country? Everyday death and killing of Christians. Everything about Nigeria is death. #BiafraExit is the answer and an end to this barbaric contraption. #NigeriaMustFall #GodBlessIPOB #ReferendumNow . . .

The hashtag #NigeriaMustFall was seen and used as a medium to advance IPOB's call for the breakup of Nigeria and emergence of Biafra. In spite of the negativity and labeling of Nigerians in South Africa, the hashtag #NigeriaMustFall was seen as a social media movement by some Nigerians, especially the Igbo, to draw attention to already existing sociocultural and ethnic disparities in the country, creating room for other forms of internal violence.

Non-Nigerians' Construction of the Hashtag #NigeriaMustFall

The non-Nigerian's construction of the hashtag #NigeriaMustFall views Nigeria as a monolithic unit without consideration that over 300 different ethnic groups make up the country. The non-Nigerians' construction concerns mostly South Africans and to them the hashtag is a figurative collapse of Nigeria and reflects the call by some South Africans for the expulsion of Nigerians from South Africa. Some of the tweets call for the reservation of employment opportunities exclusively for South Africans, ahead of immigrants from other countries. These agitators want South Africans to enjoy primary considerations for jobs and opportunities. Examples of hashtags that drove this argument include, but not limited to, "#unemployment, #PutSouthAfricanFirst, #ZimbabweMustFall, #NigeriaMustFall, #ZimbabweansMustGo, #NigeriansMustGo . . ." These hashtags were used to kick against the engagement of foreigners over South Africans. Nigerians and other nationalities are often accused of taking positions and opportunities that, in their views, should be for South Africans.

Xenophobic attacks in South Africa have been linked to perceived intimidation, oppression, and subordination of South Africans by migrants from other African countries, especially Nigerians, whom they view as successful at their expense. Perceived domination of foreigners in access to economic resources, including employment opportunities, have been identified as one of the reasons for intolerance of South Africans against migrants who are mostly of African origin.[10] In Cape Town, foreign nationals including Namibians and Angolans were accused of gaining access to land which leaves South Africans homeless and unemployed.[11] Some of the tweets with the hashtag #NigeriaMustFall lent credence to the feeling of intimidation of South Africans by the success of other nationals in South Africa. There were rallying cries such as "South Africans, you are important" "South Africa is your land, and no one must intimidate you to feel less important in your homeland" "PutSouthAfricansFirst," all aimed at bolstering the confidence and patriotic zeal of South Africans.

Pattern of Tweets by Location

An analysis of the hashtag #NigeriaMustFall by location showed that a significant number of the tweets were by users in South African cities of Durban and Johannesburg. These two locations have high numbers of black South Africans, and these locations were identified as epicenters of violence and xenophobic attacks in South Africa. In addition, the hashtag that was tweeted and retweeted by Nigerians were largely from Ebonyi State in Nigeria and London in the UK. Radio Biafra, an online radio established and used for propaganda by IPOB, operates out of London. The external activities of IPOB, in the early days of agitation, were coordinated from London. Hence, it is highly probable that larger supporters of the IPOB agenda, in the diaspora, are found in London.

SITUATING THE THEORETICAL FRAMEWORK

Group Conflict theory was used to describe intergroup prejudice and aggression, most specifically as it relates to xenophobia. The conflicts were considered in terms of power, law, and political or social interest by George Vold.[12] Individual conflicts occur between people and broader groups' conflicts between groups of interest. Examining each human dispute, Vold stresses the notion that crime is the natural reaction of ordinary people in normal circumstances who want to protect their culture and values. This means that anybody can commit violence at any time, and the purpose of such violent acts may just be to keep some of its subjective conditions, social norms, and standards. For instance, as observed in this study, threats and xenophobic actions were carried out by South Africans as measures to protect their neighborhoods and rid the streets of crime, rape, drug use, human trafficking, and internet fraud, mostly attributed to Nigerian migrants. A twitter user supporting this twitted that "Nigerians keep calling us criminals to deflect from their global crime and Boko Haram rape religion. They are hated in every country they immigrate to #NigeriansMustGo #NigeriaMustFall

. . ." Extending these narratives, another user twitted that "these people are a problem all over the world. #NigeriaMustFall #NigeriansMustGo."

In the wider society, however, communities are finding state protection in pursuit of their rights. Deeply ingrained in the law process and in controlling the structure and rules is the fundamental conflict of most interest groups. Almost every group of interests wants laws supporting their standards and values to be implemented in the broader society, in terms of either laws protecting their interests or criminalizing behavior that goes against the standards of their group.

The theory concentrates on the way in which demonstrated differences, conflicting aims, and competition between resource groups lead to intergroup conflicts by fixating on subjective norms that amplify social differences and structurally establish the boundaries of intergroup identity. Similarly, studies have shown that where vital resources or capital are considered to be confined and restricted, intergroup conflict may occur, even if perhaps the restriction is construed or pragmatic.[13] The pragmatic scarcity of these resources or capital and its imperative is however most likely to induce the socio-reflex of group identity which is the foundation of xenophobic movements. Matsumoto identifies xenophobia as an unnatural fear of people who are living as either strangers or foreigners and have various traditions, ways of living, values, societal structures, or groups. However, these fears are often expressed by means of hostilities or violent behavior, which could be interpreted as a defensive mechanism in preserving their territorial integrity.[14]

This is usually the product of a profound contempt or hate of a group based on its supposed origin, gender, faith, or sexual orientation and is articulated in aggression, to harm or degrade the perceived out-group.[15] In comparison, Cherry describes xenophobia as a distrust of something alien, unreasonable, and irrational, mostly alien individuals, locations, or objects, while using the concepts of racism and bigotry interchangeably, whereas these words may have separate definitions.[16]

DISCUSSION OF FINDINGS

The concept of Xenophobia is represented as a widespread, unsubstantiated extreme rejection or fear of people who have cultural characteristics that vary widely from each other, goes further than the usual prejudices or racism, and are often unjustified. However, considering the turn of events and present-day reality, the concept of xenophobia may seem to be engaging and covering a larger unusual scope where xenophobic threats are carried out using various online social platforms like Twitter and Facebook, away from physical violence. There are certain conflicts between those who hold similar socioeconomic status but do not share the same rights to services in South Africa.[17]

The reports that focus on growing insecurity, competitiveness for wealth, and the belief that foreigners take up "what rightfully belongs to the South African people" are often legitimized reasons for attacks and civil animosity. In addition to the increasingly obvious aggression to foreign nationals and the presumed effects on society, a further premise within the context of this discourse should also be looked at. In other words, this form of gang violence by the "in-group" often tends to demonstrate how such levels of society shield themselves from "imported criminals."[18]

The Criminality and Labeling Card as a Xenophobic Tool

From criminology studies, one major assumption of labeling, not just as a concept but as a theoretical perspective, concerns the impact of criminality labels on potential offenders; in particular, a greater likelihood is expected if communities apply a criminal label on a person or group. The theory predicts labels to modify the personality of individuals so that they view themselves, in fact, as offenders and then change their conduct. In brief, as most xenophobic communities continue to identify and treat others as offenders, such groups or individuals are likely to begin to internalize this identity. The labeled person or group will likely respond to this negative reaction of society through potential violence, which has been demonstrated throughout the observed events of Xenophobia in this study. Similarly, various tweets analyzed in this study revealed the unprofessional and a hasty generalization of the out-group (Nigerians) by the in-group (South Africans). This generalization of the out-group as criminals with and through the powerful tool "new media" could influence, impact, and questionably challenge the coherencies of "agenda setting" as against the imperative of a standard and functional society purged of crime. Nonetheless, the criminality labeling, as observed in this study, could be responsible for the victimization of Nigerians in South Africa who have the legal and legitimate right to work and do business in South Africa, making them easy and soft targets of xenophobic destruction. Although the study does not negate the fact that some Nigerians in South Africa may be involved in criminal activities like trafficking, drug peddling, or theft, the general labeling and the continuous scoring of criminality card by one group against the other could further widen the cracks in relationships between the two countries.

From the findings of this study, it was observed that the proliferation of narcotics and other banned substances on South African streets produced great negative effects on both the social and psychological lives of South African youths who mostly constitute the drug community, and all these are blamed on Nigerians.

The tweet below communicates this narrative:

> Nigerians must be responsible for the fact that SA consumes twice as much cannabis, cocaine and tik, they are also responsible for the country having over 2 million problem drinkers. Since SA have morals Nigerians must be forcing the drugs on them to grab land #NigeriaMustFall

The Cognitive Role of Agency through Agenda Setting in Xenophobia

Contextually, cognitive activities such as the "interpretation" of events and actions of out-groups, "strategy" to control such actions, "forecasting" the implications of such actions, and remedies of potential errors through agenda setting require a broad definition of cognitive management by the in-group who maybe striving to uphold its societal values.[19] It begins when routine behavioral stimulation is no longer enough to achieve optimum efficiency. This helps one to practice wise, intentional actions through cognitive regulation as observed in this study.[20]

In a similar context, Hayam elaborates the cognitive role of agency in protecting the society, most especially the youths, from engaging in drugs and other related crimes that were perceived as precipitated and motivated by Nigerian nationals in South Africa. This, however, has become the basis for the xenophobic struggle between the in-group (South Africans) and the perceived out-group (Nigerians) in South Africa, as well as in-group (Biafra/Oodua Republic apologists) and out-group (the federal government of Nigeria) within Nigeria. An interesting narrative from a respondent practically underpins the above discussion:

> This video is the reason why #NigeriansMustFall is trending, South Africans on twitter claim the lady in this video was drugged by the "Nigerians." And some useless people are defending this nonsense. The lady is drugged and paid to do this nonsense. Will they allow their sisters to do that? You are using the same money you got from them to corrupt their children, and you are expecting them to keep quiet?

The above tweet was a reaction to a video which was circulated at the time of the hashtag trend. In the video, a young South African lady, in her late teens or early 20s, is seen dancing erotically in a drunken and drugged state with a small object (sex toy) inserted in her anus. In the video, a group of five Nigerian boys could be seen enjoying the erotic display. This video went viral and inflamed many South Africans, especially the blacks, and contributed to the call for the expulsion of Nigerians from South Africa. Such reactions by

South Africans could be interpreted as a reflexive means of identifying with some of their problems (which could be youth involvement in hard drugs) and dishing out a protective track of cognitive agency and action through retributive justice.

The In-Group versus the Out-Group

The out-group is viewed as competitive rather than most groups within the population. It is therefore in the process that the out-group is perceived as different, not only from the in-group but as well as from other social groups present within the in-group. The out-group whose characteristic is very different from the in-group themselves is almost certain to be possibly competitive out-groups and could include various considerations related to population size, social presence, and also behavioral comportment. Interestingly, these groups often also have things in common with the main in-group sect like race, color, language, and so on.[21]

However, the level to which groups are substantially different is the level to which an out-group is viewed and determined as a competitor. For instance, the out-groups who are like the in-groups are supposed to be the rivals in things that required traits or essential skills necessary for the acquisition of capital or access to certain resources. The ability to acquire capital such as talents, sales, or geographical areas requires certain attributes. Indicators like nationality and ethnic origin could be applicable in those other aspects, and therefore, in such situations, the out-groups which vary considerably from the in-groups are likely to be perceived competitive. Ultimately, out-groups with a resource benefit and willing to defend their access to these resources are indeed a significant competitive out-group, since they have a higher likelihood or capacity to utilize resources. This was portrayed in the xenophobic attacks on Nigerians in South Africa where Nigerians were regarded as profiting from the susceptibility and vulnerability of the indigenous population.

There is also the perception by South Africans that their government and security forces are also in a corrupt union with perceived Nigerian competitors, and this heightened the level of their distrust of the South African government. The government is seen as opposed to the grievances of the in-group, especially with the reluctance of the government to deport all Nigerians and other foreigners accused of depleting their national resources and perpetrating crime.

The following tweets from some South Africans practically support the above opinion:

> To every South African you are important!!! South Africa is your land, and no one must intimidate you to feel less important in your Homeland. #PutSouthAfricansFirst

#unemployment. #PutSouthAfricanFirst #Zimbabwemustfall #nigeriamustfall #ZimbabweansMustGo #NigeriansMustGo.

This thing of drugs is just evil, call us self-hating or whatever you want, you are Devils for defending drug dealers, the children of SA will not be destroyed coz of your own thirst for expensive labels & Whisky, No, who's kids? #NigeriaMustFall #EFFMustFall #PearlThusiMustFall.

I believe that HUNDREDS of missing girls and woman that are never found are somewhere in Nigeria being sold as prostitutes' #NigeriaMustFall

The game of identity is a major card that defines the situated argument of Group Conflict theory which also seems consistent with the primordialist premise that argues that identity, through nationality, ethnicity, race or, color is ascriptive, given the fact that association is allotted from birth and so becomes difficult to change or manipulate.[22] It further emphasizes how identity ties are intrinsic in humans and most times display attributes and traits that easily join them with some groups and individuals, and may also bring about disunions and conflicts with other groups clinging to factors like nationality, language, religion, race, and so on.[23,24] This may also explain the discrete behavioral hostilities targeted at Nigerians amid other immigrants who may also be engaged in one form of crime or the other. The issue of identity which has pronounced the xenophobic perception of group competition may as well serve as a catalyst for the reoccurring and escalating xenophobic attacks, both physically and online via social media platforms (Twitter). This, however, seems consistent with Morris and Tshitereke who state that there seems to be a second aspect on xenophobia that negates the conventional assumption of perceived competition.[25,26] It is however on the basis of actual observation that such xenophobic anxiety, hatred, or hostility could be unfounded, unjustified, or irrational, in line with the bogeyman assumption that xenophobia is linked to the need for individuals and out-groups outside themselves to be blamed for a crisis or violent event. Primordialism describes the concern that the bulk of identity-related conflicts are focused on conquest, ejection, and even fear of contamination and corruption.[27] Primordialism exposes its commitment to values that trigger a depth of identity and strength motivated by the brutal violations perpetrated in these identity wars. On a similar note, there are several cases of conflicts in Nigeria (for instance, the many intergroup and interfaith conflicts) that Nigerians may have underestimated perhaps because they do not result in mass killings, as the history of certain incidents has documented in the past at varying periods,[28] and because they do not attract public attention as it has its own consequences for overall social health and development.

The violence and hatred toward others exist somewhat inexorably and as a commonplace in social interactions. This however depicts a redefinition of the concept of disintegration of Nigeria as observed in the findings of this study where the same hashtag #NigeriaMustFall was used in Nigeria by Nigerians to register their dissatisfaction with the political structure of Nigeria.

This is likely engrained in the ethno-religious rivalries, class oppression and manipulation, and resource conflict among other factors that have plunged Nigeria into decades of social violence and conflict. However, xenophobia does not only apply to the cases in South Africa when there has been violent altercation and abuse of most Nigerian nationals.

There are many forms of intolerance that have played out in Nigeria as well. More so, intolerance of other ethnic groups is reflected in the behavior toward language, cultures, gestures, and comments made about others who are likely to be strangers, visitors, or hosts depending on the situation. Verbal abuse and death wishes, online or physically, can also be categorized as xenophobic expressions. A major drift of this expression from online into a physical violent attack and hostility is the outcome of cumulative dent or provocation. From the findings of this study, it is evident that, on a much larger scale and scope than in the cases of South Africa, Nigeria has become an epicenter of unrest. Given the obvious reality of renewed and continuous violence which has ravaged Nigeria and undermined its structure of unity and nationalism, now there seems to be a greater scale of conflict and turmoil than what has been experienced in South Africa. However, xenophobes come in various forms: prejudice-based government officials, religious fanatics indoctrinating innocent children, and ethnic separatists preaching hate. Much of the time, this phenomenon of intolerance is viewed as ethno-religious uprising, because what in one part of the world seems to be an ethno-religious riot can snowball to looting and arson targeted at certain groups of people. The spike in conflicts in Nigeria springs from the activities and utterances of ethnic jingoists, political leaders expected to be champions and advocates of unity, who, instead, expose the discrepancies and portray some other individuals or groups as superior to others. Xenophobia runs through the media write-ups, thoughts, comments, and views of a number of bloggers, even educated ones.

Social media may spread hatred through multiple platforms. In the first place, social media cuts facilitation and organizational expenses.[29] This encourages political dissent due to its proximity and anonymity. Fostered social media collaboration could be clearly crucial for unlawful and stereotyped operations, such as homicides: the social media could facilitate the discovering of others with same view and motives (through specified groups of people) and minimize the cost of self-exposure through the establishment of more anonymized peer interaction platforms like Twitter and Facebook. Social media may also impact people's perspectives; compassionate people may be even more responsive to xenophobic views and hateful people may end up in the online space making their thoughts ever more severe.[30,31] This further unifies the long-standing expressions of hate and negatively influences the decisions of vulnerable in-group members who might not be open to xenophobic actions. More so, similar studies suggest that it depends on assumptions of the population whether or not content from media could influence and lead individuals to engage in aggressive expressions of xenophobic views. For instance, Nazi radio misinformation was efficacious only in traditionally anti-Semitic communities in the early 1930s.[32]

This shows substantively that in the social media space, the position of the underpinning context is probably much higher, because the social media material and content often clearly represent the public's attitude as regards xenophobia. This applies specially to hate crimes perpetrated by many offenders, and which was promoted by social media. Admittedly, apart from Nigeria's uproarious challenges, another very essential aspect is ethnic rivalry which stirs up secessionist provocations. Sectional discontentment, agitations for self-rule, and secession are undeniably some of the main challenges facing the Nigerian nation. These pose huge challenges to Nigeria's economic and development future. The country is directly impacted by its developmental loss played out by continuous fracas. Ethnic solidarity and sense of pride have been damaged and ethnic dissatisfaction must be addressed proximally and vigorously, if Nigeria is to remain as one indivisible nation.

XENOPHOBIA AND ITS IMPACT ON SOUTH AFRICA

Xenophobic violence against African migrants erupted in South Africa in March 2019. The attacks were allegedly stoked by a statement by Mr. Cyril Ramaphosa during one of the campaign rallies that preceded the country's general elections.[33]

In 2019, there were reprisal violence against South African business interests in Nigeria. Outlets of notable South African brands including the telecom company, MTN, as well as the retail store chain, Shoprite, and cable television service providers, Multichoice, were attacked and vandalized in some cities in Nigeria.[34] At the height of this crisis, South Africa suspended consular services in its diplomatic mission in Nigeria.[35] In other parts of Africa, the xenophobic attacks by South Africans against African migrants drew reprisal attacks against South African interests in other African countries. In the Democratic Republic of Congo, shops owned by South Africans were looted and the windows of the South African consulate in the city of Lubumbashi were broken.[36] The South African embassy in Kinshasa also witnessed several demonstrations. As a result of the xenophobic violence, Air Tanzania also suspended flights to Johannesburg, while Madagascar barred its national soccer team from traveling to South Africa for a scheduled friendly match with South Africa for reasons of security.[37] Students in Zambia forced the closure of shopping malls owned by South Africans, while Lubinda Haabazoka, president of the Zambia's Economic Association, advised the African Union (AU) not to allow Mr. Ramaphosa become its president the following year.[38]

Nonetheless, the expression of xenophobia is a denial of civil liberties and threatens social stability, sustainable coexistence, and political stability. South Africa still has legal and moral power in its commitments to counter xenophobia, by being a signatory to a number of human rights and international humanitarian protocols, in particular on migrants and refugees. South Africa is indeed not pragmatically or economically positioned to close its borders as a social democratic nation that fosters the New Partnership for Africa's Development of the South African Development Community and the AU. These organizations are established to foster brotherhood and strengthen regional coordination and cooperation. In the long term, it can be a dangerous thing to encourage people of one member state to discriminately think and behave toward nationals of other countries as such actions could undermine regional collaboration and socioeconomic development among member states. In addition to the moral ramifications of continued xenophobia, the negative reputation must be another consideration for the nation. This display of intolerance toward other Africans by South Africans has been analyzed by other interest group from around the world because of its hypocrisy.[39]

CONCLUSION

One attractive thing that makes the internet interesting in this century is that everyone can draw diverse materials from the internet, and at the same time, anyone can put up inciting and provocative information in various social communication spaces, even with all the checks and penalties. Similarly, the internet has both important and real knowledge but also slothful talk, and a good number of people fail to grasp the overriding power and influence of the internet. However, the freedom and ease of publishing on the internet can be massively exploited by the supply of offensive contents such as xenophobic and racial content, indecent literature, and violence-inciting photographs and videos.

Regular agenda setting models hold that the mass media control the public agenda by reporting on such topics of violence (xenophobia) and making them relevant to the public. The typical agenda setting influence of mass media, however, is undermined by increased selectiveness and civic polarization in today's news media climate. The increased use of social media for information and entertainment is an emerging priority to recognize in terms of this transition and has significantly influenced agenda setting from the standpoint of this xenophobia discourse.

The primary role of hashtag activism is to draw public attention to specific topics and to also raise indictment for wrongs and praises for commendable actions in today's world. It, however, empowers the agenda setting process which influences the mainstream media as well. People may not decide or form their perspectives based on the media they consume, but the media possesses the capabilities of influencing one's attention, and it plays a role in the development of opinions grounded in narratives and subjects in a negative or positive dimension. It also defines what one needs to believe and what might be labeled critical within a given period of time.

Before now, such role was played by pressure groups, journalists, and mainstream media groups. However, the hashtag trend has evolved as a type of agenda setting that can involve, manipulate, and even elevate the opinion of common citizens, as observed in this study. Although the xenophobic violence in South Africa may seem to be a medium of communicating public grievances, it however sparked different individual and state responses that exacerbated the spate of reprisals and showed that it is also capable of sustaining the vicious circle of xenophobic violence.

Such response would not exist even though social media advocacy is not enough to address the long-standing issues of xenophobia in Africa. This form of response arises when digital interaction is a revolutionary medium for the emergence of up-and-down movements without necessarily having a centralized or structured leadership. However, though hashtag campaigns alone may not be able to coordinate or maintain traditional state systems on their own, they possess a force for united attention. Today, new media (hashtags) reflects on inequality, while firmly demanding reform, which of course is a strong approach to agenda setting and communication imperatives as it affects the discourse of xenophobia.

NOTES

1. Kevin Robins and Frank Webster, *Times of the Technoculture: From the Information Society to the Virtual Life* (London: Routledge, 1999), 1–307.

2. Wienner Jon, "Free Speech on the Internet," *The Nation* 258, no. 23 (1994): 825.

3. Durham Deborah, "Youth and the Social Imagination in Africa: Introduction to Parts 1 and 2," *Anthropological Quarterly* 733 (2000): 113–121.

4. Bradley Gilbert, "The Information and Communication Society: How People will Live and Work in the New Millennium," *Ergonomics* 43, no. 7 (2000): 844–857.

5. Chiluwa Innocent, "A Nation Divided Against Itself: Biafra and the Conflicting Online Protests Discourses," *Discourses and Communication* (2018): 1–25.

6. Chiluwa Innocent, "Social Media Networks and the Discourse of Resistance: Sociolingusitic CDA of Biafra Online Discourses," *Discourse and Society* 23, no. 3 (2012): 217–244.

7. Aneke Luke, *The Untold Story of the Nigeria-Biafra War: A Chronological Reconstruction of the Events and Circumstances of the Nigerian Civil War* (New York: Triumph Publishing, 2007), 1–800.

8. Chiluwa Innocent, "A Nation Divided Against Itself: Biafra and the Conflicting Online Protests Discourses," 16.

9. Alkassim, *Daily Trust Online*, 2017.

10. Nell Ian, "The Tears of Xenophobia: Preaching and Violence from a South African Perspective," *Practical Theology in Africa* 2 (2009): 229–247.

11. Mamokhosi, Choane, Stella Shulika Lukong, and Mthombeni Mandla, "An Analysis of the Causes, Effects and Ramifications of Xenophobia in South Africa," *Insight on Africa* 3, no. 2 (2011): 129–142.

12. Georg B. Vold, *Theoretical Criminology* (Oxford: Oxford University Press, 1979), 1–433.

13. Campbell Donald, "Ethnocentric and Other Altruistic Motives." *Nebraska Symposium on Motivation* 13 (Bd 1965): 283–311.

14. Matsumoto David, *The Cambridge Dictionary of Psychology* (New York: Cambridge University Press, 2009), 61.

15. United Nations, *Xenophobia. Human Right of the High Commissioner for Human Rights, Palais des Nations* (CH-1211 Geneva 10 2013), 1211.

16. Cherry Kendra, *About Education Psychology*. about.com online, 2015.

17. Dodson Belinda and Oelofse Catherine, "Shades of Xenophobia: In-Migrants and Immigrants in Mizamoyethu, Cape Town," *Canadian Journal of African Studies* 34, no. 1 (2000): 124–148.

18. Hayem Judith, "Xenophobic Violence and National Subjectivity in South Africa," *Journal of Southern African Studies* 39 (2013): 77–97.

19. Amitai Shenhav, Matthew Botvinick and Jonathan Cohen, "The Expected Value of Control: An Integrative Theory of Anterior Cingulate Cortex Function," *Neuron* (2013): 217–240.

20. Shenhav, Botvinick and Cohen, "The Expected Value of Control: An Integrative Theory of Anterior Cingulate Cortex Function," 82.

21. Crandall Christian, Mark Schaller, and T. F. Pettigrew, *Social Psychology of Prejudice: Historical and Contemporary Issues* (Lewinian Press, 2005), 167–187.

22. Isajiw Wserolod, "Definitions and Dimensions of Ethnicity: A Theoretical Framework' Statistics Canada & US Bureau of the Census. Challenges of Measuring and Ethnic World: Science Politics and Reality." *Proceedings of the Joint Canada-United States Conference on the Measurement of Ethnicity* (Washington, DC: US Government Printing Office 1993), 407-427.

23. Geertz Clifford, *The Interpretation of Cultures* (New York: Basic Books, 1973), 3–457.

24. Chandra Kanchan, *Constructivist Theories of Ethnic Conflict* (Oxford: Oxford University Press Inc., 2012), 1–520.

25. Morris Alan, "Our Fellow Africans Make Our Lives Hell: The Lives of Congolese and Nigerians Living in Johannesburg," *Ethnic and Racial Studies* 21, no. 6 (1998): 1116–1136.

26. C. Tshitereke, "Xenophobia and Relative Deprivation," *Crossings* 3, no. 2 (1992): 4–5.

27. Glazer Nathan, "Book Review Understanding Ethnic Conflict: Ethnic Groups in Conflict," *Columbia Law Review* 86, no. 2 (1986): 427–432.

28. N. Onyekpe, *Ethnic Relations in Nigeria* (Ibadan: The Caxton Press, 2004).

29. Enikolopov, Makarin, and Petrova, "Social Media and Protest Participation: Evidence from Russia," Working Paper, 2018.

30. Sunstein Cass, *Republic: Divided Democracy in the Age of Social Media* (Princeton: Princeton University Press, 2017), 1–328.

31. Settle Jaime, *Frenemies: How Social Media Polarizes America* (Cambridge: Cambridge University Press, 2018), 1–316.

32. Adena Maja, Enikolopov Ruben, Petrova Maria, Santarosa Veronica, and Zhuravskaya Ekaterina, "Radio and the Rise of the Nazis in Prewar Germany," *Quarterly Journal of Economics* 130, no. 4 (2015): 1885–1939.

33. K. Hairsine, *South Africa's Politicians Feed Anti-Foreigner Violence* (DW, 2019).

34. VOA, *Nigerians Attack South African Businesses in Retaliation* (www .voanews.com, 2019).

35. France24 online, *S-Africa Closes Embassy in Nigeria amid Escalating Row over Xenophobic Violence*, 2019.

36. Aljazeera-News, "South African consulate, Shops Attacked in DRC," Aljazeera .com, 2019.

37. Ateba Simon, "Air Tanzania Suspends All Flights to South Africa Over Xenophobic Attacks," *TodaynewsAfrica Online*, 2019.

38. LusakaTimes, "South African Business in Lusaka Close Today Amid Security Concerns," *LusakaTimes Online*, 2019.

39. Crush Jonathan and Pendleton Wade, *Regionalising Xenophobia? Citizen Attitudes to Immigration and Refugee Policy in Southern Africa* (Canada: SAMP, 2004), i-49.

BIBLIOGRAPHY

Adena, Maja, Enikolopov Ruben, Petrova Maria, Santarosa Veronica, and Zhuravskaya Ekaterina. "Radio and the Rise of the Nazis in Prewar Germany." *Quarterly Journal of Economics* 130, no. 4 (2015): 1885–1939.

Aljazeera-News. 2019. "South African Consulate, Shops Attacked in DRC." Aljazeera.com. September 5. Accessed November 9, 2020. https://www.aljazeera .com/news/2019/9/5/south-african-consulate-shops-attacked-in-drc.

Alkassim, B. 2017. *Daily Trust*. August 15. Accessed December 17, 2020. https://www.dailytrust.com.ng/news/group-cautions-kanu-over-hate-speeches-against-north/210303.html.

Aneke, L. 2007. *The Untold Story of the Nigeria-Biafra War: A Chronological Reconstruction of the Events and Circumstances of the Nigerian Civil War*. New York: Triumph Publishing.

Ateba, Simon. 2019. *Air Tanzania Suspends All Flights to South Africa over Xenophobic Attacks*. September 5. Accessed December 9, 2020. https://todaynewsafrica.com/air-tanzania-suspends-flights-to-south-africa-over-xenophobic-attacks/.

Bradley, Gilbert. "The Information and Communication Society: How People will Live and Work in the New Millennium." *Ergonomics* 43, no. 7 (2000): 844–857.

Campbell, D. T. 1965. "Ethnocentric and other Altruistic Motives." *Nebraska Symposium on Motivation Bd* 13: 283–311.

Chandra, K. 2012. *Constructivist Theories of Ethnic Conflict*. Oxford: Oxford University Press Inc.

Cherry, K. 2015. *About Education Psychology*. about.com.

Chiluwa, Innocent. "Social Media Networks and the Discourse of Resistance: Sociolingusitic CDA of Biafra Online Discourses." *Discourse and Society* 23, no. 3 (2012): 217–244.

Chiluwa, Innocent. "A Nation Divided Against Itself: Biafra and the Conflicting Online Protests Discourses." *Discourses and Communication 12*, no. 4. (2018): 1–25.

Crandall, C.S., M. Schaller, and T. F. Pettigrew. 2005. *Social Psychology of Prejudice: Historical and Contemporary Issues*. Lewinian Press.

Crush, J., and W. Pendleton. 2004. Regionalising Xenophobia? Citizen attitudes to immigration and refugee policy in Southern Africa. Canada: SAMP.

Dodson, B. O., and C. Catherine. 2000. "Shades of Xenophobia: In-Migrants and Immigrants in Mizamoyethu, Cape Town." *Canadian Journal of African Studies* 34, no. 1 (2000): 124–148.

Durham, Deborah. "Youth and the Social Imagination in Africa: Introduction to Parts 1 and 2." *Anthropological Quarterly* 733 (2000): 113–121.

Enikolopov, R., A. Makarin, and M. Petrova. 2018. "Social Media and Protest Participation: Evidence from Russia." Working Paper.

France24. 2019. *S. Africa Closes Embassy in Nigeria amid Escalating Row over Xenophobic Violence*. Accessed November 8, 2020. https://www.google.com/url?sa=t&rct=j&q=&esrc=s&source=web&cd=4&cad=rja&uact=8&ved=2ahUKEwjzl63TpXkAhXOMMAKHSILAVIQFj ADegQIARAB&url=https%3A %2F%2F www.france24.com% 2Fen%2F20190905-southafrica-nigeria-embassyxenophobic-violencediplomacy&usg=AOvVaw38yJ.

Geertz, Clifford. 1973. *The Interpretation of Cultures*. New York: Basic Books.

Glazer, Nathan. "Book Review Understanding Ethnic Conflict: Ethnic Groups in Conflict." *Columbia Law Review* 86, no. 2 (1986): 427–432.

Hairsine, K. 2019. *South Africa's Politicians Feed Anti-foreigner Violence, DW*. Accessed October 12, 2020. https://www.google.com/url?sa =t&rct=j&q=&esrc=s&source=web&cd=4&cad=rja&uact=8& ved=2ahUKEwieiNiVpZTiAh X0VBUIHb9MBL gQFjADegQ IAhAB&url=https%3A%2F%2 Fwww.dw.com%2Fen%2Fsout h-afr icas-politicians-feed-antiforeigner-violence%2Fa48157900&usg=AOvVaw0GO CEQ.

Hayem, Judith. "Xenophobic Violence and National Subjectivity in South Africa." *Journal of Southern African Studies* 39, no. 1 (2013): 77–97.

Isajiw, Wserolod W. 1993. "Definitions and Dimensions of Ethnicity: A Theoretical Framework' Statistics Canada & US Bureau of the Census. Challenges of Measuring and Ethnic World : Science Politics and Reality." Proceedings of the Joint Canada-United States Conference on the Measurement of Ethnicity April 1–3, 1992. Washington, DC: US Government Printing Office, 407–427.

LusakaTimes. 2019. "South African Business in Lusaka Close Today Amid Security Concerns." *Lusaka Times.com*. September 4. Accessed 12 12, 2020. https://www .lusakatimes.com/2019/09/04/south-african-business-in-lusaka-close-today-amid -security-concerns/.

Mamokhosi, Choane, Stella Shulika Lukong, and Mandla Mthombeni. "An Analysis of the Causes, Effects and Ramifications of Xenophobia in South Africa." *Insight on Africa* 3, no. 2 (2011): 129–142.

Matsumoto, D. 2009. *The Cambridge Dictionary of Psychology*. New York: Cambridge University Press.

Morris, Alan. "Our Fellow Africans Make Our Lives Hell: The Lives of Congolese and Nigerians Living in Johannesburg." *Ethnic and Racial Studies* 21, no.6 (1998): 1116–1136.

Nell, Ian. "The Tears of Xenophobia: Preaching and Violence from a South African Perspective." *Practical Theology in Africa* 24, no. 2 (2009): 229–247.

Onyekpe, N. 2004. *Ethnic Relations in Nigeria*. Ibadan: The Caxton press.

Robbins Kevin, and Frank Webster. 1999. *Times of the Technoculture: From the Information Society to the Virtual Life*. London: Routledge.

Settle, J. E. 2018. *Frenemies: How Social Media Polarizes America*. Cambridge: Cambridge University Press.

Solomon, Hus., and H. Kosaka. "Xenophobia in South Africa: Reflections, Narratives and Recommendations." *Southern African Peace and Security Studies* 2, no. 2 (2015): 5–30.

Sunstein, C. 2017. *Republic: Divided Democracy in the Age of Social Media*. Princeton: Princeton University Press.

Tshitereke, C. 1992. "Xenophobia and Relative Deprivation." *Crossings* 3 (2): 4–5.

United Nations. 2013. Xenophobia. Human right of the High Commissioner for Human Rights, Palais des Nations, CH-1211 Geneva 10, Switzerland, United Nations.

VOA. 2019. "Nigerians Attack South African Businesses in Retaliation." www.voanews.com. Accessed 11 09, 2020. https://www.google.com/ url?sa =t&rct=j&q=&esrc=s&source= web&cd=1&cad=rja&uact=8& ved=2ahUKEwiptfH9xt3kAhU OlhQKHazEDGEQFjAAegQI AxAB&url= https%3A%2F%2F www.voanews.com%2Fafrica %2Fnigerians-attack-southafric an-businessesretaliation&usg=AOvVaw22gQ yNU6dTu.

Vold, G. B. 1979. *Theoretical Criminology*. Oxford: Oxford University Press, 1–433.

Wienner, Jon. 1994. "Free Speech on the Internet." *The Nation* 258 (23): 825.

Part II

SOUTH AFRICA AND ANTI-FOREIGN NATIONAL SENTIMENT

XENO- OR AFRO-PHOBIA?

Chapter 6

Are South Africans Really Anti-Heterogeneity?

A Discourse Analysis of the Extent of Xenophobia in South Africa

Happy Mathew Tirivangasi and
Samukezi Mrubula-Ngwenya

The interest of the study is derived from observations that xenophobia in South Africa threatens and puts the lives of many people in danger. The 2008 South African xenophobic attacks claimed 62 lives. Two hundred and thirteen houses were burnt down, 342 shops were looted, hundreds of people were wounded, and it left thousands of foreign nationals displaced in just a week;[1] and seven people died during the 2015 xenophobic attacks.[2] Xenophobia represents everything against the well-articulated vision prophesied by former South African president Nelson Mandela. At the dawn of democracy, the then president of South Africa, Nelson Mandela, described South Africa as a rainbow nation, meaning a nation that can accommodate all people regardless of color, race, or religion.[3] Harris[4] states that in 1994 South Africa became a new nation and represented a fundamental shift in the social, political, and geographical landscapes of the past. Unity replaced segregation, equality replaced legislated racism, and democracy replaced apartheid in terms of the law and the way of doing things. Despite the transition from authoritarian rule to democracy, xenophobia continues to be a feature in South Africa.

Given the gravity of the problem, this chapter seeks to identify the extent of xenophobic attacks in South Africa. It gives a literature analysis of the manifestation of xenophobia in different parts of the world. The different case studies give a picture to the readers on other factors which give rise to xenophobic attacks in these countries. However, this study looks at the various incidences in the different provinces of South Africa as well as providing the effects of xenophobia. The chapter presents xenophobia as a problem that has the potential to disrupt the peace and security of the African countries, with specific emphasis on Southern Africa. This is a region that has not been synonymous with violence or wars. However, with each xenophobic incident, relations between the peace-loving nations are threatened. In 2019 there were xenophobic attacks on Nigerian citizens in Durban and Johannesburg which resulted in a standoff between Nigeria and South Africa. Nigerian citizens retaliated by attacking the South African embassy in Nigeria. Further, the Nigerian government temporarily closed its embassy in South Africa and the South African government did the same in Nigeria.[5] This is antagonistic to the peaceful overtures expected from the leading African nations.

XENOPHOBIA IN THE GLOBAL CONTEXT

Xenophobia has a long history in the existence of human beings. This is evidenced by the presence of the problem in every part of the world. The difference is usually seen by the different contexts in which it manifests. However, the consequences which xenophobia poses on minorities like immigrants, ethnic groups, women, and children remain immense. This section presents analysis of four European countries: Germany, France, Hungary, and Czech Republic. Germany and France represent the Western democracies whereas Czech and Hungary represent the former socialist states. The literature analysis of the countries established under different democracies helped the authors in understanding the extent of xenophobia in South Africa. Buthelezi[6] notes that

> xenophobia is a global problem that has been experienced in both industrialized democracies of the north and the developing countries of the south. It is a reality in Germany, Belgium, and the United Kingdom as it is in China, Ivory Coast and South Africa.

This is a true reflection of what is revealed by this chapter.

Germany represents a classic example of the society where the problem of xenophobia is well-documented. Zatlin[7] provides a case study of an era when German and Polish people had problems. In 1972, Germany and Poland signed an agreement to relax border restrictions. This was done to promote cultural relations between the two nations. Moreover, this agreement was forged to ensure that ordinary citizens maintain their friendships as well as maintaining the relationships between the two countries. The liberalization of the border ensured the free movement of people from both countries. Zatlin[8] provides the estimates of the movement of people and the cultural exchange rates. In the first 11 months of 1972, the German immigration officers recorded 9 million visitors coming into Germany whereas about 6.5 million Germans moved into Poland.[9] This movement resulted in approximately 10,000 marriages between the two nations. The migration laws came because of the consensus between the two nations and that was done without any consultation to the people at grassroots level. The consequences of these marriages of convenience were short-lived. Zatlin[10] points out that the enactment of the law did not help to bury the long-standing animosity between the Polish and the Germans.

Consequently, the relationship was bound to end with disagreements or clashes of interest between citizens of the two nations. The East Germans became critical of the Polish. They accused the Poles of buying all the essential goods from the shops and leaving the Germans vulnerable. The local people living at the border post argued that the Polish consumers bought all the goods which are essential to the lives of the Germans. Zatlin[11] points out that the native Germans argued that the Poles were causing the depletion of the already short supplied goods, as a result threatening the living standards of the East Germans. The economic downslope of East Germany helped to trigger xenophobic behavior. The East Germans started portraying the Poles as people who were engaged in crooked behavior at their expense.

Lolashvili[12] highlights the signs of xenophobic behavior in Czech Republic. Foreigners complain about the unwelcoming behavior of the Czechs. The scholar notes that this was the mark which was left by the socialist regime. Lolashvili[13] also gives an example of political xenophobia. This was exemplified by the establishment of the Workers' Party in 2003; it was described as anti-Semitic, xenophobic, homophobic, and neo-Nazi. The party was banned primarily because it was exploiting the economic downturn. Furthermore, Lolashvili[14] observes that political xenophobia is rife in most countries. For instance, a Hungarian Party which is anti-Semitic and anti-Roma garnered 11% of the votes in the 2010 election and the popularity of its ideas doubled over time.

In Slovakia, the Czech Republic's eastern neighbor is not different. Its Slovak National Party Leader, Ján Slota, has been in parliament since 1990 but he is known for his anti-Hungarian sentiments. The Bulgarian's Right-Wing Party, Alaka, is also known for its hostile notions against Turkish immigrants but it has gone to win 20 seats in every election. The bad economy presents pro-xenophobic elements in the society the opportunity to stir xenophobic sentiments.[15] The recent manifestation of xenophobia around Europe indicates that countries are becoming more and more nationalistic in the wake of the high influx of migrants from different countries.

XENOPHOBIA AND AFRICA

Xenophobia globally is not a new phenomenon. It is something that has been happening for a long time. Castles and Miller[16] note that increased economic disparities between the poor and the rich countries have contributed to the high level of international migration which in turn results in xenophobic attacks against migrants. Campbell[17] gives an extensive review of the case of Ghana. Ghana was the first African country to gain independence which resulted in the influx of the foreign immigrants flocking to look for means to better their lives. However, in the wake of high unemployment and inflation rates in Ghana in the 1960s, the civilian government of Ghana identified immigrants as the cause of the economic problem.

The Ghanaian government introduced Aliens Compliance Act in 1969 which directed all the irregular immigrants in Ghana to legalize their stay within two weeks or leave the country.[18] The order was impractical and resulted in the deportations of many foreigners, Nigerians in particular. It is estimated that approximately 1.5 million people were deported.[19] The Ghanaians went further to develop policies which restricted foreigners from owning any business in their country. The government of Nigeria similarly implemented a Parliamentary Act in the 1980s which saw about 1.5 million people, mostly Ghanaians, being expelled from the country. Adepoju[20] notes that the population of those affected comprised 180,000 deportees from Ghana while 120,000 were the Cameroonians, 150,000 Chadians, 5,000 Togolese, and 5,000 Beninese.[21] This population migrated to Nigeria mostly after the discovery of oil. In 1982 high inflation and unemployment led the politicians to scapegoat the foreigners for the mass expulsion. The public responded with violence in the case where the political leadership had started the initiative. The policies implemented were too harsh and did not give the immigrants time to organize their papers hence creating the culture of exclusion.

PROBLEM STATEMENT

The South African xenophobic attacks result in the loss of people's lives and vandalism of property. At the dawn of democracy, the then president, Nelson Mandela, described South Africa as a rainbow nation, meaning a nation that can accommodate all people regardless of color, race, or religion.[22] Xenophobia however goes against all that. Harris[23] states that in 1994 South Africa grew into a new state and represented important change in the social, political, and geographical landscapes of the past.[24] "Unity replaced segregation, equality replaced legislated racism and democracy replaced apartheid in terms of the law and the way of doing things." Despite the transition from oppression rule to democracy, xenophobia continues to be a feature in South Africa.

The impact of xenophobia and xenophobic attacks are astonishing. Misago, Landau, and Monson[25] note that in the wake of the 2008 xenophobic attacks, 62 people were reported dead, at least 670 wounded, dozens raped, more than 150,000 displaced, and property worth millions of Rands looted, destroyed, or appropriated by local residents. The problem with xenophobia is that it is not a protest but a crime. It displays the inhuman nature of human beings hence the need for a permanent solution. It is also important to note that the damages conceded have a great impact on the lives of the people. Looking at the statistics of rape cases provided by Misago et al.,[26] one can note that some people will contract diseases during xenophobic attacks. Moreover, families displaced will experience disruptions in their normal life.

In addition, one can note that emotional scars and mistrust against South Africa will continue to increase among the foreign African community. Rukema and Khan[27] note that several African states in the wake of the xenophobic attacks expressed displeasure. For example, during attacks on Somali nationals, the prime minister of Somalia, Abdi Farah Shirdon, made an appeal to the South African government to protect Somali citizens as a matter of urgency to intervene and contain this unnecessary and unfortunate violence against Somali business communities to preserve peace and stability. This is not an isolated incident; the Nigerian government recalled its envoys from Pretoria.[28] South Africa closed its consulate in Nigeria for a few days following the protest by the Nigerians over the xenophobic attacks in South Africa.[29] This reflects the sour relationship created by xenophobia between the two nations. The standoff between these two nations was also noted during the 2019 occurrences of xenophobic attacks in South Africa.

THEORETICAL FRAMEWORK OF THE STUDY

In this chapter we used Scapegoat Theory to probe xenophobic attacks in South Africa. Scapegoat Theory is a theoretical framework which is used mainly in sociology and psychology. The theory can be traced to the biblical act performed by Aaron for the Jews to cleanse the Israelites of their sins. Gollwitzer[30] provides this explanation with an insert from the Bible as follows:

'And Aaron shall lay both his hands upon the head of the live goat and confess over him all the iniquities of the people of Israel, and all their transgressions, all their sins'; and he shall put them upon the head of the goat, and send him away

into the wilderness . . . (Leviticus 16:21-22 RSV). One of two goats was slaughtered and sacrificed to God; the other was burdened with the folk's sins and
dismissed into the wilderness, carrying away the sins. This metaphor has been
adopted by several sociological and psychological theories and transformed into
what has become known as the scapegoat hypothesis[31]

This scapegoat hypothesis was used by various scholars to explain a wide range
of social phenomena such as prejudice, discrimination, and xenophobia.[32,33]
The theory was first applied to explain the situation experienced by black
Americans where black people paid a price for the fluctuations of the price
of cotton. Another case study is one about the Jews who were killed in Nazi
Germany for economic problems.[34]

The proponents of the Scapegoat Theory posit that, in times of national
crisis, people instinctively seek groups upon whom to assign blame for their
misfortunes.[35] European societies certainly experienced significant trauma after
1879, including major wars and a series of economic and social upheavals, and
for many groups, Jews became the object of their frustration and aggression.[36]
The Scapegoat Theory holds that in times of significant national trauma, the
host population tends to blame minorities for its misfortunes.

In South Africa, hate or hostility against foreigners is deemed to be a
result of limited resources such as employment, housing, education, medical
services, and other public services which are entirely the expectation of the
people during transitional periods.[37,38] Allport[39] points out that frustrations
lead to prejudice, especially among disadvantaged people and, in this context,
they identify a scapegoat, and these are usually foreigners. At the turn of
transition into democracy, the black majority had higher expectations of the
new government. With time, they soon realized that their expectations were
never going to be fulfilled.[40] This gap between the expectations and the reality
was filled with frustration.[41] This made the black South African population to
turn their anger on immigrants. Immigrants became the scapegoat by South
African citizens; instead of directing their anger toward the government they
embarked on violence against foreigners as a form of protest.

The Scapegoat Theory provides the necessary framework to understand
the different mechanisms through which local communities in South Africa
direct their anger to those who seem "foreign" to them. More crucially, the
theory explores the process of "othering" that is mostly associated with the
phenomenon of xenophobia. The adaptation of the Scapegoat Theory in this
study helps in teasing out the circumstances leading to local South Africans
displacing their frustrations to those who are perceived as the "foreign other."

In this study, the Scapegoat Theory was used to examine this interplay
(intersection) between disillusionment and displacement (of anger or
frustration). Moreover, the theory provided useful lenses of examining the

ways through which governmental agencies respond to incidences of popular disillusionment that carry xenophobic undertones. By placing more emphasis on the process of interaction between those in positions of governmental authority and local citizens, the Scapegoat Theory helps in the process of theorizing xenophobia as not only a social question but a political one. For this reason, the theory will be adapted and applied in this study to examine both the social and political aspects of xenophobia and how these are being attended to by the South African government. Unlike any other existing theories, the Scapegoat Theory was useful in providing illumination on how foreign nationals living in South Africa become "targets" of xenophobic attacks especially whenever the state is perceived as falling short in meeting the day-to-day survival needs to its citizens. It is this interplay between citizens and the state that theory helps in unraveling as it remains crucial in understanding the dynamics of xenophobic experiences in contemporary South Africa.

The Study Area

South Africa is divided into nine provinces. This study covered extensive literature of xenophobia from all provinces. The provinces are namely Limpopo, Gauteng, Mpumalanga, North West, Free State, KwaZulu-Natal, Northern Cape, Eastern Cape, and Western Cape. This was used to understand the extent of xenophobia in each province and this can also reflect on some of the hot spots for xenophobic attacks in South Africa.

METHODOLOGY

Research Approach

A qualitative research approach was adopted for this study. Qualitative research is flexible and unstructured, it captures verbatim reports or observable characteristics and yielding data that usually do not take numerical form. Words, films, postcards, art, and all sensory data are considered qualitative data unless they are transformed into some numerical system.[42] This is an appropriate research approach for this research as the researchers sought to extract secondary information on the extent of xenophobia in South African provinces.

Sampling Procedure

Data was collected from the purposive samples which consisted of the contents from secondary sources. The researchers employed purposive sampling to select the documents. The sample units were chosen because they have certain characteristics or features, for example, information pertaining to xenophobia. Patton[43] points out that the logic of criterion sampling is to review and study all cases that meet some predetermined criterion of importance. Qualitative information was collected from the documents which contain relevant information pertaining to xenophobia in South Africa, incidences of xenophobia, and effects of xenophobia.

Data Collection

The secondary information collected by the researchers consisted of online newspapers and articles. The newspaper information was retrieved from the following five newspapers agencies: *News24*, *Mail & Guardian*, *Mpumalanga News*, *Times Live*, and *Chronicle*. More data was collected from three online articles accessed from South African Broadcasting Cooperation news, Farmitraker and Khulumani Support Group.[44] The researchers collected data over a period of 12 weeks of reading and assessing the relevance of the documents to the study.

Data Analysis

The researchers adopted Critical Discourse Analysis (CDA) to analyze study results. The Fairclough[45] model for conducting CDA was followed. This model allows the researchers to study three levels of discourse namely text, process, and social context. Janks[46] points out that according to Fairclough, each of these dimensions requires a different kind of analysis, which she characterizes as follows: Text analysis (description), Processing analysis (interpretation), and Social analysis (explanation).

RESULTS AND DISCUSSION

The Extent of Xenophobic Attacks in South Africa

To understand the extent of xenophobia in South Africa, this section specifically identifies the 2015 xenophobic attacks within the context of xenophobia in South Africa. The researchers provide a trajectory of ongoing and steadily increasing xenophobic violence against the foreign nationals from the past five years. Below is the illustration of the time line of xenophobic attacks as they happen in different provinces of South Africa.

Incidences of Xenophobia in Limpopo Province

The Limpopo Province recorded 10 xenophobic incidents from 2010 to 2015. These incidences were characterized by brutal attacks on foreigners which resulted in three reported dead people in the process. The xenophobic attacks in this province involved the looting of goods from the shops belonging to Somalians, Zimbabweans, and Ethiopians. In these incidences, foreigners lost their property and basic things such as food and shelter (table 6.1).

Incidences of Xenophobia in Gauteng Province

There were approximately 12 reported incidents of xenophobia from 2010 to 2015 in the province of Gauteng. These attacks resulted in the killing of foreigners, looting of goods, and displacement of people in the process. In addition, about 42 shops were destroyed in the year of 2012 alone. The number increased during the widespread xenophobic attacks of 2015. Moreover, police records indicate that about 273 people were arrested in connection with xenophobic attacks in the year 2012. This resulted in the displacement of about 600 people within the same year as highlighted by the statistics given above. The results of the incidents cited above reveal that there were about 569 protests between November 1, 2013 and February 1, 2014 in the Gauteng province and 122 of them were violent protests. The crowd used weapons of violent protest such as the use of bottles, stones, clubs, and knobkerries to attack foreigners. In turn the police were armed with guns wielding rubber bullets (table 6.2).

Incidences of Xenophobia in Mpumalanga Province

There was one incident recorded in Mpumalanga province which included violence. However, the incident was triggered by the shooting of a student by a Somalian national. This looked like retaliation. However, it resulted in the outbreak of more attacks on foreign-owned shops. The locals burned shops belonging to the foreigners. In addition, it resulted in the arrest of 13 people. What is peculiar about the incident in Mpumalanga was the role played by the community elders in calming down the students and the youth from engaging in more violence (table 6.3).

Incidences of Xenophobia in Free State Province

Free State province did not record any xenophobic attacks during the April 2015 xenophobic attacks which occurred in other provinces like Gauteng and KwaZulu-Natal. However, there is one case which occurred a month after the attacks. The looting could not be established by the police as xenophobic, but

Table 6.1   Incidences of Xenophobia in Limpopo Province

Date	Place	Incident
June 2011	Seshego	• Hundreds of Zimbabweans living in Seshego were left homeless after the attacks erupted which left one-person dead
November 2013	Lephalale Town	• Five shops, two vehicles and two houses belonging to Zimbabweans were burnt
February 2014	Tswing Village in Thohoyandou	• Two Zimbabweans were abducted from their homes and taken to a secluded place where they were brutally attacked. One died on the spot and the other sustained injuries.
19 August 2014	Tshikota Village In Makhado	• Zimbabwean attacked and killed by an angry South African mob • They used any type of weapons to beat him up until he died • The man was accused of stealing from the villagers
05 March 2015	Ga-Sekgopo	• Foreigners on the outskirts of the provincial capital Polokwane in Limpopo abandoned their shops after protesting villagers looted their shops and threatened to burn them alive. • Violent protests erupted on Sunday with villagers sending all the foreigners packing and pushing them out of 11 villages in Sekgopo. • One of the shop owners said he lost his stock and will not regain the profit lost during the looting
29 April 2015	Thabazimbi.	• Xenophobic attacks spread to Limpopo. Shops owned by Somalis and Ethiopians were set alight and looted at a township • Eight locals were arrested and there was no sign of foreign nationals. About 50 of them, including women and children, were temporarily housed in town at a community hall at a place called Tala Park. • They indicated that they lost all their belongings and had to rely on government and some humanitarian organizations to provide basic things such as food.

Source: This table draws on material from several sources such as SABC online news; Chronicle. The incidents compiled by the researchers

Table 6.2   Incidences of Xenophobia in Gauteng Province

Date	Place	Incidents
20 July 2010	Kya Sands, Johannesburg	• 16 people, most of them foreign nationals, were attacked. • Five patients were taken to Helen Joseph Hospital • 10 people arrested. • Gauteng minister for community safety Khabisi Mosunkutu insisted that it is a crime and not xenophobia. • South Africans demanded that the army be deployed to protect them, saying police were not doing enough.
2012 February	Gauteng Doornkuil	• The six reported attacks resulted in the injury of at least eight victims. • 42 shops and businesses burnt or looted, 273 people arrested and more than 600 displaced within same year. • Eight foreigners were assaulted. • The men, from Zimbabwe and Malawi were sleeping in their shack when five youths armed with knobkerries and clubs attacked and robbed them. • The police could not identify the motive for the attack However, they noted that resentment could have been a factor, as all eight men worked for a local construction company in the area.
November 1 2013 to February 1 2014	Gauteng Province	• There were 569 protest actions. • 122 turned into violent protest
21 July 2014	Thokoza Township	• Hundreds of learners were out on the streets attacking and looting from the foreign owned shops. • Silence from both the media and the leaders from Ekurhuleni
April 18, 2015	Jeppestown	• Rubber bullets were fired, and the protesters retaliated by throwing bottles and rocks at the police • People clashed with police, demanding foreigners to leave. • Many shops were looted • Many of the foreigners from the area decided to leave their homes in fear of being attacked. • The locals argued that foreigners are taking over their country. That they were stealing jobs meant for them.

(*continued*)

Table 6.2   (Continued)

Date	Place	Incidents
April 18, 2015	Alexandra	• Journalists in Alexandra reported on the xenophobic attacks taking place within the community. They witnessed the brutal killing of a Mozambican national Emmanuel Sithole, • He was stabbed by four men in full view of the public. • Groups of people looted many foreign owned shops • Some of the streets where barricaded by residents of Alexander, blocking police from entering

Source: This table draws on material from a number of sources such as Khamango News24 Farmitraker; Khulumani Support group Tromp & Oatway. Table compiled by the researchers

Table 6.3   Incidences of Xenophobia in Mpumalanga Province

Date	Place	Incidents
February 2014	Pienaar	• A Somali national killed a student by gun fire. • Thirteen people were arrested on Sunday after they went on a rampage, looting the shops of foreign nationals after the funeral • Shops were vandalised and roads blocked by students. • Elders restrained students and community members from burning all foreign owned shops.

Source: *Mpumalanga News*. The table was created by the researchers

Table 6.4   Incidences of Xenophobia in Free State Province

Date	Place	Incident
May 19 2015	Petrus Steyn	• Eleven people were arrested in the Free State • Three foreign-owned shops were burned down • 18 shops were looted

Source: Lotriet. Table created by the researchers

the researchers can still categorize it as such. This is because the lootings were directed against the foreign-owned shops. The incident is illustrated in table 6.4:

Incidences of Xenophobia in North West Province

In the North West province, there were no previous xenophobic incidents leading to the 2015 xenophobic attacks. However, the incidents were influenced by the protest for service delivery at Ledig village. The protesters burned and looted foreign-owned businesses as a way of demanding action from the local government. This was a clear scenario in which the foreigners were used as scapegoats. There was a display of frustration and anger toward the local municipalities. However, to attract the attention of the local government, foreigners became the target (table 6.5).

Incidences of Xenophobia in Northern Cape Province

In the Northern Cape Province, there was no incident leading to the 2015 xenophobic attacks and the incident cited in this study was done after the countrywide violent attacks in April 2015. The incident happened when two shopkeepers were shot. The incident reveals the vulnerability of the foreigners within the shops and spazas (tabke 6.6).

Incidences of Xenophobia in KwaZulu-Natal Province

The xenophobic attacks in KwaZulu-Natal province started the 2015 violence. The Zulu King is credited for starting the attacks when he declared that foreigners should pack their bags and leave. It resulted in the death of about seven people in the province alone. The other thing that was different was the fact that about 300 people participated in the attacks. This was the largest number of people who participated in the attacks across all the provinces.

Table 6.5   Incidences of Xenophobia in North West Province

Date	Place	Incident
April 16 2015	Ledig Village	• Foreign traders were caught in the crossfire of service delivery protests. • Shops were looted and forced to close as community member's demands action from local government. • Protestors burnt tyres and wood; foreign-owned businesses were looted.

Source: Pilane. Table created by the researchers

Table 6.6   Incidences of Xenophobia in Northern Cape Province

Date	Place	Incident
21 July 2015	Kuruman, Northern Cape	• Two foreign shopkeepers were fatally shot • A fellow shopkeeper sustained serious injuries.

Source: Pilane. Compiled by the researchers

Table 6.7   Incidences of Xenophobia in KwaZulu-Natal Province

Date	Place	Incident
8 April 2015	Durban	• Zulu King, King Goodwill Zwelithini remarked that foreigners should go back to their home countries because they were changing the nature of South African society with their goods and enjoying wealth that should have been for local people.
12 April 2015	Umlazi KwaMashu V Section	• Shops owned by foreigners were set on fire • Five people killed • A shop owned by a Somali was set on fire
14 April 2015	Veralum, North of Durban KwaNdlazi	• 300 people participated in the looting of foreign shops • locals, foreigners and police clashed in the city centre • 14-year-old boy was shot dead • Two people arrested
15 April 2015	Veralum; Durban city centre	• 58-year-old man died from the attacks by a mob • 112 people arrested in connection with the attacks • Teargas and rubber bullets were fired in the city centre. • South African companies evacuated employees from neighbouring Mozambique.
21 April 2015	Isipingo, south of Durban	• People tried to return to their homes and businesses but were attacked by violent mobs and had their possessions taken

Source: This table draws on material from several sources such as Evans and Wicks, Wicks SABC. Compiled by the researchers

Approximately, 112 people were arrested for the xenophobic attacks in the province (table 6.7).

THE EXPLANATION OF XENOPHOBIC ATTACKS IN SOUTH AFRICA

The researchers note that the April 2015 xenophobic attacks were not the first after the 2008 xenophobic attacks. The 2015 xenophobic attacks attracted the attention of the world, hence, the immediate government response to the problem. However, as noted above, there was a continuous increase in xenophobic attacks over the years. This means that the xenophobic attacks never stopped in South Africa, but it is the level of magnitude which differs. The broader patterns of xenophobic violence are a critical reference point in understanding the form and shape of xenophobic attacks.[47] This is what prompted this study to look at the trends of xenophobic attacks in South

Africa after the 2008 xenophobic attacks. In the previous studies, Nyar[48] also conducted a study in which she arrived at the same conclusion when she analyzed the trends of xenophobic attacks from the time South Africa attained democratic rule. Nyar[49] argues,

> The trajectory of the xenophobic attacks showed a trend toward increasing lawlessness, with communities often vowing to continue their anti-"foreigner" campaign even in the presence of police. Such a pattern of violence speaks to a culture of impunity in which attacks against foreign nationals have been allowed to continue in a context of a gross lack of accountability.

The incidents of xenophobic attacks have continued with many of such incidences going unreported or the police doing little to contain the situation. There is failure of a radical action to stamp out xenophobic attacks in the time of peace. The xenophobic attacks have gone from being a sentiment to being a national issue once more. Nyar[50] notes,

> What distinguishes the 2008 xenophobic violence from preceding incidences? The xenophobic attacks of 2008 denoted a marked difference in scale, for which the increasing momentum of earlier incidences of violence could well be seen as a forewarning.

This is exact scenario which was repeated by the 2015 xenophobic attacks in which the margin and extent of xenophobic attacks was the one which captured the imagination of political leaders and evoked an action.Xenophobic attacks have been going on as revealed by the incidents of violence which are cited above.

THE IMPACT OF XENOPHOBIC ATTACKS IN SOUTH AFRICA

Loss of Life

The incidents indicated through table 6.1–6.7 reveal the loss of life due to xenophobia. In Gauteng province, one death of a man is reported. Further, in KwaZulu-Natal province, seven people died during the same period. The loss of life is not something that is new. In the 2008 xenophobic attacks there was loss of life well more than the total number of human loss recorded in 2015. Matunhu[51] states that "xenophobic attacks in South Africa, which started around mid-May in 2008 in the informal settlements of Alexandria claimed 62 lives."

This information is further confirmed when he notes that "in May 2008, the country exploded into an orgy of killing, looting and burning. The outcome in Gauteng was 62 people dead of whom 21 were South Africans."[52]

This evidence reveals the gravity of xenophobic attacks in South Africa. This is what raises the eyebrows of the rest of the world and causes worry to all the humanity. The 2015 xenophobic attacks revealed the same trend of the loss of life as well. This reveals the need to protect humanity from the violence emanated from within our communities. In addition, one can note that there were approximately seven people who died during the monthlong incidents of xenophobia. Moreover, the death of people due to xenophobic incidents did not stop in 2008 as this research has revealed; many people died thereafter.

The Looting of Foreign-Owned Shops

Considering the incidents shown in all the provinces, xenophobic attacks were characterized by the looting of shops owned by foreigners. In each province where xenophobic attacks were reported, foreigners' shops were looted. This was not done in peaceful terms; in the process shopkeepers were injured. The impact of a group of people got serious consequences on the foreigners. For instance, they lost all their goods at once which reduced them to being near destitute. Further, the loss of their property and goods resulted in their business being reduced to nothing and destroying the South African entrepreneurship development in the process.

This affected the business owners, and the same community suffers from lack of access to the cheap goods which they received near their houses. However, despite the ongoing looting and violence against the foreign immigrants, these acts were categorized as xenophobic acts. The authorities urged the communities not to regard them as such. This is well noted by Crush[53] when he quotes the former minister of International Relations and Cooperation, Maite Nkoana-Mashabane, in 2013 saying, "The looting, displacement and killing of foreign nationals in South Africa should not be viewed as xenophobic attacks, but opportunistic criminal acts that have the potential to undermine the unity and cohesiveness of our communities."[54]

The looting of the foreign-owned goods as we have noted in the incidents highlighted above are part of the widespread xenophobic acts but, however, in this scenario this study can reveal that despite this being a characteristic feature of xenophobic attacks in both 2008 and the preceding years the authorities have denied the looting of goods as an effect or impact of xenophobiain South Africa.

Physical Effects of Xenophobia

The physical effects of xenophobia are outrageous; most of the foreigners who were attacked and survived suffered permanent injuries to their bodies. Some of the injuries resulted in some serious fatalities which often resulted in death. Further, some resulted in incurring injuries which led to disability. In some cases, the injuries suffered at the hands of the locals made the injured people unable to find assistance from nearby clinics. This is because some of the personnel available were shunned to touch such wounds and no one wanted to be part of those who harbor the victims of xenophobic attacks. This behavior was caused by the fear of risking their lives from the violent local perpetrators.

Mothibi, Roelofse, and Tshivhase[55] note that

> violence is understood as an act or situation that harms the health or well-being of oneself or others. It includes both attacks on a person's physical and psychological integrity, and the destructive acts that do not involve a direct relationship between victims and the institution, person or persons responsible for the harm.

This clearly reveals the devastating effects of xenophobic attacks on foreign immigrants. While this impact of the violent attack was clear for the public to see, the government of South Africa took no initiative to compensate the affected families and individuals.

Psychological Effects of Xenophobia

This discourse can reveal that victims of xenophobic attacks suffered psychological effects. At one incident, a foreigner died upon arrival at the hospital because the doctor who was supposed to attend to him was a foreigner. The doctor stayed away at his place because he was afraid of being attacked. Some of the newspapers reveal images of foreigners walking with knives in their hands fearing for their lives. This behavior reveals that most foreigners who walk in hot spots of violence still carry their knives as a defensive mechanism. Further, the xenophobic attacks revealed in the tables earlier show that most of the attacks happen within the community. This removes the foreigner's power or will of readjustment. This also affects those people who were displaced and cannot go back to the same communities they were staying in. The effects of xenophobic attacks can be radical and long-lasting. Mothibi et al.[56] note that "traumatising experiences can cast a long shadow over people's lives, including perpetrators as well as victims. That is, the effects of the experience can be radical and long lasting." This is terrible and has devastating effects on individuals involved and their families.

Family Disintegration

Xenophobic attacks had a huge impact on the families of the foreigners. This is because some foreigners had already married local women. Such foreign nationals were targets for xenophobic violence. The disintegration of families made some women to automatically become single mothers. The Zimbabwean ambassador to South Africa, Mr. Isaac Moyo, pointed out that at least 10 South African women wanted to travel to Zimbabwe with their Zimbabwean husbands but did not have the right documents. He further said that the embassy was encountering challenges in cases where undocumented South African women were insisting on traveling to Zimbabwe with their Zimbabwean husbands.[57] This apparently created a difficult time for the women who were married to foreigners. In a case where the husband was the sole breadwinner, this automatically becomes a huge impact with serious consequences.

CONCLUSION

This chapter was not meant to provide the solutions to the South African xenophobic attacks. However, it intended to reveal the gravity of the problems and the purportedly harm imposed on migrants. This study painted a clear picture of the extent of xenophobia in South Africa. It can be noted that Gauteng, KwaZulu-Natal, and Limpopo reported more incidences of xenophobic attacks. This chapter has revealed that xenophobia is not confined to South Africa alone, hence. However, the high reported incidences in South African provinces show the need to take the problem seriously. It is the continuation of xenophobic incidences which calls for the need of more sustainable preventative methods against xenophobic attacks. The effects of xenophobic attacks are so extensive as the damages result in family disintegration, psychological effects on the victims, physical effects, looting of goods, and loss of life. These are the factors which need to be taken into consideration when the government is dealing with how to handle victims of xenophobic attacks as well as creating a culture of coexistence in South Africa. The results of this study are meant to invoke further debate about xenophobia, peace, and security of the countries in the Southern African region. This will also lead to the development of mechanisms on how to protect migrants, not only in South Africa but across the globe.

NOTES

1. Matunhu, Jephias. "Re-visiting the May 2008 xenophobic attacks in South Africa." *African Journal of Criminology & Justice Studies* 5 (2011). No 95.

2. Harris, Bronwyn. "Xenophobia: A new pathology for a new South Africa." In *Psychopathology and Social Prejudice*, ed. Derek Hook and Gillian Eagle (Cape Town: University of Cape Town Press, 2002), 169–184.

3. Ibid.

4. Ibid.

5. Tirivangasi, H. M. "The efficiency of strategies for the prevention of xenophobia in post-apartheid South Africa," Doctoral dissertation, 2017.

6. Buthelezi, Msawenkosi. "An Investigation of the experiences and meaning of Xenophobia at the University of Zululand by international students." PhD diss., University of Zululand, 2009.

7. Zatlin, Jonathan R. "Scarcity and resentment: Economic sources of xenophobia in the GDR, 1971–1989." *Central European History* 40, no. 4 (2007): 683–720.

8. Zatlin, Jonathan R. "Scarcity and resentment: Economic sources of xenophobia in the GDR, 1971–1989." *Central European History* 40, no. 4 (2007): 683–720.

9. Ibid.

10. Ibid.

11. Ibid.

12. Lolashvili, Ekaterine. "Suppressed: The nature of Czech xenophobia." *The New Presence, The Prague Journal of Central European Affairs* 4 (2011): 60–65.

13. Lolashvili, Ekaterine. "Suppressed: The nature of Czech xenophobia." *The New Presence, The Prague Journal of Central European Affairs* 4 (2011): 60–65.

14. Ibid.

15. Ibid.

16. Castles, Stephen, and Mark J. Miller. *The Age of Migration International Population Movements in the Modern World* (London: Macmillan, 1988).

17. Campbell, Eugene, K. "The role of Xenophobia In Obligating Decision Toward Transnationalism and return migration," *University of Warwick*. Accessed July 16, 2009. http://www2.warwick.ac.uk/f6AF689B-9DCD-4FF7-9C13-373AEB4FBIAE/Final.

18. Ibid.

19. Ibid.

20. Adepoju, Aderanti. "Illegals and expulsion in Africa: The Nigerian experience." *International Migration Review* 18, no. 3 (1984): 426–436.

21. Ibid.

22. Harris, Bronwyn. "Xenophobia: A new pathology for a new South Africa." In *Psychopathology and Social Prejudice*, ed. Derek Hook and Gillian Eagle (Cape Town: University of Cape Town Press, 2002), 169–184.

23. Harris, Bronwyn. "Xenophobia: A new pathology for a new South Africa." In *Psychopathology and Social Prejudice*, ed. Derek Hook and Gillian Eagle (Cape Town: University of Cape Town Press, 2002), 169–184.

24. Ibid.

25. Misago, Jean Pierre, Loren B. Landau, and T. Monson. "Tensions, territory and terror: Understanding violence against foreigners in South Africa." Research conducted with the support of The International Organization for Migration (IOM), *The Atlantic Philantropies and Oxfam UK. Forced Migration Studies Programme.* University of the Witwatersrand (2008).

26. Misago, Jean Pierre, Loren B. Landau, and T. Monson. "Tensions, territory and terror: Understanding violence against foreigners in South Africa." Research conducted with the support of The International Organization for Migration (IOM), *The Atlantic Philantropies and Oxfam UK. Forced Migration Studies Programme.* University of the Witwatersrand (2008).

27. Rukema, Joseph Rudigi, and Sultan Khan. "Chronicling the effects of the 2008 xenophobic attacks amongst a select group of Congolese and Burundian women in the city of Durban." *Alternative Special Edition* 7 (2013): 176–196.

28. Ibid.

29. Ngcukana, Lubabalo, "SA closes consulate in Lagos after anti-xenophobia unrest." *Mail & Guardian.* April 22, 2015. http://mg.co.za/article/2015-04-22-sa-closes-consulate-in-lagos.

30. Gollwitzer, Mario. "Wave goodbye the scapegoat: Moral decisions and their effects on harshness of penalty." Masters Dissertation, University of Trier, 2002.

31. Gollwitzer, Mario. "Wave goodbye the scapegoat: moral decisions and their effects on harshness of penalty." Masters Dissertation, University of Trier, 2002.

32. Allport, Gordon Willard, Kenneth Clark, and Thomas Pettigrew. *The Nature of Prejudice.* Reading, MA: Addison-Wesley, 1954.

33. Tshitereke, Clarence. "Xenophobia and relative deprivation." *Crossings* 3, no. 2 (1999): 4–5.

34. Breckler, Steven J., James Olson, and Elizabeth Wiggins. *Social Psychology Alive* (Belmont: Cengage Learning, 2005).

35. Marrus, Michael Robert. "The theory and practice of anti-semitism." *Commentary* 74, no. 2 (1982): 38–42.

36. Andreski, Stanislav. "An economic interpretation of anti-semitism in Eastern Europe." *Jewish Journal of Sociology* 5, no. 3 (1963): 201–213.

37. Tshitereke, Clarence. "Xenophobia and relative deprivation." *Crossings* 3, no. 2 (1999): 4–5.

38. Harris, Bronwyn. "Xenophobia: A new pathology for a new South Africa." In *Psychopathology and Social Prejudice*, ed. Hook, Derek, and Eagle, Gillian (Cape Town: University of Cape Town Press, 2002), 169–184.

39. Allport, Gordon Willard, Kenneth Clark, and Thomas Pettigrew. *The Nature of Prejudice* (Reading, MA: Addison-Wesley, 1954).

40. Tshitereke, Clarence. "Xenophobia and relative deprivation." *Crossings* 3, no. 2 (1999): 4–5.

41. Gomo, Tapiwa. "Analysis of media reporting and xenophobia violence among youth in South Africa." Masters Dissertation., Malmo University's School of Arts and Communication, 2010.

42. Ibid.

43. Patton, M. Q. *Qualitative Methods in Research and Evaluation* (Sage Publication Inc., 1990).

44. Cornish, Jean Jacques. "South Africa: Xenophobic attacks erupt in South Africa's limpopo province." *Radio France Internationale*. March 5, 2015. http://en .rfi.fr/africa/20150305-xenophobic-attacks-south-africa-limpopo.

45. Fairclough, Norman. *"Discourse and Power." Language and Power* (London: Longman, 1989).

46. Janks, Hilary. "Critical discourse analysis as a research tool." *Discourse: Studies in the Cultural Politics of Education* 18, no. 3 (1997): 329–342.

47. Nyar, Anssilla, "'What happened'? A narrative of the May 2008 xenophobic violence," *Unpublished paper commissioned by The Atlantic Philanthropies*, 2009.

48. Nyar, Anssilla, "'What happened'? A narrative of the May 2008 xenophobic violence," *Unpublished paper commissioned by The Atlantic Philanthropies*, 2009.

49. Ibid.

50. Ibid.

51. Matunhu, Jephias. "Re-visiting the May 2008 xenophobic attacks in South Africa." *African Journal of Criminology & Justice Studies* 5 (2011), No 95.

52. Ibid.

53. Crush, J. "Doing business with xenophobia." *Workshop on Urban Informality and Migrant Entrepreneurship in Southern Africa*, 2015, 10–11 February 2014. Cape Town: SAMP.

54. Crush Jonathan. "Doing business with xenophobia." *Workshop on Urban Informality and Migrant Entrepreneurship in Southern Africa*, 2014, 25–29.

55. Mothibi, K. A., C. J. Roelofse, and Thompho Tshivhase. "Xenophobic attacks on foreign shop owners and street vendors in Louis Trichardt Central Business District, Limpopo province." *TD: The Journal for Transdisciplinary Research in Southern Africa* 11, no. 4 (2015): 151–162.

56. Mothibi, K. A., C. J. Roelofse, and Thompho Tshivhase. "Xenophobic attacks on foreign shop owners and street vendors in Louis Trichardt Central Business District, Limpopo Province." *TD: The Journal for Transdisciplinary Research in Southern Africa* 11, no. 4 (2015): 151–162.

57. News24, "Tensions looms at SADC summit in Zim over xenophobia," *NEWS 24*, April 29, 2015, http://www.news24.com/Africa/News/Xenophobic-attacks-loom -over-SADC-summit-in-Zimbabwe.

BIBLIOGRAPHY

Adepoju, Aderanti. "Illegals and expulsion in Africa: The Nigerian experience." *International Migration Review* 18, no. 3 (1984): 426–436.

Allport, Gordon Willard, Kenneth Clark, and Thomas Pettigrew. *The Nature of Prejudice.* (Reading, MA: Addison-Wesley, 1954).

Andreski, Stanislav. "An economic interpretation of anti-semitism in Eastern Europe." *Jewish Journal of Sociology* 5, no. 3 (1963): 201–213.

Breckler, Steven J., James Olson, and Elizabeth Wiggins. *Social Psychology Alive* (Belmont: Cengage Learning, 2005).

Burns, Nancy and Susan K. Grove. *The Practice of Nursing Research: Conduct, Critique and Utilisation* (Philadelphia: Saunders, 2003).

Buthelezi, Msawenkosi. "An Investigation of the experiences and meaning of Xenophobia at the University of Zululand by international students." PhD diss., University of Zululand, 2009.

Campbell, Eugene, K. "The role of Xenophobia In Obligating Decision Toward Transnationalism and return migration" *University of Warwick.* Accessed July 16, 2009. http://www2.warwick.ac.uk/f6AF689B-9DCD-4FF7-9C13 -373AEB4FBIAE/Final.

Castles, Stephen, and Mark J. Miller. *The Age of Migration International Population Movements in the Modern World* (London: Macmillan, 1988).

Chronicle. (2014). "Xenophobia: Zimbabwean man beaten to death by South Africans". http://www.myzimbabwe.co.zw/news/1036-xenophobia-zimbabwean -man-beaten-to-death-by-south-africans.html. Accessed 10 January 2016.

Cornish, Jean. Jacques. "South Africa: Xenophobic attacks erupt in South Africa's Limpopo Province." *Radio France Internationale.* March 05, 2015. http://en.rfi.fr/ africa/20150305-xenophobic-attacks-south-africa-limpopo.

Crush, J. "Doing business with xenophobia." *Workshop on Urban Informality and Migrant Entrepreneurship in Southern Africa,* 2015, 10–11 February 2014. Cape Town: SAMP.

Crush, Jonathan. "Doing Business with Xenophobia." *Workshop on Urban Informality and Migrant Entrepreneurship in Southern Africa,* 2014: 25–29.

Evans, Jenni and Wicks, Jeff, "Sixth person killed in KZN xenophobic violence," *NEWS 24,* April 17, 2015, http://www.news24.com/SouthAfrica/News/Sixth -person-killed-in-KZN-xenophobic-violence-20150417.

Fairclough, Norman. *"Discourse and Power." Language and Power* (London: Longman, 1989).

Farmitraker. "Rioting in Gauteng province 569 protest of which 122 turned violent since November 1 2013 - Feb 1 2014." 2014. http://www.censorbugbear.org/farmi- tracker/reports/view/2120. Accessed 10 January 2016. Statistics.

Gollwitzer, Mario. "Wave goodbye the scapegoat: moral decisions and their effects on harshness of penalty." Masters Dissertation, University of Trier, 2002.

Gomo, Tapiwa. "Analysis of media reporting and xenophobia violence among youth in South Africa." Masters Dissertation., Malmo University's School of Arts and Communication, 2010.

Harris, Bronwyn. "Xenophobia: A new pathology for a new South Africa." In *Psychopathology and Social Prejudice,* ed. Derek Hook and Gillian Eagle (Cape Town: University of Cape Town Press, 2002), 169–184.

Janks, Hilary. "Critical discourse analysis as a research tool." *Discourse: Studies in the Cultural Politics of Education* 18, no. 3 (1997): 329–342.

Khamango, Thembela. "Kya sands attacks not xenophobia-related." *Mail & Guardian*, July 20, 2010, http://mg.co.za/article/2010-07-20-kya-sands-attacks -not- xenophobiarelated.

Khulumani Support Group. "Xenophobic attacks on foreign shop owners in Ekurhuleni go unreported in national media: A worrying new development." 2014. http://www.khulumani.net/khulumani/statements/item/995-xenophobic-attacks-on -foreign-shop-owners-in-ekurhuleni-go-unreported-in-national-media-a-worrying -new-development.html. Accessed 10 January 2016.

Lim, Young Joon. "Anti-Chinese sentiment in Zambia and the African continent: Comparative coverage of the phenomenon by Zambian, Chinese, and South African newspapers." *International Journal of Information and Communication Technology Research* 2, no. 7 (2012).

Lolashvili, Ekaterine. "Suppressed: The nature of Czech xenophobia." *The New Presence, The Prague Journal of Central European Affairs* 4 (2011): 60–65.

Lotriet, D. "Foreign-owned shops burned and looted in free state town," *NEWS 24*, May 19, 2015, http://www.news24.com/SouthAfrica/News/Foreign-owned-shops -burnt- looted-in-Free-State-20150519.

Mafukata, M. A. "Xenophobia-the evil story of the beginnings of fascism in post-apartheid South Africa." *The International Journal of Humanities and Social Studies* 3, no. 3 (2015): 30–44.

Marrus, Michael Robert. "The theory and practice of anti-semitism." *Commentary* 74, no. 2 (1982): 38–42.

Matunhu, Jephias. "Re-visiting the May 2008 xenophobic attacks in South Africa." *African Journal of Criminology & Justice Studies* 5 (2011), No 95.

Misago, Jean Pierre, Loren B. Landau, and T. Monson. "Tensions, territory and terror: Understanding violence against foreigners in South Africa." Research conducted with the support of The International Organization for Migration (IOM), *The Atlantic Philantropies and Oxfam UK. Forced Migration Studies Programme.* University of the Witwatersrand (2008).

Mireille de Villiers and Mbekezeli Mdluli. "13 arrested after xenophobic attacks in Pienaar." *Mpumalanga News*, March 4, 2014, http://mpumalanganews.co.za/46503 /13-arrested-after-xenophobic-attacks-in-pienaar/.

Mothibi, K. A., C. J. Roelofse, and Thompho Tshivhase. "Xenophobic attacks on foreign shop owners and street vendors in Louis Trichardt Central Business District, Limpopo Province." *TD: The Journal for Transdisciplinary Research in Southern Africa* 11, no. 4 (2015): 151–162.

Myburg, Daisy. "Xenophobia cannot re-emerge in Northern Cape." *DA MPL Assistance Network,* July 21, 2015, http://www.dampl.co.za/category/xenophobia/.

News24. "No xenophobia in looting of shops- Limpopo gvt," *NEWS 24*, April 29, 2015, http://www.news24.com/SouthAfrica/News/No-xenophobia-in-looting-of -shops-Limpopo-govt-20150429.

News24. "Tensions looms at SADC summit in Zim over xenophobia," *NEWS 24*, April 29, 2015, http://www.news24.com/Africa/News/Xenophobic-attacks-loom -over-SADC-summit-in-Zimbabwe.

News24. "Xenophobic attacks - pattern changing," *News 24*, July 24; 2012, http://www
.news24.com/SouthAfrica/News/Xenophobic-attacks-pattern-changing-20120724.

Ngcukana, Lubabalo. "SA closes consulate in Lagos after anti-xenophobia unrest."
Mail & Guardian. April 22, 2015. http://mg.co.za/article/2015-04-22-sa-closes
-consulate-in-lagos.

Nyamnjoh, Francis B. *Insiders and Outsiders: Citizenship and Xenophobia in
Contemporary Southern Africa.* Zed Books, 2006.

Nyar, Anssilla, "'What happened'? A narrative of the May 2008 xenophobic
violence," *Unpublished paper Commissioned by The Atlantic Philanthropies*,
2009.

O'Brien, John, Dan Remenyi, and Aideen Keaney. "Historiography-A neglected
research method in business and management studies." *Electronic Journal of
Business Research Methods* 2, no. 2 (2004): 135–144.

Patton, M. Q. *Qualitative Methods in Research and Evaluation.* Sage Publication
Inc., 1990.

Pontsho, Pilane. "Protesters in Ledig, North West turn on foreign owned shops."
SowetanLive, April 17, 2015, http://www.sowetanlive.co.za/news/2015/04/17/
protestors-in-ledig-north-west-turn-on-foreign-owned-shops.

Popper, T., A. Fenyvesi, and C. Keszthelyi. "Research: Xenophobia at record high
in Hungary," *Budapest Business Journal*, May 6, 2015, http://www.bbj.hu/bbj/
research-xenophobia-at-a-record-high-in-hungary.

Roemer, John E., and Karine Van der Straeten. "Xenophobia and the size of the
public sector in France: A politico-economic analysis." *Journal of Economics* 86,
no. 2 (2005): 95–144.

Rukema, Joseph Rudigi, and Sultan Khan. "Chronicling the effects of the 2008
Xenophobic attacks amongst a select group of Congolese and Burundian women in
the city of Durban." *Alternative Special Edition* 7 (2013): 176–196.

SABC. "Xenophobic attacks spread to Limpopo." *SABC*, April 29, 2015, http://www
.sabc.co.za/news/a/d808e98048319b259a3bff4d1170398b/Xenophobicundefined
attacksundefinedspreadundefinedtoundefinedLimpopo-20152904.

SABC. "Xenophobic violence flares up again in Durban." *SABC*, April 21, 2015,
http://www.sabc.co.za/news/a/5fae75004818029fadaded78423ca9af/xenophobic
-violence-flares-up-again-in-durban-20152104.

Sello, Lenyaro. "Xenophobic violence reignites in Jeppestown." *eNCA,* April
17, 2015, https://www.enca.com/south-africa/jeppestown-hostel-dwellers-clash
-police.

Sibindi, Lloyd. ""Xenophobia: Zimbabwean man beaten to death by South Africans."
My Zimbabwe News. August 19, 2014. https://www.myzimbabwe.co.zw/news
/1342-xenophobia-zimbabwean-man-beaten-to-death-by-south-africans.html.

Tirivangasi, Happy M. "The efficiency of strategies for the prevention of xenophobia
in post-apartheid South Africa." Doctoral dissertation, 2017.

Tromp, Beauregard and James Oatway. "The brutal death of Emmanuel Sithole."
TimesLive, April 19, 2015, http://www.timeslive.co.za/local/2015/04/19/the-brutal
-death-of-emmanuel-sithole.

Tshitereke, Clarence. "Xenophobia and relative deprivation." *Crossings* 3, no. 2 (1999): 4–5.

Wicks, Jeff. "KZN xenophobic violence spreads to KwaMashu." *NEWS 24*, April 13, 2015. http://www.news24.com/SouthAfrica/News/KZN-xenophobic-violence -spreads-to-KwaMashu-20150413.

Zatlin, Jonathan R. "Scarcity and resentment: Economic sources of xenophobia in the GDR, 1971–1989." *Central European History* 40, no. 4 (2007): 683–720.

Chapter 7

Restoring the Fading Rainbow

Live Liyengcayelwa as a Philosophico-Ethical Resource to Addressing Xenophobic Tensions in South Africa

Sunday Paul C. Onwuegbuchulam

Agyeno rightly notes that "xenophobic violence has become recurring and a disturbing feature of Post-Apartheid South Africa. It jolted the attention of South Africa and the international community to another form of crisis added to the peace and security challenges in Africa."[1] Suffice it to say that xenophobic vehemence in South Africa is becoming analogous to the story of Sisyphus in Greek mythology, in which Sisyphus is condemned by Zeus to roll up a rock to the top of a mountain, only to have the rock roll back down to the bottom every time he manages to reach the top. Similarly, despite all the proffered solutions by all stakeholders toward solving the xenophobia problem, so as to realize the so-called rainbow nation, South Africa still sees itself falling to the depth of national disparagement by other African countries and the world because of xenophobic occurrences in the country. On this, it is central to note that the attacks have led to the suggestion that perhaps the problem is not hate against foreigners (xenophobia in the true sense of the word) but Afrophobia (specific hate against African immigrants). Evidence is legion in extant literature to substantiate the fact that it is mostly African immigrants who have borne the brunt of xenophobic attacks in South Africa.[2]

The problem has become protracted and xenophobic attacks in South Africa rear their ugly head now and then especially in recent times. These attacks perpetrated against mostly immigrant African groups have called into question the will among the country's citizens to build a rainbow nation as touted by its liberation icons like Nelson Mandela. The attacks further raise the question of whether or not the country has really risen from and divested itself of the cloak of its history and legacy of racial hate, violence, and intolerance. There is a need to interrogate this issue of xenophobia and always seek sustainable solutions to the problem. Against this backdrop, this chapter problematizes the recurring xenophobic tensions and violence in South Africa and utilizesqualitative desktop methods, and, based on the African philosophy and constructivist agenda, the study theorizes on realizing true transformation of xenophobic tensions in South Africa. The study proposes the Siswati adage *live liyengcayelwa* as an African philosophico-ethical resource and basis on which mutual respect among citizens and immigrants in South Africa could be built on toward eschewing all xenophobic tendencies.

LITERATURE PERSPECTIVES ON XENOPHOBIC VIOLENCE IN SOUTH AFRICA

Adebajo reveals that

> since the end of South Africa's Apartheid system in 1994, there have been at least 569 incidents of xenophobic violence in the country. Of these, 529, recorded up till December 2018, led to 309 deaths, 901 physical assaults, 2,193 looted shops, and over 100,000 people displaced.[3]

This revelation is staggering considering that this is happening in a country that purports to be a rainbow nation and which has acknowledged the assistance of other African nations in its fight against colonialism and apartheid. For Mangu the "violent systemic and endemic xenophobic attacks against migrants from other African countries in South Africa dramatically undermine the dream of an 'African renaissance' propounded by the South African government under Nelson Mandela's and Thabo Mbeki's presidencies."[4]

Extant literature has dwelt on this issue thoroughly and views with regards to the cause(s) and reason(s) behind the problem have been varied. Notably, Lombard underscores what the author called the "scapegoat hypothesis" which tried to explain the reasons behind the xenophobic attacks in South Africa.[5] The first premise concerns the frustration among South Africans concerning the issue of failed service delivery in the country since the demise of apartheid. With regards to the first theory, some studies[6] have alluded to the reality that xenophobic violence in South Africa could be linked to the fact that citizens have to compete with foreigners for the use of available housing and other services from government in their different localities. Related to this is the issue of the politics of economic livelihoods and competition for economic opportunities in the country as alluded to in some studies[7] which posit that some locals are dissatisfied that foreign nationals have taken over jobs and are involved with small business enterprises in the country (which should be exclusively left for citizens) thus depriving the locals of such economic opportunities. Summarily, Claassen's multilevel regression analysis reveals that there is prevalent support in literature toward the view that xenophobia in South Africa is as a result of "poverty, relative deprivation, frustration with government, and social mobilization, with mixed evidence for resource competition. Taken together, the results point toward a mechanism of scapegoating, where frustrations and hopelessness produce aggression that is targeted at African immigrants."[8]

Additionally, it is also pertinent to note that some studies[9] have shown that some South Africans blame the issue of xenophobia on their frustration with the level of crime (drug dealing, human trafficking, and other forms of organized crimes) perpetrated by foreign nationals in their country.

The second suggestion surrounding xenophobic violence in South Africa according to Lombard is the "isolation theory" which alludes to the supposed reality that South Africans are not used to foreigners consequent on the country's divisive and alienating apartheid past.[10] On this, Mutanda suggests that "xenophobic violence in South Africa existed before the end of the Apartheid in 1994."[11] Mangu rightly observes that "under Apartheid in South Africa, being black, coloured and to some extent, Indian was considered a 'crime against humanity.' It is now a crime to be a foreigner or a migrant, especially a black migrant from an African country."[12] Other studies[13] note that xenophobic violence in South Africa can be linked to the history of nationalism/decolonization and the culture of crime and violence in the country. These supposedly have had a negative impact on the collective psyche of Black South Africans leading to utilizing violence as a form of conflict resolution strategy.[14] This view could be understood against the backdrop of Fanon's thesis on violence which points to violence as an instrument to bring about decolonization.[15] And, having been learnt as a strategy to achieve some desired change in the status quo, citizens have found it difficult to unlearn and have resorted to the use of violence as a conflict resolution tool.

Similar to the isolation theory is the view in extant literature that xenophobic violence could be related to the notion of South African exceptionalism.[16] Exceptionalism is the understanding "that South Africa can be likened to European countries and does not share similar characteristics with other African countries."[17] Related to this is the claim to autochthony, which has led South Africans to be intolerant of those considered to be non-natives.[18] The issue is that globalization and migration have necessitated the movement of people from one country to another for different socioeconomic and political reasons, a phenomenon which South Africans are apparently not used to. This also borders on identity politics which "holds that the cultural 'flows' that characterize globalization induce a state of hybridity, flux, and moral anomie that triggers the impulse to violently recreate social boundaries."[19]

Conversely, some South African politicians have taken the route of denial-ism and minimalism and have not agreed that there is a problem of Xenophobia in South Africa. This is evident in the views of Thabo Mbeki and later Jacob Zuma who during their times in office continually denied and minimized the facts surrounding the xenophobic attacks on mostly African immigrants.[20] The sentiment that attacks against foreign nationals in South Africa are not as a result of xenophobia but acts of criminality are captured in this statement by the former minister of International Relations and Cooperation, Maite Nkoana-Mashabane: "Cabinet is cautious not to label this violence as xeno-phobia because preliminary evidence indicates that these acts may be driven primarily by criminality."[21] Concerning this claim, it is central to understand that even though the South African government denies the attacks as xeno-phobic, they however do not deny that such attacks (which they attribute to criminality) are real and perpetrated against foreign nationals.

Maina et al. recommend ending the denialism and minimalism and that there should be an acknowledgment that xenophobia is a problem in South Africa so that adequate solutions be found to address the root causes of the problem.[22] For Tella an effective solution "requires a conscious and com-prehensive diagnosis of the manifestation of xenophobia at the individual, state and inter-state levels."[23] Hence, different solutions have been offered in extant literature toward addressing the problem of xenophobia in South Africa. The solutions have included a suggestion to address economic dispar-ity and problems of poverty in the country, toward ameliorating the problem of scarce resources, which has led to competitions between citizens and foreign immigrants.[24] Other solutions as found in literature have focused on government and policy-level interventions toward addressing the xenopho-bia problem. On this Lombard suggests enacting and employing policies and programs at the local government level toward reducing incidences of xenophobic attacks in the country's local communities.[25] Similarly, Muchiri proposes that a multidisciplinary approach comprising both legal and extra-legal measures is needed to address the problem.[26] Relatedly, some studies[27] have proposed the development and deployment of different continental and regional strategies to address issues of migration that impinge on the problem of xenophobia in South Africa.

The current chapter acknowledges the significance of the diagnoses of the problem of xenophobic violence in South Africa and agrees with the numerous solutions and suggestions proffered in extant literature toward combating the problem. The existing anti-xenophobic solutions and strategies indeed take into cognizance some of the sociopolitical *cum* economic causes, effects, and corollaries of the problem of xenophobia in South Africa. Conversely, this chapter takes another route to suggest a solution to the problem of xenophobia and violence in South Africa. The study envisages that perhaps it is central to foray into the area of African indigenous knowledge toward yet another solution that could appeal to the collective psyche of South Africans, to aid in smoothening their relationship with foreign immigrants. The strategy of suggesting African philosophical resources to combat the problem of xenophobic violence is by no means new as some studies[28] have also in different ways suggested the *Ubuntu* ideality as a resource to addressing the issue of xenophobia. This is important because, notably, the xenophobia problem goes against a central African philosophical ethos *Ubuntu* (belonging together, with its values of solidarity and cordiality) which has been touted as some of the founding values of the South African society. For Agyeno, "the reoccurrence of xenophobic violence in South Africa is due to the fact that the government has neglected mainstreaming the African *Ubuntu* philosophy into the fabric of social existence."[29] Against this backdrop, it is posited that it could be valuable to mainstream and utilize values from African philosophy/ indigenous knowledge systems toward responding to societal problems (like xenophobic violence) that face African countries. This will be further argued in the next section.

PHILOSOPHICAL PERSPECTIVES

The philosophical approach of this chapter could be understood as embedded in the agelong debate on whether or not there is such a thing as African philosophy. The debate was precipitated by the apparent racial prejudiced remarks by notable modern philosophers like Hume, Hegel, Kant, and so on. These Western thinkers argue that rationality and reflective thoughts are not synonymous with African people.[30] For example, Hegel in his thesis on universal history relegated Africa to the level of inconsequential and "Hume declares, in the essay on 'National Characters,' that blacks are incapable of eminence in action or speculation."[31] Kant's racial prejudice also comes to light when we look at his comments on the (in)capability of the Negro race to have rational thought. Eze in his *Colour of Reason* placed this in Kant's Anthropology and noted that for Kant the Negro race is full of passion, very lively, and talkative and vain and can only be trained or educated as servants (slaves); "the African, according to Kant . . . is 'exclusively idle,' lazy, and prone to hesitation and jealousy, and the African is all these because, for climate and anthropological reasons, he or she lacks 'true' (rational and moral) character."[32] Against the backdrop of these racial remarks presenting a picture that says Africans are incapable of rational thought and philosophy, some African scholars have risen in defense. Nwosimiri affirms that "the philosophical writings of some modern philosophers like Hume, Kant, and Hegel aroused psychological defensiveness by most modern African intellectuals when they came across intellectual racial discrimination and anti-African prejudices."[33]

Some of the earliest known defense of African philosophy can be seen in the works of Placide Tempels, who argues in his *Bantu Philosophy* that Africans do indeed have a system of philosophy. For Tempels "all the customs of the Bantu depend upon a single principle—knowledge of the inmost nature of beings, that is to say, upon their ontological principle."[34] In this principle (Vital Force) lies the existence of things, knowledge of being, and the realm of myth or mystery. Tempels could be said to lead the strand of African philosophy known as Ethno-philosophy. According to Ethno-philosophers, a "genuine African philosophy consists . . . of descriptive comments on ethnological concepts of time, ethics, personhood and general cosmology."[35] The position of Ethno-philosophers, especially the thoughts of Tempels, has been criticized by some contemporary African thinkers majorly because of the perception that the school of thought is not critical enough. Hountoundji is of the view that Ethno-philosophy is uncritical and lacking in logic and cannot qualify as a form of philosophy on its own.[36] For "ethno-philosophy is as stiff as the dogmas it propagates. While pretending to rehabilitate African culture, Ethno-philosophy works not at revealing veracious African thought but at concealing it."[37] Hence, as a reaction against Ethno-philosophy, Professional Philosophy rose as a trend in African philosophy. For Professional Philosophers, "African philosophy is philosophy done by Africans whether it be in the area of logic, metaphysics, ethics, or history of philosophy and it is desirable that the works be set in some African context."[38] Hountoundji further argues that contrary to ethno-philosophers' presentation, philosophy has to be modern, scientific, and able to compete with Western thoughts with universalizable methodology and logic.[39]

The above critic forms the foundation of the entrance of this paper to the debate. In response, it is important to underscore that the history of human thought cannot be taken as a monolith. It can be argued that whatever body of knowledge we regard today as constituting "objective truth" must itself have originated from a particular context. For example, the history of Western philosophy reveals that philosophy and the concept of rational thought with its logic and method as embellished by modern philosophers could be traced to the thoughts of early Greek philosophers. It can then be further argued that the so-called rigorous and strict "logical" approach as understood in Western philosophy is itself rooted in the thoughts of a particular people (in this case the Greek). Hence, the question of what really constitutes objective truth subsists and could be said to be at the root of the debate between the logical positivist school and the constructivist school. Positivists/empiricists opt for an empirical, verifiable, and objective method to achieving knowledge.[40] For constructivists, knowledge is constructed and is essentially an active process dependent on time and context.[41] Notably, in the spirit of postmodern constructivism and the incredulity toward metanarratives that characterized the modern era, François Lyotard opted for what the author called little narratives; what obtains in the area of construction of knowledge is just people's understanding of things based on their perspectives.[42] This agrees with the "Positional objectivity" thesis which posits that "what we can observe depends on our position vis-à-vis the objects of observation."[43]

This article agrees that knowledge emerges and can be constructed from and based on peoples' understanding and contexts. As such, knowledge systems can emerge from a particular set of people depending on their worldview and indeed their ethnic, cultural, and religious thoughts and concepts. Notably, a central criticism against the position of the Professional African philosophy school concerns their focus on modern Africa thus inadvertently relegating into antiquity traditional African thoughts and values. On this, the most profound criticism was offered against Hountoundji by Ruch in his book *African Philosophy*. As already stated, Hountoundji does not agree with Tempels that traditions, myths, and beliefs should form part of African philosophy. Ruch agrees that a sole focus on ancient mythical beliefs is not sufficient to establish African philosophy; however, if people do not want to lose their identity, they must connect with their past.[44] Also, for Ruch, "if African philosophy is not a creation *ex nihilo*, it must know, use and critically sift the patrimony of ideas, thoughts beliefs and even actions of past generations."[45] Thus, traditional African thoughts, ideas, sayings, and belief systems could constitute the contents of philosophy.[46] Agreeably, Mbiti is of the view that African philosophy is in essence religious philosophy as it focuses on "religious practices, folktales, proverbs and myths."[47] Notably, here philosophy is not as construed in Western positivistic sense as a rigorous, critical, and scientific enterprise, rather philosophy becomes intuitive, figurative, un-theorized, and analogical. Philosophy is hence not only scientific but also an art in which is located the concept of "mythical consciousness." This is the first form of philosophizing as seen with early Greek thinkers and "is a concrete, existential and actively lived conception of being as a whole, which affirms the fundamental unity and harmony between man and the universe in which he lives."[48] African philosophy as such is also post-scientific because it tends to focus on areas that are beyond the scope of scientific reasoning including ethics, values, moral options, and practical choices.[49]

Against the backdrop of the above perspectives, this study links the African Ethno-philosophy and constructivist paradigms and theorizes on how to curb the spate of xenophobia and violence in South Africa. Significantly, this paper forays into the philosophical thoughts of the people of Eswatini, focusing on the philosophico-ethical concept of *live liyengcayelwa*. The concept is proposed as an aspect of the collective knowledge of African indigenous people, which could serve as a utility to understanding human relations and as such help in addressing the issue of xenophobia and violence in South Africa. Notably, the South African society also prides itself to be the custodian of another African philosophical concept *Ubuntu*.[50] *Ubuntu* as an African philosophico-ethical concept allows us to understand the importance of the other in the African worldview.[51] On its own *liveliyengcayelwa* goes beyond the prescriptions of the *Ubuntu* concept to underscore the importance of respect for all beings, starting with the respect for life.

LIVE LIYENGCAYELWA AS A PHILOSOPHICO-ETHICAL RESOURCE TO ADDRESSING RECURRING XENOPHOBIC TENSIONS IN SOUTH AFRICA

Conceptualizing *Live Liyengcayelwa* as an African Ethical Concept

The phrase *live liyengcayelwa* is made up of two Siswati words "live" (which could denote earth, land, a country, place, or territory) and "liyengcayelwa" (which means respect or care). The phrase as such could be understood as translating to "respect the earth/land," "respect where you go." The controlling word in this phrase is the word *liyengcayelwa*—respect. According to the Swati understanding, people say *kwengcayela* which is an instruction to tread carefully around certain places. For example, the word is used to advise people to tread carefully while walking barefooted through a thorny path. Here the words "respect" and "carefulness" converge and as understood in the concept of *live liyengcayelwa*, people are advised to show respect and to thread carefully around all beings.

The above etymological explication allows us to understand how the concept *live liyengcayelwa* could be seen as an African ideologico-ethical concept. The concept is very central to the relationship between people in traditional authority and the ordinary people. According to Swati tradition, high-ranking officials and decision-makers are known to go out and mingle with the common people, and there was a need for them to understand that they should carry with them the value of respect for everybody they interact with wherever they go. This means that when they are with the common masses they should not presume to lord it over the people and carry themselves with arrogance amid the masses. The instruction *live liyengcayelwa* as such creates the ethical awareness among those with power that they should tread carefully and respect people where they go since, despite their power and influence, they might still need the common people. In this also is embedded the understanding of the call to everyone to behave ethically and any human interaction should be done with care and respect despite people's socioeconomic standing. As noted by

Magagula, "*live liyengcayelwa. Kufanele kutsi letinye tintfo utihloniphele labanye noma tingakuhluphi wena.*"[52] This could be translated thus: "In other things, have respect for others even when they are not important to you or even when they are of no value to you."

Furthermore, *live liyengcayelwa* could be seen as grounding the prescripts of traditional and customary laws among the people. In this, there is an understanding that the land must be given respect and cared for by any being beneath and above the land. As such *live liyengcayelwa* ethos grounds the peaceful coexistence and cordial relationship between peoples. By extension, it also means that people should value and treat the environment with care and respect since they constitute part of life. This as we recall links to Ruch's view of African understanding of mythical consciousness which emphasizes the fundamental unity and harmony between humans and the cosmos.[53] Hence, for the Swati people, traditional and customary laws are geared toward ensuring that every individual abides by all natural laws that regulate the relationship between peoples and their interaction with the wider cosmos. This indeed is realized through and guided by the spirit and ethos of the saying *live liyengcayelwa*. Relatedly, the *live liyengcayelwa* ethico-ideological concept could be applied to the broader effort to get people to help build the nation. *Live* as a nation and country is understood here as integral to the existence of the people who live in it, and as the nation has the responsibility to care for the people, the people also have the duty to respect and build the nation through carrying out their duties and responsibilities. In this, the *live liyengcayelwa* ethos is used to encourage people to build up the nation and its reputation based on the responsibilities people hold among themselves and the duty to be kind, to show respect and to care for all that is within the nation.

Live Liyengcayelwa in the Light of Xenophobic Tensions in South Africa

Against the backdrop of the above explications, this chapter proposes *live liyengcayelwa* as an ethical resource toward responding to xenophobic tensions in South Africa. *Live liyengcayelwa* becomes important from two injunctive vantage points which are the respect for human lives/dignity and the respect for the land.

From the conceptualization, it can be seen that the *live liyengcayelwa* ethos allows people to coexist in an understanding of mutual respect and this arguably is important in the effort to curb xenophobic violence in South Africa. Notably, a central aspect of this ethic of respect is the respect for human lives. *Live liyengcayelwa* allows us to understand that in stripping people of their dignity and taking people's lives, we go against the fundamental understanding of unity and harmony among all creatures, which is part of the African understanding of mythical consciousness.[54] In abiding by the *live liyengcayelwa* ethos we agree to the value of respect of all beings especially the respect for the sanctity of human life and the respect of human dignity. This means that the desire to hate and exterminate foreigners (for whatever possible cogent sociopolitical and economic reason) can only be seen as going against this African ethos. The argument is that what should come first is the fact that people are human beings before they are part of any geographical location and or artificial border. On this, it can be further argued that artificial borders which now separate African peoples are also a problem. It will seem that because of these borders, people who happen to fall out of a geographical space have been regarded by natives and indigenes as "the others" and possibly seen as less than human. Hence Duffield rightly observes that "the South African paradox is between an internal identification based on liberal universalism and the ambiguous social boundary of autochthony, which is diametrically opposed to African humanism or a human rights culture."[55] Consequently, foreigners are beaten, dehumanized, and killed during xenophobic flare-ups, an action which reveals that perhaps the perpetrators have lost sight of the ethos of *Ubuntu* and the value of respect for the sanctity and dignity of human life which can be inferred from the live liyengcayelwa ethos. As the Swati say, *"Kufanele kutsi letinye tintfo utihloniphele labanye noma tingakuhluphi wena";*[56] respecting people even when they are not important or valuable to you means that citizens should respect people despite where they come from or the country they are born into. Also, for the Swati, those in traditional authority should learn to respect the commoner wherever they go as part of the *live liyengcayelwa* injunction. Hence those who see themselves as having the right to exercise authority and power in a place should understand that they might need others when they leave their areas of influence. This is actually instructive and advises that those who consider themselves as citizens who have rights should be aware that they can also be foreigners in another land in the future.

Secondly, in the live liyengcayelwa ethos there is also a call that people should respect the earth including all above and beneath it. It all comes down to the Swati instruction *kwengcayelwa* to tread carefully around certain places. This also means for there to be a solution to the issue of xenophobic violence in South Africa, the visitors also need to learn to respect the land that hosts them. This becomes important in the face of the numerous allegations of crime perpetrated by foreigners in South Africa. South Africans sympathetic to the call that foreigners should go back to their country give numerous reasons which include the fact that foreigners from different countries have been complicit in drug dealing, human trafficking, and all forms of organized crimes, thus constituting security challenges for the country from different documented sources.[57] Hence the outrage of the citizens could be understood since as we say in Africa "nobody would be happy to sit and watch as his house is razed by fire." The degradation of cities and townships through different acts of crime is a degradation of the land and this is what *live liyengcayelwa* preaches against. It does not matter who has been identified as complicit in these acts of criminality (since we cannot also deny that there are citizens who may be complicit in these acts of crime), *live liyengcayelwa* calls on people to respect the land. Respecting the land means that foreigners in South Africa should desist from criminal acts since through these they are desecrating the land that hosts them. The call for mutual respect as proposed by the *live liyengcayelwa* ethos also demands that the respect for foreigners is earned when they in turn respect citizens and their land. In addition, respect for the land means the respect for the properties owned by foreigners and desisting from all forms of destruction of property and businesses owned by people from other countries. Respecting the land could also be interpreted as understanding that the economic resources from the land belong to all and could be benevolently shared by all who live on the land. As such, the issue of economic resources competition which also impinges on xenophobic tensions in South Africa could be arguably attenuated when people understand this and learn to accommodate and share. This is not in any way arguing that the constitutional rights belonging to citizens should be denied and given to non-natives; rather this should be understood in the spirit of the same constitution which asserts in its preamble that "South Africa belongs to all who live in it." That stipulation was echoed severally by one of the founding fathers of South African democracy, Nelson Mandela; one would further argue was borne out of the understanding of the spirit of Ubuntu and *live liyengcayelwa*. Ultimately as can be deduced from the *live liyengcayelwa* ethos, it is the land that owns all that live on it and there is a need to respect the land and to value mutual respect.

CONCLUSION

The stated dream of the founding fathers of South Africa's democracy was to build a rainbow nation in which all who live in it will find a home, where they are treated equally and with respect. It will however seem that the continuous resurgence of xenophobic violence in the country has put a hiatus to this dream, leading to a possible scenario in which the rainbow in the so-called rainbow nation is fading out. Building on extant literature, this study takes another route to suggest a solution to the problem of xenophobia and violence in South Africa. The study envisages that perhaps it is central to foray into the area of African indigenous knowledge toward finding a nonviolent and ethical solution that can appeal to the collective psyche of South Africans, to help their relationship with foreign immigrants. This is so considering that this continuous resurgence of xenophobic attacks and violence goes against the *Ubuntu* value which Africans hold in esteem. To overcome this and as such establish a basis for mutual coexistence of people in the spirit of *Ubuntu*, this study suggests mainstreaming the Swati principle *live liyengcayelwa* as an African philosophical resource toward fostering mutual respect between South African nationals and foreigners. *Live liyengcayelwa* as a philosophico-ethical concept encourages people to build up the nation and its reputation through the responsibility and duty to be kind, to show respect, and to care for all that is within the nation. It is envisaged that following this ethos will go a long way to conscientize both South African citizens and foreign nationals to learn to coexist in mutual respect thus realizing the stated dream of a rainbow nation.

NOTES

1. Oboshi Agyeno, "Xenophobic Violence and the African Philosophy of Ubuntu in South Africa." *African Journal of Democracy & Governance*, 6, no. 1 (2019): 25.

2. Michael Neocosmos, "The Politics of Fear and the Fear of Politics: Reflections on Xenophobic Violence in South Africa." *Journal of Asian and African Studies* 43, no. 6 (2008): 586–594; Michael Neocosmos, *From "Foreign Natives" to "Native Foreigners": Explaining Xenophobia in Post-apartheid South Africa* (Dakar: CODESRIA, 2010); André Mangu, "Xenophobia and Migration in Post-Apartheid South Africa: Myths and Realities." *Journal of Democracy & Governance*, 6, no. 1 (2019): 45; Agyeno, "Xenophobic Violence."

3. Kunle Adebajo, *DATA: 309 Reported Killed, Over 100,000 Displaced Due To Xenophobia in SA Since 1994*, 2019. https://www.icirnigeria.org/data-309-reported -killed-over-100000-displaced-due-to-xenophobia-in-sa-since-1994/.

4. Mangu, "Xenophobia and Migration," 48.

5. Felicia Lombard, "Policies and Programmes to Reduce Xenophobic Violence against Black African Foreign Nationals in South Africa: A Case Study of the City of Cape Town's Metro Police and Business Areas Management: 2008-2013," Master's Thesis, University of the Western Cape, 2015.

6. Rome Sigworth, Collet Ngwane and Angelica Pino, "The Gendered Nature of Xenophobia in South Africa," 2008. https://www.files.ethz.ch/isn/101368/Gender _Xenophobia_Dec08.pdf; Human Sciences Research Council (HSRC), "Citizenship, Violence and Xenophobia in South Africa: Perceptions from South African Communities," 2008. http://www.hsrc.ac.za/en/research-outputs/view/3853; Brij Maharaj, "Migrants and Urban Rights: Politics of Xenophobia in South African Cities," 2009. http://journals.openedition.org/espacepolitique/1402; Oluwaseun Tella, "Understanding Xenophobia in South Africa: The Individual, the State and the International System," *Insight on Africa*, 8, no. 2 (2016): 142–158; Clara D. Viltoft,

"Xenophobia and Intergroup Conflict: An Inquiry through the Concept of Health," Bachelor of Arts, Thesis, Malmö University, 2018, etc.

7. HSRC, "Citizenship, Violence and Xenophobia"; Mamokhosi Choane, Stella S. Lukong and Mandla Mthombeni, "An Analysis of the Causes, Effects and Ramifications of Xenophobia in South Africa," *Insight on Africa*, 3, no. 2 (2011): 129–114; Live Hågensen, "Understanding the Causes and the Nature of Xenophobia in South Africa: A Case Study of De Doorns" (Master's Thesis, Stellenbosch University, 2014); Gabriel T. Wose Kinge, "International Dimensions of Xenophobic Attacks on Foreign Nationals in South Africa" (Master's Thesis, North-West University, 2016); Damian, C. Ukwandu, "Reflections on Xenophobic Violence in South Africa: What Happens to a Dream Deferred?" *African Journal of Public Affairs*, 9, no. 9 (2017): 43–62; Champion Masikane C., Magda L. Hewitt and Joyce, Toendepi, "Dynamics Informing Xenophobia and Leadership Response in South Africa," *Acta Commercii*, 20, no. 1, (2020): a704; etc.

8. Christopher Claassen, "Explaining South African Xenophobia," *AfroBarometer Working Paper* no. 173 (2017): 1. http://afrobarometer.org/sites/default/files/publications/Documents%20de%20travail/afropaperno173_xenophobia_in_south _africa.pdf.

9. Jean Pierre Misago, Loren B. Landau and Tamlyn Monson, "Towards Tolerance, Law, and Dignity: Addressing Violence against Foreign Nationals in South Africa," 2009. https://www.atlanticphilanthropies.org/wpcontent/uploads/2015 /09/IOM_Addressing_Violence_Against_Foreign_Nationals.pdf; Hussein Solomon and Hitomi Kosaka, "Xenophobia in South Africa: Reflections, Narratives and Recommendations," *Southern African*, 5 (2013): 5–30; Shanta B. Singh, "'Voices from behind Bars': Xenophobia and Foreign Nationals Incarcerated in a South African Correctional Centre," *Alternation Special Edition*, 7 (2013): 215–240; Didier Ruedin, "Attitudes to immigrants in South Africa: personality and vulnerability," *Journal of Ethnic and Migration Studies*, 45, no. 7 (2019): 1108-1126; etc.

10. Lombard, "Policies and Programmes"; Jonathan Crush, "The Perfect Storm: The Realities of Xenophobia in Contemporary South Africa," 2008. http://samponline .org/wp-content/uploads/2016/10/Acrobat50.pdf.

11. Darlington Mutanda, "Xenophobic Violence in South Africa: Mirroring Economic and Political Development Failures in Africa," *African Identities*, 15, no. 3 (2017): 278.

12. Mangu, "Xenophobia and Migration," 48.

13. Nahla Valji, "Creating the Nation: The Rise of Violent Xenophobia in the New South Africa" (Master's Thesis, York University, 2003); Pumla Gqola, "Brutal Inheritances: Echoes, Negrophobia and Masculinist Violence," In Shireen Hassim, Tawana Kupe, and Eric Worby, E. (Eds.), *Go Home or Die Here: Violence, Xenophobia and the Reinvention of Difference in South Africa* (Johannesburg: Wits University Press, 2008), 209–224; Sally Peberdy, *Selecting Immigrants: National Identity and South Africa's Immigration Policies, 1910-2008* (Johannesburg: Wits University Press, 2009); Simon M. Kang'ethe and Vusumzi Duma, "Exploring Dimensions of Post-apartheid Xenophobic Sentiments towards African Immigrants in South Africa," *Insight on Africa*, 5, no. 2 (2013): 157–168; Jason Hickel,

"'Xenophobia' in South Africa: Order, Chaos, and the Moral Economy of Witchcraft," *Cultural Anthropology*, 29, no. 1 (2014): 103–127; etc.

14. Norman Duncan, "Reaping the Whirlwind: Xenophobic Violence in South Africa," *Global Journal of Community Psychology Practice*, 3, no. 1 (2012): 104–112.

15. Franz Fanon, *The Wretched of the Earth* (Harmondsworth: Penguin, 1967).

16. Deirdré Kruger and Razia Osman, "The Phenomenon of Xenophobia as Experienced by Immigrant Learners in Johannesburg Inner City Schools," *Perspectives in Education*, 28, no. 4 (2010): 52–60; Mario D. Matsinhe, "Africa's Fear of Itself: The Ideology of 'Makwerekwere' in South Africa," *Third World Quarterly*, 32, no. 2 (2011): 295–313; Nic Cheeseman, "South Africans Are Learning that They're Not That Exceptional After All," *The Conversation*, 2017. https://theconversation.com /south-africans-are-learning-that-theyre-not-that-exceptional-after-all-75884; Faith Mabera, "The Impact of Xenophobia and Xenophobic Violence on South Africa's Developmental Partnership Agenda," *Africa Review*, 9, no. 1 (2017): 28–42; Ellen Wagner, "Exploring Exceptionalism in Foreign Policy Discourses: How Can We Understand South Africa's Unconstitutional and Ineffective Withdrawal from the Rome Statute?" (Bachelor's Degree Thesis, Malmö University, 2020); etc.

17. Tella, "Understanding Xenophobia," 144.

18. Valerie C. Duffield, "Exploring the Discursive Nuances of the South African Xenophobic Experience: Exclusionary Tactics and Tensions" (Master's Thesis, University of Cape Town, 2008); Timothy M Anderson, "Identity and Exclusion in Africa: An Examination of Autochthony and Xenophobia" (Honour's Degree Thesis, Ohio University, 2013); Laurent Fourchard and Aurelia Segatti, "Introduction of Xenophobia and Citizenship: The Everyday Politics of Exclusion and Inclusion in Africa," *Africa*, 85, no. 1 (2015): 2–12; Mary L. Casey, "Understanding Violence against Foreigners in Cape Town: Conceptions of Autochthony and Xenophobia in Post-Apartheid South Africa," 2018. https://cupola.gettysburg.edu/cgi/viewcontent .cgi?article=1802&context=student_scholarship; etc.

19. Hickel, "Xenophobia," 104.

20. Neocosmos, "The Politics of Fear"; Neocosmos, "Foreign Natives"; Jonathan Crush and Sujata Ramachandran, *Xenophobic Violence in South Africa: Denialism, Minimalism, Realism* (Cape Town: Southern African Migration Programmme, 2014); Mangu, "Xenophobia and Migration"; etc.

21. In Crush and Ramachandran, *Xenophobic* Violence, 9.

22. Grace Maina, Nonjabulo Mathonsi, Christy McConnell and Genevieve Williams, "It's not just Xenophobia Factors that Lead to Violent Attacks on Foreigners in South Africa and the Role of the Government," *Accord*, no. 005, March 2011.

23. Tella, "Understanding Xenophobia," 142.

24. Malemela A. Mamabolo, "Drivers of Community Xenophobic Attacks in South Africa: Poverty and Unemployment," *The Journal for Transdisciplinary Research in Southern Africa*, Special Edition, 11 no. 4 (2015): 143–150; Gideon R. Muchiri, "Xenophobia: A Critical Study of the Phenomenon and Pragmatic Solutions for South Africa" (Doctor of Law Dissertation, University of Pretoria, 2016); Isaac

Khambule and Babalwa Siswana, "How Inequalities undermine Social Cohesion: A Case study of South Africa," 2017. https://www.g20-insights.org/wp-content/uploads/2017/05/10_Inequality_How-Inequalities-undermine-Social-Cohesion.pdf; Ukwandu, "Reflections"; Claassen, "Explaining South"; etc.

25. Lombard, "Policies and Programmes."

26. Muchiri, "Xenophobia."

27. Paulin Mbecke, "Anti-Afrophobia Policy Shortfall and Dilemma in the New Partnership for Africa's Development and South Africa," *The Journal for Transdisciplinary Research in Southern Africa*, 11, no. 4 (2015): 71–82; Romola Adeola, "Preventing Xenophobia in Africa: What Must the African Union Do?" *The African Human Mobility Review*, 1, no. 3 (2015): 253–272; Mathew H. Tirivangasi and S.A. Rankoana, "South Africa and Xenophobia: Regional Peace Strategies for Xenophobia and Xenophobic Attacks Prevention," 2015. https://www.researchgate.net/publication/297734668.

28. Francis Nyamnjoh and Patience Mususa, "Migration and Xenophobia." In C. Saunders, G.A. Dzinesa, and D. Nagar (Eds.), *Region-Building Southern Africa. Progress, Problems and* Prospects (London: Zed Books, 2012); Kingsley Okoro and Chinyere Nkama, "Ubuntu Ideality: The Solution to Xenophobic Practice in South Africa," *World Journal of Research and Review*, 6, no. 3 (2018): 115–124; Mangu, "Xenophobia and Migration"; Agyeno, "Xenophobic Violence."

29. Agyeno, "Xenophobic Violence," 27.

30. Tsenay Serequeberhan, "Is There an African Philosophy?" In Tsenay Serequeberhan (Ed.), *African Philosophy: The Essential Readings* (New York: Paragon, 1991), 136.

31. Ovett Nwosimiri, "Do the Works of the Nationalist– Ideological Philosophers Undermine Hume's and Kant's Ideas about Race?" *Sage Open*, January-March (2017): 6.

32. In Emmanuel C. Eze, "The Color of Reason: The Idea of 'Race' in Kant's Anthropology." In Emmanuel C. Eze (Ed.), *Postcolonial African Philosophy A. Critical Reader* (Lewisburg: Blackwell Publishers, 1997), 116.

33. Nwosimiri, "Do the Works," 6.

34. Placide Tempels, *Bantu Philosophy* (Paris: Presence Africaine, 1959), 33.

35. Serequeberhan, "Is There," 137.

36. Paulin J. Hountondji, "Contemporary African Philosophy: The Search for a Method." In Tsenay Serequeberhan (Ed.), *African Philosophy: The Essential Readings* (New York: Paragon, 1991).

37. Lansana Keita, "Africa and the Imperative of Philosophy: A Skeptical Consideration." In Tsenay Serequeberhan (Ed.), *African Philosophy: The Essential Readings* (New York: Paragon, 1991): 191.

38. Didier N. Kaphagawani, "What is African Philosophy?" In Peter H. Coetzee and Abraham P.J. Roux (Eds.), *Philosophy from Africa: A Text with Readings* (Johannesburg: International Thomson Publishing, 1998), 96.

39. Hountondji, "Contemporary African."

40. Richard Creath, "Logical Empiricism," 2017. https://plato.stanford.edu/entries/logical-empiricism/.

41. Richard Fox, "Constructivism Examined," *Oxford Review of Education*, 27, no. 1 (2001): 23–35.

42. Jean-François Lyotard, *The Postmodern Condition* (Minneapolis: University of Minnesota Press, 1984).

43. Amartya Sen, "Positional Objectivity," *Philosophy & Public Affairs*, 22, no. 2 (1993): 126.

44. E. A. Ruch, *African Philosophy: An Introduction to the Main Philosophical Trends in Contemporary Africa* (Rome: Catholic Book Agency, 1981).

45. Ruch, "African Philosophy," 13.

46. Odera Oruka, "Sagacity in African Philosophy." In Tsenay Serequeberhan (Ed.). *African Philosophy: The Essential Readings* (New York: Paragon, 1991).

47. In Serequeberhan, "African Philosophy," 87.

48. Ruch, "African Philosophy," 37.

49. Ibid.

50. Agyeno, "Xenophobic Violence."

51. Sunday P. C. Onwuegbuchulam, "Hell is Other People: A Critical Appraisal of Sartre's Notion of the Individual's Relation to the Other in the Light of the Notion of *Ubuntu*," *Journal of African Philosophy*, 9 (2014): 28–47.

52. H. M. Magagula, *Live Liyengcayelwa.* (Manzini: Longman Swaziland, 1995).

53. Ruch, "African Philosophy."

54. Ruch, "African Philosophy."

55. Duffield, "Exploring the Discursive," 31.

56. Magagula, *"Live Liyengcayelwa."*

57. Albuquerque A. Nazare, "The Impact of International Migration on Security and Stability," *Canadian Foreign Policy Journal*, 4, no. 1 (1996): 83; Agyeno, "Xenophobic Violence."

REFERENCES

Adebajo, Kunle. *Data: 309 Reported Killed, Over 100,000 Displaced Due To Xenophobia in SA Since 1994.* 2019. https://www.icirnigeria.org/data-309-reported -killed-over-100000-displaced-due-to-xenophobia-in-sa-since-1994/

Agyeno, Oboshi. "Xenophobic Violence and the African Philosophy of Ubuntu in South Africa." *African Journal of Democracy & Governance* 6, no. 1 (2019): 25–44.

Anderson, Timothy M. "Identity and Exclusion in Africa: An Examination of Autochthony and Xenophobia." Honour's Degree Thesis, Ohio University, 2013.

Casey, Mary L. "Understanding Violence against Foreigners in Cape Town: Conceptions of Autochthony and Xenophobia in Post-Apartheid South Africa." 2018. https://cupola.gettysburg.edu/cgi/viewcontent.cgi?article=1802&context =student_scholarship

Cheeseman, Nic. "South Africans Are Learning that They're Not That Exceptional After All." *The Conversation*, 2017. https://theconversation.com/south-africans -are-learning-that-theyre-not-that-exceptional-after-all-75884

Choane, Mamokhosi, Stella S. Lukong and Mandla Mthombeni. "An Analysis of the Causes, Effects and Ramifications of Xenophobia in South Africa." *Insight on Africa* 3, no. 2 (2011): 129–114.

Claassen, Christopher. "Explaining South African Xenophobia." *AfroBarometer Working Paper* no. 173, 2017. http://afrobarometer.org/sites/default/files/publications /Documents%20de%20travail/afropaperno173_xenophobia_in_south_africa.pdf

Creath, Richard. "Logical Empiricism." 2017. https://plato.stanford.edu/entries/ logical-empiricism/

Crush, Jonathan. "The Perfect Storm: The Realities of Xenophobia in Contemporary South Africa." 2008. http://samponline.org/wp-content/uploads/2016/10/Acrobat50 .pdf

Crush, Jonathan and Sujata Ramachandran. *Xenophobic Violence in South Africa: Denialism, Minimalism, Realism.* Cape Town: Southern African Migration Programme, 2014.

Duffield, Valerie C. "Exploring the Discursive Nuances of the South African Xenophobic Experience: Exclusionary Tactics and Tensions." Master's Thesis, University of Cape Town, 2008.

Duncan, Norman. "Reaping the Whirlwind: Xenophobic Violence in South Africa." *Global Journal of Community Psychology Practice* 3, no. 1 (2012): 104–112.

Eze, Emmanuel C. "The Color of Reason: The Idea of 'Race' in Kant's Anthropology." In *Postcolonial African Philosophy A. Critical Reader*, edited by Emmanuel C. Eze. Lewisburg: Blackwell Publishers, 1997.

Fanon, Franz. *The Wretched of the Earth.* Harmondsworth: Penguin, 1967.

Fourchard, Laurent and Aurelia Segatti. "Introduction of Xenophobia and Citizenship: The Everyday Politics of Exclusion and Inclusion in Africa." *Africa,* 85, no. 1 (2015): 2–12.

Fox, Richard. "Constructivism Examined." *Oxford Review of Education,* 27, no. 1 (2001): 23–35.

Gqola, Pumla. "Brutal Inheritances: Echoes, Negrophobia and Masculinist Violence." In *Go Home or Die Here: Violence, Xenophobia and the Reinvention of Difference in South Africa*, edited by Shireen Hassim, Tawana Kupe, and Eric Worby, 209–224. Johannesburg: Wits University Press, 2008.

Hågensen, Live. "Understanding the Causes and the Nature of Xenophobia in South Africa: A Case Study of De Doorns." Master's Thesis, Stellenbosch University, 2014.

Hickel, Jason. "'Xenophobia' in South Africa: Order, Chaos, and the Moral Economy of Witchcraft." *Cultural Anthropology,* 29, no. 1 (2014): 103–127.

Hountondji, Paulin J. "Contemporary African Philosophy: The Search for a Method." In *African Philosophy: The Essential Readings*, edited by Tsenay Serequeberhan. New York: Paragon, 1991.

Human Sciences Research Council (HSRC). "Citizenship, Violence and Xenophobia in South Africa: Perceptions from South African Communities." 2008. http://www .hsrc.ac.za/en/research-outputs/view/3853

Kang'ethe, Simon M. and Vusumzi Duma. "Exploring Dimensions of Post-apartheid Xenophobic Sentiments towards African Immigrants in South Africa." *Insight on Africa,* 5, no. 2 (2013): 157–168.

Kaphagawani, Didier N. "What is African Philosophy?" In *Philosophy from Africa: A Text with Readings*, edited by Peter H. Coetzee and Abraham P.J. Roux. Johannesburg: International Thomson Publishing, 1998.

Keita, Lansana. "Africa and the Imperative of Philosophy: A Skeptical Consideration." In *African Philosophy: The Essential Readings*, edited by Tsenay Serequeberhan. New York: Paragon, 1991.

Khambule, Isaac and Babalwa Siswana. "How Inequalities undermine Social Cohesion: A Case study of South Africa." 2017. https://www.g20-insights.org/wp-content/uploads/2017/05/10_Inequality_How-Inequalities-undermine-Social-Cohesion.pdf

Kruger, Deirdré and Razia Osman. "The Phenomenon of Xenophobia as Experienced by Immigrant Learners in Johannesburg Inner City Schools." *Perspectives in Education*, 28, no. 4 (2010): 52–60.

Lombard, Felicia. "Policies and Programmes to Reduce Xenophobic Violence against Black African Foreign Nationals in South Africa: A Case Study of the City of Cape Town's Metro Police and Business Areas Management: 2008-2013." Master's Thesis, University of the Western Cape, 2015.

Lyotard, Francois. *The Postmodern Condition*. Minneapolis: University of Minnesota Press, 1984.

Mabera, Faith. "The Impact of Xenophobia and Xenophobic Violence on South Africa's Developmental Partnership Agenda." *Africa Review*, 9, no. 1 (2017): 28–42.

Maharaj, Brij. "Migrants and Urban Rights: Politics of Xenophobia in South African Cities." 2009. http://journals.openedition.org/espacepolitique/1402

Maina, Grace, Nonjabulo Mathonsi, Christy McConnell and Genevieve Williams. "It's Not Just Xenophobia Factors that Lead to Violent Attacks on Foreigners in South Africa and the Role of the Government." *Accord*, no. 005 March, 2011.

Mamabolo, Malemela, A. "Drivers of Community Xenophobic Attacks in South Africa: Poverty and Unemployment." *The Journal for Transdisciplinary Research in Southern Africa*, Special Edition, 11, no. 4 (2015): 143–150.

Mangu, André. "Xenophobia and Migration in Post-Apartheid South Africa: Myths and Realities." *Journal of Democracy & Governance*, 6, no. 1 (2019): 45–72.

Masikane, Champion C., Magda L. Hewitt and Joyce Toendepi. "Dynamics Informing Xenophobia and Leadership Response in South Africa." *Acta Commercii*, 20, no. 1 (2020): a704.

Matsinhe, Mario D. "Africa's Fear of Itself: The Ideology of 'Makwerekwere' in South Africa." *Third World Quarterly*, 32, no. 2 (2011): 295–313.

Mbecke, Paulin. "Anti-Afrophobia Policy Shortfall and Dilemma in the New Partnership for Africa's Development and South Africa." *The Journal for Transdisciplinary Research in Southern Africa*, 11, no. 4 (2015): 71–82.

Misago, Jean Pierre, Loren B. Landau and Tamlyn Monson. "Towards Tolerance, Law, and Dignity: Addressing Violence against Foreign Nationals in South Africa." 2009. http://www.atlanticphilanthropies.org/wp-content/uploads/2015/09/IOM_Addressing_Violence_Against_Foreign_Nationals.pdf

Muchiri, Gideon R. "Xenophobia: A Critical Study of the Phenomenon and Pragmatic Solutions for South Africa." Doctor of Law Dissertation, University of Pretoria, 2016.

Mutanda, Darlington. "Xenophobic Violence in South Africa: Mirroring Economic and Political Development Failures in Africa." *African Identities*, 15, no. 3 (2017): 278–294.

Nazare, Albuquerque A. "The Impact of International Migration on Security and Stability." *Canadian Foreign Policy Journal*, 4, no. 1 (1996): 83–109.

Neocosmos, Michael. *From 'Foreign Natives' to 'Native Foreigners': Explaining Xenophobia in Post-apartheid South Africa.* Dakar: CODESRIA, 2010.

———. "The Politics of Fear and the Fear of Politics: Reflections on Xenophobic Violence in South Africa." *Journal of Asian and African Studies* 43, no. 6 (2008): 586–594.

Nwosimiri, Ovett. "Do the Works of the Nationalist– Ideological Philosophers Undermine Hume's and Kant's Ideas about Race?" *Sage Open,* January-March (2017): 1–11.

Nyamnjoh, Francis and Patience Mususa. "Migration and Xenophobia." In *Region-Building Southern Africa. Progress, Problems and Prospects*, edited by C. Saunders, G.A. Dzinesa, and D. Nagar. London: Zed Books, 2012.

Okoro, Kingsley and Chinyere Nkama. "Ubuntu Ideality: "The Solution to Xenophobic Practice in South Africa."" *World Journal of Research and Review*, 6, no. 3 (2018): 115–124.

Onwuegbuchulam, Sunday P.C. "Hell is Other People: A Critical Appraisal of Sartre's Notion of the Individual's Relation to the Other in the Light of the Notion of *Ubuntu.*" *Journal of African Philosophy,* 9 (2014): 28–47.

Oruka, Odera. "Sagacity in African Philosophy." In *African Philosophy: The Essential Readings*, edited by Tsenay Serequeberhan. New York: Paragon, 1991.

Peberdy, Sally. *Selecting Immigrants: National Identity and South Africa's Immigration Policies, 1910-2008.* Johannesburg: Wits University Press, 2009.

Romola, Adeola. "Preventing Xenophobia in Africa: What Must the African Union Do?" *The African Human Mobility Review*, 1, no. 3 (2015): 253–272.

Ruch, E.A. *African Philosophy: An Introduction to the Main Philosophical Trends in Contemporary Africa.* Rome: Catholic Book Agency, 1981.

Ruedin, Didier. "Attitudes to Immigrants in South Africa: Personality and Vulnerability." *Journal of Ethnic and Migration Studies*, 45, no. 7 (2019): 1108–1126.

Sen, Amartya. "Positional Objectivity." *Philosophy & Public Affairs*, 22, no. 2 (1993): 126–145.

Serequeberhan, Tsenay. "Is There an African Philosophy?" In *African Philosophy: The Essential Readings*, edited by Tsenay Serequeberhan. New York: Paragon, 1991.

Sigworth, Rome, Collet Ngwane and Angelica Pino. "The Gendered Nature of Xenophobia in South Africa." 2008. https://www.files.ethz.ch/isn/101368/Gender _Xenophobia_Dec08.pdf

Singh, Shanta B. "'Voices from behind Bars': Xenophobia and Foreign Nationals Incarcerated in a South African Correctional Centre." *Alternation Special Edition,* 7 (2013): 215–240.

Solomon, Hussein and Hitomi Kosaka. "Xenophobia in South Africa: Reflections, Narratives and Recommendations." *Southern African,* 5 (2013): 5–30.

Tella, Oluwaseun. "Understanding Xenophobia in South Africa: The Individual, the State and the International System." *Insight on Africa,* 8, no. 2 (2016): 142–158.

Tempels, Placide. *Bantu Philosophy.* Paris: Presence Africaine, 1959.

Tirivangasi, Mathew H. and Rankoana, S.A. "South Africa and Xenophobia: Regional Peace Strategies for Xenophobia and Xenophobic Attacks Prevention." 2015. https://www.researchgate.net/publication/297734668

Ukwandu, Damian C. "Reflections on Xenophobic Violence in South Africa: What Happens to a Dream Deferred?" *African Journal of Public Affairs,* 9, no. 9 (2017): 43–62.

Valji, Nahla. "Creating the Nation: The Rise of Violent Xenophobia in the New South Africa." Master's Thesis, York University, 2003.

Viltoft, Clara D. "Xenophobia and Intergroup Conflict: An Inquiry through the Concept of Health." Bachelor of Arts, Thesis, Malmö University, 2018.

Wagner, Ellen. "Exploring Exceptionalism in Foreign Policy Discourses: How Can We Understand South Africa's Unconstitutional and Ineffective Withdrawal from the Rome Statute?" Bachelor's Degree Thesis, Malmö University, 2020.

Wose Kinge, Gabriel T. "International Dimensions of Xenophobic Attacks on Foreign Nationals in South Africa." Master's Thesis, North-West University, 2016.

Chapter 8

A Dangerous Denial

South Africa's African National Congress's Erroneous Characterization of Attacks on Foreign Nationals

Emmanuel Kasonde Matambo

Postapartheid South Africa was conceived in great expectation and optimism. Where some expected bloodletting between the long-suffering black South Africans and their previous oppressors, the negotiations leading up to the 1994 general elections went generally smoothly notwithstanding few blemishes. Nelson Mandela's magnanimity, after 27 years of imprisonment, toward apartheid apparatchiks gave the nascent democracy a moral character that was noted and respected the world over. However, the country's reputation in Africa and the world has been tarnished by spates of violent attacks on foreign nationals. Such attacks have been present from the end of apartheid, but they have grown in scope and ferocity in the new millennium—with 2008 being the worst in terms of death toll and displacement. The country is a popular hub of African migrants, some in flight from harrowing circumstances in their home countries, some pursuing a better education system, and some coming to seek economic opportunity. According to the United Nations Migration Report, the number of migrants in South Africa grew from one million in 2000, which was about 2.2% of South Africa's population to four million in 2017, which was 7.1% of South Africa's population.[1] The number of migrants approximately doubled between 2010 and 2017, from two million to four million.[2] This exponential growth occurred despite an increase in xenophobic sentiment in South Africa. The economic crisis in Zimbabwe and turmoil in the horn of Africa have been considerable contributions to this increase in immigration. Reasons for attacking foreign nationals vary; they include ingrained xenophobia that was partly forged by apartheid's racial and ethnic stratification, allegations of criminal activity by foreigners,

179

characterization of foreign nationals as threats to South Africa's public services and employment pool, and cultural hostility.

The African National Congress (ANC), South Africa's ruling party since 1994, has assumed a defensive and denialist position in its characterization of attacks on foreign nationals. Despite the plethora of evidence suggesting that some attacks on foreign nationals are driven by xenophobia, the ANC argues that these attacks are criminal rather than xenophobic. Furthermore, the ANC's failure to bring most of its population in the mainstream economy of the country has bred an antipathy to foreign nationals who are perceived as threats to South Africa's limited economic space. In *The Wretched of the Earth*, a book by Martinican scholar Frantz Fanon, a chapter titled "The Pitfalls of National Consciousness" presciently forecasts that if postcolonial or, in South Africa's case, postapartheid, leaders do not substantially change the lopsided economics of previous orders, then the perpetually disenfranchised citizens are likely to attack foreign nationals involved in small forms of industry to which citizens feel entitled. This happens mainly because the postcolonial elites merely replace the colonial elites but leave the unjust economic structure unchanged. In the same manner, citizens of a lower rung in society also want to dominate the space at their level in society and so foreign nationals who occupy that space are likely to be hounded out. It is noteworthy that, even though xenophobic sentiment permeates all levels of South Africa, its violent expression mainly takes place in low-income urban areas such as Alexandra in Johannesburg, where the failure of economic liberation after apartheid is more keenly observable.

The inequalities of apartheid in South Africa have remained largely intact, with only a small number of black South Africans inducted into the economic echelons of well-off white South Africans.[3] This, what Patrick Bond describes as class rather than racial apartheid,[4] has left most of black South Africans at the same socioeconomic station that they were confined to during apartheid. However, in lieu of confronting the ANC government for its failure to change the skewed nature of the economy inherited from apartheid, impoverished citizens project their frustrations on foreign nationals who then become the mistaken brunt of frustration. Unfortunately, this projection of the ANC's failure on foreign nationals suits the ruling party and insulates it from deserved culpability. While attacks on foreign nationals save the ANC from blame, they are also embarrassing for South Africa's international reputation and hence the government does all it can to mischaracterize the attacks and present them as something different, that is, as acts of criminality rather than xenophobia. This characterization is traced back to the ANC's response to the 2008 attacks, and it has now become a conventional ANC interpretation of attacks on foreign nationals.

The current chapter argues against the ANC's denialist position; while conceding that widespread violence and criminality play a part in attacks on foreign nationals, they do not, however, invalidate the argument that violence and criminality do not discount the existence of xenophobia in South Africa. Secondly, the ANC is caught between reining in a xenophobic citizenry and accepting blame for its economic failure, and its obligation to the safety of immigrants. In addition, statements made by some high-ranking members of the government have supported the narrative of many anti-immigrant South Africans who believe that immigrants are a burden on South Africa's resources. The denialist approach is also at odds with the reality that xenophobia is not an exclusively South African phenomenon; it exists almost in all societies. Arguably, Donald Trump's unexpected electoral victory in America in 2016 was due to his whipping up of anti-foreign sentiment among nationalistic Americans. The UK's withdrawal from the European Union was also partly due to increasing levels of immigration from non-European countries to Europe. South Africa's expression of xenophobia usually commands attention due to its violence and scope.

The first section of the chapter will outline a brief history of the ANC as a movement that was steeped in Pan-African ideals, a belief that there is a common history and a common destiny to which all Africans are inescapably bound. The shared history and destiny logically put Africans as one people and hence stand in stark contrast to intra-African xenophobia.[5] The section following that will be a brief recount of the ANC's decades as a proscribed and exiled movement that depended on international support, a significant portion of which came from Africa. That section partly forms the basis on which the ANC is loath to admit that its citizens are hostile to people from countries that helped accelerate the collapse of the apartheid edifice. Secondly, that section has also informed much of what other countries construe as South Africa's ingratitude for the suffering that African countries endured in their efforts to bring about the end of apartheid.

After decades of exile, the ANC was unbanned in 1990. It contested the 1994 general elections and became South Africa's main ruling party. Thus, the third section presents the ANC's attempt to transition from being a liberation movement to a governing party, while maintaining its pan-African moorings. Thabo Mbeki championed the idea of African Renaissance and renewal. In addition, the ANC government also sought to graft the ethics of Ubuntu onto the nascent government's internal and international politics. African Renaissance and Ubuntu drew inspiration from African history and ethics, which underscore the shared destiny of the continent and support a brand of politics couched on empathy, altruism, and interconnectedness. That section, again, helps one to understand why the ANC finds it difficult to simultaneously champion these lofty ideals and then accept that its people are actually xenophobic and perceive fellow Africans as threats and parasites.

The fourth section will then delve pointedly into the foreign national question since 1994 and how the ANC has responded. It will present the ANC's denialist approach and talk about the ANC's immigration and refugee legislation. The section will also be an outline of what could be termed extra-official realities about foreign nationals. The fifth section will be an analysis that will challenge the ANC's official perspective on the subject matter, a perspective described here and elsewhere as denialist. The analysis will rely on credible and empirical studies to controvert the ANC's dangerous, counterproductive, and irresponsible denialism.

THE ORIGINS OF THE ANC: A PAN-AFRICAN ORIENTATION

The ANC was founded on January 8, 1912. It was initially christened as the South African Native National Congress (SANNC). Its formation came a year before the adoption of the 1913 Lands Act, an egregiously crafted policy that put most of South African land in the hands of the white minority, to the disadvantage of black South Africans, who comprised the majority. Thus, the struggle for land restoration and the crusade for the rights of black South Africans have always been at the center of the ANC's struggle.[6] While the ANC had an executive leadership structure, it also initially had honorary presidents who were drawn from southern Africa, even from as far as modern-day Zambia.[7] This option demonstrated the solidarity that black people from colonial Africa felt toward minority rule in the southern Africa. It is telling that when the SANNC changed its name to become the ANC, emerging political parties in other parts of southern Africa also named themselves as ANC.

What the preceding illustrates is that the ANC's pursuit of independence and citizenship of black people was not initially confined to South Africa. The transnational nature of the ANC's struggle was also due to the economic and political influence that South Africa had in southern Africa. The country has historically been the hub of southern Africa's economy. The discovery of gold and diamond deposits in the late nineteenth century drew migrant labor from all over southern Africa. The migrant labor system was "central to the reproduction of the South African mineral-extracting industries over a century."[8] Bill Paton argued that labor immigration suited the desires of both mining and agricultural sectors, both labor-intensive sectors, that wanted the abundance of pliant and exploitable laborers who would not demand decent and high wages.[9] Desperate foreign laborers fitted this profile.

South Africa's geographic position was also strategic for the transportation of exports and imports from the region's landlocked territories. This created a dependency on South Africa that extends to this day. Not only on economic and strategic maters but even on political matters South Africa did much to shape the political situation of southern Africa. For example, after the end of the First World War, South Africa took charge of South West Africa (modern-day Namibia) and exercised influence on Bechuanaland (modern-day Botswana). These realities injected impetus in the ANC's regional rather than national orientation.

The racial stratification that compartmentalized South Africa was formally codified into law in 1948 when the National Party (NP) (dominated mainly by Afrikaner conservative nationalists) won a milestone election aided, as it were, by its promise of establishing a policy called apartheid. Literally meaning "apartness," apartheid, as Nelson Mandela put it, "was a new term but an old idea . . . [which] represented the codification in one oppressive system of all the laws and regulations that had kept Africans in an inferior position to whites for centuries."[10] Apartheid precipitated another, more militant, era in the ANC's history of struggle for the rights of native Africans. The formation of Umkhonto we Sizwe, the armed wing of the ANC, was the most radical embodiment of the emerging era of armed struggle.

It is noteworthy that at the time that the NP came to power, the ANC was not a proscribed movement. However, this changed in 1960 when protests led by the Pan-African Congress (PAC) turned violent and dozens of African protesters were mauled down by apartheid police. This was the first time when the rest of the world was conscientized to the extreme nature and brutality of apartheid. The occasion has come to be immortalized as the Sharpeville Massacre. The apartheid government reacted to the protests with violence and proscription of liberation movements including the ANC and the PAC. The South African Communist Party (SACP) had disbanded itself in 1950 after the NP formed government. The NP was a conservative white party, hostile to Jews (who had prominent roles in the SACP) and communism. A significant number of prominent ANC members was either exiled or imprisoned. The proscription of liberation movements set in motion another era of African solidarity.

THREE DECADES OF PROSCRIPTION AND EXILE: ANC AS BENEFICIARY OF AFRICAN SUCCOR

The 1960 ban of liberation movements was to remain in place for 30 years, up to 1990. During its decades as a banned movement, the ANC had to appeal for international solidarity for support to sustain its struggle. The exiled population included high-ranking members such as Oliver Tambo and Thabo

Mbeki, the armed wing Umkhonto we Sizwe, and some rank and file members. Stephen Ellis argues that

> it is no exaggeration to say that the ANC was in danger of extinction inside South Africa at one point, say from the arrest of the Umkhonto we Sizwe leadership at Rivonia in July 1963 until after the Soweto rising of 1976.[11]

Initially, the fortunes of the ANC in exile looked grim, too; the party was ill-prepared for clandestine activity, and its international connections beyond Africa were tenuous. These circumstances had at least two significant impacts on the ANC: The first was that it had to rely on the SACP's proven credentials of furtive activism. It also had to rely on the SACP to establish links with international players such as the Soviet Union and communist China, who were sympathetic to anti-colonial and anti-apartheid advocacy. The second impact the ANC's precarious existence had in exile is increasing dependency on independent African countries that offered both succor and ideological support. Countries like Angola, Botswana, Mozambique, Tanzania, Zambia, and Zimbabwe offered training grounds for the ANC's military wing and refuge for ANC members.

The southern African countries that helped exiled liberation movements from South Africa came to constitute what were known as Frontline States ranged against apartheid South Africa. Naturally, apartheid South Africa embarked on a campaign of destabilization in southern Africa under the framework of what it called the "total strategy." Douglas Anglin identified three strategies that apartheid South Africa used to try and secure the acquiescence of its neighbors. The first is what was called "transport diplomacy" which South Africa used against six of southern African neighbors that are landlocked. The second technic that it used was coercive diplomacy wherein Pretoria used some movements of African orientation such as UNITA in Angola and RENAMO in Mozambique to destabilize peace and economic progress in countries that supported liberation movements.

The third technic was direct military confrontation by South African defense forces (SADF), as happened in Angola. In May 1986, shortly before the Commonwealth Eminent Persons Group's final session with South Africa's president P. W. Botha, the SADF carried out assaults on Gaborone, Harare, and Lusaka, the three capital cities of Botswana, Zimbabwe, and Zambia respectively. South Africa's destabilizing campaign had telling impacts on southern Africa, a region that was already hampered by occasional drought and mounting debt. Mozambique seemed to have capitulated by signing the Inkomati Accord in which the country would cease to directly support liberation movements in exchange of South Africa's stopping its support for RENAMO. Nevertheless, the foregoing shows that majority-ruled southern Africa suffered in an array of ways due to its support of the liberation struggle. Naturally, this bred in some southern African mindset a sense of entitlement to South Africa's liberation after the end of apartheid rule in 1994. The ANC has also never forgotten its obligation to the region that was so significant in South Africa's liberation. It is thus discomfiting for the ANC to countenance the argument that attacks on African nationals are driven by xenophobia. In an attempt to end isolationism and imputed exclusivity from the rest of the African continent, the ANC, egged on by the efforts of Thabo Mbeki, the party's and country's president after Nelson Mandela (1997 to 2008), adopted African Renaissance as its rallying cry.

THE ANC IN GOVERNMENT: AFRICAN RENAISSANCE

Due to Mandela's reputation as a moral force and voice, and the configuration of the first postapartheid government, which included members from rival political parties, South Africa excited optimistic expectations from both Africa and outside the continent. Mandela sought to end South Africa's isolation of almost half a century, and some observers hoped that through his leadership and example, Mandela would transform South Africa from "from a pariah state to a role model for Africa."[12] Bill Clinton, who was America's president at the time Mandela became president, hoped that "if Mandela's reconciliation government succeeded, it could lift all of Africa and inspire similar efforts in troubled spots around the world."[13] Thus, Mandela's presidency could arguably be described as the country's honeymoon phase that attracted international goodwill, but great expectations, too.

When Thabo Mbeki took over as president in 1999, he sought to add economic pragmatism to the Mandela-era idealism but also to revive the centrality of Africa in South African domestic and external behavior. Thus, the term "African Renaissance" emerged as a central theme during the Mbeki years. Some aspects of African Renaissance dovetailed with Mandela's five years as president. For example, the policy to end South Africa's isolation had Africa as the priority. This was consonant with the primacy that African Renaissance gave to Africa. Mbeki spearheaded significant changes in Africa such as the transformation of the Organisation of African Unity into African Union, the establishment of the New Partnership for Africa's Development, theestablishment of the Pan-African Parliament and the African Peer Review Mechanism (APRM). Revealingly, the Pan-African Parliament and the APRM are both based in South Africa. Seen through these lenses, South Africa during Mbeki was reviving some aspects of Pan-Africanism which is logically at variance with intra-African hostility and xenophobia.

Apart from vaunting African Renaissance, South Africa evoked Ubuntu, an African value system that etymologically means "humanness." This value system highlights interconnectedness, empathy, altruism, and respect in human relations.[14] Ubuntu in a foreign policy or behavior context would mean that one African country's plight should be shared by kindred African countries. This would mean that South Africa's espousal of Ubuntu meant a feeling of responsibility and solidarity with other African countries. Muxe Nkondo has argued for the inclusion of Ubuntu ethics in (South) Africa's international relations, stating that when you espouse Ubuntu,

> the fact that you experience your life as bound up with the good for a certain community does not entail a stance of indifference, much less hostility, to outsiders. You may feel part of the South African community, but that does not mean that you should be indifferent to, say, the plight of the Sudanese in Darfur or in Southern Sudan.[15]

This, then, goes against hostility toward fellow Africans whose difficult circumstances sometimes drive them out of their native countries into South Africa.

Seen from the preceding information, the ANC has a history of Pan-African idealism that was forged at its inception and sustained through difficult years of exile when it relied on African solidarity. It is thus explicable that the ANC rejects arguments that attacks on African foreign nationals in South Africa are driven by xenophobia or what has become increasingly known as Afrophobia. The current chapter argues against ANC denialism of xenophobic elements in South African hostility and violence against other African nationals. However, the paper puts the ANC's denial in historical context. The ensuing sections will recount the ANC's quandary and how it is caught in between denying South Africans' xenophobia, but at the same recoiling from taking responsibility for the party's failure to provide basic services, economic development, and enough employment and reduce economic inequalities for an increasingly restless citizenry that takes out its frustrations on foreign nationals. In fact, according to the Gini coefficient, South Africa is one of the most unequal societies in the world. Regrettably, as figure 8.1 shows, the country's inequality has widened rather than shrunk since the end of apartheid.[16]

It is noteworthy that these alarming levels of inequality coincide with the ANC's feeble attempts to empower previously disadvantaged racial groups. Through initiatives such as Black Economic Empowerment, the ANC sought to implement a brand of affirmative action that would incorporate black South Africans into the mainstream economic structure of South Africa. Unfortunately, tokenism has infected these benign initiatives and only a

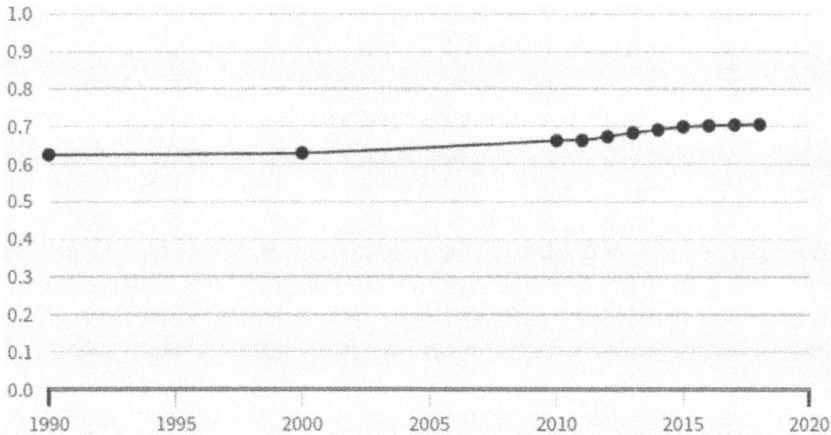

Figure 8.1 Inequality Trends in South African since 1990. *Source*: United Nations Development Programme, Human Development Reports. http://hdr.undp.org/en/countries/profiles/ZAF.

few politically connected black South Africans have enjoyed the trappings of economic empowerment. The rest of the long-suffering South Africans remain trapped in poverty and exclusion. It is in areas where impoverished black South Africans reside that violence against foreign nationals usually takes place. Thus, antipathy to foreign nationals combines with economic frustration and escalates into violence against immigrants in low-income locales of South Africa. Naturally, the ANC recoils from accepting responsibility for its failure to empower the previously disadvantaged who, in frustration, unleash their disillusionment on vulnerable foreign nationals.

THE ANC AND THE FOREIGN NATIONAL QUESTION: DENIALISM AND THE STATE-CITIZEN QUANDARY

The migration of southern Africans into South Africa is a long-standing reality. However, with the establishment of a postapartheid order, coupled with South Africa's growing prominence both politically and economically, the country started attracting migrants from as far afield as East and West Africa. The motivations for this increased migration include the pursuit of economic development and political and social respite from inauspicious conditions in home countries. The increasing number of foreign nationals brought to South Africans a new dynamic. The OECD noted that "the profile of migrants to South Africa, the sectors in which they have been hired and the reaction of the local population, recently reincorporated into the polity but still relatively marginalised socioeconomically, have been key challenges"[17] for the ANC government.

During apartheid and colonialism, many African migrants worked in the mining industry which confined their residence largely to mine quarters or hostels. The migrants that started coming after apartheid penetrated areas of South African economics that compelled them to interact with South Africans in townships. It is noteworthy that, during apartheid, Afrikaner nationalists sought to divide South Africans not only along racial lines but along tribal ones, too. For this reason, the creation of homelands and settlement areas compartmentalized South Africans to a great extent. The fact that South Africans were separated among themselves along tribal and racial lines made it difficult for them to interact with the growing number of migrants who were foreign not only on tribal but national lines as well.

Under such circumstances, anti-foreign sentiment became common among South Africans who shared their daily lives with an increasing number of African migrants. The biggest waves of attacks on foreign nationals happened in 2008, 2015, and 2019. A 2009 Human Rights Watch report stated that the 2008 widespread violence against foreign nationals "was indicative of growing xenophobia in South Africa, where isolated incidents of violence against foreign nationals have been documented since the mid-1990s."[18] The 2008 attacks came a few weeks before Africa Day which falls on May 25 of every year. In his Africa Day speech that year, Mbeki acknowledged that South Africa was commemorating this day with its head "bowed" because "the shameful actions of a few . . . blemished the name of South Africa through criminal acts against our African brothers and sisters from other parts of the continent, as well as other foreign residents especially from Asia."[19] He stated that the acts were against the urgent need for African renewal, and they were also at variance with the tenets of Ubuntu. He referred to the immense contributions that African labor has made to South Africa's economy. He also mentioned luminaries of South Africa's liberation such as Albert Luthuli, Thomas Nkobi, Joe Slovo, and Ruth First who had either foreign roots or spent part of their lives outside South Africa.

Significantly, Mbeki's Africa Day speech did not once mention the word "xenophobia" nor did he even brook the possibility that the attacks were partly ignited by anti-foreign sensibilities. He chose, rather, to characterize the attacks as criminal acts of a few South Africans. In a later speech, Mbeki maintained that the 2008 violence on foreign nationals "was not inspired by possessed nationalism, or extreme chauvinism, resulting in our communities violently expressing the hitherto unknown sentiments of mass and mindless hatred of foreigners—xenophobia."[20] Mbeki maintained his stance after leaving the presidency. During the commemoration of the APRM's 15th anniversary in 2017, Mbeki reiterated that "there isn't a population of South Africans who attack other Africans simply because of their nationality"[21] and that to label attacks on foreign nationals as xenophobic is to be simplistic and to miss the complexity of the issues involved such as competition for resources and the dearth of economic development in South Africa's townships. When challenged by Zambia's then ambassador to South Africa, Emmanuel Mwamba, Mbeki suggested a further meeting with African dignitaries but with a cynical comment that maybe they could teach him something he does not know about his own people. Mbeki's stance has become official wisdom for the ANC. During the 2019 xenophobic waves, which elicited unprecedented reactions and condemnation from the rest of Africa, the minister of International Relations and Cooperation, Lindiwe Sisulu called for a meeting with African diplomats in South Africa, while urging the police to act against the "criminal activities" without "fear or favour."[22]

While there is widespread anti-foreign sentiment in South Africa, violence against foreign nationals usually happens in low-income South African locales. When taken to urban areas, this violence occurs on foreign nationals involved in small-scale economic activity such as running tuck shops (locally known as spaza shops) or in the beauty industry such as small-scale hair salons. Foreign nationals with high levels of education, involved in areas such as academics and residing in relatively affluent or safe neighborhoods, could experience xenophobic attitudes but be spared of the violence meted out against immigrants that live in low-income, relatively unsafe, areas. The OECD report cited earlier gave a positive picture on the impact of immigrants on South Africa's labor market, economic growth, and public finance because it emphasized the high education levels of immigrants, the comparatively high taxes that they pay, and the critical skills that they introduce into the South African labor market. However, the circumstances of foreign nationals that usually suffer xenophobic violence are not so auspicious. Finally, in December 2019, South Africa's Department of Home Affairs published government regulations that enable implementation of the Refugees Amendment Act, effective January 1, 2020. Freedom House has criticized the refugee amendment for drastically limiting the rights of refugees and asylum seekers in South Africa. According to the new regulations, refugees could forfeit their refugee status if they participate in any political activity pertaining to their countries of origin. This effectively thwarts refugees from objecting to abuses in the countries from which they have fled.

The current legislation contradicts South Africa's Bill of Rights which expressly bequeaths the rights to opinion, expression, and association upon everyone. Critics of the new regulation have argued that, during apartheid, South African exiles and refugees were crucial toward forcing political change in South Africa. Hence, one would expect that the country would offer support to politically active refugees, provided they do not resort to illegal acts that could jeopardize South Africa's security. Thus, the current constraints deny refugees and asylum seekers the same opportunities that pushed for human rights in South Africa during apartheid.

Even more sinister in the amended refugee act is the threat that refugees who seek consular help from their embassies in South Africa could lose their refugee status. The dreadful implications of this condition are that refugees would not be allowed to ask for documents such as academic accreditation documents that could help them to look for employment commensurate with their qualifications. Refugees would also be prevented from asking for documents such as birth and marriage certificates which their native countries might be able to provide. These conditions arguably point to how the South African government seeks to limit the activity of immigrants residing in South Africa. The subtle limitations are not as crude as violent attacks on foreign nationals, but they nevertheless hint at a subliminal hostility to foreign nationals.

ANC'S DENIALISM AGAINST EMPIRICAL ANALYSIS

Attacks on foreign nationals in South Africa usually take different forms, from pejorative descriptions and labeling, police-sponsored harassment, looting and burning of businesses, physical attacks, to murder. The impulse to attack foreign nationals stems from a confluence of issues, such as a habitual dislike of foreign nationals, xenophobia to use the parlance of this chapter, the dearth of economic opportunities for impoverished South Africans, and the inadequacy of service delivery by the South African government. The main thrust of the chapter has been that while the ANC is discomfited by attacks on foreign nationals residing in South Africa, it is loath to accept that South Africa is xenophobic; the ANC is also reluctant to concede that its failure to provide basic necessities for its citizens usually drives impoverished citizens into attacking foreign nationals. In this case, foreign nationals become the brunt of hostility that should be correctly directed at the ANC government. The ANC has taken a position that Jonathan Crush and Sujata Ramachandran have described as a denialist approach. This position "reject[s] the argument that xenophobia plays any role in violence against migrants and refugees."[23] The ANC is a nationalist movement that has a pan-African bent in its orientation. As stated earlier, it had a wide reach in southern Africa at its inception, and during its decades as an exiled and internally banned movement, it relied on African solidarity and material support. For this reason, the ANC shrinks from accommodating the notion that South Africans could turn against the Africans whose countries were pivotal to the condemnation and isolation of apartheid South Africa. Affected African countries have also pointed to the

ANC's one-time dependency on the rest of Africa as a basis on which African nationals should not be persecuted in South Africa.

ANC denialism has been challenged by empirical studies such as the one cited from Crush and Ramachandran and the 2009 report by the Human Rights Watch which stated that the ANC government's commitment to address the country's ills, including xenophobic violence, "is inadequate."[24] A 2019 study by Pew Research Center established that more than half of South Africans blame foreign nationals for unemployment, increase in acts of terrorism, and crime (figure 8.2).

In addition, some members of the ANC, such as Aaron Motsoaledi, the current minister of home affairs in South Africa, have made comments that fuel anti-foreign sentiment; in 2018, Motsoaledi, then as minister of health, argued that foreign nationals burden the health sector in South Africa and that "when they get admitted in large numbers, they cause overcrowding [and] infection control starts failing."[25] In typical ANC fashion, though, Motsoaledi prefixed these remarks by saying that they had "nothing to do with xenophobia."[26] Apart from accusing foreign nationals of threatening South Africans'

Most South Africans hold negative views toward immigrants in their country

% who say that immigrants in South Africa today ...

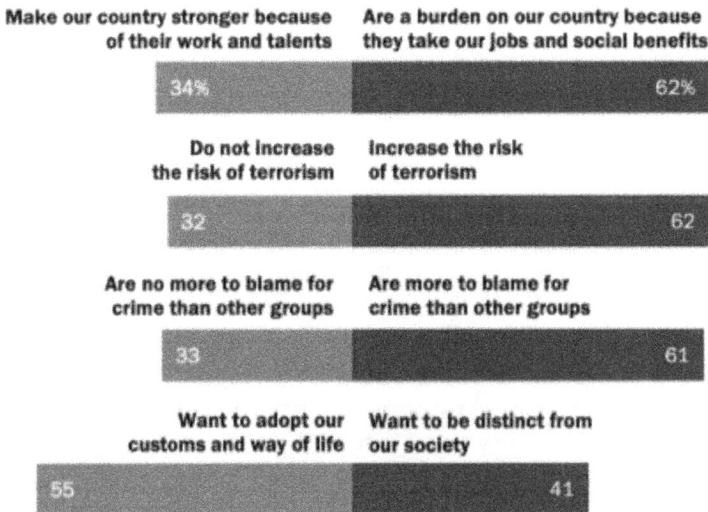

Make our country stronger because of their work and talents	Are a burden on our country because they take our jobs and social benefits
34%	62%

Do not increase the risk of terrorism	Increase the risk of terrorism
32	62

Are no more to blame for crime than other groups	Are more to blame for crime than other groups
33	61

Want to adopt our customs and way of life	Want to be distinct from our society
55	41

Figures 8.2 "Most South Africans Hold Negative Views toward Immigrants in Their Country." *Source*: Pew Research Center, Washington, D.C., May 3, 2019. https://www.pewresearch.org/fact-tank/2019/05/03/in-south-africa-racial-divisions-and-pessimism-over-democracy-loom-over-elections/ft_19-05-03_southafrica_mostsouthafricans_2/.

opportunities, some who accost foreign nationals do so on grounds that those they accost are illegal immigrants. The oblique implication of this is that legal migrants would not incur the ire of South Africans. There is a preponderance of evidence going against this logic. First, there is a specific department—home affairs—that should determine the immigration status of migrants. Mobs that attack foreign nationals do not bother, nor are they allowed, to demand documentation from foreign nationals. In addition, there have been calls for the expulsion of all foreign nationals whether legal or otherwise. In 2020, there was a trend on twitter, called #PutSouthAfricaFirst, that was championed by an unverified account under the name of Lerato Pillay. This trend called for the indiscriminate removal of all immigrants, thereby exposing a general anti-foreign sentiment, not born out of criminality.

The denialist position of the ANC has been prompted by a number of factors. First, this position became prominent following the May 2008 xenophobic attacks that were the first to claim global attention. The attacks also claimed more than 60 lives and sent thousands of foreign nationals outside the country while some were internally displaced. It is noteworthy that more than 20 of the victims were in fact South African; some of the South African fatalities were victims of mistaken identity, thought to fit some stereotyped images of foreign nationals. Preconceived ideas of what foreign nationals look like have conjured up images of the racial classification that was a notorious method that the apartheid regime used to categorize South Africans according to different races. That this still happens between South Africans and their perceived foreign threats controverts the ANC's denialism.

Thabo Mbeki, who was South Africa's president at the time of the 2008 attacks, led the denialist approach by arguing that the attacks were not xenophobic. Understandably, the ANC's approach on xenophobic attacks is informed by the party's seminal role after 1994 in forging some ideals of pan-Africanism through Mbeki's African Renaissance. Including Ubuntu as part of the driving forces of South Africa's international relations also goes against xenophobia, especially the brand that seems to disproportionately target African migrants. Mbeki argues that it is simplistic to describe attacks on foreign nationals as xenophobia. Ironically, this chapter has shown that it *is* simplistic for the ANC to describe the attacks on foreign nationals simply as criminal. While these attacks are partly prompted by economic pressure and the lack of employment, they are also prompted by visceral hostility to foreign nationals.

CONCLUSION

The chapter has argued that the ANC has taken a denialist approach to xenophobia because it is caught in a difficult quandary; admitting that some

South Africans are xenophobic or that the country itself is xenophobic might injure South Africa's standing in Africa and the world. On the other hand, the ANC, as a governing party, is reluctant to accept that attacks on foreign nationals are partly prompted by the ANC's failure to redress apartheid-era inequalities that have been detrimental to black South Africans. The only option it elects to characterize attacks on foreign nationals is that they are criminal acts. However, there is a plenitude of evidence suggesting that some fractions of South Africa are xenophobic. Furthermore, xenophobia is not consigned to impoverished South Africans who reside in low-income areas where violence against foreign nationals has been concentrated. Well-off South Africans, such as Aaron Motsoaledi who the chapter referred to, have uttered things that fuel ill-will toward foreign nationals. There are several steps that the ANC can take to reduce anti-foreign sentiment in South Africa. The first is to acknowledge the existence of xenophobia among some South Africans. Another step would be the improvement of governance in South Africa and effective implementation of economic empowerment. Improving the quality of education for previously disad-vantaged South Africans could incorporate the historically disadvantaged in more enduring ways and could bring them in the mainstream of South Africa's economy. A government that diligently provides basic services to its people, and tries to practice clean government, would go a long way to gnawing at the disenchantment that drives restive South Africans into attacking foreign nationals who are perceived as both the threats to basic services for citizens and usurpers of opportunities.

NOTES

1. United Nations Department of Economic and Social Affairs. *International Migration 2017*, 2017. https://bit.ly/3l2MAAK.

2. Christine Amir and Abby Budiman, *In South Africa, Racial Divisions and Pessimism About Democracy Loom Over Elections* (Pew Research, 2019). https://pewrsr.ch/398p6YD.

3. Michael Neocosmos, "The Politics of Fear and the Fear of Politics: Reflections on Xenophobic Violence in South Africa," *Journal of Asian and African Studies* 43, no. 6 (2008): 586–594.

4. Patrick Bond, "From Racial to Class Apartheid," *Monthly Review* 55, no. 10 (2004): 46.

5. Emmanuel Mwamba, "Zambia and South Africa Are Intertwined – Xenophobia Must Not Break that Bond," *Daily Maverick*, September 2, 2019, https://bit.ly/39bAVxi.

6. Stephen Ellis, "The ANC in Exile." *African Affairs* 90, no. 360 (1991): 439-447.

7. Thabo Mbeki, "Radio and Television Address to the Nation by the President of South Africa, Thabo Mbeki, on the occasion of Africa Day," 25 May 2008. http://www.dirco.gov.za/docs/speeches/2008/mbek0525.html.

8. OECD/ILO, *How Immigrants Contribute to South Africa's Economy* (Paris: OECD Publishing, 2018).

9. Bill Paton, *Labour export policy in the development of Southern Africa* (Basingstoke: Macmillan, 1995).

10. Nelson Mandela, *The Long Road to Freedom* (Randburg: Macdonald Purnell, 1994), 104.

11. Ellis, "The ANC in Exile," 439.

12. Colin Powell, *My American Journey* (New York: Random House, 1995), 596.

13. Bill Clinton, *My Life* (London: Hutchison, 2004), 263.

14. Bhaso Ndzendze, *Africa: The Continent we Construct* (Pretoria: Verity Publishers, 2015).

15. Muxe Nkondo. "Ubuntu as Public Policy: Challenges and Opportunities," *UJ Africa-China Occasional Paper*, No. 2 (Johannesburg: Confucius Institute, 2017).

16. United Nations, *World Social Report 2020: Inequality in a Rapidly CHANGING WORLD* (Department of Economic and Social Affairs, 2020). https://www.un.org/development/desa/dspd/wp-content/uploads/sites/22/2020/01/World-Social-Report-2020-FullReport.pdf.

17. OECD, *How Immigrants Contribute*, 40.

18. Human Rights Watch, South Africa: Events of 2008. 2009. https://bit.ly/3ft7FmS.

19. Mbeki, "Radio and Television Address."

20. Brand South Africa, "Mbeki Apologises for Attacks on Africans," July 4, 2008. https://www.brandsouthafrica.com/people-culture/democracy/xeno-040708.

21. Independent Online, "Mbeki Taken to Task Over Xenophobia Denials," *IOL*, March 10, 2017, https://www.iol.co.za/capetimes/news/mbeki-taken-to-task-over-xenophobia-denials-8121365.

22. BBC News, "Xenophobic Attacks Spark South African Response," *BBC*, March 31, 2019, https://www.bbc.com/news/world-africa-47765863.

23. Jonathan Crush and Sujata Ramachandran, *Xenophobic Violence in South Africa: Denialism, Minimalism, Realism* (Cape Town: Southern African Migration Programme, 2014): 1.

24. Human Rights Watch, South Africa, 2009.

25. SABC, "Foreign Nationals Are Burdening SA Health System: Motsoaledi" (2018). https://www.sabcnews.com/sabcnews/foreign-nationals-are-burdening-sa-health-system-motsoaledi/.

26. Ibid.

BIBLIOGRAPHY

BBC News. "Xenophobic Attacks Spark South African Response." *BBC*, March 31, 2019, https://www.bbc.com/news/world-africa-47765863

Bond, Patrick. "From Racial to Class Apartheid: South Africa's Frustrating Decade of Freedom." *Monthly Review* 55, no. 10 (2004): 45–59.

Brand South Africa. "Mbeki Apologises for Attacks on Africans." July 4, 2008. https://www.brandsouthafrica.com/people-culture/democracy/xeno-040708

Clinton, Bill. *My Life*. London: Hutchison, 2004.

Crush, Jonathan and Sujata Ramachandran. "Xenophobic Violence in South Africa: Denialism, Minimalism, Realism. Southern African Migration Programme (SAMP)." *International Migration Research Centre (IMRC) Migration Series* 66 (2014).

Ellis, Stephen. "The ANC in Exile." *African Affairs* 90, no. 360 (1991): 439–447.

Human Rights Watch. "South Africa: Events of 2008." https://bit.ly/3ft7FmS

Independent Online. "Mbeki Taken to Task over Xenophobia Denials." https://www.iol.co.za/capetimes/news/mbeki-taken-to-task-over-xenophobia-denials-8121365

Mandela, Nelson. *The Long Road to Freedom*. Randburg: Macdonald Purnell, 1994.

Mbeki, Thabo "Radio and Television Address to the Nation by the President of South Africa, Thabo Mbeki, on the Occasion of Africa Day," 25 May 2008. http://www.dirco.gov.za/docs/speeches/2008/mbek0525.html

Mwamba, Emmanuel "Zambia and South Africa Are Intertwined – Xenophobia Must Not Break That Bond," *Daily Maverick*, September 2, 2019, https://bit.ly/39bAVxi

Ndzendze, Bhaso. *Africa: The Continent We Construct*. Pretoria: Verity Publishers, 2015.

Neocosmos, Michael. "The Politics of Fear and the Fear of Politics: Reflections on Xenophobic Violence in South Africa." *Journal of Asian and African Studies* 43, no. 6 (2008): 586–594.

Nkondo. Muxe. "Ubuntu as Public Policy: Challenges and Opportunities." *UJ Africa-China Occasional Paper*, no. 2. Johannesburg: Confucius Institute, 2017.

OECD/ILO. *How Immigrants Contribute to South Africa's Economy*. Paris: OECD Publishing, 2018.

Paton, Bill. *Labour Export Policy in the Development of Southern Africa*. Basingstoke: Macmillan, 1995.

Powell, Colin. *My American Journey*. New York: Random House, 1995.

SABC, "Foreign Nationals Are Burdening SA Health System: Motsoaledi" (2018). https://www.sabcnews.com/sabcnews/foreign-nationals-are-burdening-sa-health-system-motsoaledi/

Tamir, Christine and Abby Budiman. *In South Africa, Racial Divisions and Pessimism About Democracy Loom Over Elections*. Pew Research, May 3, 2019, https://pewrsr.ch/398p6YD

United Nations. *World Social Report 2020: Inequality in a Rapidly Changing World*. Department of Economic and Social Affairs, 2020. https://www.un.org/development/desa/dspd/wpcontent/uploads/sites/22/2020/01/World-Social-Report-2020-FullReport.pdf

United Nations Department of Economic and Social Affairs. *International Migration 2017*, 2017. https://bit.ly/3l2MAAK

Part III

THE AFRICAN UNION AND XENOPHOBIA

IS PAN-AFRICANISM DOOMED?

Chapter 9

How Relevant is Pan-Africanism in Twenty-first Century Africa?

Steve Siziba

The concept of Pan-Africanism means different things to different people. For some, it recalls a precolonial past free of imperialist domination, and yet for others, it represents Africa's only chance to assert itself as an equal player in the world community of nations.

For South African poet and musician Mzwakhe Mbuli, in his popular track, "God Bless Africa," it may be viewed as a plea to bless the continent in favor of generations to come. Salif Keita from Mali also penned another well-known track *Africa* that also draws on the mystique of Africa, while Enoch Sontonga's "Nkosi Sikelel' iAfrica" (God Bless Africa) has been rendered in other languages such as Shona ("Ishe Komborera Africa") and Swahili ("Mungu ibariki Afrika").

However, beyond the divine and favor writ in Pan-Africanism, is there a bigger rationale for the concept in the twenty-first century? Some Afro-skeptics will argue that Pan-Africanism is nothing more than a romantic appeal for an unrealistic utopia long past its sell-by date. However, the coming into force of the African Continental Free Trade Area (AfCFTA), although the first day of open trade was delayed, is clear testament to the realization of the importance of African states coming together. Even the adverse impact of Covid-19 on economic growth, trade, and employment underlines the importance of ensuring that every Member State is on board. In the spirit of Pan-Africanism, none should be left behind in building resilience and renewal post-Covid-19.

PURPOSE AND STRUCTURE

This chapter acknowledges some of the obvious barriers to an integrated and developmental Africa such as weak governance, conflict, corruption, and muted political will.

However, it primarily seeks to thread the imperatives of union to show why Pan-Africanism is more relevant than ever. It briefly traces significant precolonial developmental trajectories, as well as the socioeconomic challenges wrought by the colonial experience. It then picks up the narrative from the inauguration of the Organization of African Unity (OAU) when President Kwame Nkrumah said,

> We all want a United Africa, united not only in our concept of what unity can connote, but united in our common desire to move forward together and dealing with all the problems that can best be solved only on a continental basis.

Almost three decades later, President Nelson Mandela echoed the same sentiment: "I dream of the realization of the unity of Africa, whereby its leaders combine in their efforts to solve the problems of this continent. I dream of our vast deserts, of our forests, of all our great wildernesses."[1]

In his world-famous classic, *Things Fall Apart*, Chinua Achebe dispassionately chronicles a slice of village life before the advent of colonialism.[2] While "things," as reflected in the lives of the dramatis personae are not always idyllic, the cadence of seasons and ancestral feasts, interspaced with intervillage wars, magic, and wrestling contests, define a kind of paradise which is shattered by the arrival of the white man, his religion, customs, and values.

While Achebe's narration is clearly around the change taking place in the main characters' Ibo village of Umuofia, things falling apart (e.g., governance and infrastructure) in modern-day Africa is a common talking point in the sense that the center failing to hold does so in a more dramatic and spectacular fashion, much to the disappointment and outrage of many Africans.

Writing on the subject of the relevance of Pan-Africanism in the twenty-first century, I am invariably drawn to the specter of things falling apart in Africa, and to ponder the question of whether the heady enthusiasm and optimism of a united and prosperous Africa is a dream that is too far-fetched, or whether the spirit of Pan-Africanism is precisely what is needed to begin to launch the continent on a developmental trajectory that will serve generations to come.

The paper seeks to review the concept of Pan-Africanism with a specific focus on its relevance for Africa in the twenty-first century. It starts by providing a physical geographic as well as socioeconomic context for the continent and then discusses the impediments to economic development and progress in Africa especially within the context of the much-vaunted united Africa dating back to the formation of the OAU which was transformed into the African Union (AU).

The chapter starts with an introduction followed by a brief discussion of the Pan-Africanism concept. It then focusses on the geographic, demographic, and economic context before zeroing in on the pros and cons of the AU as well as the strategic imperatives for such union.

CONCEPTUAL FRAMEWORK: DEFINITION AND HISTORY OF PAN-AFRICANISM

What Is Pan-Africanism?

Pan-continentalism is not unique to Africa. One of the most prominent examples of continent-wide union and cooperation is the European Union (EU) which began its life as the European Economic Community. Article 3 of the Lisbon Treaty defines the EU's raison d'être as being (a) the promotion of peace and the well-being of the Union's citizens; (b) an area of freedom, security, and justice without internal frontiers; (c) sustainable development based on balanced economic growth and social justice; (d) a social market economy—highly competitive and aiming at full employment and social progress; and (e) a free single market as well as to combat social exclusion and discrimination and promote social justice and protection, equality between women and men, solidarity between generations and the protection of children's rights.[3]

While definitions of Pan-Africanism are not identical, common themes in the definitions include the concept of Africans being united regardless of their location. Africans presently resident on the continent as well as those in the diaspora inclusive of recent migrants as well as those who trace their descent to Africans captured and traded as slaves winding up in different parts of the world but mostly in the Americas. Peter Kuryla refers to a Pan-Africanism where the peoples of African descent have common interests as the principal basis for their unification.[4]

Mashupye Herbert Maserumule observes that engagement around the question of whether Africa is really for Africans contributed to the development of the concept of Pan-Africanism and traces its development to such luminaries as slave trade abolitionist Martin Delany and Black Consciousness Movement proponent Robert Sobukwe.[5] Delany's "Africa for the African race and black men to rule them" idea infused all Africans' struggles against slavery, apartheid, colonialism, neocolonialism, and racism. Therefore, in this sense, Pan-Africanism is a sociopolitical worldview.

Dr. William Edward Burghardt Du Bois (W. E. B. Du Bois) is regarded as one of the fathers of modern Pan-Africanism. He was a leading African American intellectual who founded America's oldest and largest civil rights organization, the National Association for the Advancement of Coloured People. Also concerned with colonialism, Du Bois organized the very first Pan-African Congress in 1909 which called for an end to European domination.[6]

On the African continent, Kwame Nkrumah is regarded as one of the strongest proponents of the idea of Pan-Africanism as pivotal not only to the struggle for independence from colonial rule for African countries but also to the political unity of the continent into a kind of United States of Africa.[7]

At a social and political level, Pan-Africanism is therefore an idea that represents unity and integration meant to fundamentally change African society. In Nkrumah's words, Pan-Africanism "guides and seeks to connect the actions of millions of persons towards specific and definite goals" as a philosophy "based on the belief that Africans share common bonds and objectives" and that "advocates unity to achieve these objectives."[8]

At an early stage, even the formation of the OAU was informed by an underlying attitude of "unite or perish" and in the words of President Kwame Nkrumah,

> Unite we must. Without necessarily sacrificing our sovereignties, big or small, we can here and now forge a political union based on Defense, Foreign Affairs and Diplomacy, and a Common Citizenship, an African Currency, an African Monetary Zone and an African Central Bank. We must unite in order to achieve the full liberation of our continent.[9]

Years after the OAU morphed into the AU, the integration agenda is still among the priorities of the AU as exemplified by the consummation of the AfCFTA when 54 of the 55 AU nations ratified the Agreement.[10]

OUR AFRICA

Geographical Context

While many scientists may concur on the origins of mankind as being Africa, there are divergent views about where Africa as a reference to the entire continent comes from. Some associate Africa with the Greek word *aphrike* (no cold) or the Phoenician word *Afar* (dust) or the Latin word *Aprica* (sunny).[11]

Most of the African landmass lies within the 30-degree (North and South) parallels. The second largest continent on earth after Asia, it is bounded to the west by the Atlantic Ocean while to the south and east of the continent is the Indian Ocean while to the north and northeast the continent is bounded by the Mediterranean Sea and the Red Sea:[12]

Africa is home to a wide range of natural resources. Some of the top oil and gas producing countries are to be found on the continent.[13] Apart from oil and gas, Africa's natural resource bounty includes precious minerals, forests, timber, diamonds, gold, nickel, uranium, iron ore, graphite, titanium, platinum, phosphates, copper, and fish.

It is this resource base and Africa's population that constitute the potential for launching the continent on a growth and development trajectory that could address poverty, inequality, and unemployment on a massive and sustained scale.

Demographic and Economic Context

The continent of Africa has a population of around 1.4 billion and a combined GDP of US$3.3 trillion spread across the eight Regional Economic Communities (RECs) that are recognized by the AU. These RECs are the Arab Maghreb Union (AMU), Common Market for Eastern and Southern Africa, Community of Sahel–Saharan States, East African Community, Economic Community of Central African States, Economic Community of West African States, Intergovernmental Authority on Development, and the Southern African Development Community (SADC).

The RECs are building blocks with the context of the AU's development and integration agenda as mandated by the Abuja Treaty, the AU Constitutive Act, as well as the 2008 Protocol on Relations between the RECs and the AU: and the Memorandum of Understanding on Cooperation in the Area of Peace and Security between the AU, RECs, and the Coordinating Mechanisms of the Regional Standby Brigades of Eastern and Northern Africa.[14]

Using AU economic data for the different RECs in Africa shows a total GDP of US$3.3 trillion with an average per capita GDP of US$1,440 while the lowest REC per capita GDP of US$733 for CEN–SAD compared to the highest of US$3,647 for the AMU.[15] Table 9.1 presents details for the different RECs:

The variations across the RECs mask even wider variations within regions with, for example, Botswana and Malawi in the SADC Region having average GDP per capita of US$8,258 and US$389 respectively[16] (CountryEconomy.com 2020). It is instructive that Africa, with a combined population and land area that is at least six times bigger than the United States, has, comparatively, only 1/65 of the U.S. per capita GDP.

Although the picture is not uniform across or within RECs and AU Member States, unemployment and its intersection with inequality and poverty is among the most critical challenges facing the continent. The economic

Table 9.1   African RECs GDP and Population

REC	GDP (USD)	Population	Land Area	Estimated Per Capita GDP
East African Community (EAC)*	USD 188 billion	135 million	1.8 million km2	1 393
Economic Community Of West African States (ECOWAS)*	USD 623 billion	355 million	5.1 million km2	1 755
Economic Community Of Central African States (ECCAS)*	USD 204 billion	175 million	6.6 million km2	1 166
Community Of Sahel–Saharan States (CEN–SAD)*	USD 403 billion	550 million	13.8 million km2	733
Common Market For Eastern And Southern Africa (COMESA)*	USD 714 billion	406 million	12.8 million km2	1 759
Inter-Governmental Authority On Development (IGAD)**	USD 218.2 billion	247.4 million	5.5 million km2	882
Southern African Development Community (SADC)*	USD 621 billion	352 million	9.3 million km2	1 764
Arab Maghreb Union (AMU)*	USD 375 billion	102 million	6 million km2	3 647
Total	**USD 3.3 trillion**	**2.3 billion**		**1 440**

Source: (UNECA 2019)
*2019 African Regional Integration Report.
** https://www.uneca.org/oria/pages/igad-intergovernmental-authority-development.

exclusion created during colonialism has survived into the postcolonial era and while there may be success stories, the scenario can be related to the islands of prosperity in a sea of poverty which, in the medium to long term, is a clear recipe for instability.

UNION: DREAM OR PIPE DREAM?

The dream of a united Africa goes back to at least the colonial scramble for the continent when Africa was divided into territories shared by various European countries rising to a crescendo as the decolonization process took root.[17] Having successfully led his country, Ghana, to independence, Kwame Nkrumah dreamt of a union of African states[18] echoing a shared belief that not only Africa had shared history but all the continent's Member States had a common destiny beyond emancipation from colonial rule.

Many authors acknowledge that Nkrumah's vision of a united Africa that is wholly politically integrated gave way to a looser unit framework that allowed Member States to retain their sovereignty finding it somewhat difficult to give up such sovereignty having just acquired independence from the colonial powers.[19] By the same taken, Mandela envisioned an Africa at peace and working in concert:

> I dream of an Africa which is in peace with itself. I dream of the realization of the unity of Africa, whereby its leaders combine in their efforts to solve the problems of this continent. I dream of our vast deserts, of our forests, of all our great wildernesses.[20]

Addressing the Heads of State meeting of the OAU in 1994, President Mandela acknowledged the solidarity of all Africans in the quest for freedom:

> Africa shed her blood and surrendered the lives of her children so that all her children could be free. She gave of her limited wealth and resources so that all of Africa should be liberated. She opened her heart of hospitality and her head so full of wise counsel, so that we shall emerge victorious. A million times, she put her hand to the plough that has now dug up the encrusted burden of oppression accumulated for centuries. If freedom was the crown which the fighters of liberation sought to place on the head of Mother Africa, let the upliftment, the happiness, prosperity and comfort of her children be the jewel of the crown.[21]

President Mandela is also quoted as making reference to the African concept of community, unity, humanity, and harmony commonly called Ubuntu saying:

> In Africa there is a concept known as "ubuntu"—the profound sense that we are human only through the humanity of others; that if we are to accomplish anything in this world it will in equal measure be due to the work and achievement of others.[22]

Consistent with this vision of shared and united growth and development, the AU's Agenda 2063 defines *The Africa That We Want* as being integrated, prosperous, and peaceful. Agenda 2063 envisions inclusive growth and sustainable development which will translate to (a) African people having a high standard of living and quality of life, sound health, and well-being; (b) well-educated and skilled citizens, underpinned by science, technology, and innovation for a knowledge society is the norm and no child misses school due to poverty or any form of discrimination; and (c) economies that are structurally transformed to create shared growth, decent jobs, and economic opportunities for all. One of the goals is to target job creation, especially addressing youth unemployment in order to secure a high standard of living, quality of life, and well-being for all. In this regard, the African Union Commission is coordinating implementation of the Ouagadougou+10 Declaration and Plan of Action on Employment, Poverty Eradication and Inclusive Development adopted by the Assembly in January 2015.

Clearly, the sentiments contained in the above Pan-African dream of united and shared prosperity bear the hallmarks of a quest worth pursuing. And yet, skeptics and critics have dismissed the whole idea as a pipe dream. Some of them have suggested that the quest for union is impossible to achieve. The political and economic integration envisioned by the founding fathers of Pan-Africanism reportedly remains a pipe dream on the back of politicians and citizens who have little or no appetite for such integration.[23] Others point to a lack of unity at national level spiked with identity and tribal politics as a barrier to broader (regional and continental) unity and integration.[24]

Another factor which is cited by several analysts as a barrier to moving toward the dream of a united Africa is the fact that individual rulers from different Member States of the AU want to rule without let or hindrance and without worrying about their sovereignty being comprom. For some, the insistence on clinging to uninterrupted power renders the idea of Pan-Africanist integration "stillborn."[25]

Another frequently recognized impediment is the fact that Member States are at different levels in terms of their development trajectory. This variable geometry means that different Member States will have different needs for integration and hence the methodology and pace of integration adopted at Member State level will vary.[26]

Armed conflict is a persistent threat that has surfaced in the postcolonial era. Examples include the Biafran war where the eastern region of Nigeria attempted to secede to form an independent state and the Libyan crisis of 2011 which eventually toppled Muammar Gaddafi.[27] In Nigeria, Boko Haram, which was formed in 2002 by a well-known preacher (Mohammed Yusuf) of the Izala sect of Islam in the Maiduguri region of Nigeria, is linked to ongoing armed conflict and instability. The group continues to attack military and civilian targets in the country.[28]

In Ethiopia, there is fighting between the country's central government and its northern Tigray region with potential ramifications for the entire Horn of Africa. Apart from the rising death toll, there are concerns about food insecurity—which was already shaky in any case following a locust invasion and has not been helped by the outbreak of Covid-19.[29] In Mozambique, in Cabo Delgado, there is ongoing fighting between Islamist militants attempting to establish an Islamic state in the region and Mozambican security forces, while civilians have been targeted by the Islamist militants.[30]

As if the mere existence of armed conflict, regardless of its underlying causes, is not challenge enough, it is compounded by the proliferation of small arms and the recruitment of children below the age of 18 as combatants in state military and armed opposition groups and militias.[31] Young people who should be undergoing education and training in preparation to play full and productive roles in society are instead radicalized and traumatized by experiences of children high on drugs and wielding automatic rifles and forced to kill or be killed.[32]

There is no question that armed conflict gets in the way of the national, regional, and continental development agenda. Little wonder then that one of the AU's priority initiatives is that of silencing the guns. Ending all wars, civil conflicts, gender-based violence, and violent conflicts and preventing genocide in the continent by 2020 was driven by the quest for a peaceful and secure Africa as a minimum condition for development and prosperity.[33]

Corruption and poor governance are often flagged as having considerable significance for development.[34] The plague of corruption is not just about citizens' perceptions with one in four Africans reporting that they had to pay a bribe to access public services.[35] It is also about the diversion of scarce resources which undermines economic progress and impedes development.[36] Some reports show that Africa loses more than US$50 billion per year through illicit financial flows (IFFs).[37] The latest numbers for IFFs show annual losses of up to US$89 billion.[38]

According to Sandholtz and Gray, there is an interesting link between integration and corruption arguing that "greater degrees of international integration lead to lower levels of corruption."[39]

THE STRATEGIC IMPERATIVE FOR PAN-AFRICANISM

Pan-Africanism is only relevant to the extent that it fits into the agenda for the creation of decent work and rolling back multigenerational and endemic poverty in African communities. Integration at regional and continental level is a clear factor in the quest for poverty reduction and employment creation. It is a complex space requiring a number of things to be done simultaneously such as the removal of trade obstacles such as tariff barriers and nontariff barriers, activating the AfCFTA to stimulate trade growth and addressing some of the potentially negative aspects of integration.

The economic benefits associated with integration leading up to sustainable development and growth as well as the creation of decent work opportunities include (a) improved market efficiencies, (b) sharing the costs of public goods or large infrastructure projects, (c) harmonized policy frameworks, and (d) noneconomic benefits inclusive of peace and security.[40] A united Africa is a much stronger player on the world stage that has for a long time been dominated by states or coalitions with imperialist tendencies.

Major global players have benefited from close economic cooperation. The EU is one example. In the Americas, the North American Free Trade Agreement (NAFTA) came into being when in 1988 the United States and Canada signed the Canada–United States Free Trade Agreement with Mexico coming on board in 1992. The goal of NAFTA was to encourage trade between Canada, the United States, and Mexico. Africa's pursuit of political, fiscal, monetary, customs, common market, or free trade area integration is therefore not new. It has been tried and tested elsewhere and shown to deliver the development goods sought.

Does this mean that Pan-Africanism is the silver bullet, the magic solution that will address all the social, political, and economic challenges that the continent faces? Not at all. However, it is reasonable to take the position that many African states, on their own, have a little chance of successfully competing in the global arena against the largest economic players like the United States and China. Similarly, African states have a better chance of creating jobs and rolling back the advance of poverty by working in an integrated fashion.

Past failures in implementing the principles of African unity and the many challenges, inclusive of conflict, corruption, and asymmetry, do not in and of themselves take away from the importance of systematically pursuing the agenda of union especially as unpacked by the AU's Agenda 2063.

CONCLUSIONS AND RECOMMENDATIONS

This chapter has discussed the concept of Pan-Africanism in the context of a united Africa with a shared history and a common destiny. Because integration plays a central role in galvanizing sustained economic growth and development, Pan-Africanism is therefore even more relevant in twenty-first-century Africa that is yet to achieve the development status that it desires for its citizens.

Experience suggests that the journey to Pan-African development and progress is not easy. Internal and external forces will continue to counter the steady progress toward more comprehensive integration. To ensure that the continent and all its Member States stay the course, I make the following recommendations:

- Improving national, regional, and continental capacities to execute the various aspects of the integration agenda.

- Improving regulatory frameworks and harmonizing the relevant standards to make integration a reality.
- Investment in the different types of infrastructure required to facilitate the unhindered movement of people and goods from any one part of the continent to another.
- Promote a whole of society approach to regional and continental integration with partnerships between state and non-state actors as well as national, regional, and continental stakeholders and partners.
- Acknowledge integration success stories while systematically addressing and potential losses for some Member States and/or communities.

The ideas of a shared history, common ancestral heritage and cultural ties that bind communities across borders, and a shared vision for a united and prosperous Africa should underpin a shared Pan-African identity.

NOTES

1. Roze Moodley, "Nelson Mandela Famous Quotes," Accessed November 19, 2020, https://www.sanews.gov.za/south-africa/nelson-mandela-famous-quotes.

2. Chinua Achebe, *Things Fall Apart* (London: Heinemann, 1965).

3. EU, "Objectives of the EU," accessed November 16, 2020, http://en.euabc.com/word/743.

4. Peter Kuryla, "Pan Africanism," accessed November 16, 2020, https://www.britannica.com/topic/Pan-Africanism.

5. Mashupye Herbert Maserumule, "Sobukwe's Pan-Africanist Dream: An Elusive Idea that Refuses to Die," The Conversation, accessed November 16, 2020, https://theconversation.com/sobukwes-pan-africanist-dream-an-elusive-idea-that-refuses-to-die-52601.

6. New African, "WE Dubois – The Father of Pan Africanism?," November 16, 2020, https://newafricanmagazine.com/4091/.

7. Henry Kah, "Kwame Nkrumah and the Pan-African Vision: Between Acceptance and Rebuttal," *Journal of Strategy & International Relations* 5, no. 1 (October 2016): 141–164.

8. Herbert Maserumule, Sobukwe's Pan-Africanist Dream. 2016.

9. African Union, "Speeches & Statements Made at the First Organization of African Unity First OAU Summit," accessed November 16, 2020, https://au.int/sites/default/files/speeches/38523-sp-oau_summit_may_1963_speeches.

10. Len Ishmael, "Integration: Not an Option but an Imperative," accessed November 16, 2020, https://www.africaportal.org/publications/africas-integration-not-option-imperative/.

11. Elizabeth Buhungiro, "Origins of Ordinary Things: The Name Africa," *The New York Times*, accessed November 16, 2020, https://www.newtimes.co.rw/education/origins-ordinary-things-name-africa.

12. John Innes Clarke, "Africa Continent," *Britannica*, accessed November 17, 2020, https://www.britannica.com/place/Africa.

13. Aljazeera, *Mapping Africa's Natural Resources: An Overview of the Continent's Main Natural Resources*, Aljazeera, Accessed November 17, 2020, https://www.aljazeera.com/news/2018/2/20/mapping-africas-natural-resources.

14. African Union, "2019 African Regional Integration Report: Towards an Integrated and Prosperous and Peaceful Africa. Report, Addis Ababa: African Union Commission," accessed November 17, 2020, https://au.int/en/organs/recs.

15. African Union, African Integration Report (2019).

16. Country Economy, "Country Comparison: Botswana vs Malawi," Country Economy, accessed November 18, 2020, https://countryeconomy.com/countries/compare/botswana/malawi.

17. Taylor Mayol, "A United Africa? Leaders Revive a Dream," *Ozy*, accessed November 29, 2020, https://www.ozy.com/around-the-world/a-united-africa-leaders-revive-a-dream/70330/.

18. Hakim Adi, "The United States of Africa?," *History Today*, accessed November 20, 2020, https://www.historytoday.com/miscellanies/united-states-africa.

19. 19 Guy Martin, "Dream of Unity: From United States of Africa to Federation of African States," *African and Asian Studies* 12, no. 3 (2013): 169–188, accessed November 22, https://brill.com/view/journals/aas/12/3/article-p169_1.xml?language=en.

20. Roze Moodley, Nelson Mandela Famous Quotes (2020).

21. Roze Moodley, Nelson Mandela Famous Quotes (2020).

22. RelicsWorld, "Nelson Mandela Quotes," accessed November 20, 2020, https://www.relicsworld.com/nelson-mandela.

23. African News Agency, "Despite Free Trade Area Breakthrough, United States of Africa Still a Pipedream," accessed November 22, 2020, https://www.engineeringnews.co.za/article/despite-free-trade-area-breakthrough-united-states-of-africa-still-a-pipe-dream-2019-08-16/rep_id:4136.

24. The Standard, "Why Unity in Africa is a Pipedream," accessed November 25, 2020, https://www.thestandard.co.zw/2011/05/29/sundayopinion/.
https://www.thestandard.co.zw/2011/05/29/sundayopinion/.

25. Sunny Ntayombya, "The African Pipedream," accessed November 29, 2020, https://www.newtimes.co.rw/section/read/7034.

26. Ottilia Anna Maunganidze and Julian Formica, "Freedom of Movement in Southern Africa: A SADC (Pipe)dream," *Johannesburg: Institute for Security Studies* 2018, no. 17 (2018): 1–24.

27. Matebe Chisiza, "The Demise of African Unity?," SAIIA, May 25, 2016, https://saiia.org.za/research/the-demise-of-african-unity/.

28. Center for International Security and Cooperation, "Boko Haram," accessed November 29, 2020, https://cisac.fsi.stanford.edu/mappingmilitants/profiles/boko-haram#text_block_11860.

29. Anthony Irungu, "Tigray Crisis: Three Consequences of the Crisis in Ethiopia," accessed November 29, 2020, https://www.bbc.com/news/av/world-africa-55022557.

30. BBC, "Militant Islamists 'behead more than 50' in Mozambique," November 9, 2020, https://www.bbc.com/news/world-africa-54877202.

31. Martin Kalis, "Child Soldiers in Africa," accessed November 30, 2020, https://www.accord.org.za/ajcr-issues/child-soldiers-in-africa/.

32. Mohamed Sidibay, "Reminiscences of a Former Child Soldier," accessed November 29, 2020, https://www.un.org/africarenewal/magazine/special-edition -youth-2017/reminiscences-former-child-soldier.

33. Sandy Africa, "Challenges of Peacebuilding," 9 November 2020, https://www .accord.org.za/conflict-trends/challenges-of-peacebuilding-in-africa/.

34. United Nations Economic Commission for Africa. "Measuring Corruption in Africa: The international Dimension Matters," accessed November 29, 2020, https:// www.uneca.org/sites/default/files/PublicationFiles/agr4_eng_fin_web_11april.pdf.

35. Kate Whiting, "1 in 4 Africans Had to Pay a Bribe to Access Public Services Last Year," World Economic Forum, accessed November 29, 2020. https://www .weforum.org/agenda/2019/07/africa-corruption-bribe-economy/.

36. Gbenga Lawal, "Corruption and Development in Africa: Challenges for Political and Economic Change (2007)," *Humanity & Social Sciences Journal* 2, no. 1 (2007): 1–7.

37. Masimba Tafirenyika, "Africa Loses $50 Billion Every Year," *Africa Renewal*, December 2013, https://www.un.org/africarenewal/magazine/december-2013/africa -loses-50-billion-every-year.

38. UNCTAD, "Africa Could Gain $89 Billion Annually by Curbing Illicit Financial Flows," accessed November 30, 2020, https://unctad.org/news/africa-could -gain-89-billion-annually-curbing-illicit-financial-flows.

39. Wayne Sandholtz and Mark Gray, "International Integration and National Corruption," *International Organization* 57, no. 4 (2003): 761–800.

40. World Bank, "Regional Integration," accessed November 30, 2020. https:// www.worldbank.org/en/topic/regional-integration/overview.

BIBLIOGRAPHY

Achebe, Chinua. *Things Fall Apart*. London: Heinemann, 1965.

Adi, Hakim. "The United States of Africa?" 04 April 2019. Accessed November 20, 2020, https://www.historytoday.com/miscellanies/united-states-africa.

Africa, Sandy. *Challenges of Peacebuilding in Africa*, 2020. Accessed November 30, 2020, https://www.accord.org.za/conflict-trends/challenges-of-peacebuilding -in-africa/.

African News Agency. *Despite Free Trade Area Breakthrough, 'United States of Africa' Still a Pipe Dream*, 2019. Accessed November 29, 2020, https://www .engineeringnews.co.za/article/despite-free-trade-area-breakthrough-united-states -of-africa-still-a-pipe-dream-2019-08-16/rep_id:4136.

African Union. *2019 African Regional Integration Report: Towards an integrated and prosperous and peaceful Africa*. Report, Addis Ababa: African Union

Commission, 2019. *Regional Economic Communities (RECs)*. Accessed November 17, 2020, https://au.int/en/organs/recs.

African Union. *Speeches & Statements Made at the First Organization of African Unity (O.A.U) SUMMIT*. May 1963. Accessed November 16, 2020, https://au.int/sites/default/files/speeches/38523-sp-oau_summit_may_1963_speeches.pdf.

Buhungiro, Elizabeth. *Origins of Ordinary Things: The Name "Africa"*, 2018. Accessed November 29, 2020. https://www.newtimes.co.rw/education/origins-ordinary-things-name-africa.

Center for International Security and Cooperation. *Boko Haram*, 2018. Accessed November 29, 2020, https://cisac.fsi.stanford.edu/mappingmilitants/profiles/boko-haram#text_block_11860.

Chisiza, Matebe. *The Demise of African Unity?* Johannesburg: SAIIA, 2016.

CountryEconomy.com. *Country comparison Botswana vs Malawi*. 18 November 2020. Accessed November 18, 2020, https://countryeconomy.com/countries/compare/botswana/malawi.

European Union. *Objectives of the EU*. 12 June 2016. Accessed November 16, 2020, http://en.euabc.com/word/743.

Irungu, Anthony. *Tigray Crisis: Three Consequences of the Crisis in Ethiopia*, 2020. Accessed November 29, 2020, https://www.bbc.com/news/av/world-africa-55022557.

Ishmael, Len. *Africa's Integration: Not an Option, But an Imperative*. 9 March 2020. Accessed November 16, 2020, https://www.africaportal.org/publications/africas-integration-not-option-imperative/.

Ishmael, Len. *Integration: Not an Option but an Imperative*, 2020. Accessed November 16, 2020, https://www.africaportal.org/publications/africas-integration-not-option-imperative/

Kah, Henry Kam. "Kwame Nkrumah and the Panafrican Vision: Between Acceptance and Rebuttal." *Austral Brazilian Journal of Strategy & International Relations* 5, no. 1 (October 2016): 141–164.

Kalis, Martin. *Child Soldiers in Africa*, 2002. Accessed November 30, 2020. https://www.accord.org.za/ajcr-issues/child-soldiers-in-africa/.

Kröner, Alfred. *Africa*. 30 October 2020. Accessed November 17, 2020, https://www.britannica.com/place/Africa.

Kuryla, Peter. *Pan-Africanism*, 1 October 2020. Accessed November 16, 2020. https://www.britannica.com/topic/Pan-Africanism.

Lawal, Gbenga. "Corruption and Development in Africa: Challenges for Political and Economic Change." *Humanity & Social Sciences Journal* 2, no. 1 (2007): 1–7.

Martin, Guy. "Dream of Unity: From the United States of Africa to the Federation of African States." *African and Asian Studies* 12, no. 3 (2013): 169–188.

Maserumule, Mashupye Herbert. *The Conversation*. 16 February 2016. Accessed November 16, 2020, https://theconversation.com/sobukwes-pan-africanist-dream-an-elusive-idea-that-refuses-to-die-52601.

Maunganidze, Ottilia Anna and Julian Formica. "Freedom of Movement in Southern Africa: A SADC (Pipe)dream." *Johannesburg: Institute for Security Studies* 2018, no. 17 (2018): 1–24.

Mayol, Taylor. *A United Africa? Leaders Revive a Dream,* 2016. Accessed November 29, 2020, https://www.ozy.com/around-the-world/a-united-africa-leaders-revive-a-dream/70330/.

Moodley, Roze. *Nelson Mandela Famous Quotes,* 2020. Accessed November 19, 2020. https://www.sanews.gov.za/south-africa/nelson-mandela-famous-quotes.

New African. *W.E.B. Du Bois – The Father of Modern Pan-Africanism?* 3 December, 2–13. Accessed November 16, 2020, https://newafricanmagazine.com/4091/.

Ntayombya, Sunny. *The African Pipedream,* 2009. Accessed November 29, 2020. https://www.newtimes.co.rw/section/read/7034.

RelicsWorld. *Quote by Nelson Mandela,* 2020. Accessed November 29, 2020, https://www.relicsworld.com/nelson-mandela/in-africa-there-is-a-concept-known-as-ubuntu-the-profound-sense-author-nelson-mandela.

Sandholtz, Wayne, and Gray, Mark. "International Integration and National Corruption." *International Organization* 57, no. 4 (2003): 761–800.

Sidibay, Mohamed. *Reminiscences of a Former Child Soldier,* 2017. Accessed November 29, 2020, https://www.un.org/africarenewal/magazine/special-edition-youth-2017/reminiscences-former-child-soldier.

Tafirenyika, Masimba. *Africa Loses $50 Billion Every Year,* 2013. Accessed November 29, 2020, https://www.un.org/africarenewal/magazine/december-2013/africa-loses-50-billion-every-year.

Tembe, Jose. *Militant Islamists 'behead more than 50' in Mozambique,* 2020. Accessed November 29, 2020. https://www.bbc.com/news/world-africa-54877202.

The Standard. *Why Unity in Africa is a Pipedream,* 2011. Accessed November 29, 2020. https://www.thestandard.co.zw/2011/05/29/sundayopinion/.

UNCTAD. *Africa Could Gain $89 Billion Annually by Curbing Illicit Financial Flows,* 2020. Accessed November 30, 2020, https://unctad.org/news/africa-could-gain-89-billion-annually-curbing-illicit-financial-flows.

UNECA. *IGAD - Intergovernmental Authority on Development,* 1 July 2016. Accessed November 17, 2020. https://www.uneca.org/oria/pages/igad-intergovernmental-authority-development.

United Nations Economic Commission for Africa. *Measuring Corruption in Africa: The International Dimension Matters,* 2016. Accessed November 29, 2020, https://www.uneca.org/sites/default/files/PublicationFiles/agr4_eng_fin_web_11april.pdf.

Whiting, Kate. *1 in 4 Africans Had to Pay a Bribe to Access Public Services Last Year,* 2019. Accessed November 29, 2020, https://www.weforum.org/agenda/2019/07/africa-corruption-bribe-economy/.

World Bank. *Regional Integration,* 2020. Accessed November 30, 2020, https://www.worldbank.org/en/topic/regional-integration/overview.

Chapter 10

Afrocentric Development
The Model that Matters for Africa
Lehasa Moloi

The[1] following words by Afigbo[2] offer a useful starting point for discussing a development model for Africans that is Afrocentric, rather than Eurocentric:

> Why is it that almost every major situation so far known in history appears to have placed the Blackman, his historians, sociologist and other cultural interpreters to invest him with the responsibility for what happens to and around him? The central peg in which many scholars have hung the African history is . . . "a race under perpetual siege" . . . it means an African is an "effect" rather than a cause, an object on which things act rather than an active agent that act[s] on things.

Afigbo's insightful question implies that, to avoid this vision of Africans, in future, Africans need to make themselves the subjects of development rather than its objects. The question then is why this situation arises in the first place. Before one can respond to this critical question, which informs the basis of this chapter, it is imperative to historicize the African development predicament resulting from a history of European colonization of Africa and the resultant effect of coloniality. Any attempt to de-historicize or ignore the background of the African development predicament can only result in misleading and decontextualized analyses of that predicament.

Africa's experience of colonialism was not a mere episode but a process which safeguarded the systematic and well-orchestrated exploitation of the African continent and its people by the Global North. The legacy of colonialism in the postindependence era imposed a mammoth task on the newly established African governments to restore the humanity of the African peoples that colonialism had eroded. Sadly, the postcolonial state has not addressed a crucial facet of liberation, namely the dismantling of the institutional colonial legacy in all the nation-states on the continent. The reality is that even today, the African development project is not controlled by the general African populace. The African masses and their governments remain the subjects of preprogrammed Western development processes and yardsticks. This clearly reflects the fact that African governments' respective decrees of sovereignty are concealments of borrowed and misnamed political-economic autonomies, which translate into normalized postcolonial underdevelopment frameworks misguided by Western prejudice and development parameters.

Maldonado-Torres,[3] a leading philosopher in decolonial thought, explains the differences between colonialism and coloniality, which assist a clearer understanding of how Africa as a continent and its people are trapped within complex colonial matrices of power. He articulates these two concepts as follows:

> Colonialism denotes a political and economic relation in which the sovereignty of a nation or people rests on the power of another nation, which makes such a nation an empire. Coloniality, on the other hand, refers to long-standing patterns of power relations that emerged as a result of colonialism, but that define culture, labour, intersubjectivity relations, and knowledge production well beyond the strict limits of colonial administration. Thus coloniality survives colonialism. It is maintained alive in books, in criteria for academic performance, in cultural patterns, in common sense, in the self-image of peoples, in aspirations of self, and so many other aspects of our modern experience. In a way, as modern subjects we breathe coloniality all the time and every day.

For colonization to appear as a noble undertaking to Europeans' conscience and perception, it needed justification by appropriating the African people and cloning their minds into those of European subjects through a Eurocentric education system. This was the case with the Bantu Education System in apartheid South Africa. The violent and brutal nature of the invasion of Africa by Europeans enabled the dehumanization which gave birth to the enslavement of the African people for the sole reason of economic exploitation and the perpetuation of racial and cultural stereotypes. Viriri and Mungwini[4] argue that this violent encounter rendered Africans as embodiments of barbarism and other dehumanizing hierarchies of being. Mengara[5] confirms that Africa was not only erroneously viewed as the Dark Continent but also perceived as a land of despotic civilizations with no history of the democratic principles that have been enshrined in the West's self-image. The European powers sealed their control of Africa during the 1884–1885 Berlin Conference, which signaled what many scholars refer to as the "Scramble for Africa." Otto von Bismarck,[6] the then chancellor of Germany and the chairman of this Conference, invited major Western powers to Berlin to decide on the fate of the "barbaric" people of Africa. Sebeka Richard Plaatjie[7] points out that many scholars argue that the Conference began a process of imperial domination which was to open Africa, its people, and natural resources to untold exploitation and domination for years to come. The Berlin Conference invitation letter reads,

> The Conference Commission requests your immediate presence in Germany as a delegate to the Berlin Conference. You and your delegation, experts in the areas of economics, geography, ethic, military history, and international negotiations, have been appointed by your government to represent them in this process. Each nation present will be allowed to participate in a three-day review and deliberation to determine the fate of the African Continent. Your timely presence in Berlin by 15 November 1884 will allow your country to be heard. As a Chairman of the Berlin Conference I assure you that your task will be difficult, but of supreme importance to the future of Africa, Europe, and the entire world.[8]

Africans did not know that their lives and future were being decided in their absence, let alone the unspeakable atrocities that were to befall them. The aftermath of the Conference enabled European powers to remap, reshape, and rename Africa according to how they viewed the world. Viriri and Mungwini[9] mention that the indigenous African standards were replaced by monolithic African identities, as specifically reworked by the European empires, that is, the names of towns, streets, and institutions bore foreign designations and the physical environment was not spared. The invasion left Africa and its diaspora wrecked psychologically, economically, culturally, politically, and otherwise. In fact, the colonizers destroyed the philosophical and religious base of Africa and foisted the European system on Africans as a definitive shackle of the colonized.[10] Colonialism left two broad legacies on Africa, namely denial of African identity and the foisting of Western thought and cultural realities and perspectives on Africans.

Against this background, this chapter provides a critique of the Eurocentric conception of development, particularly, the modernization development theory as a Euro-ethnocentric view of development. The argument is premised on Afrocentricity as a proposed alternative theoretical framework to the mainstream imposition of Western-dictated terms of development in Africa. Apart from Molefi Kete Asante's[11] Afrocentricity theory, the research converses with other perspectives, particularly post-development theories which challenge the hegemony of the European-defined ideas of development.

EUROCENTRIC CONCEPTION OF DEVELOPMENT:
THE IDEA OF MODERNIZATION

The contemporary ideas and practice of development can be traced to the late 1940s through to the 1950s, and development studies as an interdisciplinary and transdisciplinary field of inquiry has been around for approximately 50 years.[12] Although scholars would find it difficult to provide the exact date on which the discourse of development studies emerged, many seem to agree that the 1949 inaugural speech by the then U.S. president Harry S. Truman was a defining moment in the history of the present development discourse. I quote at length from his speech to demonstrate the thinking that underpins this ongoing development discourse, which is dominated by the Global North:

> We must embark on a bold new program for making the benefits of our scientific advances and industrial progress available for the improvement and growth of underdeveloped areas. More than half the people of the world are living in conditions approaching misery. Their food is inadequate. They are victims of disease. Their economic life is primitive and stagnant. Their poverty is a handicap and a threat both to them and to more prosperous areas. For the first time in history, humanity possesses the knowledge and the skill to relieve the suffering of these people. The United States is pre-eminent among nations in the development of industrial and scientific techniques. The material resources which we can afford to use for the assistance of other peoples are limited. But our imponderable resources in technical knowledge are constantly growing and are inexhaustible. I believe that we should make available to peace-loving peoples the benefits of our store of technical knowledge in order to help them realize their aspirations for a better life. Moreover, in cooperation with other nations, we should foster capital investment in areas needing development.[13]

It is evident that the agenda behind the idea of "development" in Truman's terms was a Euro-American missionary task of saving and developing the Global South in general and Africa in particular and that this was an "investment" with the hope of lucrative returns for the United States and its allies. This Eurocentric narrative of development as an exogenous process reflects the colonial tendency to portray Africans as objects of European/American development. About a decade after Truman's speech, Daniel Lerner expresses a similar view in *The Passing of Traditional Society: Modernizing the Middle East*, when he writes that "the only hope for non-European nations is to be modernized by an injection of Western values and expertise."[14] He claims that "the dissemination of Western values and ideas through Western mass media could help transform countries of the Middle

East from traditional and primitive nations into countries with modern forms of social, economic and political organization."[15]

Modernization theory, sometimes called developmentalism or development doctrine, emerged around the 1950s. It supplied the working concepts through which Western Europe understood its "obligation" toward those it considered unindustrialized or underdeveloped: the newly independent nations in the last half of the twentieth century.[16] According to modernization theorists, their episteme is based on conscious, purposeful, and nonviolent change.[17] From their perspective, modernization involves changing social structures, changing people's behavior, and leading them to a new sense of what should be done. It is an all-encompassing process, which, in the general perception of these theorists, proposes that developing states have to undergo change for development to occur.[18] Modernization focuses on the deficiencies of countries viewed as less developed, according to Eurocentric standards. Therefore, modernization prescribes how developing countries can overcome their deficiencies to assume an accepted standard of development. Development in this context simply means that an effort must be made for the underdeveloped to catch up with the industrialized Western world. This catch-up doctrine can be clearly traced, among other places, in Rostow's growth stages.[19] Some of the problems of this approach have recently been articulated by leading African intellectual voices, such as Thandika Mkandawire:

> The idea of "catching up" entails learning not only about ideas from abroad but also about one's capacities and weaknesses. "Catching up" requires that countries know themselves and their own history that has set the "initial conditions" for any future progress. They need a deep understanding of their culture, not only for self-reaffirmation, but in order to capture the strong points of their culture and institution that will see their societies through rapid social change. [. . .] The real issue about "catching up" is not that of simply taking on every wretched instrument used by their pioneers to get what they have—wars, slave labour, child labour, colonialism, Gulags, concentration camps—but of finding more efficacious and morally acceptable ways of improving the life chances of millions of poor people. [. . .] There would be no point in investing so much in the study if it involved simply regurgitating scripts that countries must follow.[20]

The modernization theory has been challenged from the Global South, particularly by leading Latin American dependency theorists, who argue that what looks like development is often actually a process of "development of underdevelopment or of dependent development."[21] The primary argument advanced by these theorists is that the more powerful states (the center, the Global North) continue to take wealth from the weaker states (the periphery, the Global South). They believe that weaker states fund the growth of the stronger states. The very idea of development assistance from wealthy states is seen as exploitative, paternalistic, and coercive of dependent states. Modernization theory has also been challenged by critical counterpoint approaches, which criticize modernization processes for taking the form of large-scale industrialization, urbanization, and bureaucratization. Instead, these approaches suggest "another development" with diverse needs and equity-oriented development strategies rooted in local cultures and local thinking, strategies that emphasize self-management and participation, and that build on small people and small enterprises.[22] In this regard, Pieterse[23] suggests that the dissatisfaction in the 1970s with mainstream development further crystallized into alternative, people-centered, participatory approaches to development. However, he argues that the alternative development approach failed to offer a real alternative, as it was still framed within the prescriptions of Western modernity. The only thing that was different was that it proposed the attainment of these Western ideals through a different methodology.[24]

It is against the background of these ideas that I argue that the notion and practice of development remains entrapped, even at the start of the third decade of the twenty-first century, within the imperialist project that seeks to justify colonialism vis-à-vis non-Europeans, Africans in particular. What I find perplexing in this view of development is its continued inability to account historically for the immorality of European colonization and abuse of others in the attainment of development status. Ndlovu-Gatsheni rightly notes that the Eurocentric notion of development rationalizes opening up the African continent for untold economic exploitation and the permanent settlement of Europeans through force on African-occupied land:

> Development meant the dispossession of Africans, forcing them off the land and transforming them into peasants, workers and domestic servants for European masters. Development meant the rearrangement of African agrarian systems to make sure they produce the cash crops needed in Europe and America.[25]

This kind of development is possible only through dominating and taking from others, thus impoverishing them to establish and empower Europeans. Plaatjie points out that this view is at heart underpinned by the mantra of the fifteenth century, to civilize and to enlighten the "soulless" subalterns of the globe, and to rescue them from their barbarity, which from a European perspective was seen as development—at the same time, the worst possible barbaric acts were committed on the colonized, and this is the darker side of this notion of development.[26]

The groundbreaking book by Walter Rodney, *How Europe Underdeveloped Africa*, first published in 1972,[27] also exposes how European colonial regimes deliberately exploited and underdeveloped Africa. Rodney shifted the geography of analysis by clearly articulating the ripple effects of colonialism from Africa's point of view. Rodney shows the comparative nature of the concept of development by which Africa, Latin America, and Asia are only viewed as underdeveloped in comparison to Europe. An unbalanced pattern of development is created by the fact that Europe as the "exploiter" becomes developed, while the "exploited" become underdeveloped. The very vocabulary of describing some as developed and others as underdeveloped embraces a discriminatory and racist worldview which is premised on European hegemonic standards.

It is therefore the contention of this study that modernization theory has nothing to do with development, conceived as philanthropic handouts toward the non-Europeans; instead, this theory peddles colonially-anchored perspectives of conceptualizing development. This perspective's main hypocrisy is its concealment of Europe's underdevelopment effect on Africa. The modernization theory is also a smokescreen for European racism against non-Europeans, who are misrepresented as beneficiaries of European development's benevolence. In essence, the modernization theory represents a Eurocentric fundamental order. Its exclusionist insinuations suggest that Europe is the epitome of modernization and a barometer and the apex of civilization. The approach implies that Europe has the right to violently impose its autonomy on those it categorizes as underdeveloped in a bid to "redeem" them from their primitivism and traditionalism. It is in this context that Aimé Césaire's *Discourse on Colonialism* speaks of Western civilization as colonialism.[28] Césaire's question about what fundamentally constitutes colonialism unmasks the fact that much of the rhetoric of development is merely a cover-up for deeper forms of colonialism. These forms of colonialism go into the psyche of the colonized subjects while affecting and rearticulating their power, knowledge, being, and nature. If we assume that this is true, then, the question remains, should African governments still look to European countries for a development model? Or should they begin to think about the models that best suit their local circumstances? It is my contention that the idea and practice of development should never be divorced from the aspirations of the beneficiaries; instead, it should be drawn from the historical trajectory of the people intended to be the beneficiaries and elevate their living conditions.

AN AFROCENTRIC DEVELOPMENT PARADIGM

Against the background of European development ideas and practices, this chapter takes as its point of reference the idea of development as articulated by the Bandung Conference of 1955, whose point of departure is decolonization.

This conference understood development as an emancipatory counter-epistemic route from political, economic, ideological, and social domination imposed through Western colonialism and coloniality.[29] The essence of this delineation is that development entails overcoming the stumbling blocks to human happiness and the attainment of material welfare, civil and political liberties, social peace, and human security.[30] This objective entails that Africa as a continent has a right to exercise self-determination and that it must not be at the mercy of the European states or receive handouts in the form of development aid to attain its development status. While cooperation between African states and European states is necessary for development, the process should not victimize African states, as has been the case historically. Thus decolonization remains an unfinished task which requires deep commitment from African leaders. To support the validity of this position, I deploy the theory of Afrocentricity, drawing on the perspectives of the theory's leading scholar, Molefi Kete Asante. In particular, I argue that Africans must be grounded within their own knowledge and culture and advance their own agency to overcome domination.

THE THEORY OF AFROCENTRICITY AND ITS PAN-AFRICAN VISION IN THE RECONCEPTUALIZATION OF THE AFROCENTRIC DEVELOPMENT VISION

According to Asante,

> Afrocentricity is a paradigmatic intellectual perspective that privileges African agency within the context of African history and culture trans-continentally and trans-generationally. This means that the quality of location is essential to any analysis that involves African culture and behavior whether literary or economic, whether political or cultural.[31]

At the heart of Afrocentricity is the rejection of European particularism as a universal point of reference from which non-Europeans, in particular Africans, should interpret their realities. In the words of Walter D. Mignolo, the geopolitics of knowledge goes hand in hand with the politics of knowing; this implies that all knowledges are situated within a given episteme residence and every knowledge is constructed.[32] This is why Afrocentricity seeks to transcend the ontological, epistemological, and methodological hegemony of Eurocentric social sciences, by expressing an African-centered viewpoint.

In this regard, Afrocentricity aspires to overcome the tendency to interpret social phenomena based on the colonizer's precepts (Western Europe) and to assess Africa's development needs and path based on the colonizers' agenda.

The broader objective of Afrocentricity is to deal with the question of African identity from the perspective of African people as centered, located, oriented, and grounded. African people, from the viewpoint of Afrocentricity, should be relocated historically, economically, socially, politically, and philosophically. In this way, they will overcome the syndrome of merely viewing themselves as a footnote in the script of European history or objects of European experimentation waiting to be developed. In this regard, Asante asserts,

> To say that we (Africans) are decentered means essentially that we have lost our own cultural footing and become other than our cultural and political origins, dis-located and disoriented. We are essentially insane, that is, living an absurdity from which we will never be able to free our minds until we return to the source. Afrocentricity as a theory of change intends to re-locate the African person as a subject. As a pan-African idea, Afrocentricity becomes the key to the proper education of children and the essence of an African cultural revival and, indeed, survival.[33]

The Afrocentric paradigm is a revolutionary shift in thinking proposed as a constructional adjustment to African disorientation, decenteredness, and lack of agency. It is a paradigm based on the idea that African people should reassert a sense of agency in order to achieve sanity.[34] In Asante's words, "Afrocentricity represents a deepening of the conceptual frames which bring us (Africans) close to ourselves and a sharpening of the distractions which will help us rid ourselves of the peripheral vestiges of a Eurocentric reality."[35] This suggests that African people should project their experiences in their own terms. Hence, these experiences should produce paradigmatic scholarly discourses that are rooted in the consciousness of existential conditions.[36] On that note, Ama Mazama[37] also asserts that Afrocentricity is not just a theory but a liberating paradigm which emphasizes the need for a reconceptualization of the social and historical realities of African people.[38] Centeredness involves the centering of Africans in their own historical context, reality, and time. This serves to demarginalize knowledge that has been marginalized as a result of Eurocentric dominance. Viewing Africans through European lenses results in an inaccurate and misleading interpretation of their social realities. Therefore, Eurocentrism as a paradigm, although it is relevant in the study of European experiences, should not be applied in a generalized manner to interpret non-European experiences, as this would lead to a defective view of other realities. It is on this basis that the discourse of development should be rescued from the Euro-ethnocentric bias that privileges the views of European scholars and social scientists; rather, it should be localized.

This is where Afrocentricity comes in as a redemptive epistemic tool for African scholars and practitioners of development to ground their understanding of development within the living realities of the African people. This approach creates a convergence point to enable a meeting point for desirable solutions to development problems. These particular solutions are rooted within the local context, thus overcoming what Chambers refers to as the "outsiders' perspective."[39] In this regard, Archibald Mafeje, an African scholar and social anthropologist, argues that social science disciplines suffer from an "epistemology of alterity," which refers to a scholarship rooted in Western thought.[40] Mafeje emphasizes the "insistence on Africans to think, speak, and do things for themselves in the first place." This does not imply an unwillingness to learn from others, but this is rebellion to domination by others, irrespective of color or race.[41] In essence, Africans must define development for themselves and determine what best suits African circumstances, thus overcoming European paternalism. Ndlovu-Gatsheni also attests that for a meaningful and systematic decolonization of development studies to take place, there is a need to shift the geo- and biography of knowledge and begin to articulate the experience of development from Africa as a privileged epistemic site capable of formulating its own development trajectory.[42] A shift in the analysis of knowledge on development will afford Africans an opportunity to think on their terms, in particular to overcome the dismembering effect of Eurocentric knowledge, which perpetuates divisions among Africans.

While Afrocentricity is a revolutionary paradigm which combats racist Eurocentric worldviews and their negative understanding of Africa, its application should not be misinterpreted to mean the promotion of narrow African fundamentalism hidden beneath the rhetoric of nativism. As Ndlovu-Gatsheni notes,

> One of the paradoxes of the making of African nations and African identities in the postcolonial era is the metamorphoses and mutations of African nationalism from civic principles founded on the slogan of "diverse people unite" to narrow, autochthonous, nativist and xenophobic forms that breeds violence.[43]

Fanon has also warned against the crisis of impoverished postcolonial African nationalism ideology emancipation, which fails to facilitate a rebirth of African humanity free from colonialism and its racial bigotry.[44] To Fanon, such phenomena as nativism and xenophobia are a product of what he terms the pitfalls of a national consciousness reflective of the native bourgeois's intellectual laziness.[45] The consequential effect of the pitfalls of the African national consciousness that spearheaded the African national project was what Fanon termed "repetition without difference."[46] It is important to highlight the fact that the national project in the aftermath of political decolonization has continued to be held captive by the European modernist paradigm which imagines an African resurgence only within the intellectual framework of the modernization ideology. Afrocentricity, therefore, seeks to challenge such notions by inviting Africans to re-reflect on the questions of their own identities, culture, and knowledge on an ongoing basis to avoid a repetition of the same order that perpetuated racist discourses. Fundamentally, the very idea of nationhood would require Africans to reorganize themselves on the basis of their history and culture and an assertion of their own agency as they take power to live meaningfully to overcome domination by others.

TOWARD AN AFROCENTRIC
DEVELOPMENT PARADIGM

Having articulated the intellectual determinations of Afrocentricity in respect of the development epistemic crisis, it is relevant to examine what should constitute an Afrocentric development paradigm. Afrocentricity proposes that we transcend a narrow Eurocentric framework in our interpretation of the idea and practice of development in Africa. Afrocentricity challenges all faculties of social sciences and policymakers to shift the geography of reason and analysis from Euro-centeredness to Afro-centeredness. This means that the idea and practice of development should be engaged from the position of Africans as centered and rooted within their own existential realities. Africans should engage with development not as dependent beneficiaries of European ideas of development but as people capable of defining their own needs and solving their own challenges.

This implies that the idea of development should not be interpreted solely to mean economic freedom and overcoming the scourge of poverty in Africa, as this would be too narrow an interpretation. The modernization perspective has used wealth (an economic indicator) as a primary indicator to determine the level of a country's progress.[47] This way of measuring development fails to account for the social, political, and cultural aspects of development. The use of wealth as an indicator has since given way to the Human Development Index, which was devised by the United Nations Development Programme, and is now employed as a measure of development or human progress and quality of life by many countries.[48] This indicator looks at life expectancy, education, and income.

Countering this quantitative approach, there is an emerging Pan-African-centered perspective that focuses on the "human-factor" approach to development.[49] This approach holds that human capital is a valuable asset in promoting development. Therefore, development practitioners and participants must have a self-driven attitude and positive orientation toward a particular angle of development that they expect in critical areas of their respective communities' needs. This implies that the pace of any development prospect must be determined by the localized expectations premised on the worldview of the community concerned. The mandate of human-factor approach practitioners and participants is to align the expected function of development with societal growth to address critical gaps in the promotion of sustainable human livelihoods. The human-factor approach and its Afrocentric underpinning are more relevant to Africa than the modernization model, given the continent's multifaceted historical oppression, and the need to develop beyond the economic limitations which a modernization perspective to development seeks to redress. This is because the relevance of the modernization theory is curtailed by the realities of the divergent destructive effects of colonialism and slavery. These effects not only were economically and politically catastrophic to Africa's growth but led directly to the stagnation of the gradual sustainable human livelihood trajectory of the continent. The background to the realities of confronting the development question in Africa validates the call for an epistemic transition from the modernization articulation of development toward an Afrocentric paradigm. This position is informed by the merits of Afrocentricity's inclusive character in unpacking the African development agenda beyond narrow Eurocentric or economically centered aspects of development as espoused in the modernization theory (which neglects the human factor question). While the modernization school of thought indicators seek to account for the level of development of those considered as "developing nations," this chapter problematizes its narrow Eurocentric prescriptions to development. For this reason, this chapter argues that using the Eurocentric standards of the Global North would be misleading, because these standards are founded on stereotypes of what progress and development are and are then imposed on the multicultural societies of Africa. In this regard, Asante[50] asserts that the Eurocentric view has become an ethnocentric view which elevates the European experience and downgrades all others.

Afrocentric development should enable the relocation of Africans in their own cultural context. From that context they can become their own agents and subjects, rather than objects in a European frame of reference. That said, I propose that development in and for Africans, as Chukwuokolo[51] also suggests, be understood to involve a holistic evaluative process of the epistemic, cultural, economic, political, religious, normative, psychological, and sociological stance of African people. Chukwuokolo's view affirms the expressions of the Bandung Conference of 1955, which perceive development as a redemptive human aspiration; development should promote the attainment of freedom from political, economic, ideological, epistemological, and social domination that was installed through colonialism and coloniality. This conception of development offers a more holistic picture and enables us to overcome the reductionist tendency to measure development as solely an economic project, disregarding other contributing aspects of the situation that require redemption in the first place.

Such a conception of an Afrocentric development paradigm should be framed from a clear understanding of African history in the precolonial, colonial, and postcolonial periods. A historical view of the African continent would enable a proper account of the factors that have limited African people from realizing their dreams of a better quality of life. In the words of Ali Mazrui, "What Africa knows about itself, what different parts of Africa know about each other, has been profoundly influenced by the West."[52] Ndlovu-Gatsheni highlights six long-term effects of colonialism in Africa as identified by Ali Mazrui. Firstly, colonialism and capitalism forcibly incorporated Africa into the world economy, beginning with the slave trade. Secondly, Africa was excluded from the post-1648 Westphalian sovereign state system, but was partitioned and apportioned to European states in the physical scramble for Africa after the 1884–1885 Berlin Conference, and Africa was incorporated into the post-1945 United Nations state system. Thirdly, Africa was incorporated into the Euro-North American-centric world culture and forced to adopt European languages. Fourthly, Africa was incorporated into the heavily Euro-North American-centric world of international law. Fifthly, Africa was catapulted into the modern technological age, including being enmeshed into the global system of dissemination of information. Lastly, Africa has been indoctrinated into a Euro-North American-centric moral order dominated by Christian thought.[53]

When the above factors are unmasked, there is a clearer understanding of why Africa as a continent is less developed than Europe and the rest of the Global North. The historically based account dispels the myths fueled by European scholars such as Hegel who propounded that "Africa only hears the echo of the majestic march of world civilization across Europe and through which the absolute spirit fulfils and realizes itself."[54] A clear grasp of these factors would help to deconstruct and dispel the implanted negative images of Africans as zoo-bound people who lack philosophy, which is humankind's greatest intellectual achievement. Moreover, a historical analysis of the continent would end the tendency among Eurocentrists deliberately to teach half-truths as a strategy to suppress Africans, so that they do not know themselves, so as to ensure that they never rise to oppose their oppressors. In the same way, European colonization ensured the dismemberment of Africa to turn it into a replica of Europe and planted its memories in the psyche of Africans to reproduce itself, and now an Afrocentric development paradigm must undertake the re-membering of Africa to improve Africans' quality of life. An Afrocentric development idea should end the alienation of Africans and reorient them to themselves. It is within this context that Ngũgĩ wa Thiong'o in *Moving the Centre: The Struggle for Cultural Freedoms* argues that the center should be moved from its assumed location in the West to a multiplicity of spheres in all the cultures of the world.[55] What this means for the study of development is that the African worldview must inform how Africans conceptualize their own development, thus overcoming the hegemony of Euro-centeredness.

CONCLUSION

In order for Africa to experience its own development path, Africa must free itself to define and map out its key development priorities without the dictatorship of European countries. The legacy of colonialism that continues in coloniality has locked Africa into a subservient position in relation to Europe, even in the so-called postindependence period. The pervasiveness of Eurocentric thought in the sociopolitical and economic spheres has prevented African governments from making progress. It will take Afrocentric thought to counter the negative effects of the kind of Eurocentric thinking which has contributed to the denigration of African voices. The discourse of development needs to be rescued from the colonial mindset in which Africans came to be viewed as dependent beneficiaries, waiting to be developed. Instead, meaningful development should start with the local context; such development must be relevant to the people and add value to their living realities. African-centered paradigms should take priority in the articulation of the development agenda; this agenda should be mapped from a clear understanding of an African political history that privileges African people. The ideas about development and progress should not be defined by external bodies who serve their own hegemonic interests. If the path suggested in this chapter is followed, it promises contextual relevance and will indeed contribute to justice and the liberation of those who were marginalized.

NOTES

1. An earlier version of this chapter appeared in Moloi, Lehasa. "Afrocentric Development: The Model that Matters for Africa," in *The Reinventions and Contestations of Thought Power in Africa: Emerging Perspectives on Pan-Africanism*, edited by Percy-Sledge Chigora, Richard Mahomva, and Majahana Lunga. LAN Book Publishers, 2018.

2. Adiele Eberechukwu Afigbo, "History and Responsibility: A Keynote Address Delivered at the Meeting of American Studies Association of Nigeria Held at the University of Nigeria," Nsukka, February 24, 1993, 11.

3. Nelson Maldonado-Torres, "On the Coloniality of Being," *Cultural Studies* 21, no. 2–3 (2007): 240–270.

4. Advice Viriri and Pascah Mungwini, "African Cosmology and the Duality of Western Hegemony: The Search for an African Identity," *Journal* of *Pan African Studies* 3, no. 6 (March 2010): 27–42.

5. Daniel M. Mengara, *Images of Africa: Stereotypes and Realities* (Trenton and Asmara: Africa World Press, 2001).

6. Otto von Bismarck, *Otto. 1884-1885 Berlin Conference: Creating a Better Africa.* Accessed May 8, 2020. http://teacherweb.ftl.pinecrest.edu/snyderd/MWH/Projects/MUN-BC/index.htm.

7. Sebeka Richard Plaatjie, "Beyond Western-Centric and Eurocentric Development: A Case for Decolonizing Development," *Africanus*: *Journal* of *Development Studies* 43, no. 2 (2017): 118–130. doi: 10.25159/0304-615X/2306.

8. Von Bismark, Berlin Conference.

9. Viriri and Mungwini, "African Cosmology," 29.

10. J. Chidozie Chukwuokolo, "Afrocentrism or Eurocentrism: The Dilemma of African Development," *OGIRISI: A New Journal of African Studies* 6, no. 1 (2009): 24–39.

11. Molefi Kete Asante, *An Afrocentric Manifesto: Toward an African Renaissance* (Cambridge and Oxford: Polity Press, 2007), 2; Molefi Kete Asante, Afrocentricity (2009). Accessed May 8, 2020. http://www.asante.net/articles/1/afrocentricity.

12. Mogens Buch-Hansen and Laurids S. Lauridsen, "The Past, Present and Future of Development Studies," *Forum for Development Studies* 39, no. 3 (2012), 293–300. doi: 10.1080/08039410.2012.709985.

13. Harry S. Truman, Truman's Inaugural Address, January 20, 1949 (Delivered in person at the Capitol). Accessed May 8, 2020. http://www.trumanlibrary.org/whistlestop/50yr_archive/inargural20jan1949.htm.

14. Daniel Lerner, *The Passing of Traditional Society: Modernizing the Middle East* (Glencoe, IL: Free Press, 1958), 59.

15. Lerner, *The Passing of Traditional Society*, 59.

16. Nick Cullather, "Development Doctrine and Modernization Theory," in *Encyclopedia of American Foreign Policy* (The Gale Group Inc., 2002), Accessed April 15, 2021. https://www.encyclopedia.com.

17. Peter D. S. Stewart, *Development Theories: Only Study Guide for DVA3701* (Pretoria: UNISA, 2010).

18. André du Pisani, *Political Science: Study Guide 1 for PCS302N* (Pretoria: UNISA, 1980).

19. Walt Whitman Rostow, *The Stages of Economic Growth: A Non-Communist Manifesto* (Cambridge: Cambridge University Press, 1960).

20. Thandika Mkandawire, "Running While Others Walk: Knowledge and the Challenge of Africa's Development," *Africa Development* 36, no. 2 (2011): 1–36, here 13.

21. Buch-Hansen and Lauridsen, "The Past, Present and Future," 293–300.

22. Bjorn Hettne, *Development Theory and the Three Worlds. Towards an International Political Economy of* Development (London: Longman, 1990).

23. Jan Nederveen Pieterse, "My Paradigm or Yours? Alternative Development, Post-Development, Reflexive Development," *Institute of Social Studies*: Working Paper Series, 1996, No. 229.

24. Jan Nederveen Pieterse, "My Paradigm or Yours? Alternative Development, Post-Development, Reflexive Development," *Development and Change*, 29, no. 2 (1998): 343–373.

25. Sabelo J. Ndlovu-Gatsheni, Coloniality of Power in Development Studies and the Impact of Global Imperial Designs, Inaugural lecture delivered at UNISA: AMRI, 2012.

26. Plaatjie, "Beyond Western-Centric and Eurocentric Development," 118–130.

27. Walter Rodney, *How Europe Underdeveloped Africa* (London: Bogle-L'Ouverture, 1972).

28. Aimé Césaire, *Discourse on Colonialism* (New York: Monthly Review Press, 1955).

29. Mkandawire, "Running While Others Walk," 7.

30. Sabelo J. Ndlovu-Gatsheni, "The Entrapment of Africa Within the Global Colonial Matrices of Power: Eurocentrism, Coloniality, and Deimperialization in the Twenty-First Century," *Journal of Developing Societies* 29, no. 4 (2013): 331–353.

31. Asante, *An Afrocentric Manifesto*, 2.

32. Walter D. Mignolo, "Epistemic Disobedience, Independent Freedom and Decolonial Freedom," *Theory, Culture and Society* 26, no. 7–8 (2009): 159–181. doi: 10.1177/0263276409349275.

33. Asante, "Afrocentricity," 20.

34. Asante, "Afrocentricity," 1.

35. Charles C. Verharen, "Afrocentrism and Acentrism: A Marriage of Science and Philosophy." *Journal of Black Studies* 26, no. 1 (1998): 62–76.

36. Asante, *An Afrocentric Manifesto*, 9.

37. Ama Mazama, "The Afrocentric Paradigm: Contours and Definitions." *Journal of Black Studies* 31, no. 4 (2001): 387–405. Ama Mazama, *The Afrocentric Paradigm* (Trenton, NJ: Africa World Press, 2003). Ama Mazama, *Afrocentricity and the Critical Question of African Agency*. 2014. Accessed January 19, 2018. https://www.dyabukam.com/index.php/en/knowledge/ philosophy/item/136-afrocentricity.

38. Asante, *Afrocentric Manifesto*, 9.

39. Robert Chambers, *Rural Development: Putting the Last First* (Harlow: Prentice Hall, 1983), 2–3.

40. Nontyatyambo Pearl Dastile, "Beyond Euro-Western Dominance: An African-Centred Decolonial Paradigm." *Africanus: Journal of Development Studies* 43, no. 2 (2017): 93–104. doi: 10.25159/0304-615X/2304, 97.

41. Archie Mafeje, "Africanity: A Combative Ontology," *CODESRIA Bulletin* 1 & 4 (2000): 66–71.

42. Ndlovu-Gatsheni, Coloniality of Power, 21.

43. Sabelo J. Ndlovu-Gatsheni, "Do 'Africans' Exist? Genealogies and Paradoxes of African Identities and the Discourses of Nativism and Xenophobia," *African Identities* 8, no. 3 (2010): 281–295, here 281.

44. Frantz Fanon, *The Wretched of the Earth* (New York: Grove Press, 1968).
45. Fanon, *The Wretched of the Earth*, 157.
46. Fanon, *The Wretched of the Earth*, 170.
47. Colm Regan, *80:20: Development in an Unequal World*, 6th ed. (Oxford: New Internationalist, 2006), 22.
48. United Nations Development Programme, "Human Development Index (HDI)." Accessed May 23, 2020. http://hdr.undp.org/en/content/human-development-index-hdi.
49. Vimbai G. Chivaura and Claude G. Mararike, *The Human Factor Approach to Development in Africa* (Harare: University of Zimbabwe Publications, 1998).
50. Molefi Kete Asante, *Facing South to Africa: Towards an Afrocentric Critical Orientation* (Cambridge and Oxford: Lexington Books, 2014), 3.
51. Chukwuokolo, "Afrocentrism or Eurocentrism," 28.
52. Ali Al-Amin Mazrui, *The Africans: A Triple Heritage* (London: BBC Publication, 1986).
53. Sabelo J. Ndlovu-Gatsheni, "Decoloniality as the Future of Africa," *History Compass* 13, no. 10 (2015): 485–496. doi: 10.1111/hic3.12264.
54. Hegel, cited in Chukwuokolo, "Afrocentrism or Eurocentrism," 29.
55. Ngũgĩ wa Thiong'o, *Moving the Centre: The Struggle for Cultural Freedoms* (London: James Currey, 1993).

BIBLIOGRAPHY

Afigbo, Adiele Eberechukwu. "History and Responsibility: A Keynote Address Delivered at the Meeting of American Studies Association of Nigeria held at the University of Nigeria," Nsukka, February 24, 1993.

Asante, Molefi Kete. "Afrocentricity." (2009). Accessed May 8, 2020. http://www.asante.net/articles/1/afrocentricity.

Asante, Molefi Kete. *An Afrocentric Manifesto: Toward an African Renaissance.* Cambridge and Oxford: Polity Press, 2007.

Asante, Molefi Kete. *Facing South to Africa: Towards an Afrocentric Critical Orientation.* Cambridge and Oxford: Polity Press, 2014.

Buch-Hansen, Mogens and Laurids Sandager Lauridsen. "The Past, Present and Future of Development Studies." *Forum for Development Studies* 39, no. 3 (2012): 293–300. doi: 10.1080/08039410.2012.709985.

Césaire, Aimé. *Discourse on Colonialism.* New York: Monthly Review Press, 1955.

Chambers, Robert. *Rural Development: Putting the Last First.* Harlow: Prentice Hall, 1983.

Chivaura, Vimbai G. and Claude G. Mararike. *The Human Factor Approach to Development in Africa.* Harare: University of Zimbabwe Publications, 1998.

Chukwuokolo, J. Chidozie. "Afrocentrism or Eurocentrism: The Dilemma of African Development." *OGIRISI: A New Journal of African Studies* 6, no. 1 (2009): 24–39.

Cullather, Nick. "Development Doctrine and Modernization Theory." In *Encyclopedia of American Foreign Policy*, Gale Group Inc., 2002. Accessed April 15, 2021, https://www.encyclopedia.com.

Dastile, Nontyatyambo Pearl. 2017. "Beyond Euro-Western Dominance: An African-Centred Decolonial Paradigm." *Africanus: Journal of Development Studies* 43, no. 2 (2017): 93–104. doi: 10.25159/0304-615X/2304.

Du Pisani, André. *Political Science: Study Guide 1 for PCS302N*. Pretoria: UNISA, 1980.

Fanon, Frantz. *The Wretched of the Earth*. New York: Grove Press, 1968.

Hettne, Bjorn. *Development Theory and the Three Worlds. Towards an International Political Economy of* Development. London: Longman, 1990.

Lerner, Daniel. *The Passing of Traditional Society: Modernizing the Middle East*. Glencoe, IL: Free Press, 1958.

Mafeje, Archie. "Africanity: A Combative Ontology." *CODESRIA Bulletin*, 1 and 4 (2000): 66–71.

Maldonado-Torres, Nelson. "On the Coloniality of Being." *Cultural Studies* 21, no. 2–3 (2007): 240–270.

Mazama, Ama. *Afrocentricity and the Critical Question of African Agency*, 2014. Accessed January 19, 2018. https://www.dyabukam.com/index.php/en/knowledge/philosophy/item/136-afrocentricity.

Mazama, Ama. *The Afrocentric Paradigm*. Trenton, NJ: Africa World Press, 2003.

Mazama, Ama. "The Afrocentric Paradigm: Contours and Definitions." *Journal of Black Studies* 31, no. 4 (2001): 387–405.

Mazrui, Ali Al-Amin. *The Africans: A Triple Heritage*. London: BBC Publication, 1986.

Mengara, Daniel M. *Images of Africa: Stereotypes and Realities*. Trenton and Asmara: Africa World Press, 2001.

Mignolo, Walter D. "Epistemic Disobedience, Independent Freedom and Decolonial Freedom." *Theory, Culture and Society* 26, no. 7–8 (2009): 159–181. doi: 10.1177/0263276409349275.

Mkandawire, Thandika. "Running While Others Walk: Knowledge and the Challenge of Africa's Development." *Africa Development* 36, no. 2 (2011): 1–36.

Ndlovu-Gatsheni, Sabelo J. *Coloniality of Power in Development Studies and the Impact of Global Imperial Designs*. Inaugural lecture delivered at UNISA: AMRI, 2012.

Ndlovu-Gatsheni, Sabelo J. "Decoloniality as the Future of Africa." *History Compass* 13, no. 10 (2015): 485–496. doi: 10.1111/hic3.12264.

Ndlovu-Gatsheni, Sabelo J. "Do 'Africans' Exist? Genealogies and Paradoxes of African Identities and the Discourses of Nativism and Xenophobia." *African Identities* 8, no. 3 (2010): 281–295.

Ndlovu-Gatsheni, Sabelo J. "The Entrapment of Africa Within the Global Colonial Matrices of Power: Eurocentrism, Coloniality, and Deimperialization in the Twenty-First Century." *Journal of Developing Societies* 29 no. 4 (2013): 331–353.

Ngũgĩ wa Thiong'o. *Moving the Centre: The Struggle for Cultural Freedoms*. London: James Currey, 1993.

Pieterse, Jan Nederveen. "My Paradigm or Yours? Alternative Development, Post-Development, Reflexive Development." Institute of Social Studies: Working Paper Series, 1996, No. 229.

Plaatjie, Sebeka Richard. 2017. "Beyond Western-Centric and Eurocentric Development: A Case for Decolonizing Development." *Africanus: Journal* of *Development Studies* 43, no. 2 (2017): 118–130. doi: 10.25159/0304-615X/2306.

Regan, Colm. 80:20: *Development in an Unequal World*, 6th edition. Oxford: New Internationalist, 2006.

Rodney, Walter. *How Europe Underdeveloped Africa*. London: Bogle-L'Ouverture, 1972.

Rostow, Walt Whitman. *The Stages of Economic Growth: A Non-Communist Manifesto*. Cambridge: Cambridge University Press, 1960.

Stewart, Peter D. S. *Development Theories: Only Study Guide for DVA3701*. Pretoria: UNISA, 2010.

Truman, Harry S. Truman's Inaugural Address, January 20, 1949 (Delivered in person at the Capitol). Accessed May 8, 2020. http://www.trumanlibrary.org/whistlestop/50yr_archive/inargural20jan1949.htm.

United Nations Development Programme. "Human Development Index (HDI)." Accessed May 23, 2020. http://hdr.undp.org/en/content/human-development-index -hdi.

Verharen, Charles C. "Afrocentrism and Acentrism: A Marriage of Science and Philosophy." *Journal of Black Studies* 26, no. 1 (1998): 62–76.

Viriri, Advice and Pascah Mungwini. "African Cosmology and the Duality of Western Hegemony: The Search for an African Identity." *Journal* of *Pan African Studies* 3, no. 6 (March 2010): 27–42.

Von Bismark, Otto. "1884-1885 Berlin Conference: Creating a Better Africa." Accessed May 8, 2020. http://teacherweb.ftl.pinecrest.edu/snyderd/MWH/Projects /MUN-BC/index.htm.

Chapter 11

Xenophobia in South Africa, 2008–2010

Is Pan-Africanism Still Alive or Dying?

Sky Mkuti

The struggles of Africans in the postcolonial era have been for complete economic, social, and political emancipation. These historical events were shaped by Pan-Africanism—an ideology of adaptable variations. This is because Pan-Africanism shaped a large part of the events of Africa in the twentieth century which remain imprinted in the twenty-first century. In its classic form, Pan-Africanism began in the mid-nineteenth century with struggles against slavery in the diaspora. However, as an "adaptable" ideology it transcended into the twentieth century and saw Marcus Garvey's radical demand of "Africa for the Africans" ideals being pursued.[1] Over the centuries, Pan-African ideas evolved and the second millennium brought additional changes for Africans as struggles against colonial powers gained momentum. The decolonization process of the twentieth century brought historical changes of African states' liberation and the eradication of colonial rule. Additionally, the twentieth century also saw a shift in Pan-African ideals with an increased need for cooperation and integration among African states. Thus, calling for greater economic growth and development guided by the first Pan-African organization, namely the Organization of African Unity (OAU), currently known as the African Union (AU), whose vision is highlighted in its Constitutive Act,[2] as attractive as the vision for an integrated, prosperous, and peaceful Africa is, challenges for its accomplishment remain a reality. The wake of xenophobic sentiments toward foreign nationals in South Africa created mixed feelings regarding the much-sought unity and integration of African people. Questions whether Africans still appreciate Pan-Africanism have surfaced due to the sporadic violent xenophobic outbreaks that took place during the 2008–2020 period. The incidents of violent xenophobic attacks in South Africa portray a negative image of what constitutes Pan-Africanism. This chapter revisits the prospects of Pan-Africanism in the twenty-first century in light of the xenophobic attacks against foreign nationals in South Africa. It postulates the psychological implications of xenophobic attacks to examine the status of Pan-Africanism: to determine whether this ideology is *alive* or *dying*. It gives a brief analogy of the successes advanced by ideals of early Pan-Africanists such as Kwame Nkrumah and W. E. B. Du Bois. The chapter concludes by answering an intrinsic, yet complex, question: Is Pan-Africanism still alive and appreciated as an essential belief for a unified Africa, or is it a dying ideology?

THE CONCEPT OF XENOPHOBIA: CONTEXTUALIZING SOUTH AFRICAN FEAR OF *THE OTHER*

The *Longman Dictionary of Contemporary English* defines xenophobia as an unreasonable fear and dislike of strange or foreign people. It is a term that originates from the Greek word *xenos* which means "strange" and *phobos* meaning *fear*.[3] Despite appearing to be a straightforward term, xenophobia remains a complex concept. Many debates have presented distinct views on the state of South Africa's xenophobic manifestations.[4] Despite rich explanations, there are omissions on how this societal ill called xenophobia impacts Pan-Africanism as an ideology that contributed to the establishment of a *free* and *democratic* nation in South Africa.

Several definitions construe xenophobia as an outcome of historical socio-economic disparities and innate insecurities among the masses to an overlooked problem by the government of South Africa. On the one hand xenophobia is also defined as a "deep and pervasive phenomenon":[5] a phenomenon that is not pursued by an individual effort, but collective, often arising due to poverty and lack of opportunities among the youth.[6] Another segment explains xenophobia as a hostile exclusion of foreigners or strangers on the basis of cultural or religious incompatibility. This forms the basis for exclusion through a discriminatory "economic self-interest" of which foreign nationals are perceived as the "other" group that quenches the already scarce economic opportunities, thus viewing foreign nationals as "strangers" who "steal" jobs from South Africans. The latter view instilled in their minds suggests that these economic benefits are reserved for South Africans alone.[7] This mentality toward others propelled the 2008 xenophobic attacks, although to some "xenophobic attitudes do not always or automatically translate into violence."[8] However, the 2008 manifestations of xenophobia against foreign nationals in South Africa proved that mass mobilization of xenophobic sentiments can lead to deadly violence.

Another noneconomic dimension suggests that xenophobia is also drawn from individuals' innate preferences.[9] This dimension relates to the psychological factors drawn from the apartheid segregation policies based on racial discrimination which remained dormant in the postapartheid era. Psychological factors vary from fabricated beliefs about foreigners, ignorance, misinformation, and emotional dynamics.[10] As a result, the hatred seen toward foreign nationals can be regarded as a "scapegoat" of an existing racial intolerance caused by the socioeconomic and political imbalances left by the apartheid legacy. This, then, frames xenophobia in South Africa as an outcome of a much deeper case of intolerance among its own citizenries. This intolerance has been diverted to the *Other* who became the weakest link in the existing racial violent-hate paradoxical coexistence in South Africa.

To put this assumption into context: (a) The incitement of racist incidents aired publicly in 2016 illustrate the underlying racial intolerance within the nation. For instance, when racial slurs are uttered by the likes of Penny Sparrow, who referred to blacks as "monkeys," a can of worms is loosened. (b) Further hate speech was aired in the public domain when Benny Morota, a black male advocate lecturing at a South African University, incited hate speech on social media (Facebook platform). He called his white colleague a "cockroach," which fueled a series of hate speech and racial intolerance among South African citizens. (c) The proponents of racism incorporate people with no influential social positioning to socially and somewhat culturally and politically affluent citizens such as the businessman Adam Catzavelos on the other hand, whose racial utterances were also aired on social media. (d) Other examples are the well-known South African musician Steve Hofmeyr and the Democratic Alliance leader Helen Zille whose insensitive utterances justifying colonialism enraged many South Africans. (e) This further stimulated racial intolerance and prompted the daughter of the liberation icons Nelson Mandela and Winnie Madikizela-Mandela, the late Zindzi Mandela, to get entangled in racial slurs on social media. To many this incident was in bad taste because at the time she was also serving as ambassador to Denmark with the responsibility to serve the people of South Africa impartially.[11]

Against the above background, it is not surprising that racial intolerance influences the dislike of *the Other*. As such, xenophobia in South Africa is a phenomenon that does not emerge in isolation. The historical patterns of racial, socioeconomic, cultural, and political discrimination have had psychological impacts on its citizens. The impact of xenophobic tendencies has weighed on foreign nationals' dignity as human beings. Apart from violent attacks they also suffer from discriminatory connotations such as calling them *makwerekwere* and body profiling which are attributed by the virtue of being an African of distinct nationality or an Asian immigrant.[12] In this sense, the unresolved sociopolitical circumstances of the apartheid regime created an intolerant and somewhat "hateful" populace whose discriminatory behavior is exposed in their hate speech utterances as exemplified above.

Evidently, racism and xenophobia are a bad combination for South Africa's progressive and leading role in Africa. Racism not only opens historical wounds but also aggravates the ideals of a unified rainbow nation and in many respects it negatively affects the larger portion of foreign nationals through acts of xenophobia. Hence, xenophobia presents the features of a new racism based on the discriminatory treatment meted out to foreign nationals who are regarded as the Other. This means that the instigation of discrimination is based on "the other's national origin or ethnicity."[13] In this sense, xenophobia in South Africa is also a phenomenon that unfortunately challenges any Pan-African idea despite South Africa having accomplished a peaceful democratic transition in 1994 and being regarded as a nation that embraces constitutional rights for everyone.[14]

The economic dynamics and human rights protection enshrined in the Bill of Rights of the South African Constitution (1996) became instrumental in attracting foreign nationals whose fate was met with distasteful intolerance instigated by the proponents of xenophobia. The 2008 xenophobic developments undermined South Africa's efforts in unifying Africans through its influential commitment toward regional, continental, and global development. Recurring xenophobic attacks tarnish the much-applauded sense of Pan-Africanism that embraces all cultures and creeds without traces of discrimination because its main unifying ideal negates all forms of discriminatory behavior. In South Africa, these ideals resonate with the term "rainbow nation" used since the inception of the Mandela Administration. It describes the coexistence of diversified cultures that embrace and value human rights. However, in recent years this has been clouded by intolerable and recurring incidents of racism and xenophobia that make one suspect that "the rainbow nation is dead."[15] This is due to the fact that many unresolved socioeconomic and political drivers of xenophobia are still part of the South African society, which fuel discrimination and intolerance. Subsequently, we find a high occurrence of racism and therefore a civil society that engages in violent xenophobic behavior. Additionally, the lack of an early government-intervention plan to address the manifestations of intolerance and discriminatory sentiments catalyzed the deadly incidents of xenophobia in 2008 and those that followed in the subsequent years. Furthermore, the then Mbeki Administration was perceived to have showed minimal commitment to fully acknowledge and take decisive steps to address the root causes of xenophobia despite engaging in certain isolated efforts.[16] These efforts did not deter the recurring incidents of xenophobia in the following years.

The lack of a National Action Plan (NAP) capable of addressing specific drivers of xenophobia meant that the recurring violent xenophobic attacks on foreign nationals were perceived as a *normal* affair. The socioeconomic gap is one of the drivers influencing xenophobic sentiments against foreign nationals. Until the end of 2019 the unemployment rate stood at 31% among the black majority and only 6% among the white group, with the colored population at 22%.[17]

The above figures represent a large unemployment percentage gap which is to a greater extent attributed to the economic legacies of apartheid. Foreign nationals are caught up in this historic problem and are continuously blamed for these socioeconomic maladies. There is also a distorted myth that foreign nationals are the major contributors of these economic woes despite their countries having been instrumental in mobilizing the attainment of South Africa's liberty from apartheid. The successful eradication of the apartheid regime gave hope to Pan-Africanism. The values and ideals of Pan-Africanism are enshrined in the governing agenda of the South African government through its committed economic and political objective of steering the "Africa Agenda." This is also endorsed in the Constitutive Act of the AU which vaunts the, "noble ideals which guided the founding fathers of our Continental Organization and generations of Pan-Africanists in their determination to promote unity, solidarity, cohesion and cooperation among the peoples of Africa and African States."[18]

The Ramaphosa Administration showed commitment in addressing the damaging effects of xenophobia and all forms of associated intolerance in theory through the implementation of the NAP.[19] As such, although xenophobia is a phenomenon which undermines Pan-Africanism and tarnishes the concept of rainbow nation, these two ideals remain significant transformational beliefs that cannot be allowed to die down. Their revitalization is necessary to advance a true sense of solidarity and unity among Africans and eradicate the myth that the Other is a stranger while having roots on the African soil, although there is more to what constitutes an African. Former South African president Thabo Mbeki asserts that the definition of what constitutes an African goes beyond racial identity and interweaves with the national identity of migrants who left their nation to find a new home in South Africa.[20] This view positions Pan-Africanism as a concept that does not only appropriate the identity of a traditional understanding of "black" Africanism but includes all people of Asian and mixed-race origin. In the South African context, Pan-Africanism suggests that South Africa does belong not only to native South Africans but to all who live in it and thus share the human rights values contained in the constitutional Bill of Rights.[21] Xenophobic violence negates this progressive view of Pan-Africanism.

DEALING WITH PAN-AFRICANISM
IN A XENOPHOBIC SOCIETY

Pan-Africanism is not a strange ideology but a concept that can be reinvented to accomplish desirable and progressive ideals. A concept that emerged in the twentieth century, Pan-Africanism can be regarded as an ideology or political movement traditionally premised by the desire to eradicate oppression such as slavery. Pan-Africanism emerged when people of African descendance moved around the world in search of greater freedom and liberty against the oppressive and discriminatory set of rules imposed by colonialism.[22] Throughout history Pan-Africanism survived challenges presented by conditions in distinct centuries. However, despite the hardships the unifying factor which remained the core purpose for its pursuit resulted in the eradication of a common ill: colonialism.

Furthermore, history dictates that in Africa "two advocates of African socialism, Kwame Nkrumah and Julius Nyerere—created institutional and ideological openings to realize African unity."[23] In essence, the unifying ideals of Pan-Africanism succeeded in freeing African states from European domination leading to the subsequent independence of Africa's 54 countries. In Africa, the struggle against colonial rule was the major driving force that intensified unity and cooperation among Africans on the continent and in the diaspora. Nkrumah knew this quite well when he became the first leader of an independent Ghana, liberated from colonial rule in 1957. This historic accomplishment paved the way for the independence of the rest of the African states, including South Africa. South Africa followed the ideals of this much-acclaimed leader of Pan-Africanism (Nkrumah) who appealed in his widely known writings *Africans Must Unite* that Africans should attain common liberties and do away with class struggle in Africa. Putting Nkrumah's ideals and appeal into practice remains a challenge and, in many respects, creates an environment prone to xenophobia and other forms of intolerance and discrimination, which in turn cripple the ideals of Pan-Africanism to this day. Xenophobia requires the same level of brotherhood commitment and determination used in the earlier century (twentieth) to eradicate colonialism and to solidify the unifying aspirations of Nkrumah, Nyerere, Samora Machel, and Nelson Mandela. For these "founding fathers" of Pan-Africanism the endurance against imperialist colonial rule led to the liberation of African states despite having been accomplished at a high cost. In the case of South Africa, Mandela endured 27 years of incarceration while Mozambique's Machel was assassinated—allegedly by the apartheid regime—in their quest for freedom from imperialism.[24] They both fought victoriously for the liberation of Africans, specifically against colonial oppression and violation of human rights. Overall, in the South African context, Pan-Africanism contributed to bring an end to what can be regarded as "the twentieth century's greatest Pan-African struggles—the civil rights and anti-apartheid battles."[25] For this reason, the efforts of the earlier Pan-Africans need not only be appreciated and honored; it is important to ensure that the values thereof are put into practice. Only then can the eradication of apartheid's challenging and historic "side effects" reflected in the existing socioeconomic conditions that have become pervasive for xenophobic sentiments among its proponents be fully redressed.

Additionally, the "diasporic" Pan-Africans such as Du Bois were also instrumental in advancing a sense of belonging among Africans on the continent and in the diaspora through nationalistic self-determination. Pan-Africanism is not simply an ideology that advances a "belief that African peoples, both on the continent and in the diaspora, share not merely a common history, but a common destiny."[26] It goes beyond that: it is an ideology imprinted in the hearts and minds of many Africans. This imprint is seen in the continuous desire for the fulfillment of a dream for brotherhood. This dream drives modern Pan-Africans to remain decisive in the pursuit of an undying desire of a "fully" unified Africa: one that is devoid of the boundaries once imposed by the colonial rule. South Africa has since the days of the freedom struggle committed itself to this dream through the development of Regional Economic Communities (RECs) such as the Southern African Development Community formed in 1992 and the subsequent transformation of the former 1963 OAU which is known as the AU since 2002. These regional and continental organizations have ushered in South Africa's role in advancing the aspirations of a united Africa. However, xenophobic attacks against Africans contradict this envisioned unity of African people.

Despite this, Pan-Africanism captivated a sense of belonging and gave birth to rights for political association and unity. Therefore, Pan-Africanism "is no different from any other broad-based and passionate political movement."[27] It could change and influence the understanding of someone's identity and pursuit of human rights. As an ideology it began as a nationalistic "black consciousness" advanced by classic diasporic Pan-Africanists such as Marcus Garvey and the sons of the African soil such as Steve Biko as well as the "black intelligentsia." This ideology went through many changes that it needed to be adaptable with time, thus shifting to a sense of Pan-Africanism that is "inclusive, hybrid and syncretic."[28] This ideal incorporates all African people regardless of race, culture, language, or nationality with an understanding that an African does not exist in isolation. Drumming up this kind of understanding in the minds of Africans has the potential to change misinformed myths about foreign migrants.

The same commitment that Du Bois's Pan-Africanism ignited and significantly linked Africa's first generation of leaders through political aspirations to free Africa from colonial oppression can still be applicable to South Africa's twenty-first-century generation to redress xenophobia.[29] Hence, reinventing Pan-Africanism in the twenty-first century will be instrumental in addressing xenophobia that manifests in intolerance, division, hate, and extreme violence toward foreign migrants seen during the 2008–2020 xenophobic attacks.

A REFLECTION ON INCIDENTS OF XENOPHOBIA IN SOUTH AFRICA (2008–2020): A CHALLENGE FOR PAN-AFRICANISM

It is no secret that the May 2008 xenophobic incidents in South Africa led to global astonishment and disparagement of the sacrificial efforts made by the forefathers of Pan-Africanism. In 2009 the Human Rights Watch *World Report* indicated that xenophobic attacks began in one of South Africa's economic provinces, Gauteng, in a squatter section of a township called Alexandra.[30] The attacks soon spread to other parts of the country. In most cases, the outbreaks of xenophobia occurred in informal settlements and when it turned violent the majority of deaths were usually among foreign nationals. In the case of the 2008 xenophobic incident, eleven Mozambicans, five Zimbabweans, and three Somalis lost their lives while thousands were injured. The report drawn from the Human Rights Watch further stated that some 40,000 foreign nationals left the country and a further 50,000 remained internally displaced.[31] This incident remains the peak of violent South African xenophobic manifestation because the victims of the brutal killings were largely African foreign immigrants.[32] However, this profiling has since changed given that in subsequent years xenophobia has been directed not only toward foreign nationals of African descent but also toward Pakistanis and other Asian migrants who have been equally blamed for all the socioeconomic struggles.[33]

Since the 2008 xenophobic incidents there have been numerous factors attributed to its occurrence and continuity over the past 12 years. The following paragraphs discuss a number of attributed reasons that have influenced xenophobic acts.

REASONS FOR CONTINUITY IN XENOPHOBIC INCIDENTS

There are two identified reasons that influence the continuity of xenophobic attacks targeted toward foreign nationals, which will be discussed further.

Inadequate Public Policing Order

There is evidence that the 1994 postapartheid government inherited numerous shortcomings from its predecessor's public policing management. Hence, in the aftermath of the 2008 xenophobic attacks the former president Thabo Mbeki stressed that "the organs of state have been fully mobilised to ensure law and order and protect everybody in our country."[34] However, reports indicate that one of the reasons for inadequacy in managing public policing has been the lack of capacity in intelligence gathering. This has led to a lack of confidence in the policing structures because victims of xenophobia feel that their rights are marginalized by the same structures that are supposed to protect them. For instance, in the aftermath of the May 2008 xenophobic attacks, government officials were merely reacting to the xenophobic outbreaks instead of putting into place stringent measures to uproot the xenophobic views that spread among the perpetrators of such attacks. The government's reaction to these attacks was to label them as criminal acts and not motivated by underlying xenophobic perceptions. The government spread the message that a so-called *third force* was responsible for instigating the attacks. These attacks tarnished South Africa's democracy as well as the Pan-African ideals that drive the national and international leadership of democratic South Africa.[35] Over the years the South African government strongly stressed this view, until March 2019 with the enactment of a NAP.[36]

Stagnant Rectification of Extreme Public Hostility toward Immigrants

Foreign nationals have over the years been demonized and blamed for numerous socioeconomic ills such as crime, unemployment, and cultural differences.[37] This has contributed to a never-ending cycle of violence toward foreign nationals with threats of xenophobic incidents being experienced almost annually in South Africa. It is, therefore, essential to redress the attitudes of the general South African public about xenophobia and what it entails. However, government efforts to do so have been stagnant. For example, despite being outlined in the Government Gazette, the Immigration Act of 2002 gives "blind" evidence on the measures intended to halt xenophobia.[38] These measures are considered "blind" in the sense that, although they are written in black and white, in most cases they are not followed or implemented as they should be. Subsequently, there has been no difference in the attitude of South Africans toward foreign nationals. This has, to a large extent, contributed to the recurring cases of xenophobic violence since the gruesome acts of May 2008. Several other xenophobic incidents followed in South Africa. For instance, in mid-April 2015 a number of xenophobic incidents made front-page headline news. The most graphic and inhumane was showing the fatal stabbing of a Mozambican named Emmanuel Sithole in Alexandra near Sandton. The murder of yet another Mozambican, Ernesto Nhamuave, who was burned alive in the Ramaphosa informal settlement on the East Rand, further serves as a grim reminder of what can happen when people view others as their enemies. These are only a few of the numerous examples of graphically inflicted hate that caused a grisly wave of xenophobia in South Africa.[39] Although these actions were also projected as criminal intent, xenophobic acts misrepresent Pan-African ideals that are meant to embrace "brotherhood" among a people of African descent, whether on the African continent or the diaspora.

Attack on foreign nationals do not only make South Africa look bad but are also "opposed to everything that our freedom from apartheid represents," stressed the then South African president Thabo Mbeki.[40] The xenophobic incidents of 2008 brought many questions, such as (a) Where did South Africa go wrong? (b) Was Mandela's long walk to freedom insignificant? (c) Where have the Pan-African ideals been stored? (d) Is Pan-Africanism dying?

This chapter cannot stress enough that the revival of the ideals of Pan-Africanism is essential to stimulate brotherhood and collaboration among Africans. Contemporary Pan-Africanists Mbeki and the Ugandan Yoweri Museveni have been instrumental in attempting to establish a "step-by-step" approach to Pan-Africanism with the reinforcement of the RECs. However, despite being instrumental in establishing regional economic cohesion and cooperation among African states, RECs have some shortcomings. They have produced limited solidarity in terms of the sociopolitical experience among the civil society. Critics argue that the lack of a people-focused Pan-African integration influences intolerance among Africans. Hence the need to reinvent Pan-Africanism because thus far greater emphasis has been on economic and state development by the RECs.[41] Subsequently, this has blindsided the Pan-African rhetoric of a unified African people through a sense of brotherhood solidarity. Instead, the successes have been fully visible by a mere establishment of states' regional economic development. It would thus be significant if a shift in the tenets of Pan-Africanism would focus on the formulation of strategies that focus strongly on the combat of disinformation and hate speech that instigates xenophobic manifestations and violence.[42] Figure 11.1 depicts a long-standing feature of xenophobia in South Africa. It further shows that there has been a sharp increase in the incidents of xenophobic attacks against foreign nationals since 2008, specifically in 2019 when xenophobic incidents nearly matched those of 2015. This is concerning because instead of reducing, xenophobia seems to have become a stronghold that hinders the sense

Total Number of Xenophobic Violence Incidents in South Africa by Year: 1994-April 2021

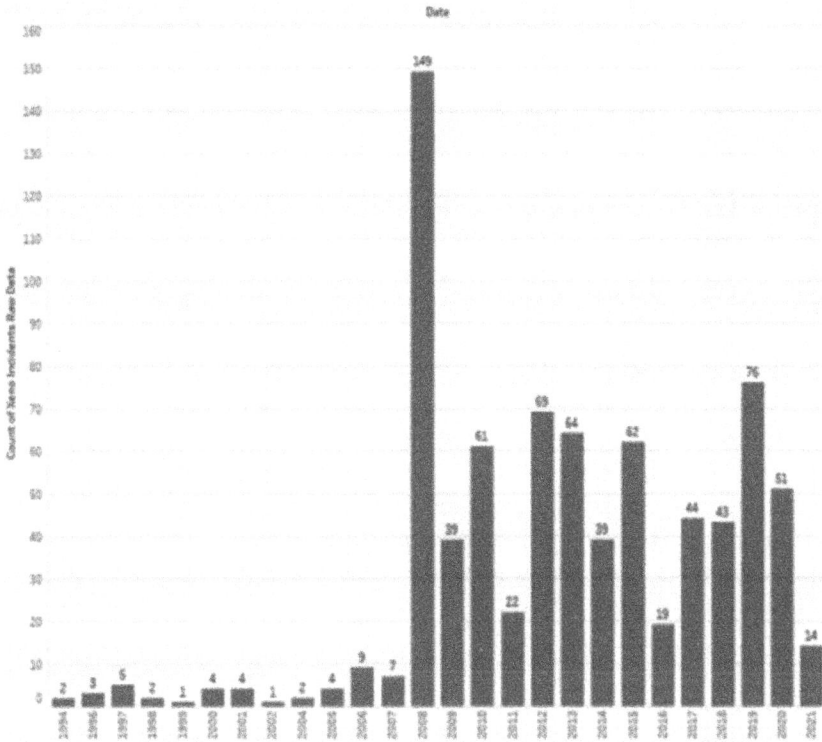

Figure 11.1   Incidents of xenophobic violence in South Africa.

of brotherhood and solidarity that Pan-Africanism is meant to nurture among African people and humanity as a whole.

As indicated earlier, figure 11.1 presents a clear indication of an increase in the incidents of xenophobic attacks against foreign nationals. This further suggests the need for formulation and implementation of strategic approaches that would effectively counter the resurgence of xenophobic acts. Most importantly, strategies that will intensify the eradication of disinformation are needed.[43] In many cases this disinformation strengthens extreme discriminatory behavior seen in the attribution of derogatory terms such as *makwerekwere*—a term used to describe foreign nationals. People are often profiled by their looks, language, and physical appearances that are distinct from national citizens. The United Nations High Commissioner for Refugees agrees that "stereotyping foreigners and other outsiders assists in their victimisation, and uninformed opinions are often reproduced unexamined by the media."[44] As such, because of the exacerbation of xenophobic manifestations through harmful stereotypes and disinformation which is often spread through social media, there is a need to educate the masses against this harmful behavior. Moreover, despite having a legislative plan in place to address xenophobic challenges, the effectiveness in combating xenophobia and related acts of intolerance by the National Action Plan (NAP), as enacted in 2019, is yet to be seen.[45]

The implementation of the NAP thus represents a shift in the manner in which the South African government has prioritized and finally acknowledged the chronic problem that xenophobia causes. This could be viewed as a resolute step in addressing this challenge. The government's historical dragging of their feet on acting proactively against xenophobia has in many respects undermined its efforts in advancing development-oriented policy initiatives and programs. These policies and programs are to a larger extent driven by Pan-African ideals as in the case of the "Africa Agenda."

It is also worth noting that for over a decade since the 2008 violent xenophobic outbreaks, the South African government has been somewhat reluctant in acknowledging the existence of xenophobia.[46] On many occasions the South African government and law enforcement authorities have been reported to repeatedly claim that the waves of violence have been purely acts of crime instead of xenophobia.[47] Hence, the government leaders have been categorically regarded as "denialists" for repeatedly rejecting the argument that the increased violence against migrants and refugees was due to xenophobia and as "minimalists" for acknowledging xenophobia but disregarding its potential as an "epiphenomenon" which does not reach to the underlying origins of violent manifestations. On some occasions they were called "realists" for acknowledging that xenophobia is indeed an extant phenomenon and that a number of South Africans are prone to violence and xenophobia.[48]

In this manner, a proactive response to the regular incidents of xenophobic attacks is necessary: one that takes South Africans back to the basics of humanity and to the realization of what truly constitutes an African irrespective of national, racial, cultural, and language distinctions. Interestingly, in the aftermath of the violent 2008 xenophobic attacks, the South African government reminded South Africans that they

> must never forget that our struggle for liberation has always been both national and Pan-African. . . . We must never forget that our economy was built by the combined labour of Africans drawn from all countries of our region, many of whom died in our mines together with their fellow South African workers.[49]

However, this did not deter the proponents of xenophobia from acting violently toward foreign nationals or rethinking how xenophobia negates the ideals of Pan-Africanism. Instead of a behavioral change more incidents of xenophobia were experienced giving an indication of greater intolerant behavior. For instance, from 2008 until end of 2018 Xenowatch recorded 529 incidents of violent xenophobia that resulted in 309 deaths, 901 physical assaults, 2,193 shops looted, and the displacement of over 100,000 people.[50] Furthermore, in September 2019, South Africa awakened to yet another xenophobic incident toward foreign nationals in Hillbrow, Johannesburg. Additionally, a large number of immigrants was displaced leading to massive homelessness. Factors such as endemic corruption and poor economic planning by the South African Government have also compounded criminal acts against foreign nationals when xenophobic attacks ensued.[51]

In September 2020 Human Rights Watch documented, yet again, mob attacks against foreign nationals: this time the target was not only African descendants but people of Asian descent as well. More than 1,000 Bangladeshi shops were looted. Foreign nationals are still "scapegoated and blamed for economic insecurity, crime and government failures to deliver services."[52] To compound matters further, the preconceived notion that foreign nationals steal jobs and women, deplete the country's basic services, spread diseases, and run crime syndicates brings alienation among Africans. It also tarnishes the prospects of establishing a harmonious and united Africa through acceptance of fellow Africans and a sense of brotherhood. In fact, violent xenophobic actions and their undesirable stereotypes constitute a betrayal to the South African constitutional promise and the government's commitment to "preventing and deterring xenophobia within the Department [Department of Home Affairs], any sphere of government or organ of State and at community level."[53]

To this end, the continuity of xenophobic outbreaks in the face of an extant legislative measure suggests that the real drivers that motivate the proponents of violent xenophobic attacks are, firstly, the lack of respect for the country's laws and policies; secondly, the lack of trusted, prompt, and effective conflict resolution mechanisms; thirdly, the existence of local community political vacuums capable of creating a false consciousness of what it means to be a "noncompliant" foreign national; and finally, the absence of a culture of impunity toward attacks on foreign nationals.[54] When these aspects are not accurately addressed, intolerance toward immigrants and continued exacerbation of xenophobic outbreaks become inevitable. This chapter goes a step further to identify the lack of the advocacy for appreciation and celebration of a unique and diversified Africa. This diversity is shown by Africa's socioeconomic composition that is made up of distinct languages and religions, race and ethnicities, and gender and class. The continuous advocacy of all these aspects can strengthen government's decisiveness in pursuing Pan-Africanism at a social level. The absence of this will pose questions on the position of the government in addressing the continuous incidents of violent intolerance toward migrants despite the enactment of a legislation created to respond to the challenges that intolerance and xenophobia bring to South Africa's global image.

THE STATE OF PAN-AFRICANISM: ALIVE OR DYING?

Pan-Africanism is more than a mere ideology. It represents the interconnectedness of African people's past, present, and an envisioned united future. As such it cannot die and it remains relevant. As an ideology it is continuous and requires reinvention for it to remain relevant in the twenty-first century. It remains relevant because of the interconnectedness of the past and future that the African people share with each other and which continue to shape their Pan-African aspirations despite the challenges seen throughout centuries, specifically when opposing racism, colonialism, oppression, and exploitation against African descendants.[55] So, to answer the pressing question whether Pan-Africanism is still alive or dying, it is equally vital to identify the reasons behind its initial pursuit and impactful worldview.

Pan-Africanism is an ideology that emerged in the diaspora and was a highly desirable political ideology. It was also a unifying force by Africans on the continent and in the diaspora. The ideals of Pan-Africanism were guided by common struggles and a desire to fight against racial segregation brought by colonialism. These ideals fertilized in the minds of the African intellectuals in the diaspora whose vision created a response against European domination.[56] The consequences of these divisions are visible and can be identified through societal ills that challenge the prospect of Pan-Africanism in many distinct forms, from isolated incidents of racism to current xenophobic upheaval seen in South Africa. Nonetheless, the original movement of Pan-Africanism driven by the likes of Marcus Garvey, Du Bois, C. L. R. James, Nkrumah, and George Padmore imagined a nonracial, independent, and a unified Africa: one that would certainly never have been a playground for xenophobia and its damaging repercussions.

History suggests that the founders of Pan-Africanism popularized a global sentiment of "Africa for the Africans at home and abroad."[57] In the same vein, modern Pan-Africanists such as Mbeki, Ramaphosa, Nkosazana Dlamini-Zuma, and Graça Machel still preserve Pan-Africanism under the auspices of an African Renaissance. It is an ideology that pursues the political and ideological vision that matches with the aspirations of African people, although each country from all four corners of our continent has distinct historic experiences with colonial exploitation. In many regards this influences the strengths and weaknesses in the achievement and sustainability of Pan-Africanism. Undoubtedly, the remnants of colonial exploitation created an array of shortcomings, leaving an unalterable "dark period of our history."[58] It is essential to identify these weaknesses and strengths of our common historic experiences in order to remodel Pan-Africanism in a manner that would address the current and future challenges of xenophobia. This view resonates with the argument that the beginning of any proactivism requires acknowledgment of weaknesses and strengths because a "struggle that does not inventory what it can do for itself, and then rely on that as its starting base, is doomed to fail."[59] It is in Africa's interest to have an African citizenry that thinks and acts through the lenses of Pan-African values to build a society that does not abhor fellow Africans but realizes that anyone deserves basic human rights such as freedom, dignity, and respect to life. This would build a united society in which all people play a vital role in building an African continent that is devoid of violent discrimination and xenophobic tendencies despite the existence of diverse cultures, languages, and religions. What then should we say: Is Pan-Africanism dying? It might be dormant but definitely not dead or dying. It would be absurd to let the efforts of many liberation leaders such as Nkrumah, Nyerere, Machel, Amilcar Cabral, Agostinho Neto, and Mandela go down the drain. It is in principle still the responsibility of every African to revitalize Pan-Africanism by embracing its ideals and advocating its values among the masses.

In its contemporary form, Pan-Africanism remains an ideology which can propagate unity in a reinvented manner. The initial vision of achieving freedom and independence from colonial rule has to a certain degree been successfully accomplished. However, the advocacy of Pan-African ideals needs to be more accessible to the masses instead of being pursued by a few educated Pan-Africanists as it was in its classic form. While Pan-Africanism spread across Africa, it created an exclusive African class, an elite movement comprised of African intellectuals who were also by-products of Western education. The shortcoming of this was that they "identified more with one another than with 'uneducated' Africans."[60] Although the educated African elite had a mission of prefabricating a "rational" Pan-African culture that was capable of elevating and politicizing the consciousness of the common people, the masses were not actively involved in politicizing Pan-Africanism themselves.[61] As a result, only the elite was avid in raising the consciousness for the ideals of Pan-Africanism necessary to free Africans from the shackles of their regressive beliefs and values.

Therefore, in the twenty-first century the culture of Pan-Africanism requires reinvention, popularization, and a more avid engagement of the civil society at the grassroots. This will enable all people to thrive together with the state leaders who have thus far been instrumental in leading Pan-Africanism through political and economic models that are largely embedded in the AU's development goals. These goals entail among others the promotion of unity and solidarity of the African states.[62]

In its broader sense, Pan-Africanism is driven by good intentions despite remaining a movement that requires adaptability to address the socioeconomic and cultural challenges affecting African people, specifically South Africans within the context of xenophobia. This suggests that the attainment of unity and solidarity of African peoples requires nurturing in order to redress the continuity of xenophobic violence which depicts a gloomy Pan-African scenario that exposes the existence of intense intolerance toward foreign nationals.

Despite being a society that is "inherently" violent due to its oppressive historical background, there is an urgent need for a mindset shift to revive the most pressing Pan-African drivers embedded in South Africa's foreign policy: a policy that is premised on the "Africa Agenda" that contributes toward regional and continental peace and security and plays a significant role in developmental integration and investments as well as the building of African institutions such as the AU. Apart from playing a significant role in the reform of the former organizational structure, namely the OAU which resulted in the 2002 launch of the AU in Durban, South Africa also led the development of many other projects such as the Programme for Infrastructure Development in Africa and the creation of a Pan-African Parliament.[63]

Against the above backdrop, South Africa has over the years gained credibility as the key African voice that positions African affairs on the continent and internationally. It advances an "African Agenda" that addresses among other issues global marginalization through multilateral relations and South-South engagements such as BRICS. This alone symbolizes the existence and appreciation of living Pan-African values. Nonetheless, it is a responsibility of all African descendants to embrace the unifying ideals of Pan-Africanism to fight against xenophobia, for "none of us alone can save the nation or the world. But each of us can make a positive difference if we commit ourselves to do so."[64] This assertion is, therefore, an indication of the need for a collective commitment as a step toward the revitalization of Pan-Africanism.

CONCLUSION

The May 2008 xenophobic outbreaks in South Africa heightened an analysis of the causes and factors that led to its occurrence. Despite an array of speculated reasons for its outbreak largely assumed to have emanated from the socioeconomic and political conditions, the historic conditions from the mid-seventeenth to the latter half of the twentieth century in South Africa played a crucial role in the violent manifestations of intolerance toward foreign nationals. This prompted a further analysis of the prospects of Pan-Africanism as a unifying ideology that has brought together people with common interests, values, and aspirations to attain a much-desired liberty against all forms of oppression. As such, inasmuch as the South African government received much criticism for not being decisive in putting into place legislation that would eradicate increasing xenophobic tendencies, in theory the Ramaphosa Administration showed huge commitment to tackle xenophobia and related intolerance through the inception of the NAP. However, the effectiveness of this in eradicating future xenophobic attacks and advancing Pan-Africanism among the civil society, in particular the proponents of xenophobic acts, is yet to be seen. This chapter takes the position that revitalizing Pan-Africanism in South Africa is an approach that needs serious consideration. It further argues that Pan-Africanism is not dead because its values of "brotherhood," "African Renaissance," and "unity" are embedded in the very institutions that govern South Africa and the entire continent through RECs and the AU. The reinvention of Pan-Africanism in the twenty-first century is nonetheless necessary to eradicate the myths surrounding foreign nationals. Only then can xenophobia be alienated and Pan-Africanism appreciated by putting its ideals into practice. The starting point would be to reconstruct the essence of the African culture among the people of African descent. This would not only shape our contemporary lives but ensure that we continuously embrace one another despite having distinct features.

NOTES

1. Adom Gatechew. "A Fuller Freedom: The Lost Promise of Pan-Africanism," *The Nation*, October 29, 2019. https://www.thenation.com/article/archive/pan-africanism-history-hakim-adi-review/.

2. African Union Constitutive Act. "The Constitutive Act of the African Union: Adopted by the Thirty-Sixth Ordinary Session of the Assembly of Heads of State And Government," July 11, 2000. https://au.int/sites/default/files/pages/34873-file-constitutiveact_en.pdf.

3. M. Mayor, *Longman Dictionary of Contemporary English*, 6th Edition (London: Pearson Education, 2015), 1223.

4. Laurence Caromba. "Imagined Liberation: Xenophobia, Citizenship and Identity in South Africa, Germany and Canada." *Politikon*, 42, no. 2 (2015): 296. doi: 10.1080/02589346.2015.1057676.

5. Crush, "Face of Xenophobia."

6. Sechaba Koapa. "Xenophobia in Southern Africa: A Pan-Africanist Perspective for Modern Times." *Open Access Library Journal*, 3 (2016): e2415. doi: 10.4236/oalib.1102415.

7. Jonathan Crush. "The Perfect Storm: The Realities of Xenophobia in Contemporary South Africa." Southern African Migration Project (SAMP), *Migration Policy Series*, no. 50 (Cape Town: Idasa, 2008b), 3: 29.

8. Philippa Kerr, et al. "Xenophobic Violence and the Struggle Discourse in South Africa." *JAAS*, 54, no. 7 (2019): 999.

9. Caromba, *Imagined Liberation*, 296.

10. Steven Laurence Gordon. "Understanding Xenophobic Hate Crime in South Africa." *Wiley Journal of Public Affairs* (2020): 9. doi:10.1002/pa.2076.

11. Judith Geldenhuys and Michelle Kelly-Louw. "Hate Speech and Racist Slurs in the South African Context: Where to Starts?" Pioneer in Peer Reviewed (P.E.R) Open Access Online Law Publications, 23 (2020): 22–25.

12. David Mario Matsinhe. "Africa's Fear of Itself: The Ideology of Makwerekwere in South Africa." *Third World Quarterly*, 32, no. 2 (2011): 303.

13. Carol Adjai and Gabriella Lazaridis. "Migration, Xenophobia And New Racism in Post-Apartheid South Africa," *Redframe* 1, no. 1 (2013): 192.

14. Dewa Mavhinga, "Cyril Ramaphosa Should Revive South Africa's Human Rights Agenda." *Human Rights Watch News*, March 17, 2020. https://www.hrw.org/news/2020/03/17/cyril-ramaphosa-should-revive-south-africas-human-rights-agenda.

15. Pearl Mncube. "The Rainbow Nation Is Dead." *News24*, May 23, 2019. https://www.news24.com/news24/columnists/guestcolumn/the-rainbow-nation-is-dead-20190523.

16. Crush, "Face of Xenophobia."

17. Mncube, "The Rainbow."

18. African Union Constitutive Act, "The African Union," 2.

19. South African Government National Action Plan (NAP). "National Action Plan to Combat Racism, Racial Discrimination, Xenophobia and Related Intolerance." March 2019, 14.

20. Mark Gevisser. *The Dream Deferred: Thabo Mbeki* (Johannesburg: Jonathan Ball Publishers, 2007), 326.

21. The Constitution of the Republic of South Africa. "Bill of Rights: Chapter 2," Section 7-39, 10 December 1996. https://www.justice.gov.za/legislation/constitution/chp02.html.

22. Gatechew, "Promise of Pan-Africanism."

23. Ibid.

24. Augusta Conchiglia. "Was Mozambique Air Crash an Assassination? The Mysterious Death of Samora Machel," *Le Monde diplomatique*, November 2017. https://mondediplo.com/2017/11/12Machel.

25. Adekeye Adebajo. "Mandela, Pan-African Prophet." *International Peace Institute: Global Observatory*, December 9, 2013. https://theglobalobservatory.org/2013/12/mandela-pan-african-prophet/.

26. Minkah Makalani. "Pan-Africanism." *Africana Age*, 2011. https://wayback.archive-it.org/11788/20200108191610/http://exhibitions.nypl.org/africanaage/essay-pan-africanism.html.

27. Dambudzo Mapuranga. 2019. "Is Pan-Africanism dead?" *The Patriot*, May 23, 2019. https://www.thepatriot.co.zw/old_posts/is-pa-africanism-dead/.

28. Gevisser, "The Dream," 326.

29. Brandon Kendhammer. "DuBois the pan-Africanist and the Development of African Nationalism." *Ethnic and Racial Studies*, 30, no. 1 (2007): 53.

30. Human Rights Watch. "South Africa Events of 2008." World Report, 2009. https://www.hrw.org/world-report/2009/country-chapters/south-africa.

31. Human Rights Watch. "South Africa Events of 2008."

32. SABC NEWS. "Cape Mounts Relief Effort as Xenophobia Spreads." May 23, 2008. https://web.archive.org/web/20080612135405/http://www.sabcnews.com/south_africa/general/0%2C2172%2C170109%2C00.html.

33. Human Rights Watch. "They Have Robbed Me of My Life": Xenophobic Violence Against Non-Nationals in South Africa. September 17, 2020c. https://www.hrw.org/report/2020/09/17/they-have-robbed-me-my-life/xenophobic-violence-against-non-nationals-south.

34. Department of International Relations and Cooperation (DIRCO). "Radio and Television Address to the Nation by the President of South Africa, Thabo Mbeki, on the occasion of Africa Day." *News and Events*, May 25, 2008. http://www.dirco.gov.za/docs/speeches/2008/mbek0525.html.

35. Betuel Ngcamu and Evangelos Mantzaris. "Xenophobic Violence and Criminality in the KwaZulu-Natal Townships." *The Journal for Transdisciplinary Research in Southern Africa*, 15, no. 1 (2019): 1–8.

36. NAP, "Intolerance," 14.

37. Daniel Tevera, "African Migrants, Xenophobia and Urban Violence in Post-apartheid South Africa. Alternation." *Special Edition*, 7 (2013): 16.

38. South African Government Gazette. "Immigration Act No 13." 443, no. 23478 (2002): 14. http://www.saflii.org/za/legis/num_act/ia2002138.pdf.

39. Kwanele Sosibo. "Xenophobia: What Did We Learn from 2008?" *Mail & Guardian News Analysis*, April 23, 2015, https://mg.co.za/article/2015-04-23-xenophobia-what-did-we-learn-from-2008/.

40. DIRCO, "Africa Day."

41. Emmanuel Kisiangani. "The Dream of Uniting Africa Has Persisted for Some Time Now. Its Undoing, however, Remains Attempts to Unite the Political Class Rather than African People." *Institute for Security Security (ISS) Today*, 2013. https://issafrica.org/iss-today/au-and-pan-africanism-beyond-rhetoric%20.

42. United Nations Educational, Scientific and Cultural Organization (UNESCO). "Fight Against Xenophobia in the Age of Disinformation and Artificial Intelligence." February 2, 2020. https://en.unesco.org/news/fight-against-xenophobia-age-disinformation-and-artificial-intelligence.

43. UNESCO, "Fight."

44. Jean Pierre Misago, Iriann Freemantle, and Loren Landau. "Protection From Xenophobia: An Evaluation of UNHCR's Regional Office for Southern Africa's Xenophobia Related Programmes," *UNHCR*, February (2015):23. https://www.unhcr.org/55cb153f9.pdf.

45. NAP, "Intolerance," 14.

46. David Monda. "Long Walk to Freedom: Xenophobia Continues Against African Migrants in Johannesburg, South Africa." *Political Animal Magazine*, October 4, 2019. https://www.politicalanimalmagazine.com/2019/10/04/long-walk-to-freedom-xenophobia-continues-against-african-migrants-in-johannesburg-south-africa /.

47. Human Rights Watch. "South Africa: Widespread Xenophobic Violence Implement National Action Plan; Hold Attackers Responsible." September 17, 2020b. https://www.hrw.org/news/2020/09/17/south-africa-widespread-xenophobic -violence.

48. Jonathan Crush and Sujata Ramachandran. "Xenophobic Violence in South Africa: Denialism, Minimalism, Realism." Migration Policy Series No. 66. The Southern African Migration Programme (SAMP). (Cape Town: Bronwen Dachs Müller, 2014), 11.

49. DIRCO, "Africa Day."

50. Jean Pierre Misago and Silindile Mlilo. "Xenophobic Violence in South Africa: 1994-2018 An Overview," Xenowatch, March 2019, 2. The African Centre for Migration & Society (ACMS). https://www.xenowatch.ac.za/wp -content/uploads/2019/03/Xenophobic-Violence-in-South-Africa-1994-2018_An -Overview.pdf.

51. Monda. "Long Walk."

52. Mia Swart. "'There will be Blood': Xenophobia in S Africa Routine and Lethal,"*AlJazeera*, September 17, 2020. https://www.aljazeera.com/news/2020/09/17 /there-will-be-blood-xenophobia-in-s-africa-routine-and-lethal/.

53. South African Government Gazette, "Immigration Act," 14.

54. Jean Pierre Misag, et al. "Towards Tolerance, Law, and Dignity: Addressing Violence against Foreign Nationals in South Africa." *International Organisation for Migration* (IOM), 1 (2009): 1-63. https://web.archive.org/web/20160711045229 /http://www.iom.int/jahia/webdav/shared/shared/mainsite/media/docs/reports/ violence_against_foreign_nationals.pdf.

55. Makalani, "Pan-Africanism."

56. Ngũgĩ wa Thiong'o. "African Identities: Pan-Africanism in the Era of Globalization and Capitalist Fundamentalism," *Macalester International*, 14, Article 9 (2004): 21–42.

57. Thiong'o, "African Identities," 32.

58. Jean-Baptiste Natama. "Message on Pan-Africanism on the Occasion of the Fiftieth Anniversary of the Organisation of African Unity." *African Union*, May 25, 2013. https://au.int/sites/default/files/newsevents/workingdocuments/29152-wd -message_on_pan-africanism_-_english_0.pdf.

59. Thiong'o, "African Identities," 27.

60. Tshabalala, "A History."

61. John McCall, "The Pan-Africanism We Have: Nollywood's Invention of Africa." *Film International*, 5, no. 4 (2007): 92–97.

62. African Union Constitutive Act, "The African Union," 5.

63. Neuma Grobbelaar and Chen, Yunnan. "Understanding South Africa's Role in Achieving Regional and Global Development Progress," *IDS Policy Briefing*, no. 64, May 2014. https://assets.publishing.service.gov.uk/media/57a089c040f0b65 2dd0003c0/PB64.pdf.

64. Cornel West. *Race Matters* (New York: Vintage Books, 1994), 109.

BIBLIOGRAPHY

Adebajo, Adekeye. 2013. Mandela, Pan-African Prophet. International Peace Institute: Global Observatory, December 9. Accessed on September 20, 2020. https://theglobalobservatory.org/2013/12/mandela-pan-african-prophet/ .

Adjai, Carol. & Lazaridis, Gabriella.. "Migration, Xenophobia and New Racism in Post-Apartheid South Africa." *Redframe* 1, 1 (2013): 192–205.

African Union Constitutive Act. 2000. The Constitutive Act of the African Union: Adopted by the Thirty-Sixth Ordinary Session of the Assembly of Heads of State And Government, July 11. Accessed on September 20, 2020. https://au.int/sites/default/files/pages/34873-file-constitutiveact_en.pdf.

BBC News. 2019. South Africa: How Common are Xenophobic Attacks? October 2. Accessed on October 20, 2020. https://www.bbc.com/news/world-africa-47800718.

Caromba, Laurence. "Imagined Liberation: Xenophobia, Citizenship and Identity in South Africa, Germany and Canada." *Politikon* 42, 2 (2015): 295–298. doi:10.108 0/02589346.2015.1057676.

Conchiglia, Augusta. 2017. "Was Mozambique Air Crash an Assassination? The Mysterious Death of Samora Machel." *Le Monde diplomatique*, November. Accessed on October 01, 2020. https://mondediplo.com/2017/11/12Machel.

Crush, Jonathan. 2008a. "South Africa: Policy in the Face of Xenophobia." *Migration Policy Institute,* July. Accessed on October 01, 2020. https://www.migrationpolicy .org/article/south-africa-policy-face-xenophobia.

Crush, Jonathan. 2008b. "The Perfect Storm: The Realities of Xenophobia in Contemporary South Africa." Southern African Migration Project (SAMP) *Migration Policy Series* Issue Nr. 50. Cape Town: Idasa, pp. 1–68.

Crush, Jonathan & Ramachandran, Sujata. 2014. *Xenophobic Violence in South Africa: Denialism, Minimalism, Realism.* Migration Policy Series No. 66. The Southern African Migration Programme (SAMP). Cape Town: Bronwen Dachs Müller, pp. 1–49.

Department of International Relations and Cooperation (DIRCO). 2008. "Radio and Television Address to the Nation by the President of South Africa, Thabo Mbeki, on the Occasion of Africa Day." *News and Events*, May 25. Accessed on October 10, 2020. http://www.dirco.gov.za/docs/speeches/2008/mbek0525.html.

Gatechew, Adom. 2019. A Fuller Freedom: The Lost Promise of Pan-Africanism. *The Nation*, October 29. Accessed on September 20, 2020. https://www.thenation.com /article/archive/pan-africanism-history-hakim-adi-review/.

Geldenhuys, Judith & Kelly-Louw, Michelle. 2020. "Hate Speech and Racist Slurs in the South African Context: Where to Starts?" *Pioneer in Peer Reviewed (P.E.R) Open Access Online Law Publications* 23: 1–46.

Gevisser, Mark. 2007. *The Dream Deferred: Thabo Mbeki*. Johannesburg: Jonathan Ball Publishers.

Gordon, Steven Laurence. "Understanding Xenophobic Hate Crime in South Africa." *Wiley*, (2020): 1–9. doi:10.1002/pa.2076.

Grobbelaar, Neuma & Yunnan, Chen. "Understanding South Africa's Role in Achieving Regional and Global Development Progress." IDS Policy Briefing Issue Nr.64, May, (2014). Accessed on August 01, 2020. https://assets.publishing.service .gov.uk/media/57a089c040f0b652dd0003c0/PB64.pdf.

Human Rights Watch. 2009. South Africa Events of 2008. *World Report*. Accessed on June 15, 2020. https://www.hrw.org/world-report/2009/country-chapters/south -africa.

Human Rights Watch. 2020a. World Report: South Africa Events of 2019. *World Report*. Accessed on June 15, 2020. https://www.hrw.org/world-report/2020/ country-chapters/south-africa.

Human Rights Watch. 2020b. "South Africa: Widespread Xenophobic Violence Implement National Action Plan; Hold Attackers Responsible." September 17. Accessed on September 20, 2020. https://www.hrw.org/news/2020/09/17/south -africa-widespread-xenophobic-violence.

Human Rights Watch. 2020c. "They Have Robbed Me of My Life": Xenophobic Violence Against Non-Nationals in South Africa. September 17. Accessed on September 20, 2020. https://www.hrw.org/report/2020/09/17/they-have-robbed -me-my-life/xenophobic-violence-against-non-nationals-south.

Kendhammer, Brandon. DuBois the Pan-Africanist and the Development of African Nationalism. *Ethnic and Racial Studies* 30, 1 (2007): 51–71.

Kerr, Philippa, Durrheim, Kevin & Dixon, John. 2019. "Xenophobic Violence and the Struggle Discourse in South Africa." *JAAS* 54, 7 (2019): 955–1011.

Kisiangani, Emmanuel. 2013. "The Dream of Uniting Africa has Persisted for Some Time Now. Its Undoing, However, Remains Attempts to Unite the Political Class rather than African People." *Institute for Security Security (ISS) Today*. Accessed on September 20, 2020. https://issafrica.org/iss-today/au-and-pan-africanism -beyond-rhetoric%20.

Koapa, Sechaba. 2016. "Xenophobia in Southern Africa: A Pan-Africanist Perspective for Modern Times." *Open Access Library Journal*, 3: e2415. Accessed on September 20, 2020. doi:10.4236/oalib.1102415.

Makalani, Minkah. 2011. *"Pan-Africanism"*. New York: Africana Age. Accessed on June 15, 2020. https://wayback.archive-it.org/11788/20200108191610/http:// exhibitions.nypl.org/africanaage/essay-pan-africanism.html.

Mapuranga, Dambudzo. 2019. Is Pan-Africanism Dead? *The Patriot*, May 23. Accessed on June 20, 2020. https://www.thepatriot.co.zw/old_posts/is-pa-africanism-dead/.

Matsinhe, David Mario. 2011. "Africa's Fear of Itself: The Ideology of Makwerekwere in South Africa." *Third World Quarterly* 32, 2 (2011): 295–313.

Mavhinga, Dewa. 2020. "Cyril Ramaphosa Should Revive South Africa's Human Rights Agenda." *Human Rights Watch News*, March 17. Accessed on September 20, 2020. https://www.hrw.org/news/2020/03/17/cyril-ramaphosa-should-revive -south-africas-human-rights-agenda.

Mayor, M. *Longman Dictionary of Contemporary English*. 6th edition. London: Pearson Education, 2015.

McCall, John. 2007. The Pan-Africanism We Have: Nollywood's Invention of Africa. *Film International* 5, 4 (2007): 92–97.

Misago, Jean Pierre, Freemantle, Iriann & Landau, Loren. 2015. "Protection From Xenophobia: An Evaluation of UNHCR's Regional Office for Southern Africa's Xenophobia Related Programmes," *UNHCR*, February, pp. 1–108. Accessed on June 15, 2020. https://www.unhcr.org/55cb153f9.pdf.

Misago, Jean Pierre, Landau, Loren & Monson, Tamlyn. 2009. Towards Tolerance, Law, and Dignity: Addressing Violence against Foreign Nationals in South Africa. *International Organisation for Migration (IOM)*, 1: 1–63. Accessed on June 15, 2020. https://web.archive.org/web/20160711045229/http://www.iom.int/jahia/webdav/shared/shared/mainsite/media/docs/reports/violence_against_foreign_nationals.pdf.

Misago, Jean Pierre & Mlilo, Silindile. 2019. "Xenophobic Violence in South Africa: 1994-2018 An Overview." *Xenowatch*, 1–7. The African Centre for Migration & Society (ACMS). Accessed on June 15, 2020. https://www.xenowatch.ac.za/wp-content/uploads/2019/03/Xenophobic-Violence-in-South-Africa-1994-2018_An-Overview.pdf.

Mncube, Pearl. 2019. "The Rainbow Nation is Dead." *News24*, May 23. Accessed on September 20, 2020. https://www.news24.com/news24/columnists/guestcolumn/the-rainbow-nation-is-dead-20190523.

Monda, David. 2019. "Long Walk to Freedom: Xenophobia Continues Against African Migrants in Johannesburg, South Africa." *Political Animal Magazine*, October 04. Accessed on June 15, 2020. https://www.politicalanimalmagazine.com/2019/10/04/long-walk-to-freedom-xenophobia-continues-against-african-migrants-in-johannesburg-south-africa/.

Natama, Jean-Baptiste. 2013. "Message on Pan-Africanism on the Occasion of the Fiftieth Anniversary of the Organisation of African Unity." *African Union*, May 25. Accessed on June 25, 2020. https://au.int/sites/default/files/newsevents/workingdocuments/29152-wd-message_on_pan-africanism_-_english_0.pdf.

Ngcamu, Betuel & Mantzaris, Evangelos. "Xenophobic Violence and Criminality in the KwaZulu-Natal Townships." *The Journal for Transdisciplinary Research in Southern Africa* 15, 1 (2019): 1–8.

SABC NEWS. 2008. *Cape Mounts Relief Effort as Xenophobia Spreads*. May 23. Accessed on June 12, 2020. https://web.archive.org/web/20080612135405/http://www.sabcnews.com/south_africa/general/0%2C2172%2C170109%2C00.html.

Sosibo, Kwanele. 2015. "Xenophobia: What did We Learn from 2008?" *Mail & Guardian News Analysis*, April 23. Accessed on 01 August, 2020. https://mg.co.za/article/2015-04-23-xenophobia-what-did-we-learn-from-2008/.

South African Government Gazette. 2002. "Immigration Act No 13." 443(23478): 1–43. Accessed on August 01, 2020. http://www.saflii.org/za/legis/num_act/ia2002138.pdf.

South African Government National Action Plan. 2019. *National Action Plan to combat Racism, Racial Discrimination, Xenophobia and Related Intolerance*, pp. 1–67. https://www.gov.za/sites/default/files/gcis_document/201903/national-action-plan.pdf.

South African History Online (SAHO). 2018. Xenophobic Violence in Democratic South Africa. Accessed on June 15, 2020. https://www.sahistory.org.za/article/xenophobic-violence-democratic-south-africa.

Swart, Mia. 2020. "'There will be Blood': Xenophobia in S Africa Routine and Lethal." *Al Jazeera*, September 17. Accessed on September 20, 2020. https://www.aljazeera.com/news/2020/09/17/there-will-be-blood-xenophobia-in-s-africa-routine-and-lethal/.

Tevera, Daniel.African Migrants, Xenophobia and Urban Violence in Post-apartheid South Africa. *Alternation Special Edition* 7 (2013): 9–26.

The Constitution of the Republic of South Africa. 1996. "Bill of Rights: Chapter 2," Section 7-39, December 10. Accessed on July 15, 2020. https://www.justice.gov.za/legislation/constitution/chp02.html.

Thiong'o, Ngũgĩ wa. 2004. "African Identities: Pan-Africanism in the Era of Globalization and Capitalist Fundamentalism." *Macalester International*, 14, Article 9: 21–42. Accessed on July 20, 2020. http://digitalcommons.macalester.edu/macintl/vol14/iss1/9.

Tshabalala, Mpumelelo. 2019. Pan-Africanism: A History. *Review of African Political Economy*. Accessed on September 20, 2020. http://roape.net/2019/05/30/pan-africanism-a-history/.

United Nations Educational, Scientific and Cultural Organization (UNESCO). 2020. "Fight Against Xenophobia in the Age of Disinformation and Artificial Intelligence." February 02. Accessed on 20 September, 2020. https://en.unesco.org/news/fight-against-xenophobia-age-disinformation-and-artificial-intelligence.

West, Cornel. 1994. *Race Matters*. New York: Vintage Books.

Chapter 12

"We versus Them"

National Identity and the African Union's Pan-Africanist Vision

Akinkunmi Afeez Akinlabi

The transformation of the Organization of African Unity (OAU) into the African Union (AU) was aimed at promoting the development of Africa in line with the premise of Pan-African ideology of collectivism. The movement which evolved through the activities of the African descendants in the new world and transcended onto Africa in postindependence underpinned the unity of Africans for the development of ideas to liberate the African continent. The movement was formed as a voice against racial discrimination encountered by blacks throughout the world. Considering its evolution, Legum argues that the problem of racial prejudice necessitated the conduct of the first conference by African descendants in the United States and West Indies.[1] Hence, the movement started with the 1900 conferences held in London.[2] At the conference, the participants deliberated on British activities in African colonies and the racial prejudice in both South Africa and Rhodesia.[3] Subsequently, other conferences held in Paris (1919), London and Brussels (1921), London and Lisbon (1923), and New York (1927) demanded international laws to protect the natives, African participation in governance, and the right of Africans to local self-government, while the 1945 Manchester Conference attended by some future African leaders demanded the independence of African colonies.[4] The Manchester Conference of 1945 was significant in the history of the movement because it paved way for the transition of the movement to the African continent and likewise it influenced the anti-colonial struggle in the continent. At the conference, the participants argued that "economic democracy is the only real democracy and condemned the rule of private wealth and industry for private profit alone."[5]

Coming down to Africa, the ideology transcended into a nationalist struggle against colonialism and imperialism. After Ghana's independence in 1957, Kwame Nkrumah, a participant at the last conference of Pan-Africanism in 1945, spearheaded the call for the Pan-African Conference of Independent African States. According to Legum, the 1958 "Conference of Independent Africa State" had representatives from eight independent African states that included Ghana, Liberia, Egypt, Tunisia, Libya, Sudan, Morocco, and Ethiopia to deliberate on issues bordering on the liberation of African states that were still under colonialism.[6] At the end of the conference, participant states resolved that all independent African states should have "direct involvement in securing the emancipation of the continent; they declared war on colonialism and apartheid in South Africa and gave full support to the National Liberation Front (FLN) struggle in Algeria."[7] Another Pan-African conference which was a nongovernmental conference of political parties and African nationalists was held at Accra in 1958 tagged "All African Peoples Organization." The idea of unification of the African continent surfaced at that conference.[8]

However, the dreams and aspirations of the movement waned down with the various challenges that bedeviled Africa in the postcolonial era. Despite the existence of the OAU, established in 1963, the continent faced the challenges of war of separations and underdevelopment that militated against the integration process of the continent. The quest to overcome these challenges and others necessitated the transformation of the OAU into the AU in 2002 that was designed for the realization of the Pan-Africanist ideology of greater unity and solidarity between the African countries and the peoples of Africa.[9] Unlike the OAU, the AU adopts a bottom-up approach in its quest to realize regional citizenship and the development of the region through collective efforts of countries on the continent. This process is designed to start with subregional integration under the seven recognized Regional Economic Communities (RECs) and, afterward, the various subregional organizations integrating into a united, peaceful, sovereign, independent, confident, and self-reliant continent. As stipulated in "Agenda 2063: The Africa We Want,"

> The regional level—the RECs will serve as the fulcrum for the implementation at the member states level. They will adopt the Agenda 2063 results framework to regional peculiarities and facilitate/coordinate the implementation by member states and develop/implement monitoring and evaluation frameworks at the regional level [while] the continental level (AU Organs, especially the AUC) will be responsible for setting the broad results framework and broad monitoring and evaluation based on inputs from the RECs.[10]

Hence, the expected unification of the member states is projected to materialize by 2063. Agenda 2063, a 50-year strategic framework rooted in

Pan-Africanism and African Renaissance, provides a robust framework for addressing past injustices and the realization of the twenty-first century as the African Century. Succinctly put, AU's Agenda 2063 is a "continuation of the Pan-African drive over centuries, for unity, self-determination, freedom, progress and collective prosperity pursued under Pan-Africanism and African Renaissance."[11] This is built on the seven aspirations that include the following:

1. A prosperous Africa based on inclusive growth and sustainable development;
2. An integrated continent, politically united and based on the ideals of Pan-Africanism and the vision of Africa's Renaissance;
3. An Africa of good governance, democracy, respect for human rights, justice, and the rule of law;
4. A peaceful and secure Africa;
5. An Africa with a strong cultural identity, common heritage, shared values, and ethics;
6. An Africa whose development is people-driven, relying on the potential of African people, especially its women and youth, and caring for children; and
7. Africa as a strong, united, and influential global player and partner.

Emphatically, aspiration two and five of Agenda 2063 revolve around the creation of a politically united continent with a strong cultural identity, common heritage, shared values, and ethics. These aspirations form the core values of Pan-Africanism from its inception in the new world. As a movement, Pan-Africanism is both a political and cultural phenomenon that sets out to exalt the values of Africanness under a united front.

Contrary to this AU's Pan-Africanist vision of a united front leading to common citizenship on the continent, national identity, association with the territorially defined state that emerged during the colonial era and transcended into postcolonial Africa is associated with the division of the people into nationalities such as Kenyan, Nigerian, South African, and Algerian. Prior to colonialism, citizenry in Africa was affiliated with ethnic groups but later metamorphosed to affiliation with territorially defined states during and after colonialism. Thereafter, identity with modern states defines the sociopolitical and economic relations of states and individuals on the continent from independence. These new national identities in Africa beget a "we versus them" syndrome embedded in the wave of a new nationalism in post-independence Africa.[12] This "we versus them" contributes to the factors that fuel attacks on foreign African nationals in some African states. Attacks influenced by the syndrome are well exhibited in the xenophobic attacks in

South Africa, the attacks on Nigerian traders and their businesses in Ghana, and the stereotyping and enslavement of blacks in the Maghreb region of the continent. In return, the several attacks and discriminatory behaviors influence the patterns of economic, political, and social interactions among the various nationalities of the continent.

Attacks and stereotypes triggered by the "we versus them" syndrome and its divisive effect within the continent are antithetical to the main principle of AU's Pan-Africanist vision. While some subregional organizations on the continent set out mechanisms to promote integration that include the creation of common citizens, the national identity of citizens builds a dichotomy of "we and others" on the continent as against AU's projected common citizenship. The inability of foreign nationals to be integrated into the nationality of host countries results in politics of identity of inclusion and exclusion on the continent leading to divisive nationalism. This chapter argues that identity with territorially defined states triggering anti-immigrants sentiments and attacks is an impediment to the realization of the AU's Pan-Africanist vision of African citizens through a united continent by 2063. Against this background, this chapter examines the potential danger of the "we versus them" syndrome in the attainment of AU's Pan-Africanist vision of common citizenship.

In terms of structure, this chapter has five sections. The second section that follows this introductory section centers on the concept of national identity in relation to nationality. The third and the fourth sections discuss Pan-Africanism and then analysis. The final section is the conclusion of the chapter.

NATIONAL IDENTITY

Literature has approached the concept of identity and its different forms from both the sociological and psychological perspectives. These two perspectives explain identity as association with a particular collection of features that differentiate members from nonmembers. For both perspectives, the existence of "others" who possess different attributes is an underlying factor in explaining any forms of identity. Hence, identity is the construction of the sense of inclusion that involves the absorption of certain values and beliefs which differentiate the self-acknowledgment from others. Individuals' self-acknowledgments are consequences of self-views that materialize from reflexive activity of self-categorization or identification in terms of membership in particular groups or roles as against others.[13] Self-categorization entails the sense of belonging of an individual either on personal or group identity. For instance, an individual can identify herself with a female gender role and still identify herself with a profession. Generally, individuals have multiple identities that form their patterns of interactions and relations with other individuals who are either members of their identity or not. As a social and psychological construction, identity aids individuals in answering the question of "Who am I/are we?" This question is an explicit indication of the importance of the concept of "others" in understanding either personal or collective identity. This imaginary construct of "self and others" plays a crucial role in the interactions and relations of members and perceived nonmembers. Association with identity can be built on political, gender, social, economic, ideological, ethnic, or national grounds.

National identity, like other forms of identity, is based on a set of common features that bind the members of the nation together.[14] Here, members are defined based on the fact of sharing common features as against nonmembers who are perceived as foreigners in the collective identity. In another view, Parekh opines that the term "national identity" should be dropped and replaced with the term "collective identity of a polity" because national identity conveys the wrong impression that every polity is or should be constituted as a nation which refers to a homogeneous and collectively self-conscious ethno-cultural unit, a spiritual whole that shapes the substance and identity of its members. Rather, he suggests that the term "national identity" may be used provided we constantly bear in mind what we mean by it nothing more than the collective identity of a polity and that we remain agnostic about whether a well-ordered polity needs to be constituted as a nation.[15]

Thus, national identity entails the way a polity is constituted and what makes it the kind of community it is. It includes the central organizing principles of the polity, its structural tendencies, characteristic ways of thinking and living, the ideals that inspire its people, the values they profess and to which its leaders tend to appeal, the kind of character they admire and cherish, their propensities to act in specific ways, their deepest fears, ambitions, anxieties, collective memories, traumatic historical experiences, dominant myths, and collective self-understandings.[16]

Moreover, Parekh posits that national identity can be used in two related but different senses. First, national identity refers to an individual's identity as a member of a political community as different from that of other kinds of communities such as "English," "British," "American," or "French," and the second perspective refers to the identity of a political community, as when we ask what makes France or Sweden this community rather than some other.[17] The first explanation centers on the psychological sense of belonging of an individual to a polity or state while the second perspective entails the ideological features that separate states from one another.[18] Here, national identity is associated with the notion of the psychological bonds an individual has toward a state and likewise what a state stands for that differentiate the individuals or state from others. This binary explanation of national identity has effects on the level and patterns of relationship and interactions between the imaginary members and nonmembers of a state. Relations and interaction among member individuals differ from the relations between members and nonmembers that are often stereotyped with negative images.

Meanwhile at the functional form of national identity is nationality which has to do with the bond of personal connection to the nation and belonging to the national community having as its basis a social fact of attachment, a genuine connection of existence, interest, and sentiments together with the existence of reciprocal rights and duties.[19] Nationality is one of the important components of national identity.[20] National identity finds expression in the nationality possessed by an individual because nationality is an individual connection to the nation and sense of belonging to territorially defined states. The consciousness created by the national attachment cum collective features produce nationality that comprises of effective solidarity of interests, reciprocity of rights and duties, feelings of solidarity, and social bonds.[21]

PAN-AFRICANISM AND AU

Pan-Africanism as both ideology and movement evolved with the black descendants in the new world to build unity and solidarity among the African descendants in the diaspora. In its historical trajectory, Pan-Africanism, transited from the new world movement to Africa-centered ideology, anchored on the unity of the African states as a united front. Earlier from its inception in the new world, the movement focused on the plight of African descendants and later changed to finding African solutions to African problems.

The movement in the new world started with the 1900 London conference chaired by Dr. Williams Du Bois under the call of Sylvester Williams.[22] At this conference, British activities in African colonies and racial prejudice in South Africa and Rhodesia were discussed with a communique sent to Queen Victoria who replied through Mr. Joseph Chamberlain that "Her Majesty's Government will not overlook the interests and welfare of the native races."[23] Apart from the first conference, other conferences were held in 1919 at Paris, 1921 at London and Brussels, 1923 at London, 1927 at Lisbon, and 1945 at Manchester with various demands in the interest of black people both within and outside the African continent. For instance, the 1919 conference had demands that included the need for international laws to protect the natives, land to be held in trust, the prevention of exploitation by foreign capital, the abolition of slavery and capital punishment, the right of education, and the natives of Africa to participate in the Government as fast as their development permits.[24]

Unlike the 1900, 1919, 1921, 1923, and 1927 conferences, the 1945 Manchester Conference was significant in the history of the Pan-Africanist movement. The conference which was the last conference held outside the African continent had African nationalists such as Kwame Nkrumah, Jomo Kenyatta, Samuel Akintola, H. O. Davies, and Otto Makomen who turned out to be future African leaders after independence.[25] In addition to this, the conference demanded for African independence and the adoption of economic democracy.[26] As the last conference held outside the African continent, the 1945 conference served as the passage for the transformation of the movement from abroad to the African continent and laying foundation for the new movement in Africa.

Upon attaining independence, Ghana under Kwame Nkrumah organized the first Pan-African conference on the continent in April 1958 tagged the "Conference of Independent African States."[27] The conference attended by eight independent African states centered on the liberation of African states under colonialism through direct involvement in the anti-colonial struggles. After the April conference another conference was held at Accra in 1958 tagged "All African Peoples Organization," which was a nongovernmental conference of political parties and African nationalists. According to Legum, the idea of the creation of a "United State of Africa or regional federation" came up during this conference.[28] This idea embraced the collapse of the colonial-created boundaries and the erosion of state sovereignty on the continent for a singular federation of the African states.

To achieve this aim two major schools of thought, gradualist and radical, emerged. The gradualist school led by Nigeria favored functional approach to African cooperation while the radical approach led by Ghana favored political integration as a prerequisite to economic integration and a socialist path to economic development.[29] Succinctly put, Legum quotes Maitama Sule, Nigerian representative at the second 1960 conference of Independent African States:

> Pan-Africanism, said Mr. Sule, is the only solution to our problems in Africa. . . . No one in Africa doubts the need to promote Pan-Africanism. . . . But we must not be sentimental; we must be realistic. It is for this reason that we would like to point out that at this moment the idea of forming a Union of African States is premature. On the other hand, we do not dispute the sincerity and indeed the good intentions of those people who advocate it. But we feel such a move is too radical-perhaps too ambitious-to be of lasting benefit. Gradual development of ideas and thoughts is more lasting.[30]

The division among the African states on the approach for creating a United Africa was reconciled with the establishment of the Organization of African

Unity (OAU) in 1963 with the major aim of promoting unity and solidarity across Africa. In its 39 years of existence, the organization, OAU, succeeded in the decolonization of the African continent but failed to promote economic development and unification.[31] The failure of OAU to solve African challenges necessitated the transformation of the organization into AU formed in 2002 with the major aims of achieving greater unity and solidarity among African countries and people of Africa and accelerating the political and socioeconomic integration of the continent.[32] These aims are projected to be achieved through the integration of members of the various subregional organizations which should subsequently spill into continental integration.

In its vision to achieve its major aim, the AU spells out its modus operandi in "Agenda 2063: The Africa We Want." The 50-year plan document with 7 aspirations is built on the "continuation of the Pan-African drive over centuries, for unity, self-determination, freedom, progress and collective prosperity pursued under Pan-Africanism and African Renaissance."[33] Among the seven aspirations, aspiration 2 and 5 entail the union's vision of a united African continent. For instance, aspiration 2 of the document "An integrated continent, politically united and based on the ideals of Pan-Africanism and the vision of Africa's Renaissance" envisages a united, strong, sovereign, independent, and self-reliant continent that realizes full economic and political integration.[34] The union shall consist of a united Africa with world class, integrative infrastructure that crisscrosses the continent; dynamic and mutually beneficial links with her diaspora; and a continent of seamless borders, and management of cross-border resources through dialogue.[35] Aspiration 5 "Africa with a strong cultural identity, common heritage, shared values and ethics" focuses on the sociocultural harmonization of the continent built on Pan-Africanism. These two aspirations revolve around the creation of single identity for the Africans and Africa in the global politics.

NATIONAL IDENTITY AND AU'S UNITED AFRICA

Nationality, which is the personal and legal connection individuals have with states, is one of the major components of national identity claimed by the individuals. In Africa, nationality evolved from the colonially established legal framework that transited into the independence era.[36] Even though independent African states have amended some of the colonial legal statutes, the laws guiding the acquisition of nationality are not unconnected to the colonial definition of membership of the territorially defined states. These laws of the African states spell out the modus operandi for acquiring nationality through naturalizations and marriage. States on the continent have separate laws establishing the procedures and basic requirements for nationality acquisition. For instance, language and religion are among the commonest requirements in the Maghreb region of the continent while the issue of race is a parameter in Liberia and Sierra Leone. Hence, the legal admission and recognition of an individual as member of a state automatically attaches to certain characteristics that include language, race, origin, and religion.

National identity, individual's identity with territorially defined states, is one of the driven forces in the sociopolitical and economic relations not only at state level but also at the micro-level of relations among individuals on the continent. Relations at the individual level, mostly economic, on the continent are patterned in line with national affiliation thereby promoting inclusiveness and exclusiveness within the continent. At state level, however, the African states key themselves into subregional cooperation that includes the establishment of free movement of people and goods and rights of residence and employment. The various RECs recognized by the AU all have interstates migration protocols/articles aimed at promoting the creation of subregional citizens as planned by the AU. At the center of the subregional integration is the intra-migration and the creation of common citizens that enjoy certain legal privileges in every member state on the continent. This idea is in line with AU's projection that the African continent should be a continent where free movement of persons, capital, goods, and services leading to significant increases in trade and investments among African countries is achieved by 2063.[37] As one of the aims of the African integration process, intra-migration within Africa is expected to foster economic development and the creation of a single common citizenship on the continent. With globalization and widespread labor mobility in the world, intra-migration on the continent becomes an inexorable event that requires collective laws to guide it and thereby resulting in partial erosion of states' sovereignties on the continent.

The processes of actualizing common African citizenship vis-à-vis nationality are guided by various declarations and articles at both regional and subregional levels of the continent. For instance, the ECOWAS member states in 2015 adopted the Abidjan Declaration on the Eradication of Statelessness aimed to

> prevent and reduce statelessness by reforming constitutional, legislative and institutional regimes related to nationality in order to include appropriate safeguards against statelessness, in particular to ensure that every child acquires a nationality at birth and that all foundlings are considered national of the state in which they are found.[38]

This with other various articles such as Article 2, 3, 5, 7, and 12 of the African Charter on Human and Peoples' Rights, though existing concurrently with the state laws of nationality, are set to safeguard the rights of nonnational

Africans in host African states and fast-track the process of creating African citizens across the continent.[39] Safeguarding the rights and privileges of foreign Africans in host African states is an imperative means for the AU to dissuade African states from making legal frameworks that promote the divisiveness of "we versus them" on the continent. For this reason, the AU through the African Commission on Human and Peoples Rights continues to provide frameworks guiding nationality acquisition and migrant rights. An example of such frameworks is Article 6 (1) of "Right to a Nationality and the Eradication of Statelessness in Africa," which provides that naturalization shall in principle be open to foreigners on the basis of habitual residence, though other reasonable conditions may also be applied.[40]

Despite the existence of the available articles and declarations, the procedures of acquiring nationality through naturalization, common form of national acquisition, in some African countries is an exacting and difficult task. The strict requirements and bureaucratic procedures have become impediments to the integration of foreign Africans into the nationality of their host states. Supporting this claim, Manby argues that, in principle, all African states allow the acquisition of nationality by naturalization on the basis of long-term residence and the fulfillment of other conditions but the process of obtaining it can be very difficult and highly discretionary in many countries.[41] Contrary to the AU's goal, the process of naturalization in the host African states is often mitigated by various discriminatory requirements that include religion, language, gender distinction, race, and ethnicity. For instance, Egyptian law shows preferential terms to Arab origin or Muslims; Libyan laws accept persons of Arab descent while Ethiopian law requires that the applicant must be "able to communicate in any one of the languages spoken by the nations/nationalities of the Country and Liberia offers eligibility to only Africans with black ancestry."[42] Existence of discriminatory requirements is against Article 16(5) of the Right to a Nationality and the Eradication of Statelessness in Africa. It states that "the arbitrary deprivation of nationality, especially on discriminatory grounds such as race, colour, sex, language, religion, political or other opinion, national or social origin, property, birth, or other status, including disability, is a violation of human rights and fundamental freedoms."[43]

The strict requirements and bureaucratic procedures against the acquisition of nationality by foreign Africans arouse the psychological configuration of "we versus them" that triggers divisive nationalism and stereotypical attitudes against foreign nationals. Divisive nationalism and derogatory stereotypes associated with the anti-immigrant sentiments promote hostility and hatred hereby facilitating attacks on the African foreign nationals and their businesses. Anti-immigrant rhetoric on the continent has been one of the major raison d'être for attacks on foreign African nationals in South

Africa and Ghana.[44] With the aid of the media and state institutions, the self-other sentiment grows on the continent. In South Africa, for instance, xenophobic attacks are directed at African migrants who are perceived as threats to the national identity of the rainbow nation by both citizens and state institutions. This act is not limited to South Africa. In Ghana, the government has continued to reinforce individual, systemic, and institutional anti-immigration sentiments leading to attacks on foreign African nationals, especially Nigerians.[45] Xenophobic attacks and hostilities against African migrants grow widely among the citizens of Africans with experiences in Côte d'Ivoire, Gambia, Senegal, Botswana, Libya, Tunisia, and Sierra Leone. Resentments and stereotypes across the continent materialized through the various derogatory images associated with nationals. For example, the black Africans are popularly regarded as *kwerekwere* which means unintelligible by South Africans while South Africans are also perceived as lazy and violent citizens by some nationals. Generally, Nigerians are stereotyped as internet fraudsters, drug dealers, and human traffickers on the continent.

CONCLUSION

This chapter establishes the AU's vision of forming a politically and culturally unified African continent by 2063. This vision rooted in the Pan-African vision of a unified Africa is geared toward the creation of a common African citizenry and front in the global community by the year 2063. However, the various stereotyping and anti-immigrant sentiments that stem from the binary discussion of national identity are antithetical to the AU's Pan-African vision embedded in the Agenda 2063 document. Taking aspiration 2 and 5 of the document that center on the creation of a unified identity for Africa, this chapter argues that for such visions to be feasible the "we versus them" syndrome fueling divisive nationalism and anti-immigrant sentiments on the continent needs to be resolved. Stereotyping and xenophobic attacks facilitate resentment that has the potential of thwarting aspiration 2 and 5 of Agenda 2063. While it is evident from this chapter that the AU puts many legal frameworks in place to promote easier acquisition of nationality and protect the rights of African migrants in host states, it also establishes that the acquisitions of nationality on the continent is still mitigated by discriminatory requirements that are prohibited by the AU.

The noncompliance of states to the various supranational treaties and lack of harmonization of states' laws with the supranational cum AU's treaties are bottlenecks to aspirations 2 and 5 of the AU's Agenda 2063. This chapter opines that there is still a large gap between the national laws and regional articles in relations to nationality acquisition on the African continent. The various impediments in terms of requirements for acquisition of nationalism contribute to the formation of psychological sense of inclusiveness and exclusiveness by Africans within the continent. Due to the continuous exacerbation of divisive nationalism on the continent, the AU's vision of united front as presented in Agenda 2063 seems elusive. Evidently, states are fostering cooperation at the subregional level. However, the creation of a common African citizenship on the continent which is one of the aims of the AU's Pan-African mission is drawing back with the spread of new territorial nationalism among the citizens. By and large, this chapter has provided insight into national identity and AU Pan-African vision of common citizenship.

NOTES

1. Colin S. Legum, *Pan-Africanism: A Short Political Guide* (New York: Frederick A. Praeger, 1965), 25.

2. Legum, *Pan-Africanism: A Short Political Guide*, 24; Pakinso T. Tondi, "Pan-African Thought and Practice," *Alternative Special Edition* 2 (2005): 312; Tesema Ta'a, "Pan-Africanism: A Historiographical Analysis," *EJSSLS*, 1, no. 1 (2014): 65; Yusuf S. Omoiya, "Pan Africanism, the OAU and the African Union," in *African Culture and Civilization*, ed. Ademola S. Ajayi (Ibadan: Ibadan Cultural studies Group, 2005), 383.

3. Legum, *Pan-Africanism: A Short Political Guide*, 25.

4. Legum, *Pan-Africanism: A Short Political Guide*, 28-31; Tondi, "Pan-African Thought and Practice," *Alternative Special Edition*, 316–317; Ta'a, "Pan-Africanism: A Historiographical Analysis," *EJSSLS*, 69–72.

5. Legum, *Pan-Africanism: A Short Political Guide*, 32.

6. Legum, *Pan-Africanism: A Short Political Guide*, 41.

7. Legum, *Pan-Africanism: A Short Political Guide*, 43; Ta'a, "Pan-Africanism: A Historiographical Analysis," *EJSSLS*, 73.

8. Legum, *Pan-Africanism: A Short Political Guide*, 43.

9. Yusuf S. Omoiya, "Pan Africanism," 390; Paul Adogamhe, "Pan-Africanism Revisited: Vision and Reality of African Unity and Development," *African Review of Integration* 2, no. 2 (2008): 15; Edwin H. Moshi, *Organization of African Unity/African Union and The Challenges of Realizing its Objectives*, Workshop to Commemorate 50 years of OAU/AU, May 25 (J.K. Nyerere Hall, MUCCoBS, 2013), 50.

10. African Union Commission, *Agenda 2063: The Africa We Want* (Addis Ababa: AUC, 2015), 3.

11. Ibid., 2.

12. Norbert Kersting, "New Nationalism and Xenophobia in Africa – A New Inclination?," *Africa Spectrum*, 44, no. 1(2009): 7–18; Dirk Kohnert, "New Nationalism and Development in Africa," *Africa Spectrum*, 44, no. 1 (2009): 111–123.

13. Jan Stets and Peter Burke, "Identity Theory and Social Identity Theory," *Social Psychology Quarterly*, 63, no. 3 (2000): 224.

14. Varun Uberoi, "National Identity – A Multiculturalist's Approach," *Critical Review of International Social and Political Philosophy*, 21, no. 1 (2018): 46–64; Anna Triandafyllidou, "National Identity and the 'Other,'" *Ethnic and Racial Studies*, 21, no. 4 (1998): 593–612.

15. Bhikhu Parekh, "The Concept of National Identity," *Journal of Ethnic and Migration Studies*, 21, no. 2 (1995): 255–256.

16. Bhikhu Parekh, "The Concept of National Identity," 257.

17. Bhikhu Parekh, *A New Politics of Identity: Political Principles for an Interdependent World* (Basingstoke: Palgrave Macmillan, 2008), 56.

18. Ibid., 56.

19. Bronwen Manby, *Citizenship Law in Africa: A Comparative Study* (Cape Town: African Minds, 2016), ix; Agnė Juškevičienė, "What Does Nationality Mean Today? Construction of National Identity of the Students Who Are Attending Lithuanian Schools," *Mediterranean Journal of Social Sciences*, 5, no. 22 (2014), 21.

20. David Miller, *Citizenship and National Identity* (Maldon: Polity Press, 2000), 31; Agnė Juškevičienė, "What Does Nationality Mean Today?," 20.

21. African Commission on Human and Peoples' Rights (ACHPR), *The Right to Nationality in Africa* (Banjul: ACHPR, 2015), 8.

22. Legum, *Pan-Africanism: A Short Political Guide*, 24; Pakinso T. Tondi, "Pan-African Thought and Practice," *Alternative Special Edition* 2 (2005): 312; Tesema Ta'a, "Pan-Africanism: A Historiographical Analysis," *EJSSLS* 1, no.1 (2014): 65; Yusuf S. Omoiya, "Pan Africanism, the OAU and the African Union," in *African Culture and Civilization*, ed. Ademola S. Ajayi (Ibadan: Ibadan Cultural studies Group, 2005), 383.

23. Legum, *Pan-Africanism: A Short Political Guide*, 25.

24. Ibid., 29.

25. Ibid., 31; Pakinso T. Tondi, "Pan-African Thought and Practice," 320; Tesema Ta'a, "Pan-Africanism: A Historiographical Analysis," *EJSSLS* 72.

26. Legum, *Pan-Africanism: A Short Political Guide, EJSSLS* 32.

27. Legum, *Pan-Africanism: A Short Political Guide*, 41; Tesema Ta'a, "Pan-Africanism: A Historiographical Analysis," *EJSSLS* 73.

28. Legum, *Pan-Africanism: A Short Political Guide*, 42.

29. Legum, *Pan-Africanism: A Short Political Guide*, 46; Omoiya, "Pan Africanism, the OAU and the African Union," 385; Paul Adogamhe, "Pan-Africanism Revisited," 10.

30. Legum, *Pan-Africanism: A Short Political Guide*, 46.

31. Paul Adogamhe, "Pan-Africanism Revisited," 14.

32. Omoiya, "Pan Africanism, the OAU and the African Union," 390; Paul Adogamhe, "Pan-Africanism Revisited," 15; Edwin H. Moshi, *Organization of African Unity/African Union and The Challenges of Realizing its Objectives*, Workshop to Commemorate 50 years of OAU/AU, May 25 (J.K. Nyerere Hall, MUCCoBS, 2013), 50.

33. African Union Commission, *Agenda 2063: The Africa We Want* (Addis Ababa: AUC, 2015), 2.

34. ibid., 7.

35. Ibid., 4.

36. Bronwen Manby, *Nationality, Migration and Statelessness in West Africa*, Report of the International Organisation for Migration and UN High Commissioner for Refugee, (Dakar: IOM and UNHCR, 2015), 9; Bronwen Manby, *Citizenship Law in Africa*, 38; Bronwen Manby, *Citizenship in Africa: The Law of Belonging*, (Oxford: Hart Publishing, 2018), 315.

37. African Union Commission, *Agenda 2063*, 3.

38. ECOWAS, "Abidjan Declaration of Minister of ECOWAS Member States on Eradication of Statelessness," ECOWAS Report, 2015, http://citizenship rightsafrica.org/midsa-conclusions-and-recommendations-2016/ (accessed on 21, 2020), 4.

39. African Commission on Human and Peoples' Rights (ACHPR), *The Right to Nationality in Africa*, 1-86; Bronwen Manby, *Citizenship Law in Africa: A Comparative Study* , 34.

40. African Commission on Human and Peoples' Rights (ACHPR), *Draft Protocol to the African Charter on Human and Peoples' Rights on the Specific Aspects of the Right to a Nationality and the Eradication of Statelessness in Africa: Explanatory Memorandum* (Banjul: ACHPR, 2018), 13.

41. Bronwen Manby, *Citizenship Law in Africa*, 7.

42. Bronwen Manby, *Nationality, Migration and Statelessness in West Africa*, Report of the International Organisation for Migration and UN High Commissioner for Refugee (Dakar: IOM and UNHCR, 2015), 17; Bronwen Manby, *Citizenship Law in Africa*, 5-8; African Commission on Human and Peoples' Rights (ACHPR), *The Right to Nationality in Africa*, 27.

43. African Commission on Human and Peoples' Rights (ACHPR), *Draft Protocol to the African Charter on Human and Peoples' Rights on the Specific Aspects of the Right to a Nationality and the Eradication of Statelessness in Africa*, 21.

44. Adeoye Akinola, "Nigeria: The Politics of Ghana's Xenophobic Attacks on Nigerians," *Premium Times*, 6 July 2020, https://opinion.premiumtimesng.com/2020 /07/06/the-politics-of-ghanas-xenophobic-attacks-on-nigerians-by-adeoye-o-akinola/ (accessed November7, 2020); Olubunmi Akande, Hilary Musarurwa, and Sylvia Kaye, "Students' Attitudes and Perceptions on Xenophobia: A Study of a University in Durban," *Journal of Student Affairs in Africa* 6, no. 2 (2018), 1–17.

45. Adeoye Akinola, "Nigeria."

BIBLIOGRAPHY

Adogamhe, Paul. "Pan-Africanism Revisited: Vision and Reality of African Unity and Development." *African Review of Integration* 2, no. 2 (2008): 1–34.

African Commission on Human and Peoples' Rights (ACHPR). *Draft Protocol to the African Charter on Human and Peoples' Rights on the Specific Aspects of the*

Right to a Nationality and the Eradication of Statelessness in Africa: Explanatory Memorandum. Banjul: ACHPR, 2018.

African Commission on Human and Peoples' Rights (ACHPR). *The Right to Nationality in Africa.* Banjul: ACHPR, 2015.

African Union Commission. *Agenda 2063: The Africa We Want.* Addis Ababa: AUC, 2015.

Akande, Olubunmi D., Musarurwa, Hilary, and Kaye, Sylvia. "Students' Attitudes and Perceptions on Xenophobia: A Study of a University in Durban." *Journal of Student Affairs in Africa* 6, no. 2 (2018): 1–17.

Akinola, Adeoye. "Nigeria: The Politics of Ghana's Xenophobic Attacks on Nigerians." *Premium Times*, July 6, 2020. https://opinion.premiumtimesng.com /2020/07/06/the-politics-of- ghanas-xenophobic-attacks-on-nigerians-by-adeoye-o -akinola/ (accessed November 7, 2020).

ECOWAS. "Abidjan Declaration of Minister of ECOWAS Member States on Eradication of Statelessness." ECOWAS Report, 2015. http://citizenshiprightsafrica .org/midsa- conclusions-and-recommendations-2016/ (accessed on 21, 2020)

Juškevičienė, Agnė. "What Does Nationality Mean Today? Construction of National Identity of the Students Who Are Attending Lithuanian Schools." *Mediterranean Journal of Social Sciences* 5, no. 22 (2014), 20–26.

Kersting, Norbert. "New Nationalism and Xenophobia in Africa – A New Inclination?" *Africa Spectrum* 44, no. 1 (2009): 7–18.

Kohnert, Dirk. "New Nationalism and Development in Africa." *Africa Spectrum* 44, no. 1 (2009): 111–123.

Legum, Colin S. *Pan-Africanism: A Short Political Guide.* New York: Frederick A Praeger, 1965.

Manby, Bronwen. *Citizenship in Africa: The Law of Belonging.* Oxford: Hart Publishing, 2018.

Manby, Bronwen. *Citizenship Law in Africa: A Comparative Study.* Cape Town: African Minds, 2016.

Manby, Bronwen. *Nationality, Migration and Statelessness in West Africa.* Report of the International Organisation for Migration and UN High Commissioner for Refugee, Dakar: IOM and UNHCR, 2015.

Miller, David. *Citizenship and National Identity.* Maldon: Polity Press, 2000.

Moshi, Edwin H. *Organization of African Unity/African Union and The Challenges of Realizing its Objectives*, Workshop to Commemorate 50 years of OAU/AU, May 25 (J.K. Nyerere Hall, MUCCoBS, 2013), 50.

Omoiya, Yusuf S. "Pan Africanism, the OAU and the African Union." In *African Culture and Civilization*, edited by Ademola S. Ajayi, 381–394. Ibadan: Ibadan Cultural studies Group, 2005.

Parekh, Bhikhu. *A New Politics of Identity: Political Principles for an Interdependent World.* Basingstoke: Palgrave Macmillan, 2008.

Parekh, Bhikhu. "The Concept of National Identity." *Journal of Ethnic and Migration Studies* 21, no. 2 (1995): 255–256.

Stets, Jan, and Burke, Peter. "Identity Theory and Social Identity Theory." *Social Psychology Quarterly* 63, no. 3 (2000): 224–237.

Ta'a, Tesema. "Pan-Africanism: A Historiographical Analysis." *EJSSLS* 1, no. 1 (2014): 63–77.

Tondi, Pakinso T. "Pan-African Thought and Practice." *Alternative Special Edition* 2 (2005): 301–328.

Triandafyllidou, Anna. "National Identity and the 'Other'." *Ethnic and Racial Studies* 21, no. 4 (1998): 593–612.

Uberoi, Varun. "National Identity – A Multiculturalist's Approach." *Critical Review of International Social and Political Philosophy* 21, no. 1 (2018): 46–64.

Chapter 13

The African Union and the Problem of Xenophobia in South Africa

Festus Chibuike Onuegbu

The frictions and fallouts of globalization doubtlessly have given room to a lot of conflicts in twenty-first-century Africa, thus creating not only a huge challenge but also a big role for the African Union (AU). In as much as the frequency of traditional armed conflicts in Africa including interstate and civil wars has receded, new variants of tensions have emerged. One of these new tensions is xenophobia, and one country in Africa that has been the major hot spot is South Africa. Though South Africa is the epicenter of the xenophobic crisis, developments therein have affected the entire continent with the attacks directed on other African nationals and their livelihoods. The point is that xenophobia in South Africa is an all-African problem, a common source of conflict capable of endangering peace, security, development, and relations between and among states in Africa; thus, it deserves some collective action at the continental level to address it. It is in this context that the role of the AU becomes crucial. As an important African institution saddled with the responsibility to promote unity, peace, security, integration, and development in the continent, the AU not only has a moral obligation but political responsibility to address xenophobia in South Africa as a common African problem. No doubt, on a state actor level, South Africa and other countries in Africa affected by the acts of xenophobia thereof have made significant efforts both in response and reactions to confronting the problem.

Owing to the need and conviction emphasized above, the AU has made some significant efforts in the fight against xenophobia in "the rainbow nation in Africa"[1] like it has done in any other common conflicts on continent, thus making the institution a critical actor on such questions not just particularly in South Africa but in the entire continent. However, the problem lies in the fact that despite these important efforts of the AU in relation to curbing xenophobia in South Africa, construction of discourses and analysis on the question has hardly featured those efforts. By implication, the role of AU in that regard has not received the attention it deserves. It is on the strength of this gap that the present contribution derives its essence and merit. Therefore, the aim of this chapter is to examine the role of the AU toward addressing the problem of xenophobia in South Africa as a common African problem. The chapter looks at the dynamics of xenophobia in South Africa, the rationale for the AU engagement, the role and approach of the AU in the engagement proper as well as the challenges thereof. To achieve this objective, the qualitative historical method of analysis is employed. For clarity, convenience, and coherence the chapter is divided into seven sections. The first is the introduction, followed by analysis of the background and dynamics of xenophobia in South Africa. The third part captures the reasons for the AU intervention, while the fourth section analyzes the response role of the AU. The fifth section assesses the role approach of the AU in combating xenophobia in South Africa, while the penultimate section highlights the challenges thereof. The last section is the conclusion.

CONCEPTUALIZING "XENOPHOBIA"

Defining and understanding xenophobia is not as simple as the concept generally appears. However, one common fact about the idea of xenophobia is its closeness to racism, but its distinction lies in the fact that it is rooted on nationality while racism is based on race. Bronwyn Harris posits that "xenophobia is a manifestation of racism."[2] They are both negative identity constructions and assumptions. Thus, xenophobia shares the same prejudiced discourses with racism. Going by the definition advanced by the South African Human Rights Commission, xenophobia is "the deep dislike of non-nationals [foreigners] by nationals [citizens] of a recipient state."[3] In other words, it simply suggests hatred for foreigners. Leaning on a similar prism, C. Adjai and G. Lazaridis posit that xenophobia is a sociopsychological as well as cultural orientation on identity where nationality or nativity is the basis of action which often is expressed in a violent manner.[4] It is a prejudiced violent behavior against foreigners in their host country; thus, the concept of xenophobia does connote not only hatred and rejection but also violence against someone on the basis of one's nationality. Michael Neocosmos notes that consequential violent actions of xenophobia are often triggered by public incitements, falling economic fortunes, social exclusion, and the question of national pride, and though foreigners are generally affected, refugees, asylum seekers, and undocumented migrants are often the main targets.[5] This is obviously why D. Everatt defines xenophobia as "a toxic and contagious construction of hatred for the others."[6] By implication, xenophobia breaks down intergroup relationships, leads to social and economic destructions, and threatens peace in the society.

The "contagious nature" of xenophobia brings in the question of reprisals into focus. One xenophobic attack in one country may lead to another xenophobic attack(s) in another country. Put in different words, xenophobia brews tensions between and among states and/or nations. In this context, xenophobia is understood as a potential source of conflict and conflict in itself. It destroys trust that exists between nations. Therefore, xenophobia as an operational concept in this discussion is understood as acts of violence and maltreatment of foreign nationals by the nationals of their host country based on their nationality in a manner that raises concern beyond the shores of that country. It attracts condemnation as well as reprisals from the countries whose nationals were the victims of such violent acts.

XENOPHOBIA IN SOUTH AFRICA: BACKGROUND AND DYNAMICS

Xenophobia is not a new phenomenon in South Africa. It has been a common experience with the country's society even before the liquidation of the apartheid regime and enthronement of African majority rule.[7] South Africa has recorded series of xenophobic violence against foreigners, particularly other African nationals. The anti-immigrant sentiments largely derived their strength and push factors from South Africa's ugly racial past. So, to have a better grasp of the problem and dynamics of xenophobia in South Africa, understanding the background that feeds it is important. South Africa emerged from the shackles of apartheid history to become a leading economic and political powerhouse in Africa and thus became a popular destination for groups of African immigrants: refugees, asylum seekers, and both documented and undocumented migrants. Though the country has had some elements of immigrant population, the number and frequency of the movement dramatically increased in the post-apartheid era. Statistics show that before the close of 2018 there were 3.9 million immigrants living in South Africa, a country of 58.4 million people, and about 85% of these foreign nationals are from other African countries.[8] Though nationals from Zimbabwe, Mozambique, Malawi, Lesotho and Namibia are in the majority there are substantial numbers from Nigeria, Ethiopia, Democratic Republic of Congo, Kenya, Somalia, and Tanzania; and the motivation for this new immigration is not utterly unconnected to good business and investment opportunities, job prospects, efficient infrastructure, quality education, and relative political stability.[9] In fact, South Africa is one of the few countries in Africa with uncommon attributes that could fast-track the future and sustainable development of the continent anchored on the integration agenda. The argument of Mutanda in this direction is apt:

> South Africa offers a rare hope and prides itself as a model of development in Africa where many others have failed to govern and provide for their citizens, thus, providing an escape for a good number of other African nationals who saw migration therein as a huge relief.[10,11]

Despite the promise and prospects that South Africa holds, all is not well with it. The country is confronted by several challenging problems rooted mostly in the obnoxious legacies of its apartheid past. Martin Meredith gives a lucid description of South Africa at the end of apartheid. The entire system inherited by the new and democratic South Africa had been designed largely to serve white interests. All the key institutions—the media, civil service, security forces, business community, universities, banks, stock exchange, and agriculture—were dominated by the whites. South Africa's fortunes still depended heavily on the skills, expertise, and capital of the whites. The average white income was eight times greater than that of the average black. Whites, comprising 13% of the population, earned 61% of the total income while 39% of it was pitiably shared by blacks who constitute 87% of the population.[12] In other words, the country's political economy was unduly skewed in favor of the white population. The United Nations Human Development Report further painted a picture of South Africa before the close of 1996:

> If white South Africa were to be treated as a separate country, its standard of living would rank twenty-fourth in the world, just below Spain; black South Africa on the same basis would rank one hundred and twenty-third, below Lesotho and Vietnam. Yet, overall, in terms of human development South Africa ranked only ninety-third in the world. Out of a population of 40 million where about 34 million are blacks, 22 million mostly blacks lacked adequate sanitation, including 7.5 million in urban areas; 12 million lacked clean water supply; 23 million had no access to electricity; and some 3 million children were out of school. Almost half of all the households lived below the poverty line; a quarter lived on an income of less than half of the poverty-line income; some 8 million were estimated to be "complete destitute." One third of the population was illiterate.[13]

In other words, there was a massive disparity in wealth accumulation, ownership, and control between the whites and blacks in the country. Thus, since the end of apartheid, economic challenges have disrupted efforts to establish a society of inclusive growth and prosperity.[14,15] Understandably, black South Africans anticipated that the post-apartheid state would change the status quo and equitably restructure the country's societal systems. Yet, while recognizing the need to reassure whites about their future under black rule, the government of South Africa has been daunted with an avalanche of black expectations which includes at least better jobs, housing, education, health services, and equal public income. But the ability and chances of meeting these expectations by the government continued to appear very slim against existing social, economic, and structural realities of the country's society. The growing impatience for change coupled with further economic decline as well as continuous rise in unemployment in recent years has consequentially become a source of frustration and anger particularly for most native countrymen and women.[16] The height of the frustration has given room for scapegoats (some people had to take the blame) and series of violent attacks against them. Successive governments in the new dispensation in South Africa have battled to redress economic issues with minimal success[17] and thus have had cause to contend with street violence and township riots reminiscent of the apartheid years. Meredith observes that outbreaks of lawlessness were commonplace: students seized teaching staff as hostages and vandalized buildings and looted shops; corrupt police harassed and brutalized people at will; taxi and bus drivers blocked roads in major cities; squatters invaded vacant homes; and shop workers went on a looting rampage.[18] What all this succeeded in doing was to breed a cycle xenophobic violence.

The toxic expression that xenophobia gained was largely driven by the aftermaths of apartheid[19] Xenophobia, thus, could be seen as one of the oppressive legacies of apartheid. The other two mutual elements are disharmonious interracial relations and inequality that is most manifest in the country's persistent economic imbalance, social marginalization, and exclusion. However, it was not so much a problem per se to the country and how it was perceived, at least, before the end of the first decade of the post-apartheid period. It first began as occasional restricted township unrests that could be quelled by simple police action. But, over the past one-and-a-half decades it has taken a worrisomely dangerous dimension, not only within South Africa but also in the way the country is seen outside its borders. Xenophobia has risen to constitute a significant blind spot in the country's foreign policy relations as it has on different occasions dealt a huge blow to the country's image abroad, especially in Africa. The African Centre for Migration and Society reports recent attacks appeared over a wide geographic area, with hot spots in South Africa's major cities of Johannesburg, Durban, Pretoria, Cape Town, and their surrounding urban areas.[20] The fact is that xenophobic violence in recent years has graduated from occasional restricted township unrest to a widespread phenomenon.

Though there are isolated cases of attacks on immigrants and their economic livelihood in many parts of South Africa that mostly go unreported, the experiences of 2008, 2015, and 2019 were widespread and made international headlines. A number of immigrants, particularly from African countries, were killed; several other hundreds wounded; and thousands lost their businesses and jobs; and some were made homeless. Although the percentage of the immigrant population in relation to total percentage of South Africa's population is small, foreigners are mostly blamed for the country's economic and social ills. Tella observes that "when it comes to the cause of poverty, unemployment, and social vices immigrants are made the scapegoats."[21] They are accused of taking over jobs from South Africans, perpetrating criminality and corrupting the country's society. Despite the fact that the blames appear untenable and evoke a sense of wrong judgment they often find dangerous expression among many South African youths who act on those impulses to vent their anger and frustration. Bronwyn Harris posits that anti-immigrant rhetoric did not only come from the streets, it was common among the country's elites—including traditional leaders and government officials.[22] These unfortunate behaviors and actions of South Africans have elicited strong international condemnations and the seemingly inability of the South African government to credibly live up to its obligation to protect fellow Africans against these "hate attacks" that some occasions have brought tensions in the relations between South Africa and some countries in Africa. It was on this point that the AU began to carve out some engagement role for itself on the issue.

RATIONALE FOR THE AU ENGAGEMENT

Regional organizations tend to intervene in conflict situations when elements of peace and security within its geopolitical space are substituted with tension and chaos.[23] On this note, Makinda et al. contend that one of the reasons that compel the AU to intervene in a conflict situation in Africa relates to the question of peace and security of the continent.[24] In other words, the need to maintain peace and regional stability is a major factor that motivated the AU's engagement against xenophobia in South Africa. The trend of reactions from other African countries whose nationals were attacked in South Africa was already creating some serious tension capable of undermining regional peace. Those reactions came in the forms of repatriation of nationals from a number of other African states, calling back diplomatic missions, suspension of flights to and from, withdrawal of participation in international forums or summits where South Africa was the host, and reprisal attacks on South African investments.[25] In other words, the AU considered the incidence of xenophobia in South Africa a huge threat to peace, stability, and human rights in the continent. It is noteworthy that among the high points outlined in the

Constitutive Act of the AU, "promotion of peace, security and human rights" are fundamental.[26] In other words, maltreatment and violent attacks on other Africans in any other African country did constitute not only a threat to peace and security but also a gross abuse of human rights capable of igniting a regional conflict; hence, the AU could not be silent as these noble objectives were abandoned in South Africa.

Aside being a threat to peace and undermining the ideals of African solidarity, resentment and attacks on other African nationals in South Africa or any other country in Africa for that matter are a serious violation of international human rights law and constitute a willful disruption of international migration. The xenophobic attacks, therefore, did not just violate the principles of the African Charter on Human and Peoples' Rights[27] but other existing international human rights instruments which South Africa was expected to honor.[28] As an important African institution that places strong emphasis on the promotion of human and peoples' rights, and with the machinery to address same, when violated it was not only morally expedient but also a question of political responsibility that the AU has to rise up to the occasion when and where the rights and freedoms of African citizens are grossly violated.

Again, there was pressure on the AU both on the continental and international level to engage South Africa on the crisis. A number of African statesmen, international groups, and civil society organizations were calling on the AU to engage the government of South Africa to probe and end the xenophobic attacks on foreigners. For instance, against the backdrop of 2019 attacks, Nigeria's former president Olusegun Obasanjo appealed to the AU to impose sanctions on South Africa for what he described as "continued molestation of other Africans and abandonment of the ideals of African solidarity."[29] Amnesty Group said that "it was time for the AU to put pressure on South Africa, and seriously remind it of its obligation to protect the rights of everyone therein."[30] In fact, more than 130 civil society organizations wrote to the AU urging it to call upon South Africa to take concrete steps to end the attacks.[31] Calls also came from the United Nations and some other notable international organizations for the AU as a principal actor on human rights and peace and security architecture in the continent to meaningfully engage the government of South Africa to combat xenophobic violence. The reports of these organizations further exposed the level of human rights abuses in the xenophobic attacks and the urgency it required on the part of the AU to address such.

Furthermore, the AU had serious concerns that if the problem of xenophobia in South Africa and elsewhere in Africa is left unaddressed it will disrupt the growing flow of inter-African remittances and investment from African Diaspora communities within the continent, and South Africa is said to be playing host to significant number of these Diaspora Africans in Africa. One of the most obvious impacts of migration and existence of Diaspora communities in Africa, likewise elsewhere in the world, is most visible in remittances and investments they do bring in for the development of their home countries and the continent at large. Economic Commission for Africa reports that remittances and investments for sub-Saharan Africa grew from the range of $21 billion in 2005 to $46 billion in 2018 an average growth rate of 7% annually with significant inflow of 37% of the increase coming from within the continent.[32] While the vibrant and growing African Diaspora communities in America and Europe are gaining in visibility, it is communities of Africans within Africa that will have the most transformative impact on the continent's future particularly with regard to continental free trade and economic integration agenda.

In 2012, the AU proclaimed the African Diaspora as the continent's sixth region with over 30 million Africans living outside their home countries, and about 55% of this number resides within the continent.[33] There was a realization that inter-African migration will play a big role in shaping Africa's future in the twenty-first century. The point, therefore, is that the AU has not just a moral obligation but political and economic responsibility to engage the problem of xenophobia in South Africa as a common African problem. In as much as it directly and indirectly affects a good number of other Africans it was no longer a problem that is country-specific; hence, the role of the AU became imperative. As an African institution with the mandate of fostering cohesion, promoting peace, security, stability, and development among African States, on the one hand, and between Africa and the international community, on the other hand, the AU has the responsibility and the capacity to be a significant actor in addressing xenophobia in South Africa and in any other country in Africa for that matter.

THE EFFORTS OF THE AU

The AU has made some significant efforts in combating xenophobia not just in South Africa but in other parts of Africa where such problems have occurred in recent years. Nevertheless, our concern here remains on how it has engaged the problem in South Africa. The 2008 xenophobic attacks in South Africa were said to be the launching pad for the AU's spirited intervention thereof. Though there were occasional cases of attacks on foreign nationals and their businesses in the country, prior to the time the AU response did not go beyond issuing official press statements condemning the acts. The initial nonintervention response could be taken on the following grounds: (a) the AU just got launched and was still trying to get its institutions to work; (b) it needed time to understand the complexity of the problem in South Africa and how best to engage it; and (c) the attacks were relatively isolated and were considered a mere "township unrest" which was not seen to have posed a serious threat to regional stability and peace.

However, the AU's perception and approach to the problem of xenophobia in South Africa shifted from mere condemnation to proper engagement following the widespread attacks in 2008 and in the years after. Though the reasons for the AU's decision to meaningfully engage the problem are already highlighted here in the preceding section, it must be stressed that the primary goal was to find a lasting solution to the problem, as "a broader and higher level of engagement or intervention in a conflict is not just meant to de-escalate but to permanently resolve the conflict by treating its underlying causes."[34] At the wake of the attacks in 2008, the AU called on the government of South Africa to rise to its obligation under the African Charter to protect the rights, lives, and properties of foreign nationals and appealed to other African countries whose nationals were attacked to remain calm and be cautious in their possible reactions. The African Union Commission (AUC) opened a special line of communication with relevant authorities in Pretoria through the office the Permanent Representative of South Africa to the AU and sent a special envoy whose recommendations would help articulate better ways for the AU institution to effectively respond to the problem.[35] Even though it appears the AU efforts in the event of the attacks were spontaneous there were some important coordinated and enduring institutional responses. In May 2008, the African Commission on Human and Peoples' Rights (ACHPR)—a primary organ of the AU with the mandate to promote and protect human and people's rights in Africa—acted on the weight of petitions before it adopted a high-powered resolution condemning the xenophobic attacks in South Africa.[36]

In 2013, the AU while marking the 50th anniversary of its inherited history adopted the Solemn Declaration—a springboard for the development of the Agenda 2063 policy document which outlines Africa's aspirations and the framework to pursue them for the next 50 years from 2013. Among these important aspirations is the need to combat and eradicate xenophobia and other forms of racial conflict in Africa.[37] By this commitment, the AU enjoined South Africa and other member-countries of Africa to be more proactive and strengthen their state machinery and institutions while taking cognizance of the ideals and obligations of the "African Charter" and explore room for cooperation both on bilateral and sub-regional collective arrangement among them in the fight against xenophobia. Following the March–April 2015 xenophobic attacks in South Africa, the AUC chairperson Dr. Nkosazana Dlamini-Zuma condemned the violence and described it as "unacceptable."[38] The attacks came less than two months to the 25th Ordinary

Session of the AU Summit in Pretoria, and the AUC chairperson feared the damaging impact that xenophobic violence might have on the summit: (a) it could raise some moral questions about the credibility of South Africa hosting the summit; (b) it could write off chances for consensus decision and action expected on the agenda for the summit; and (c) it could possibly put the country's political image and position in the AU in some jeopardy.

Aside the palpable fear about the fate of unity and stability in the AU expressed by the AUC and which informed its prompt response, the weightier issue relates to gross deterioration of human rights and abuses that the violent attacks on foreign nationals represent. On April 21, 2015, the ACHPR in its 56th Ordinary Session in Banjul adopted a fresh resolution condemning xenophobic attacks in South Africa and called on the government and people of South Africa to protect the rights of foreign nationals.[39] On the strength of this resolution, the ACHPR Country Rapporteur in South Africa and other human rights offices associated to it were requested to identify, track, and report any further xenophobic actions thereof that qualify as human rights abuses for early warning response. As part of larger social, economic, and political challenges facing the continent, the Peace and Security Council (PSC) of the AU on April 30, 2015 in its 503rd Meeting condemned xenophobic violence in all its forms and manifestations. It recommended that a special session be convened by the Assembly of Heads of State and Government on the issue of migration, and its challenges, thus, articulate a comprehensive solution to the problem of xenophobic violence.[40,41] On September 1, 2019, another cycle of xenophobic attacks erupted in the Gauteng, KwaZulu-Natal, and Mpumalanga provinces and spread to other regions like the Western Cape Province and Limpopo in South Africa. The AUC chairperson Moussa Faki Mahamat on September 3 in a press statement rose to condemn it.[42] The attacks were already generating a serious political and economic tension between South Africa and many countries in the AU. For instance, Nigeria recalled its High Commissioner to South Africa, embarked on repatriation of about 600 of its nationals, and issued South Africa travel advisory. It further pulled out of World Economic Forum on Africa held in the South African city of Cape Town and attempts were made by mobs to attack South African business investments in Nigeria. Air Tanzania suspended flight operations to South Africa; Botswana also issued South Africa travel advisory; anti-South Africa protests erupted in the Democratic Republic of Congo (DRC); Zambia shut three South African malls; Madagascar canceled a football match with South Africa; and Rwanda, Malawi, and the DRC also had to withdraw their participation from the World Economic Forum.[43] In other words, the provocative attacks not only created some diplomatic tensions between South Africa and a number of countries in Africa but also isolated cases of reprisal attacks against South Africa in some countries in

Africa. Considering the level of tensions the attacks have generated and the possible threat it posed to the continent, the PSC on its 879th Meeting held on September 11, 2019 adopted a position of action on xenophobic violence in South Africa. By its decision, the PSC requested the AUC chairperson to fully engage the government of South Africa on the recent acts of xenophobic violence. It also urged the commission chairperson to expedite the holding of a continental conference in collaboration with the AU Assembly that will serve as a platform for all AU member states to thoroughly highlight the issue of xenophobia including its root causes with a view to finding a collective approach on how best to prevent its reoccurrence on the continent. It further requested the AUC chairperson to report on the conclusion of the conference to the PSC and subsequently to the AU Assembly.[44]

THE AU APPROACH AND ITS MERIT

The AU approach in combating xenophobia in South Africa made use of the dialogue machinery of its relevant institutions to bring its influence to bear on the government of South Africa. The AU took the path of appeals, dialogues, and building common positions of moral norms against the violent attacks on foreign African nationals. It was persuasive. Though many derided the AU approach as being less radical against a problem that posed a serious threat to peace, human rights, and security in the continent, it was not less proactive. A number of people, mostly in the victim countries, claimed the AU appeased the South African sentiments rather than put pressure on the country's authorities to do the needful. Economic and political sanctions as well as diplomatic isolation against the country were widely touted but, in spite of the wild and repercussive reactions from a number of African states that trailed the xenophobic attacks and the agitations within the AU for a tougher stand against South Africa, sanctions or any other enforceable coercive measures were not invoked against the country. The AU rather opted for persuasions and dialogue and appealed to the sensibilities of the South African government to live up to its obligations to put an end to the problem, even when the government of South Africa appeared not too committed or/ and, perhaps, seen as an accomplice in the acts of xenophobia. The AU felt it would be in the "best interest" of South Africa, the AU, and other countries of Africa to continue to support the government of South Africa to strengthen its legitimate responsibility and efforts to address the problem; hence, the victims' countries in Africa were advised not to retaliate—a possible reprisal that could escalate tensions and jeopardize regional security.

In as much as the path taken by the AU could be said to have fallen short of the demands and expectations of some member states whose nationals were victims of the xenophobic attacks in South Africa, it did not lack substance, merit, and wisdom. The fact is not so much about reposing faith in the sovereign ability and capacity of South Africa, but because "the AU is always required to play its role within the frame of its Constitutive Act and in the manner that promotes, not threatens, the unity and solidarity of the African States."[45] Therefore, the AU's primary responsibility in a conflict situation in Africa is to pursue peace through collaboration and dialogue; it can only initiate military or/and other punitive options as the last resort in extreme cases of war and genocide, and where the state has willfully refused every peaceful means advanced to it to pursue that very peace. The AU Constitutive Act in Article 3 stipulates "the right of the Union (AU) to 'intervene' [suggesting military solution] in a member-state pursuant to a decision of the Assembly in respect of grave circumstances, namely war, war crimes, genocide and crimes against humanity."[46] In a similar connection, Article 23(2) of the Act further states inter alia

> any member that fails to comply with the decisions and policies of the Union may be subjected to other sanctions, such as the denial of transport and communications links with other member-states, and other measures of a political and economic nature to be determined by the Assembly.[47]

The implication is that the AU could only take punitive actions against South Africa if the problem involved instances of war crime, genocide, and crimes against humanity, and the country willfully refused every pacific overture to resolve it. But the case of xenophobia in South Africa is way too far to qualify for punitive actions. Though, technically, it could be argued to have constituted a "crime against humanity," and that there was a prejudiced lack of commitment (complicity) on the part of the state authorities in South Africa to put an end to the attacks, the government of South Africa has never refused to cooperate with the decisions and recommendations of the relevant AU institutions on the issue. It has always collaborated with the AU toward finding a lasting solution to the problem. The argument is that the AU took the right step and did what it was legally expected to do by ruling out sanctions and any other coercive measures for that matter as a necessary option to addressing xenophobia in South Africa.

Beside the legal correctness of the approach, there is the larger picture of peace. The AU engagement to address xenophobia in South Africa was primarily conceptualized in the context of *Ubuntu*.[48] Thus, the essence of the AU's role was not just to end the attacks but to promote peace and harmonious living between South Africans and other Africans in the spirit of African brotherhood and solidarity. Imposing sanctions or initiating any other coercive measures in the face of the escalating tensions and violence would further deteriorate the prevailing security and human rights conditions and alienate South Africa as a critical AU member state. Tahir Gashendi rightly posits that "coercion always wins fragile peace but persuasion and dialogue often lead to lasting peace."[49] Taking from the ideals of this notion, the AU had little choice than tread the path of persuasions, dialogues, and instituting common norms through its relevant organs. Moreover, xenophobic violence is not a civil war situation, and the South African state acknowledges it has an obligation to protect the rights of its citizens as well as other nationals in the country, only that it is constrained by complex challenges in the way of combating the problem. Therefore, it would be premature and illogical to go with sanctions or military solutions in a situation that did not substantially warrant it, whereas there are suited options readily available to exploit.

Political economy wise, South Africa is one the few countries in Africa that is critical in determining Africa's future in the twenty-first century. Apart from the advancing level of industrialization and the size of gross domestic product, the country is a major investment exporter and immigration hub in Africa. For instance, in the Southern African Development Community region South Africa accounts for about 25% of foreign direct investment and 7.3% average in the entire continent more than any other country in Africa. It absorbs more than 10% average of African migrants annually since 2000.[50] The point is that leaning on the country's economic projectiles and development initiative is critical to the implementation of Africa's integration and development agenda. Africa and the AU need to leverage on South Africa's potentials as an emerging actor in the globalization process than to shut themselves out of such opportunities. The fact remains that AU needs South Africa as much as the country needs the AU. Thus, the AU has more to gain for Africa if it chooses dialogue and persuasions to put South Africa on the right track to end the xenophobic attacks on other Africans than employing coercive measures or sanctions to do so, which may damage relations between it and South Africa, on one hand, and between South Africa and other African countries, on the other hand. It is in this context that, again, one can understand the wisdom and merits of the AU approach in engaging South Africa on addressing the problem of xenophobia.

SOME CHALLENGES OF THE AU

The AU was presented with a number of challenges in its engagement to address the problem of xenophobia in South Africa. The first challenge relates to the nature and racial composition of the South African society. One thing that cannot be taken away from South Africa as a country is its complex but fragile interracial relations shaped by its troubled past. The underlying issues that lay beneath xenophobia in the country are much more than the visible occasional violent attacks directed at foreign nationals. J. Bordeau posits that xenophobia in South Africa is rooted in racist and hate beliefs cultivated by the long years of apartheid oppression.[51] Thus, one of the problems that were bound to challenge the AU peace engagement in the country was its racial complex under which emotions and survival are always mixed to produce varying degrees of violence. According to B. Moller, it is easier to deal with circumstance than to deal with fractured orientation;[52] hence, it was difficult to get many South Africans convinced that their actions amounted to violations of the dignity and rights of human persons. Rather, they saw those dehumanizing acts as a way of gratifying their yearnings for a better South Africa. People cared less about appeals and messages for accommodation and tolerance of immigrants in the face of frustration due to economic marginalization and social exclusion. It is possible that among the people who carried out these attacks on foreign immigrants there were those who did not actually hate the immigrants but attacked them due to economic frustrations. The Centre for Human Rights said, "Until the huge imbalance in the structures of the South African society is fairly and equitably addressed, xenophobic orientation would likely continue to be reinforced."[53] The point is that the common orientation that feeds xenophobia among South Africans has a way of undermining the AU's efforts against xenophobia in the country.

Similarly, some local leadership and institutional failure in South Africa were not helpful to the AU's efforts to addressing the problem of xenophobia. The alleged bias and selective operation of some of South Africa's law enforcement agents, especially in the police, against foreign immigrants was a major source of worry. Instead of getting protection from the police, immigrants often got labeled criminals and were further harassed and intimidated. There was tacit complicity of some local police authorities in the xenophobic violence instead of being agents of cooperation in the fight against it. Human Rights Watch observed that

> the vicious cycle of the violence is further encouraged by lack of effective policing to protect foreign nationals and their properties. Those responsible for previous waves of xenophobic attacks in South Africa have rarely faced any penalties or punishment for their crimes. When the attackers are not held to account, others will not be deterred from perpetuating further acts of xenophobic violence. Despite the increasing degree of this unwarranted violence the government has done little to address the attacks except to issue the National Action Plan to Combat Xenophobia and Other Forms of Racism.[54]

It is largely on this context that the government of South Africa was variously criticized for not showing enough commitment to put a stop to xenophobic attacks.

Outside the weakness in the local law enforcement system, a number of local leaders and politicians are using xenophobic rhetoric to push their political agenda. They exploit the xenophobic orientation to gain mass appeal by making careless and inciting statements that further raise the level of these violent attacks. For instance, at the height of attacks on other African immigrants in 2008 the African National Congress Youth Leader Julius Malema called on South African youths to rise up and wrestle their jobs and society from *makwerekwere*. Again, the xenophobic comment from the Zulu King Goodwill Zwelithini that "immigrants must take their bags and go where they came from" heightened the tempo of 2015 attacks on immigrants. The point is that some local leaders and agents of public institutions who would have been part of the instrument through which the AU message of peace, accommodation, and respect for the rights of other nationals could have effectively filtered into the base level of South African society were actually promoting acts of xenophobia. This, in no small way, is another society problem that the AU faced in its efforts to address xenophobia in South Africa.

Moreover, not every challenge to the AU engagement with the problem of xenophobia in South Africa is rooted in the character of the country's society. Some are within the AU itself as an institution. First, the AU Commission did not have an effective mechanism on ground to monitor the progress of the implementation of the AU decisions, resolutions, and appeals in relation to xenophobic violence in South Africa. Apart from the ACHPR Special Rapporteur in South Africa, the AU often had to rely on South Africa Country Representatives of the United Nations High Commissioner for Refugees and the United Nations Office of the High Commissioner on Human Rights, offices of Amnesty International and Human Rights Watch in South Africa, and reassurances from the government of South Africa to keep itself on track with the true development of events therein. The fact that the AU can propose and adopt initiatives is significant but the real issue lies on how it ensures those initiatives are followed up for implementation. In other words, lack of active follow up of mechanism was also a challenge that the AU has had to face in its engagement of xenophobia in South Africa.

CONCLUSION

The AU saw the rising spates of xenophobic attacks in South Africa in recent years as one common African problem in the twenty-first century and on that conviction has made significant efforts in addressing the problem. Though its approach to South Africa's xenophobia toed the path of sounding appeals, initiating dialogue and articulating common moral norms, its merits were evident. The steps taken were not only morally justified but also politically expedient. The AU engaged the government of South Africa on many occasions to commit itself to its primary obligation to protect the rights and property of foreign nationals in the country. That the AU sought the synergy of the South African government was not out of place but the right decision as the organization still operates on association level where sovereignty of the member states is still sacrosanct. The AU cannot take up an engagement that is beyond what its Constitutive Act requires it to do. Notwithstanding some variegated criticisms from a number of countries, mostly those affected by the problem of xenophobia in South Africa, the AU efforts were significant and commendable. However, that is not to say all was well in the role it played thereof. Based on the kind of challenges it encountered, the organization needs to expand its engagement role on common African problems of this nature. First, it has to design a workable follow-up mechanism to track and monitor the implementation of its decision on any issues of concern in the African continent. The experience of xenophobia made limits of action open. The second is that it needs to adopt a grassroot initiative to peace. Too much engagement with the elites and top leaders often left the larger population it seeks to reorient at a loss and alienated to its programs. Above all, the role of the AU to addressing xenophobia in South Africa has merits and deserves attention.

NOTES

1. Archbishop Desmond Tutu once described South Africa as "a rainbow nation in Africa" because of its complex multiracial composition and the nature of intergroup relations therein.

2. Bronwyn Harris, "Xenophobia: A New Pathology for a New South Africa?" South Africa History Online accessed October 12, 2020, https://www.sahistory.org/collection/article/xenophobia-a-new-pathology-for-a-new-south-africa.html.

3. South African Human Rights Commission, "Xenophobia in South Africa and Human Rights," *Policy* Brief3, SAHRC Pretoria, September 2017.

4. C. Adjai and G. Lazaridis, "Migration, Xenophobia and New Racism in Post-Apartheid South Africa," *International Journal of Social Science Studies* 1, no. 1 (2013): 196.

5. M. Neocosmos, "The Politics of Fear and the Fear of Politics: Reflections on Xenophobic Violence in South Africa," *Journal of Asian and African Studies* 43, no. 6 (2008): 1120.

6. D. Everatt, "Xenophobia, State and Society in South Africa 2008-2010," *Politikon: South African Journal of Political Studies* 38, no. 1 (2011): 14.

7. Tella Oluwaseun, "Understanding Xenophobia in South Africa: the Individual, the State and the International System," *Insights on Africa* 8, no. 2 (2016): 145. doi: 10.1177/09755087816655014.

8. Statistics South Africa, National Population Review Chart, August 2019.

9. G. Nwakikagile, *African Immigrants in South Africa* (Pretoria: New Africa Press, 2008), 26.

10. D. Mutanda, "Xenophobic Violence in South Africa: Mirroring Economic and Political Development Failures in Africa," *African Identities* 15, no. 3 (2017): 279, doi: 10.1080/14725843.2017.1291325.

11. Martin Meredith, *The States of Africa: A History of Fifty Years of Independence* (London: Simon and Schuster, 2006), 647.

12. United Nations Development Programme, *South Africa: A Country Report* (UNDP, December 1994).

13. UNU-WIDER, "Turnin' It up a Notch: Can Foreign Direct Investment Help South Africa Increase the Complexity of Its Exports?" *Research Brief* 002 (Helsinki: UNU-WIDER, 2020), 1.

14. William Gumede, "A Tarnished Rainbow," *New African*, no. 521 (October 2012): 54.

15. Push Commey, "Economic Apartheid Lives On," *New African*, no. 489 (November 2009): 26.

16. Meredith, *The States of Africa*, 648.

17. M. Duponchel, "Who is the Alien? Xenophobia in Post-Apartheid South Africa," *WIDER Working Paper* 003, (Helsinki: UNU-WIDER, 2013).

18. African Centre for Migration and Society, "Xenophobia in South Africa: Repercussions on African Migration," *Occasional Report*, no. 11 (Johannesburg: ACMS University of Wits, December 2016).

19. Oluwaseun, "Understanding Xenophobia," 144.

20. Bronwyn Harris, "Xenophobia: A New Pathology for a New South Africa," in *Psychopathology and Social Prejudice*, ed. D. Hook and G. Eagle (Cape Town: University of Cape Town Press, 2002), 169–84.

21. Sam Obiegbu, *Regional Organizations: On the Theory and Practice of Intervention in Conflicts* (Uyo: Elite Publishing Co., 2013), 31.

22. S. M. Makinda, F. W. Okuma, and D. Mickler, *The African Union: Addressing the Challenges of Peace, Security and Governance* (Oxford, UK: Rutledge, 2016).

23. John Ameh, "Xenophobia: Nigeria Recalls High Commissioner to South Africa, Shuns WES," *Punch*, September 4, 2019, 3.

24. The Constitutive Act of the African Union, adopted on July 11, 2000, and entered into force on May 26, 2001, provides inter alia in Article 3(f) that the objective of the Union shall be "to promote peace, security, and stability on the continent," and as in Article 3(h) the objective shall be "to promote and protect human and peoples' rights in accordance with the African Charter on Human and Peoples' Rights and other relevant human rights instruments."

25. The African Charter on Human and Peoples Rights or "the African Charter" is a human rights instrument of the African Union primarily inherited from the parent Organization of African Unity in 2001. It was originally adopted by the defunct OAU on June 27, 1981 at Banjul and came into force on October 21, 1986 after substantial number of member states ratified it and deposited their instrument of ratification.

26. Other international human rights instruments include the Universal Declaration of Human Rights 1946, United Nations Convention on Migrant Rights 1990 (International Convention on the Protection of the Rights of All Migrant Workers and Members of their Families), and the Vienna Declaration and Plan of Action 1993.

27. O. Kayode, "Xenophobia in South Africa - Obasanjo Urges Nigeria, Others to Report South Africa to the African Union," *Premium Times* accessed September 18, 2020, https://www.premiumtimesng.com/newss/top-news/352552-xenophobia -Obasanjo-urges-nigeria-others-to-report-south-africa-to-african-union.html.

28. Amnesty International, "African Union Should Call on South Africa to Protect Refugees and Migrants from Xenophobic Attacks," accessed September 16, 2020, https://www.amnesty.org/en/search/?issue.

29. African Union, "Open Letter to the AU on Resurgence of Xenophobic Violence in South Africa," *Pambazuka News* accessed September 21, 2020, https:// www.pambazuka.org/governance/open-letter-au-resurgence-xenophobic-violence .html.

30. Economic Commission for Africa, *Africa Report* (Addis Ababa: UNECA, 2019), 67.

31. A. Odieng, and G. Thwaites, "The Future of Africa's Diaspora is in Africa," CNBCAFRICA, accessed October 6, 2020, https://www.cnbcafrica.com/news/the -future-of-africa-diaspora/html.

32. Obiegbu, *Regional Organisations*, 37.

33. Dr. Alfa Umar Konaye, former President of Mali was sent as AU Special Envoy to South Africa on Xenophobic Violence in April 2008 by the African Union Commission.

34. ACHPR/Res. 131 (XXXXIII) was adopted in May 2008. See: African Commission on Human and Peoples' Rights Official Press Statement on Xenophobic Attacks in South Africa, September 4, 2019.

35. Romola Adeola, "Preventing Xenophobia in Africa: What Must the African Union Do?" *AHMR* 1, no. 3 (Third Quarter 2015): 261.

36. African Union, "Xenophobic Attacks on Foreign Nationals in South Africa," accessed September 18, 2020, https://www.au.int/fr/node/25802.

37. ACHPR/Res. 304 (LVI) was adopted in April 2015. See: African Commission on Human and Peoples' Rights Official Press Statement on Xenophobic Attacks in South Africa, September 4, 2019.

38. African Union, "The 503rd Meeting of the Peace and Security Council on Acts of Xenophobic Violence in South Africa," PSC/PR/COMM.1 (III), April 30, 2015.

39. A. A. Shaban and D. Mumbere, "Xenophobia: South Africa Calls out Degraded African Countries," *Africanews* accessed September 21, 2020, https://www .africanews.com/news/xenophobia-south-africa-call-out-degraded-african-leaders .html.

40. Ameh, "Xenophobia: Nigeria Recalls," 3.

41. African Union, "The 879th Meeting of the Peace and Security Council on Acts of Xenophobic Violence against African Migrants in South Africa," accessed September 21, 2020, https://www.peaceau.org/en/article/the-879th-meeting-of-the -peace-and-security-council.

42. Lawrence Ogbuzu, "From the OAU to AU: the Challenges of African Unity and Development in the Twenty-first Century," *NIIA Lecture Series*, no. 83 (Lagos: Nigeria Institute of International Affairs, 2004), 27.

43. African Union, *The Constitutive Act of the African Union*, July 2001 (art. 3, parag. 1).

44. African Union, *The Constitutive Act* (art. 23, parag. 1).

45. *Ubuntu* is a traditional African peace philosophy as well as mechanism geared toward resolving African conflicts with African solutions. It is peace in its own value. It emphasizes "humaneness" and respect for "the other."

46. Tahir Gashendi, *The Africa Union Search for Peace in a Troubled Sudan: Between Diplomacy and War* (Asmara: Academic Books Ltd, 2010), 71.

47. Economic Commission for Africa, *South Africa and Globalisation in Africa: A Special Report* (Addis Ababa: UNECA, March 2017), 32.

48. J. Bordeau, *Xenophobia: the Violence of Fear and Hate* (New York: Rosen Publishing Group, 2010), 103.

49. B. Moller, "The African Union as a Security Actor: African Solution to African Problems," *DIIS Working Paper*, no. 57 (Amsterdam: Dutch Institute for International Studies, August 2009).

50. Centre for Human Rights, *The Nature of South Africa's Legal Obligations to Combat Xenophobia* (Pretoria: CHR South Africa, December 2009).

51. Human Rights Watch, "South Africa: Punish Xenophobic Violence," accessed October 6, 2020, https://www.hrw.org/news/south-africa-punish-xenophobic -violence/html.

52. *Makwerekwere* is a derogatory stereotyping word used to refer to 'wretched and never do well foreign immigrants' among native South Africans. It is a common local xenophobic abuse of foreigners.

53. Human Rights Watch, "South Africa: Punish."

54. Datti Aboderin, *The African Union Agency in African Conflict* (Accra: Advance Press Ltd, 2016), 77.

BIBLIOGRAPHY

Aboderin, Datti. *The African Union Agency in African Conflict*. Accra: Advance Press Ltd, 2016.

Adeola, Romola. "Preventing Xenophobia in Africa: What Must the African Union Do?" *AHMR* 1, no. 3 (Third Quarter 2015): 253–72.

Adjai, C. and G. Lazaridis. "Migration, Xenophobia and New Racism in Post-Apartheid South Africa." *International Journal of Social Science Studies* 1, no. 1 (2013): 192–205.

African Centre for Migration and Society. "Xenophobia in South Africa: Repercussions on African Migration." *Occasional Report* 11, Johannesburg: University of Wits, December 2016.

African Commission on Human and Peoples' Rights. "Press Statement on Xenophobic Attacks in South Africa." September 4, 2019.

African Union, *Constitutive Act of the African Union*, July 2001.

African Union. "Open Letter to the AU on Resurgence of Xenophobic Violence in South Africa." Accessed September 21, 2020. https://www.pambazuka.org/governance/open-letter-au-resurgence-xenophobic-violence.html.

African Union. "The 503rd Meeting of the Peace and Security Council on Acts of Xenophobic Violence in South Africa." PSC/PR/COMM.1 (III), April 30, 2015.

African Union. "The 879th Meeting of the Peace and Security Council on Acts of Xenophobic Violence against African Migrants in South Africa." Accessed September 21, 2020. https://www.peaceau.org/en/article/the-879th-meeting-of-the-peace-and-security-council.

African Union. "Xenophobic Attacks on Foreign Nationals in South Africa." Accessed September 18, 2020. https://www.au.int/fr/node/25802.

Ameh, John. "Xenophobia: Nigeria Recalls High Commissioner to South Africa, Shuns WES." *Punch*. September 4, 2019.

Amnesty International. "African Union Should Call on South Africa to Protect Refugees and Migrants from Xenophobic Attacks." Accessed September 16, 2020. https://www.amnesty.org/en/search/?issue.

Bordeau, J. *Xenophobia: the Violence of Fear and Hate*. New York: Rosen Publishing Group, 2010.

Centre for Human Rights. *The Nature of South Africa's Legal Obligations to Combat Xenophobia*. Pretoria: CHR South Africa, December 2009.

Commey, Push. "Economic Apartheid Lives On." *NewAfrican* 489, November 2009.

Duponchel, M. "Who's the Alien? Xenophobia in Post Apartheid South Africa." *WIDER Working Paper* 003, Helsinki: UNU-WIDER, 2013.

Economic Commission for Africa. *Africa Report*. Addis Ababa: UNECA, 2019.

Economic Commission for Africa. *South Africa and Globalisation in Africa: A Special Report*. Addis Ababa: UNECA, March 2017.

Everatt, D. "Xenophobia, State and Society in South Africa, 2008-2010." *Politikon: South African Journal of Political Studies* 38, no. 1 (2011): 7–36.

Gashendi, T. *The Africa Union Search for Peace in a Troubled Sudan: Between Diplomacy and War*. Asmara: Academic Books Ltd, 2010.

Gumede, William. "A Tarnished Rainbow." *NewAfrican* 521, October 2012.

Harris, Bronwyn. "Xenophobia: A New Pathology for a New South Africa." In *Psychopathology and Social Prejudice*, edited by D. Hook and G. Eagle, 169–84. Cape Town: University of Cape Town Press, 2002.

Harris, Bronwyn. "Xenophobia: A New Pathology for a New South Africa?" South Africa History Online, Accessed October 12, 2020. https://www.sahistory.org/collection/article/xenophobia-a-new-pathology-for-a-new-south-africa.html.

Human Rights Watch. "South Africa: Punish Xenophobic Violence." Accessed October 6, 2020. https://www.hrw.org/news/south-africa-punish-xenophobic-violence/html.

Kayode, O. "Africa: Xenophobia – Obasanjo Urges Nigeria, Others to Report South Africa to the African Union." Accessed September 18, 2020. https://www.premiumtimesng.com/newss/top-news/352552-xenophobia-Obasanjo-urges-nigeria-others-to-report-south-africa-to-african-union.html.

Makinda, S.M., F.W. Okuma, and D. Mickler. *The African Union: Addressing the Challenges of Peace, Security and Governance.* Oxfordshire, UK: Rutledge, 2016.

Meredith, Martin. *The State of Africa: A History of Fifty Years of Independence.* London: Simon and Schuster UK Ltd., 2006.

Moller, B. "The African Union as a Security Actor: African Solution to African Problems." *DIIS Working Paper* 57 (August 2009). Dutch Institute for International Studies.

Mutanda, D. "Xenophobic Violence in South Africa: Mirroring Economic and Political Development Failures in Africa." *African Identities* 15, no. 3 (2017): 278–94. doi: 10.1080/14725843.

Neocosmos, N. "The Politics of Fear and the Fear of Politics: Reflections on Xenophobic Violence in South Africa," *Journal of Asian and African Studies* 43, no. 6 (2008) 1116–36.

Nwakikagile, G. *African Immigrants in South Africa.* Pretoria: New Africa Press, 2008.

Obiegbu, Sam. *Regional Organisations: On the Theory and Practice of Intervention in Conflict.* Uyo: Elite Publishing Co., 2013.

Ochieng, A. and G. Thwaites. "The Future of Africa's Diaspora is in Africa." CNBCAFRICA. Accessed October 6, 2020. www.cnbcafrica.com/news/the-future -of-africa-diaspora/html.

Ogbuzu, Lawrence. "From the OAU to AU: the Challenges of African Unity and Development in the Twenty-first Century." *NIIA Lecture Series* 83. Lagos: Nigeria Institute of International Affairs, 2004.

Oluwaseun, Tella. "Understanding Xenophobia in South Africa: the Individual, the State and the International System." *Insight on Africa* 8, no. 2 (2016): 142–58. doi: 10.1177/0975087816655014.

Shaban, A.A. and Mumbere, D. "Xenophobia: South Africa Calls Out "Degraded" African Countries." *Africanews*, Accessed September 21, 2020. https://www .africanews.com/news/xenophobia-south-africa-call-out-degraded-african-leaders .html.

UNU-WIDER. "Turnin' It up a Notch: Can Foreign Direct Investment Help South Africa Increase the Complexity of Its Exports?" *Research Brief* 002. Helsinki: UNU-WIDER, 2020.

Conclusion

Xenophobia, Nativism, and the Prospects for Pan-Africanism in Twenty-First-Century Africa: The Story So Far

Emmanuel Kasonde Matambo

One of the most certain assertions that this book has made is that nationalistic, nativist, and xenophobic sentiments abound in all societies.[1] Poverty, inequality, unemployment, and shrinking opportunities usually breed resentment toward those considered as foreign usurpers. Atavistic impulses to always find a scapegoat for one's woeful circumstances play a part in singling out the most vulnerable in society as sources of misfortune. Major crises, especially if they assume international proportions, stir nationalistic and xenophobic sentiment. The uncertain future that the world faced after the end of Cold War opened up avenues for emerging regional powers that could easily be characterized as new challengers to time-honored Western dominance. Among the emerging powers, China is the most prominent and hence caused the most concern in the United States, the preeminent embodiment of Western dominance and the custodian of Western values and universalism. It is thus not surprising that American foreign policy to China usually comes with hints of containment and, among ordinary Americans, sentiment toward China often lends itself to xenophobia and thinly disguised racial anxiety.

The rise and spread of terrorism, especially after 9/11, has exacerbated xenophobia against people of Arab provenance and the Muslim religion. The 2008 economic crisis is another event that provoked agitations for protectionism and an antipathy toward globalization—with its attendant consequences on the movement of persons, ideas, and goods. Instability in the developing world has forced a rapid increase in North- and West-ward migration, which has in turn caused anxiety about the dilution of Western mores and identities by the increasing numbers of people of different color, religion, and cultures. The coronavirus pandemic is another crisis that is likely to entrench insular sentiments that could easily escalate into xenophobia. For example, in January 2021, South Africa's former minster of health, Zweli Mkhize, announced that the vaccines that the country had procured were for South African citizens only, a move that Russell Pollitt, a Catholic priest and director of The Jesuit Institute in South Africa, argued was xenophobic "even though the government denies it."[2]

This background provides justification for the premise that the subject of the current book, while based on observations of Africa, is present elsewhere in the world. However, xenophobia in Africa usually carries more import because of the mighty odds stacked against the continent; Africa remains the least integrated continent in economic terms. This stymies the prospects of attaining Pan-African ideals. To some extent, the identity-based structures that were established and entrenched during colonialism have found expression in postcolonial Africa, only that now the discord took on an ethnic and Afrophobic manifestation.

DEBATES ON XENOPHOBIC IMPULSES
IN POSTCOLONIAL AFRICA

Even though Pan-Africanism sounds anachronistic, Africa still needs continental approaches for common challenges. However, there are factors that stand in the way of achieving continental approaches to continental challenges. This book sought to bring to the fore the vices of xenophobia and nativism and how they foreclose prospects of a unified Africa. The knotty challenges that postcolonial Africa inherited from the colonial structures were more than formidable for the crop of untrained African leaders, with limited or no experience at all of national leadership. In addition, ethnic and tribal divisions in newly independent countries were so inflamed that the future of unified African nations was fraught with social, political, and economic hazards. Typical of the developing world, Africa is often afflicted by what Ernest Gellner describes as ethnic nationalism, which almost always caries within it underlying xenophobia.[3]

Ethnic nationalism is distinct from civic nationalism because the latter is mostly based on ideological persuasion, one's political sympathies, and fidelity to certain institutions. Ethnic nationalism usually runs along language, culture, religion, and kinship. With the fluidity of political ideologies in Africa, ethnic nationalism usually enjoys more salience than its civic counterpart, thereby spurring possibilities of discord that are largely driven by language, religion, and wistful references to a common origin. If, due to ethnic, tribal, or racial cleavages, a nation's peoples cannot unite in pursuit of common national goals, one can only imagine how the presence of foreign nationals could inflame the already present fissures of identity politics. In addition, xenophobia in contemporary Africa followed the shift of colonial-era nationalism directed at colonial powers, to postcolonial nationalism, which Claude Ake describes as a "new nationalism" which is often directed at fellow Africans because of their different languages, culture, religions, and, yes, nationality.[4]

There is a legion of arguments on why Africa is limitedly integrated and why Africans harbor xenophobic sentiments toward each other. In chapter 2 of this book, Okeke argued that xenophobes and nativists act out of an intense irrational fear of what is foreign. In addition to this psychological argument, writers such as Frantz Fanon and René Dumont present structural and instrumentalist arguments for xenophobia in postcolonial Africa. They argue that changes of personnel from colonial to independent administrations left the lopsided colonial-era structures intact. In the long run, while the indigenous elite occupied positions of power and privilege, ordinary Africans were in the main left on the fringes of economic, social, and political progress. This bred resentment for which certain groups in African societies were the victims. In chapter 4, Seun Bamidele argues that lack of substantial transformation in South Africa is attributable to the embitterment toward the presence of foreign nationals in the country. While the emerging South African middle class has joined the economic echelons of the apartheid-era middle class, those trapped at the lowest end of the food chain abhor having to compete for or share their socioeconomic station with immigrants. Thus, autochthonous impulses become more salient in deciding who should enjoy the perquisites (i.e., employment, land, and social welfare) of origin (citizenship) and who should not.

Fanon submits an instrumentalist argument for xenophobia; whenever the shortcomings of postcolonial African leaders were pointed out, the leaders often appealed to the role they played in liberating the continent. Once this defense failed to secure acquiescence, they appealed to ethnic sensibilities, and this degenerated into internecine strife and, when foreigners are present, into xenophobia. This was the case, for example, in the then Zaire (now the Democratic Republic of Congo) when in 1981 Mobutu Sese Seko repealed his 1972 edict that granted citizenship to people of Rwandan and Burundian descent. He took advantage of long-held discomforts against people of foreign ancestry among Congolese and used them to deflect attention from his government's excesses.[5] Fanon's arguments, written in the 1960s when independence fever was in full bloom, remain valid today as the continent has made only tentative strides for economic inclusivity and the fight against identity-based politics. While this is applicable to many countries on the continent, the book should conclude with explaining the obvious attention that South Africa has incurred in this book.

SPOTLIGHT ON SOUTH AFRICA:
THE REASONS BEHIND

As mentioned in the introduction, 7 of the 13 chapters comprising this book focused on South Africa. Many reasons could be adduced for this, without denying the presence of xenophobia elsewhere in Africa. In addition to the attention-grabbing violence and frequency that accompany South Africa's xenophobia, the problem partly stems from the skewed apartheid-era edifice that has proved sclerotic for the post-apartheid order. When Nelson Mandela was inaugurated as South Africa's first democratically elected president, South Africa moved, almost overnight, from being a "polecat to model citizen" of Africa and the world.[6] The relatively peaceful manner with which South Africa's political players negotiated the transition and the credible election that had ushered in the new dispensation combined to paint South Africa as both a moral and democratic or political paragon. Amid all the fanfare, however, lurking in the background was the enormous responsibility of redressing centuries-old pervasive injustices.

The undeniable verdict is that South Africa's efforts toward redress have proved to be very limited. The majority of previously marginalized demographics still remain trapped at the fringes of upward mobility. To compound South Africa's challenges was the increasing number of African foreign nationals streaming through South African borders for a variety of reasons. Some were fleeing dreadful circumstances in their home countries, while some came to South Africa on their way to the more developed world. Still, some came to South Africa in search of education and employment. These dynamics caused strain on South Africa's limited resources and opportunities. The country still battles with soaring levels of unemployment, and any impression that foreign nationals further diminish opportunities for citizens understandably excites anti-foreign passions. That apartheid-era structures have proved impervious to change gives the consequent xenophobia a historical basis which, to some extent, absolves the ruling ANC government of culpability in South African citizens' antipathy to foreign nationals. However, some writers have argued that spates of xenophobic violence in South Africa can be understood as a direct consequence of corruption.[7] This argument indicts the ANC for the country's failure to rein in vices such as corruption and miscarriage of well-intentioned policies such as affirmative action.

Currently, post-apartheid South Africa finds itself in an embarrassing quagmire; on the one hand, it is constantly reminded of the role that the rest of Africa played in ending apartheid. It is thus understandable that the government feels a certain indebtedness to the continent, meaning Africans seeking refuge in South Africa should not be harmed. On the other hand, the ANC's difficulties with providing public goods and combatting economic decline and inequality play a part in exacerbating anti-foreign violence, especially within the ranks of the historically and currently marginalized. Understandably, the ANC shirks responsibility in admitting its inadvertent role in the country's xenophobia. For this reason, the ANC's dominant interpretation of attacks on foreign nationals has been that such attacks are driven by criminality rather than xenophobia. Chapter 8 of this book debunked this denialism and argued, in concert with Kerstin, that "xenophobic attacks in South Africa and elsewhere [are] not a sudden eruption and not the action of criminals but were a latent mindset in the midst of society."[8]

Xenophobic violence partly erupts from ethnic nationalism and the long-standing ethnic cleavages that the apartheid regime had enforced through the creation of regimented Bantustans. A cynical reading of the ANC's stance on xenophobia could be that targeting foreign nationals somewhat works in the governing party's favor because blame for the country's woes is apportioned to foreign nationals rather that the ANC government. It is worth mentioning, though, that the ANC has made tentative initiatives to stem xenophobia though, as Onuegbu argues in chapter 13, more decisiveness is needed. While South Africa attracted the most attention in this book, defeating xenophobia, nativism, and other impediments to Pan-Africanism cannot be left in the hands of a single country. Going forward, it will need a continental effort.

CONCLUSION: GOING FORWARD

The sad news for people harboring xenophobic sentiments is that globalization is irreversible and "with its new information and communication technologies as well as its new transport systems, has greatly enhanced the mobility of capital and labour."[9] With the passage of time, this inexorable trend is changing conceptions of the nation-state, and national identities are constantly constructed and reconstructed. The result of this is anxiety in some quarters that want to retain what they conceive as unsullied cultural or national identities. Just as post-independent Africans cast off colonial shackles in an attempt to reclaim what they considered precolonial pristine Africa, Africans that are currently confronted with droves of immigrants from other African countries are anxious about losing their conceptions of the nation and national identity as they were prior to the arrival of immigrants.

In addition, the reality that the replacement of colonial with indigenous leadership was an elite project left socioeconomic problems and inequalities unabated. While the African middle class and leaders (in South Africa these would comprise liberation activists) could "see people from African countries as comrades who supported the liberation struggle, in the low income areas perceptions of citizens from other African countries are different." Poor immigrants are often loathed by impoverished natives, and this explains why violent expressions of xenophobia often occur in low-income locales. In sum, while African leaders and the middle class could retain some semblance of commitment to Pan-Africanist ideals, this sentiment is not usually shared by ordinary, low-income Africans desperate to monopolize opportunities available at their socioeconomic station.

Ecological factors (such as environmental catastrophes) and civil war have been prominent triggers of rising levels of immigration in Africa. There is also the constant search of economic opportunity that has prompted a rapid increase in both external migration and internal migration, otherwise known as rural-urban drift. An Africa that is not responsive to the material needs of its citizens risks conjuring nativist sentiments in impoverished citizens who are forced to share meager economic opportunities with exponential numbers of desperate immigrants. Going forward, the African Union, through instruments such as the African Continental Free Trade Agreement and the African Peer Review Mechanism, has the responsibility of ensuring compliance to good governance and the free movement of persons and goods, which could limit the number of desperate refugees or asylum seekers risking their lives through perilous flight and straining the resources of host countries. Article 12(5) of the 1986 African Charter forbids "mass expulsion" of nonnationals, mass expulsion "being that which is aimed at national, racial, ethnic, or religious groups."[10] Noble as this ideal might be, it could limit the actions of governments, but have no bearing on anti-foreign sentiment among ordinary Africans, especially when governments are failing to provide sufficient public goods. An Africa that is effectively governed and set on a growth trajectory could blunt the anxiety of otherwise despairing and unskilled Africans, unwilling to share their polities with foreign nationals. The prospects of Pan-Africanism could be enhanced by effective governance, but this mode of governance is dependent on candor at the level of the AU, and a willingness to punishing errant and odious regimes, whose brand of rule often provokes a spike in unregulated and undocumented migration.

NOTES

1. Mikael Hjerm, "Education, Xenophobia and nationalism: A comparative analysis," *Journal of Ethnic and Migration Studies* 27, no. 1 (2001): 37.

2. Linda Bordoni, "South Africa: Xenophobia and corruption threaten fair and effective distribution of Covid vaccine," *Vatican News*, February 8, 2021, https://bit.ly/3B60II2.

3. Ernest Gellner, *Nations and Nationalism* (Ithaca: Cornell University Press, 1983).

4. Claude Ake, *Democracy and Development in Africa* (Washington: Brookings, 1996).

5. Georges Nzongola-Ntalaja, "Citizenship, political violence and democratisation in Africa," *Global Governance* 10, no. 4 (2004): 403–409.

6. Nic Von Wielligh and Lydia von Wielligh-Steyn, *The Bomb: South Africa's Nuclear Weapons Programme* (Pretoria: Litera Publikasies, 2014), 305.

7. Regis Wilson Lulu Magam, "Frustration-aggression, Afrophobia and the psycho-social consequences of corruption in South Africa," in *The Political Economy of Xenophobia in Africa. Advances in African Economic, Social and Political Development*, ed. Adeoye Akinola (Cham: Springer, 2018). 93–107.

8. Norbert Kersting, "New nationalism and xenophobia in Africa–A new inclination?" *Africa Spectrum* 44, no. 1 (2009): 16.

9. Kersting, "New nationalism," 7.

10. African Union, *African Charter on Human and Peoples' Rights*. Addis Ababa: African Union, 2016.

REFERENCES

African Union. *African Charter on Human and Peoples' Rights*. Addis Ababa: African Union, 2016.

Ake, Claude. *Democracy and Development in Africa*. Washington: Brookings, 1996.

Bordoni, Linda. "South Africa: Xenophobia and corruption threaten fair and effective distribution of Covid vaccine." *Vatican News*, February 8, 2021. https://bit.ly /3B60lI2

Gellner, Ernest. *Nations and Nationalism*. Ithaca: Cornell University Press, 1983.

Hjerm, Mikael. "Xenophobia and nationalism: A comparative analysis," *Journal of Ethnic and Migration Studies* 27, no. 1 (2001): 37–60.

Kersting, Norbert. "New nationalism and xenophobia in Africa–A new inclination?" *Africa Spectrum* 44, no. 1 (2009): 7–18.

Nzongola-Ntalaja, Georges. "Citizenship, Political Violence and Democratisation in Africa," *Global Governance* 10, no. 4 (2004): 403–409.

von Wielligh, Nic and Lydia von Wielligh-Steyn. *The Bomb: South Africa's Nuclear Weapons Programme*. Pretoria: Litera Publikasies, 2014.

Wilson, Regis and Lulu Magam. "Frustration-aggression, Afrophobia and the psycho-social consequences of corruption in South Africa." In *The Political Economy of Xenophobia in Africa. Advances in African Economic, Social and Political Development*, edited by Adeoye Akinola, 93–107. Cham: Springer, 2018.

Index

About the Editor and Contributors

Victor Onyilor Achem holds a first and second degree in Sociology from Ahmadu Bello University Zaria and University of Ibadan. He is presently a researcher and doctoral candidate at the University of Ibadan. He specializes in Social Research and Data deconstruction toward informed Policy baiting and justified intervention. His areas of interest include Ethno-politics, Victimology, Armed Conflict, Forced Migration, and Restorative Justice. He is particularly interested in social problems resulting from protracted human interaction most specifically as it relates to collective identity, shared values, and goals. Substantively, Victor is interested in analyzing sustained conflict, renewed violence, victimization, and forced migration, which are relative to "identity politics" and resource control that have led to several sectarian games in the African sociopolitical space. Victor has several publications and has won several research and travel grants. He is one of the winners of the 2020 New-Med Research Network Youth call 3rd edition (Exploring New Approaches to Economic Cooperation, Security and Migration) by Istituto Affari Internazionali in Rome, Italy.

Akinkunmi Afeez Akinlabi is a first year PhD candidate at the Department of Political Science, Obafemi Awolowo University, Ile-Ife, Osun state. He graduated with a BSc Political Science and MSc Political Science from the same university in 2013 and 2018 respectively. His research concentrates on international relations, Nigeria's foreign relations, political Islam, terrorism, and African politics.

Seun Bamidele is presently a lecturer in the Department of Peace and Conflict Studies, Federal University Oye-Ekiti, Nigeria. He is a recipient of many international awards and fellowships, notably the Next Generation

Social Sciences in Africa Program, Social Science Research Council and Carnegie Corporation of New York; CODESRIA College of Academic Mentors Institute, Council for the Development of Social Science Research in Africa (CODESRIA), Dakar, Senegal and Carnegie Corporation of New York, United States; Women in International Security (WIIS), Washington, United States; Trust Africa Illicit Financial Flow; and Equator Peace Academy, Uganda Martyrs University, Uganda. My scholarly work has been published in top-notch peer-review international journals including *GeoJournal, Social Change, African Conflict and Peacebuilding Review, India Quarterly: A Journal of International Affairs, International Journal on World Peace, International Journal on Minority and Group Rights, Jadavpur Journal of International Relations*, and *African Journal of Legal Studies*.

Adeniyi Semiu Basiru (PhD) is an independent researcher, consultant, and policy analyst. He obtained his first degree in Political Science from the University of Ilorin, Ilorin, Nigeria, and his second and third degrees in the same discipline from the University of Lagos, Lagos, Nigeria. He has had teaching experiences in various universities in Benin Republic and Nigeria, spanning a period of 16 years. His research interests cover international economic relations, foreign policy analysis, conflict and peace studies, African politics, and governance and security studies. He has contributed chapters to several books and attended local and international conferences, where he presented academic papers. Since 2013, he has had the privilege of reviewing articles for notable international journals including *African Journal of Democracy and Governance, African Security Review, Africa Review, Democracy and Security*, and *Politea*. Dr. Basiru, a member of the Nigerian Society of International Affairs (NSIA), has published widely in local and international journals. His articles have appeared in *Africa Insight, Africa Review, Inkanyiso, Ibadan Journal of Sociology, Unilag Journal of Politics, Contemporary Journal of African Studies, Taiwan Journal of Democracy, Ufahamu, Journal of International Studies, Democracy and Security, Africanus, African Journal on Conflict Resolution, International Social Science Review, The African Review, Brazilian Journal of African Studies*, and *Journal of Asian and Africaan Studies*. He coauthored "Foreign Policy Analysis: Conceptual and Theoretical Logic" (ISBN: 978-0-9844840-2-7) with Solomon Oladele Akinboye in 2014.

Happy Mathew Tirivangasi has a Master of Arts in Sociology from the University of Limpopo in South Africa as well as a Master of Science in Governance and Development from the University of Antwerp in Belgium. He is a proficient researcher in the field of political and environmental sociology. He has researched governance issues namely xenophobia, Democracy, that is,

Elections and electoral violence, and Transitional Justice in Zimbabwe, social movements, climate change, and food security. Happy has currently completed funded research by South Africa DSI-NRF Centre excellence in human development: project entitled "Evaluation of the Humanitarian Response Strategies in the Aftermath of Climate-Induced Disasters in Southern Africa." Happy is affiliated to the University of Limpopo and Jyväskylä in Finland as a research associate and PhD researcher, respectively.

Feyisitan Ijimakinwa is a research fellow in the Institute of African Studies at the University of Ibadan, Ibadan, Nigeria. He is also a research fellow of the *Institut Francais de Recherche en Afrique* (IFRA), Nigeria, with core focus on Migration, Diaspora Connections, and Transnationalism. He holds research interests in New Media and Cultural Studies, Environmental Anthropology, and Cultural Diplomacy. His works have been presented at national and international conferences, and he has published in the *Journal of African Studies*, *African Historical Review*, *Journal of Migration Studies*, and *KUJUUA*. A campaigner against plastic pollution, Feyisitan is a regular social commentator and political analyst on radio and television across Nigeria.

Robert Maseko holds a PhD in Industrial Sociology from Rhodes University, South Africa, and is currently a postdoctoral research fellow at the Department of Development Studies, University of South Africa (UNISA). He researches on the social condition of black mine workers in South Africa and labor-related studies in the Platinum Belt of South Africa. His other research interests also include issues of decoloniality, decolonization, and colonialism.

Emmanuel Matambo (PhD) is the research director for the Centre for Africa-China Studies at the University of Johannesburg, South Africa. He holds a doctorate of Political Science from the University of Kwa-Zulu Natal (UKZN). From 2018 to 2019, he was a postdoctoral research fellow at UKZN specializing in Africa-China relations. He is an alumnus of the Africa Program at the Woodrow Wilson Center for International Scholars in Washington, DC. In 2020, he was selected for the Millennium Fellowship program for the Atlantic Council, class of 2020 to 2021. He has published academic articles on a range of topics from Africa-China relations conflict resolution, contemporary terrorism, and educational theory to African agency. This is his first sole-edited book.

Sky Mkuti is pursuing a PhD in International Relations at the UNISA. She obtained a Bachelor of Social Sciences (*Cum Laude*) from the University of Limpopo (Turfloop Campus, South Africa) where she previously tutored

Political Sciences and International Politics. She later earned an MA degree in Security Studies with the emphasis on Information Terrorism and Cyber-terror from the University of Pretoria (South Africa) and thereafter worked as a sessional lecturer at the University of Monash, South Africa. Her research focuses on counterterrorism, exploring concepts of terrorism, and violent extremism. Sky has a keen interest in aspects related to Pan-Africanism and xenophobia in the context of Africa's peace and security stability. Furthermore, her ambition remains to contribute invaluably toward the mitigation of factors that exacerbate societal ills and all forms of violence toward humanity.

Lehasa Moloi is a lecturer of Development Studies at UNISA. He holds a master's degree in development studies and is currently working on his doctoral studies under the title "Towards an Afrocentric Development Paradigm in Africa." He is passionate on decolonization debates, in particular, as grounded on the African soil. He presented papers and webinars on numerous Academic conferences, internationally and nationally. He is an active participant in decolonization debates, in particular, he pursues scholarship in Afrocentricity. He has been privileged to work closely with Professor Molefi Kete Asante, the leading scholar in Afrocentricity, and Professor Sabelo Ndlovu-Gatsheni, the leading African scholar in decoloniality. His scholarship is primarily dedicated to the project of African Renaissance in search to overcome the dominant colonial paradigm of difference, which has hegemonized African people into political, economic, epistemological, and spiritual bondage.

Samukezi Mrubula-Ngwenya holds Masters in Women and Gender Studies from San Francisco State University, United States. A Fulbright Scholar, Samukezi Mrubula-Ngwenya was appointed into a New Generations of Academics lecturer position at the University of Limpopo in 2017. Her research focuses on democracy, sexuality, social movements, and LGBTIQ+ narratives and experiences. Her teaching and research area is Gender Studies. Her major task is to create and implement a fully-fledged undergraduate Gender Studies and Social Change program. Samukezi is also a PhD candidate in Political Science at the University of Limpopo.

Janet Abosede Ogundairo is a doctoral candidate in the Department of Sociology, Faculty of the Social Sciences, University of Ibadan, Ibadan, Nigeria. She is also a research fellow with *Institut Francais de Recherche en Afrique*, Nigeria, based in the University of Ibadan, Ibadan, Nigeria. Her field is Medical Sociology/Anthropology and her main research interests are Anthropology of Fulani pastoral group, Conflict, Anthropology of anti-microbial resistance, and Health care delivery systems. She is also interested in New media and New technologies and how these inform change.

Kizito N.C. Okeke did his graduate studies in psychology at the University of Georgia, and West Georgia University, and earned a master's degree in Educational Psychology and a PhD in Psychology, respectively. Previously, he studied philosophy and theology in Nigeria and was awarded a Bachelor of Sacred Theology degree by the Pontifical Urbaniana University in Rome, Italy. His interest in psychology is in the philosophy and methodological foundations of psychology, and these have engendered a kind of epistemological dialogue with other branches of psychology. His dissertation and subsequent publication examined the phenomenon of authenticity, and this empirical research is symbolic of his main area of research on Social Justice. He is currently an employee of Alabama State University, as assistant professor of psychology, where he teaches courses in psychology in the department of psychology.

Festus Chibuike Onuegbu is a senior researcher in African Affairs, African International Relations, and International Political Economy. He holds MA and PhD in Diplomatic History and International Studies respectively. His research interest touches on areas that relate to Africa in the global affairs, African regional institutions, contemporary African history, and Africa and international development frameworks in the areas of aid, economic cooperation, peace and security, human rights, and environment. Some of his published works include "Neo-colonial Imperialism: The Trend and the Plight of African States," *International Journal of Research in Arts and Social Sciences*, 7(1), 2014; "The Role of US and Her Multinational Companies in the Nigeria-Biafra War: Beyond the Threshold of Neutrality," *Ogrisi: A New Journal of African Studies*, 12(2), 2016; and "Rethinking the Challenges of a Multilateral Development Bank in African Society: The African Development Bank in Nigeria, 1986-2015," *UJAH: Unizik Journal of Arts and Humanities*, 20(2), 2019. He is currently working on "Controversy of Engagement or Disengagement: The African Union and the International Criminal Court in Africa." Dr Onuegbu is currently a senior lecturer in Department of History and International Studies at Nnamdi Azikiwe University, Awka, Nigeria, where he is also the coordinator of Continuing Education Programme. He belongs to a number of academic professional bodies which include Historical Society of Nigeria, NSIA, and Society for Research and Academic Excellence, University of Nigeria, Nsukka.

Sunday Paul C. Onwuegbuchulam (PhD) has taught and published research in the areas of Africa Political Environment, Democracy and Governance in Africa, Religion and Politics, Political Theory and Philosophy, Conflict Transformation and Peacebuilding, and Civil Society and Faith-based Organizations.

Steve Siziba is a Strategy, Monitoring and Evaluation consultant presently based in Johannesburg, South Africa. He is also involved in performance improvement programs and change management. He studied his bachelor's degree in Sociology at the University of Zimbabwe. He did his MPhil in Business Management and Leadership with South Valley University's Global Centre for Academic Research focusing on the relationship between financial audit outcomes and human capacity in the public sector. His current research focus is on the role of public libraries in advancing digital literacy and closing the digital divide.